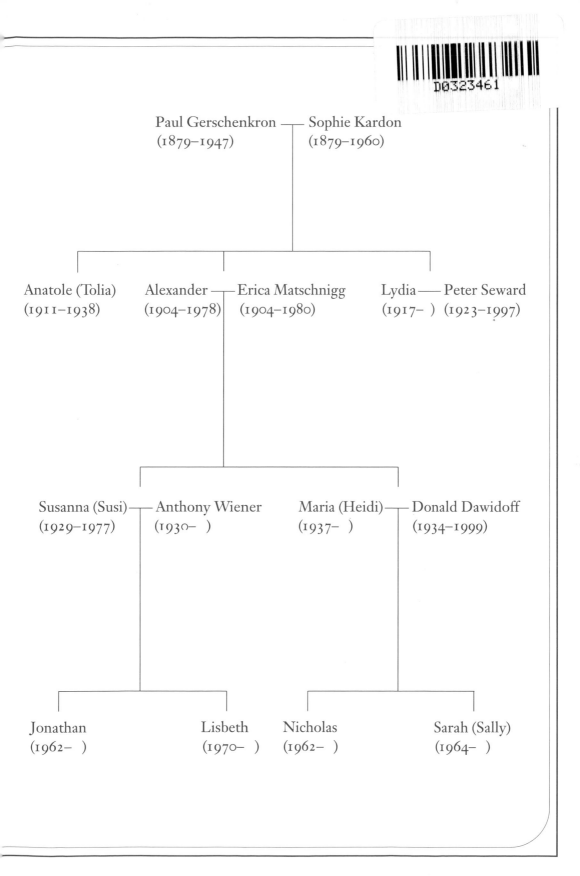

Paul Gerschenkron — Sophie Kardon
(1879–1947)   (1879–1960)

Anatole (Tolia)   Alexander — Erica Matschnigg   Lydia — Peter Seward
(1911–1938)   (1904–1978) (1904–1980)   (1917–) (1923–1997)

Susanna (Susi) — Anthony Wiener   Maria (Heidi) — Donald Dawidoff
(1929–1977)   (1930–)   (1937–)   (1934–1999)

Jonathan   Lisbeth   Nicholas   Sarah (Sally)
(1962–)   (1970–)   (1962–)   (1964–)

THE FLY SWATTER

THE FLY SWATTER

HOW MY GRANDFATHER MADE

HIS WAY IN THE WORLD

Nicholas Dawidoff

PANTHEON BOOKS

NEW YORK

All rights reserved under International and Pan-American
Copyright Conventions. Published in the United States
by Pantheon Books, a division of Random House, Inc., New
York, and simultaneously in Canada by Random House
of Canada Limited, Toronto.

Pantheon Books and colophon are registered
trademarks of Random House, Inc.

Library of Congress Cataloging-in-Publication Data
Dawidoff, Nicholas.
The fly swatter : how my grandfather made his way
in the world / Nicholas Dawidoff.
p. cm.
ISBN 0-375-40027-3
1. Gerschenkron, Alexander. 2. Economists—United States—
Biography. 3. Harvard University. Dept. of Economics. I. Title.
HB119.G47 D39 2002   330'.092—dc21   [B]   2001052042

www.pantheonbooks.com
Book design by Anthea Lingeman
Printed in the United States of America
First Edition
2 4 6 8 9 7 5 3 1

For Jonathan, Sally, and Lisbeth
Just the grandchildren Alexander Gerschenkron always wanted

And in memory of
Susanna Gerschenkron Wiener, 1929–1977
Donald Jay Dawidoff, 1934–1999

It is those we live with and love and should
know who elude us. Now nearly all those I
loved and did not understand when I was
young are dead, but still I reach out to them.

NORMAN MACLEAN,
A River Runs Through It

CONTENTS

THE FLY SWATTER

PROLOGUE

Crossing the Border Disguised as
a Saint Bernard and Other Mysteries

He's a clever man, your grandfather.

Maxim Gorky, *My Childhood*

M Y GRANDFATHER, ALEXANDER GERSCHENKRON, WAS AL-
ways making dramatic declarations, and one day when he
was in his fifties he appeared in front of his family to
announce that he was giving up the morning newspaper. He had been
looking into the matter, he said, and had discovered that the number of
books even a non-newspaper-reading man could get through in a lifetime was so small—five thousand, according to my grandfather's calculations—that permitting himself such a daily distraction was simply out
of the question. My grandfather had been an avid reader of newspapers
since the age of six, and he freely admitted that they had their pleasures
and their virtues, but now, with some force, he promised that he would
no longer submit to them. And he didn't; he never read the newspaper
again.

My mother inherited her father's moral and literary views, and for
that reason I reached the age of twelve without ever having seen a
newspaper in my house. That changed on a late spring day in 1975,
when my mother received a telephone call from a neighbor, hung up,
went rushing out the front door, was back a few minutes later, and then,
without even shedding her dripping raincoat, came to find my sister

Sally and me. "Kids! Kids!" she cried, pressing the day's *New York Times* into my hands. "Look! Your grandfather's in the paper!"

There he was. Just below a headline that read "Harvard's Scholarly Model Ends His Career" was a lengthy profile of my grandfather, accompanied by a photograph of him dressed in the most rumpled of his many rumpled tweed jackets. That my grandfather had posed for one of the nation's leading newspapers in such embattled attire was no surprise to us. He considered fashion to be an even greater waste of time than newspapers, and was always inveighing against fops and dandies. As far as my grandfather was concerned, what made the man were books, and the photograph showed him surrounded by a turmoil of them. There were portly editions of Marx over his left shoulder, stout volumes of Tocqueville beyond his right, and so many husky tomes in front and behind him that, set against them all, he looked like what he would have called "a little fellow." The exception was his hands. As he leaned back in his desk chair, he held a pipe to his lips with fingers that were so oddly oversized that they obscured most of the pipe bowl, if not the beautiful gold watch on his wrist.

I was so glad to see my grandfather that I got a sudden whiff of tobacco, and damp wool, and brandy, and aftershave, and strong tea, and old paper. Nobody treated me with more uncomplicated warmth and good humor than he did, and, when you are twelve years old and come across a photograph of your grandfather in the newspaper, you see him as you know him. It doesn't occur to you that someone else who has had less affectionate dealings may be gazing at his copy of the *Times* and noticing that even in this valedictory moment, the old man is wearing a distinctly churlish expression that says "if you don't stay the hell off my land, you'll surely regret it."

At the time I saw the newspaper photograph showing my grandfather in his office, I had never been there and had no idea that he kept the room double-stacked up, down, and sideways with so many thousands of books that they even covered the light switch on the wall. Very few people knew where that light switch was, and that was how my grandfather wanted it. When he went away for a semester or two, he departed confident that the visiting professor assigned to the office would spend several hours in darkness and misery until he finally pulled out the right book. It took one guy a day and a half.

The *Times* article turned out to contain much information about my grandfather that was news to me. Along with describing a reputation that placed him among the world's most respected economists since Keynes, it went on to report that he was "the dean of academic one-upmanshippers." That is to say, when his close friend, the Nobel Prize–winning economist Paul Samuelson, told my grandfather that he was reading a biography of Ludwig Wittgenstein and wondered if he had ever come across two names mentioned in the book, my grandfather was the sort of man who replied, "But Paul, every educated person knows Bühler and Glöckel." My grandfather was said to know all about everything—German historiography, the emigration theory in Romanian history, the complexities of infinitely divisible time. He understood Kant, Chekhov, Aristotle, and Schopenhauer better than people teaching them at Harvard for a living, and had once critiqued Vladimir Nabokov with such brio that the novelist retaliated by lampooning my grandfather in his next book. Even his vacations were erudite. He spent a pleasant summer with my grandmother examining one hundred translations of Hamlet's quatrain to Ophelia, "Doubt thou the stars are fire," in languages ranging from Catalan to Icelandic to Serbo-Croatian to Bulgarian—all as preparation for an essay in which they argued that translation inevitably distorts meaning.

My grandfather was already frail and sick when I was born, and he remained so sedentary for all the years I knew him that once, when I opened his closet door and saw an old pair of hiking shoes, I wondered whose boots had got mixed up with his belts and sandals. Yet the newspaper article said that there had been a more vigorous time when he'd moonlighted as a steelworker in a California shipyard during the Second World War. This had been such a pleasing experience that he claimed he had considered throwing over Adam Smith for the docks. "I liked the contact with the anonymous mass of Americans," he said. "And the work doesn't follow you home at night into your leisure and your dreams. Is scholarship pleasure or pain? If someone cuts off your leg you know it's pain, but with scholarship you never know."

*   *   *

NOT MANY DAYS AFTER THE *TIMES* ARTICLE TOLD ME SO MANY new things about my grandfather, my father, Donald Dawidoff, telephoned with some revelations of his own. My parents had been divorced when I was very young, and my father's not being around much—he always lived in other states—was partly why I was so drawn to my grandfather. But it was more than my father's absence. It was also just him.

On this night when my father called, I answered the telephone and spoke to him, and then it was Sally's turn. Dad asked her how she was. Sally replied that she'd had a bad day. "You come by that naturally," he said. "I'm mentally ill."

After Sally hung up, she came over to the table where my mother and I were sitting and told us, "Dad says he's mentally ill."

MY FIRST MEMORY OF MY FATHER IS OF LEAVING HIM. FOR MONTHS he had been unhinged, experiencing hallucinations so powerful that he communicated with dead squirrels. Not long after he began hitting my mother, she decided it was time for us to go. I was three. It was raining steadily when my mother, Sally, and I drove away from Washington for the long ride to our new home in New Haven, Connecticut. I remember watching the water streaming down the car window and deciding that the sky was unhappy, too.

When I was a child people used to tell me stories about my father as a promising young man. He had been the valedictorian of the Manhasset (Long Island) High School class of 1952, a fine French horn and cornet player, a varsity athlete who starred in football and lacrosse with the future NFL Hall of Famer Jim Brown. His classmates voted him "Most Likely to Succeed." At Harvard, my father's skill at throwing a lacrosse ball made him one of the nation's leaders in assists. A photograph of him making a graceful feed appeared in *Sports Illustrated*. He was such an excellent student of American history and literature that he was admitted to both Harvard and Yale law schools. I also heard about my father's personal qualities: his dry sense of humor, his crackling energy, his gifts as a legal scholar, his interest in words and ideas. He collected unusual nomenclature the way some men amass stamps or coins. After a while, I couldn't stand those stories anymore. They weren't about anybody I knew.

During the next few years after we moved to New Haven, I made a couple of visits back to Washington. When I was six my father took me to the National Zoo, where he got angry and walked away from me. Only by running along after him was I able to keep the back of his bald head in sight. He went up a sloping walkway, and I followed, until finally he slowed enough for me to catch up. My father didn't look at me, but he let me follow two steps behind.

In 1970 my father moved from Washington to New York and opened his own law office. Once a month on a Sunday, he'd ride the train up to New Haven. There were times when he could be so much fun. He took Sally and me out for pancakes, he invented a belly-tickling game called "So it does that, does it?," and, after the basketball star Lew Alcindor changed his name to Kareem Abdul-Jabbar, my father made a game of that too. "Say it, Dad, say it," I would plead, and he'd repeat the name again and again, lingering on the hard vowels like an auctioneer.

He was not always that way. He was not always any way except a man whose behavior could not be predicted. I would awaken on his visiting days, go running into my sister's room, and skip around shouting, "Sally! Sally! Dad's coming!" Often, a bit later in the morning, the telephone rang and Mom would answer it. As soon as I heard her flat tone of voice and clipped sentences, I knew Dad was calling and what he was telling her. Even before she hung up, I'd be back in Sally's room. "Dad's sick again," I'd report. I thought it wasn't fair. Why did I have to have a Dad who got the flu so much?

By the time I was twelve, I was going into New York to visit my father once a month on a Sunday. I always braced myself as I got off the train at Grand Central Station because I never knew which Dad would be meeting me at the information booth. His speech was sometimes not lucid, his actions erratic. I spent our visits tensed, waiting for something horrible to happen. Often something horrible did happen. When my father got into nasty altercations with people we encountered on sidewalks or in restaurants, when he told me things I knew he shouldn't— he liked to talk about his encounters with prostitutes and to describe new women he wanted to "lay"—when he suddenly turned on me in front of a crowd of people and began screaming about what an evil person I was, I didn't know what to do. Your father is supposed to protect you, and mine was scaring the hell out of me.

The dramatic displays of instability were awful, but the mundane features of my father's sickness were also hard. There were moments when I'd observe other fathers and sons and long for what they had. During a summer vacation, my mother took me to the Baseball Hall of Fame in Cooperstown, and as I walked around the little village, looking at all the boys with their fathers, I felt diminished at having come to such a place with my mom. Father's Day for me was like Valentine's Day for the brokenhearted. It would catch me by surprise every year, and I would slump.

Not that I wanted to be with my father. Although I called him "Dad," he felt less and less like a father to me. I began to resent him. That he could never hold a job meant he could never provide anything, so we drank powdered milk and kept the thermostat all the way to the left all winter. I began to dread those monthly visits with my father and continued to go regularly to see him only because I had no choice. He insisted, and so did my mother. She thought it was important for me to have two parents in my life. I began to think of the visits as my moral obligation. Still, it was confusing; there weren't any obligations for him. Because my father was unwell, he wasn't accountable for anything. When he treated me badly, it was the illness talking, not him, and I had to forgive him.

My father's troubles were nothing if not complicated, but I was no more than twelve when it occurred to me that his situation was also very simple: my father was someone who did not know how to be. The two of us were in New York, riding a crowded bus together up Madison Avenue. At one stop an elderly woman carrying several shopping bags got on and our eyes met. I stood and offered her my seat, and she accepted. "You didn't need to do that," my father hissed, and then he refused to talk to me for the rest of the trip.

I tried in every possible way to make myself different from my father. I never talked about him, not even with family, if I could help it. I felt antipathy for everything I associated with him—for New York, for the

French horn, for lacrosse. That my father was a negative example for me was something he may have sensed long before I did, because he never tried to be much of an influence on me. Usually it was a baby-sitter, the husband of one of my mother's friends, or one of my friend's fathers who was teaching me how to catch a ball, ride a bicycle, knot a necktie, shave my face, or drive the car. What strikes me now is how vividly I remember the interactions with each of these men. I can see their faces so clearly—the curve of their jaws, the tincture of their eyes—as I am warned about the dangers of dull razor blades and instructed never to ride the clutch. From the time I was very young I always had male friends close to my father's age. I notice now that I chose men who were successful, intelligent, and almost invariably bald. I would solicit their opinions and their judgment. There was, however, the inevitable disappointment. I wasn't theirs, and sooner or later they quietly set their limits—all of them, except my grandfather.

My grandfather and I were together a lot. Several times a year I was taken from New Haven to his home in Cambridge or his summer place in southern New Hampshire. These visits sometimes lasted for weeks, and it was rare that I saw anyone on them besides family. There weren't many other children nearby, his house had few toys, no record player, no television, and, of course, no newspapers. This situation could have made things slow for a little kid, but not with my grandfather around.

Like my father, my grandfather was full of surprises, but where my father's surprises were out of control and upsetting, my grandfather's were orchestrated events. When we were very young, he liked to hoist Sally and me onto his knees—he'd named them Hoxie and Moxie—and relate the latest, lengthy installment in the lives of two bad children named Hooey and Mooey. These episodes involved a great variety of malfeasance. There was poisoning, poaching, pickpocketing, purse snatching, ponzy-scheming, pool sharking, card counting, horse-thieving, bearbaiting, rum running, safecracking, swindling, smuggling, embezzling, vandalism, and blackmail. Crime always paid.

He was very patriotic. Independence Day was celebrated by standing in an open field and shooting a few rounds into the sky from an old pistol that had once belonged to Admiral Nimitz, the commander of the Pacific Fleet. "What if the bullets come down and hit us?" I wanted to know.

"Don't be silly, Nicky Boy. Those bullets don't come down."

About the time I grew too heavy for Hoxie, I learned to read, whereupon my grandfather not only made it his business to prepare lists of books for me, but also argued the virtues of getting through them at high speed. He was not a fast reader, he explained, and was condemned to finish only five thousand books in his lifetime. But, he said, I could aspire to do better. Once he handed me a copy of Trevelyan's *History of England*, pulled out a stopwatch, and clocked me to see how many pages a minute I could manage. It is no small trick to acquaint yourself with Ethelred the Unready while an animated man with a strong Russian accent is shouting out time splits. When the minute was up, my grandfather gave me a quiz on what I'd just read. He asked a question and I answered it. Without telling me whether I was right or not, he asked me another question, and another. Then he yelled out, "The boy can do it!" and I jumped.

A lot of time was spent teaching me to be a baseball fan. My grandfather arrived in this country as an immigrant from Europe and had been instantly attracted to the national pastime. Part of it was that the game could accommodate his deeper concerns; he could use it as an oblique means of addressing the serious matters that were on his mind. Whenever I visited him in Cambridge, he impressed upon me that someone who was going to grow up to be a person of true principle would get that way by proving his loyalty to small things, like the Boston Red Sox. I was cautioned never to blame the umpire for the many disappointments suffered by the Red Sox. My grandfather wanted me to feel that a person creates his own luck. Although he accredited fate, felt that fate—like God—was immutable, he also seemed to find it oddly beside the point and believed a man stood a better chance in life if he ran out every routine ground ball to second base. "Nicky Boy, you never know," was one of his prized phrases.

We would sit together in his study listening to broadcasts of Red Sox games on his transistor radio, with my grandfather encouraging me to

hear the games the way he did, as nine-inning fables. He had given his
loyalty over to the Red Sox because they were dramatic in a style that
was familiar to him as a Russian. Every year they filled their supporters
with hope, and then in the end they found romantic ways of letting
them down. The Red Sox even had a mortal enemy, the New York Yan-
kees, whom my grandfather regarded with disdain because they always
won, leaving nothing to the imagination—nothing, as A. J. Liebling
once said, to if about.

The Red Sox players kept my grandfather company in his study
through many afternoons and evenings, and he became attached to
them in his way. When we listened to the games together, he often discussed the team's two young outfielding Conigliaro brothers, Tony and
Billy. To my grandfather, Tony was always the Good Conigliaro and
Billy was the Bad Conigliaro. Tony was a much better hitter, but that
wasn't it. In 1967, a California Angels pitcher struck Tony flush in the
face with a rising fastball. He dropped to the dirt with such a gruesome
injury that I can still remember the sports magazine photographs taken
from his hospital bed. Tony's left eye had swelled into a ripe black
lemon. Beside the socket the seams of the baseball had notched a zipper
trail deep into his flesh. It took the eye two seasons to heal well enough
for Tony to try to play again. On opening day 1969, against the Balti-
more Orioles, he walked up to the plate, settled into his stance, glared
out at the pitcher, and drove a fastball over the wall for a home run. My
grandfather admired this display of nerve immensely. Billy, meanwhile,
was a spare left fielder of middling talents who never did anything
remarkable. It was that last quality which at first made my grandfather
dismissive. Eventually, however, it occurred to him that there was
something poignant about being the mediocre foil to the heroic Tony
Conigliaro. If you emphasized how totally nondescript Billy was, he
became exceptional for being so very unexceptional—the Bad Conigliaro.
Shortly after my grandfather had gone to all the trouble of reinventing
him in this way, the Red Sox traded Billy to Milwaukee. My grandfather was a little miffed. "Nicky Boy, they didn't know what they had,"
he said sadly.

Out on his screened porch in New Hampshire, he read epic tomes
and fought epic battles. Some men just kill a fly. My grandfather had an

arsenal of swatters which he used to protect the porch from winged invaders. There was no discernible difference between any of these instruments except that the head of one flyswatter might be molded from pink plastic while another happened to be light green. My grandfather, however, was sure that each swatter had its own particular entomicidal capacities. The pink one, for instance, had supple pounce and was better for keeping up with the shifty turns and sudden swoops of the hornet. The green was a duller stick, but supplied thumping impact, making it the weapon of choice for cruising houseflies and bumblebees. My grandfather's favorite adversaries were wasps, which he admired both because they were vicious and, as he said, because "the wasp is a metaphysical animal." He fought wasps with baby blue swatters, explaining that such an innocent color lured them into letting down their guard. Once a wasp was sighted, my grandfather would loudly alert everyone else to take cover. My sister was allergic to bee stings, so she would sometimes receive urgent admonitions from him to keep clear—warnings that had the most immediate effect on my mother and grandmother. "Sally, get back!" they would be yelling as my grandfather, baby blue swatter in hand, crept forward and swung.

The truth is that he often missed; by instinct and inclination he was a rough-and-tumble practitioner of a finesse sport. Sometimes, however, there was a success, followed by much jubilation (from us) and lengthy disquisitions on swatting technique (from him). My grandfather never allowed his victims to be cleaned up. He claimed they were deterrents, that other yellowjackets would encounter their unfortunate colleague and feel inclined to keep away themselves.

Eventually, when he was off somewhere else, my grandmother would dispose of the carnage. She had heard that dead bees retain their sting and wasn't taking any chances. My grandfather was allergic too.

There was a nimbus about my grandfather. He walked into a day and instinctively shaped it with his sensibility, charging the most ordinary events in his life with conspicuous moment. After his doctor ordered him to drink a daily glass of prune juice to make digestion easier on his weakened heart, a tall helping of the thick brown stuff was placed by his plate at breakfast every morning. As he sat down, he always gave the glass a hard look and then spent the rest of the meal ignoring it. Just as we were sure that he'd forgotten all about it, he'd take it up, give it another glower, announce, "I hate it but I drink it because I am a good boy," and down the whole thing in one big gulp.

He had enthusiasms—white horses, big boulders—and he got me interested in them on his behalf. We'd head off together in his old blue Plymouth, he wearing his lumberjacket and his red-and-black wool hunting cap even in summer— both of us peering so intently into clearings for a snowy fetlock or a rise of feldspar that the car was always barely averting trees and ponds. He was a famously incompetent driver and proud of it—he liked to point out pedestrians and ask, "Should we hit that one, Nicky Boy? No. Well, what about that little fellow with the shopping bags?" He never followed through, although he did once draw Sally a cartoon detailing the adventures of a bad uncle and a wayward bicycle.

My grandfather and I rarely found what we were looking for on these drives in the Plymouth. My grandfather didn't mind. He never wanted to be associated with anything likely. We returned from one outing to discover that my Aunt Susi had seen a work crew removing some huge rocks from the roadside and persuaded the men to dump the biggest one in the middle of my grandfather's front lawn. That delighted him.

After our drives we cleaned up and sat down at the supper table where my grandfather taught all the grandchildren to praise our grandmother's terrible cooking with the same ecstasy that he himself projected. Throughout the meal we were all outdoing one another in our enthusiasm for charred roasts and scorched vegetables. After the meal it was time for the grown-ups to talk and time for us to go to bed. The day always ended with us upstairs, waiting for the slow thud and creak of my grandfather coming up the staircase. Each night, without fail, he tucked us all in and slipped us each a piece of unwrapped milk chocolate. He said it was our reward for brushing our teeth.

WHEN I TURNED FOURTEEN, I TRAVELED ALONE ON THE TRAIN TO Cambridge for the first time. Riding up the Connecticut shoreline I felt unencumbered—a traveler with a bright destination. I ran from South

DEAR SALLY,
WATCH ME DRAWING A STORY:

THIS IS MICHI AND HER MOTHER	THIS IS UNCLE UHU. HE IS A GOOD UNCLE	UNCLE UHU GIVES MICHI A BICYCLE. FOR IT IS MICHI'S BIRTHDAY
MICHI TRIES HER NEW BIKE	THIS IS A BIG TREE	MICHI HITS THE TREE
MICHI HAS A BUMP ON HER HEAD	MICHI'S MOTHER GIVES HELL TO UNCLE UHU	I SHALL NEVER GIVE MICHI A BIKE AGAIN. I'LL GIVE HER AN AUTOMOBILE

THERE. THIS IS THE END OF THE STORY. IT
WAS TOLD FOR A SWEET LITTE GIRL NAMED SALLY
BY AN UNSWEET MAN CALLED

PAPA-Vati

TELL NICKY TO WRITE ME A LETTER, SO THAT I CAN
WRITE TO HIM TOO.

Station to the Cambridge subway and from the Harvard Square stop to my grandfather's street. He greeted me at the door with a hug and a kiss. I was breathless from the sprinting and from being caught up in the smell and the feel of him—the press of his stubbly cheek on my lips, the cool of his wire-framed glasses brushing the side of my head. We went for a drive out to the town of Concord, where I was given an ice cream cone. I began to lick it on the sidewalk and he looked me over: "Nicky Boy, if you had been seen eating in public right here two hundred years ago, they would have put you in the stocks." I said I was glad I didn't live then. My grandfather sighed. This was the period of Watergate and Vietnam, and I think he must have been exercising the historian's license, which permits a man to experience feelings of wistfulness for a time in which he never lived.

This visit to Cambridge also turned out to be my first chance to see my grandfather in public among his peers. He took me to a party at the Massachusetts Institute of Technology hosted by the M.I.T. economist Franco Modigliani in celebration of Modigliani's brother. As soon as we arrived—quite late—half the room rushed over to my grandfather. He stood there, near the door, with a crescent of people in front of him and his arm around me, holding forth. I came to feel a little sorry for the guest of honor, to think of him, in a compensatory way, as the Good Modigliani, because very quickly it had become my grandfather's party. Any male not absolutely doddering was greeted with a hearty "Hello, young man." Sometimes these people received a further verbal slap on the back as he explained, "Nicky Boy, Professor Domar here is nothing but a barbarian." He was totally engaged in this banter, and they were totally engaged in him as he teased, issued puckish retorts, and told witty stories about his enemies.

There were a lot of them. My grandfather never felt right if he wasn't feuding with someone. He believed that a gentleman does not say unflattering things out of another man's hearing that he is unwilling to repeat in his presence. My grandfather took pleasure in insulting people to their faces and, since this was well known to be true, he concluded he had leave to take a few swipes at an inconveniently absent chin during a party. Over the years he had failed to get along with a spectacular range of men, from Jascha Heifetz to Nabokov to Herbert Marcuse to Walt Rostow to his noisy next-door neighbor Alan Dershowitz, but without a doubt his most durable disagreements were with his former best friend, the Harvard economist and liberal political activist John Kenneth Galbraith. Although the sources of this breach were complicated, at M.I.T. my grandfather had no trouble boiling them down for rhetorical effect. He announced that he had recently paid a visit to his old pal, the former Red Sox star outfielder Ted Williams.

"Williams, you know, is nobody's fool," my grandfather said smoothly. "In fact, Williams is an extremely literate man, and it also turns out that he has a real interest in economics." All of the economists looked very pleased. "But," my grandfather continued, "it is a characteristic of Williams's mind that he tends to express his opinions in baseball terms." The economists looked very puzzled. "And," my grandfather said, "as it happens, I can provide you with an example. Do you know who came up during our conversation?" Nobody knew. "John Kenneth Galbraith did! And at the mention of his name, Williams said to me, 'Oh, Galbraith! Certainly, Alex. I know all about him. A high fly ball to shallow left field.'"

My grandfather nodded while everyone laughed, and then he began telling another one. The skin on his cheeks was as pale and cracked as parchment. There were ditches under his eyes, his tie was poorly knotted above a shirt that was no longer white and trousers that had grown unused to pressing. Nobody would have called him tall or trim or agile. Just the same, at that moment I could not imagine any man looking finer. It was then that I noticed the number of women who were watching him with considerable admiration. He was not paying any special attention to them, something that appeared only to increase the goodwill in their eyes. When he ran his fingers through his thick white hair, two ladies reached up and touched their own.

This went on for forty-five minutes until my grandmother said it was time for him to go home and rest. He looked desolate. The crowd urged her to reconsider. She held firm, and rightly so. He wasn't well. My grandfather went into the hospital for the last time a year later. He was seventy-four.

It took me a long time to get used to his death. With my father grown so sick and strange and disappointing, I had come to rely on my grandfather as a kind of anodyne. Although my sister and I never suffered from any of my father's afflictions, I often worried that what had happened to my father would be my fate as well. After one upsetting visit with Dad, my mother asked me if I had read Virginia Woolf's novel *Mrs. Dalloway*. I hadn't. She told me about Clarissa Dalloway and Clarissa's alter ego, Septimus Smith, who is mad and constantly destroys life—"makes everything terrible," as his wife Lucrezia says. My mother showed me the part where Septimus lolls on a bench in Regent's Park and gazes at the clouds, the leaves, and the trees that he believes are signaling to him. Then my mother looked at me and said, "You don't do that, Nicky. You don't distort things." But there are some parts of life nobody can tell you how to feel about, and she never completely convinced me. Instead, it was spending days with my grandfather that had always made me seem to myself like a regular boy. Those times in Cambridge and New Hampshire were all so joyful and light and absorbing. It meant a lot to me that I came from him, to think of myself in the world not as my father's son, but as Alexander Gerschenkron's grandson. When other people talked about what they did with their fathers, I described my adventures with my amazing grandfather. Now he was gone too.

Except that he wasn't. I saw a blue Plymouth passing by on a New Haven street and was so sure it was my grandfather's that I informed my mother I'd seen him. "He was wearing his lumberjacket and the red-and-black wool hunting cap," I said. She told me that this couldn't be, but I held on to the image of him crouched at the controls, heading up Mitchell Drive. Sometimes I had sensory experiences of him—the sudden recollection of his hands spreading red preserves across a piece of toast or the hollow sound he made with his lips as he puckered them together in thought. Then I'd look, and he wasn't there, and I would feel momentarily confused and then oddly exultant—I'd had a visit with my grandfather. I never stopped dreaming about him. In one dream he was sliding into a lake and I went in after him. Grasping him around the chest, I pulled my grandfather to the surface as clear water streamed off both of us. In all sorts of ways I carried him with me. I put his photograph on my wall. I read the books he liked. I did my homework in his old desk chair. I wore his beautiful gold watch on my wrist. The older I got the closer I felt to him, and yet I had been fifteen when my grandfa-

ther died, and my memories were all those of a child. I knew my grandfather, but I knew almost nothing of Alexander Gerschenkron.

When I met my grandfather's friends and acquaintances, I would
bother them with questions. The more they told me about him, the
more curious I grew. This was partly because they all seemed to find
him as interesting as I did. They referred to my grandfather as "the
Great Gerschenkron" and they made him sound positively mythical.
"Everybody loved him," the economist and former Kennedy adviser
Carl Kaysen remembered. "He knew everything, had read everything,
and could talk about anything." Orchids of this sort piled up. To James
Billington, the librarian of Congress, my grandfather had been "a living
example of the true intelligent." Martin Peretz, the editor of the *New
Republic*, was a young Harvard political science instructor when he met
my grandfather. "I used to watch him at the Faculty Club's Long Table
and say to myself, 'This is the last man with all known knowledge," he
told me. In my grandfather's day, the Harvard economics department
paired professors with a secretary. "I shared one with him," a professor
named Jerry Green said. "It was like sharing a secretary with God.
When I got to Harvard, I wasn't sure he was alive he was such a legend.
He'd been so famous for so long, I couldn't imagine he really existed."

Many of these people had stories about my grandfather, set pieces
which they brought out like the good silver. My grandfather was a lifelong champion of what he called "French manners." A notable component of French manners was that under all circumstances you
maintained your French manners. Take my grandfather's visit to Germany. He found himself aboard a jet liner that successfully crash-
landed in Frankfurt. After the plane had come to a stop on a runway
covered with foam, the flight crew begged him to slide down the emergency chute, but my grandfather refused until he'd first gone up to the
cockpit and properly congratulated the pilot.

He not only practiced French manners, he enforced them. While
having dinner at a Cambridge restaurant, my grandfather overheard a
Harvard boy at the next table bragging that he'd taken a Wellesley girl
for a drive out into the deep countryside and coaxed her into granting
him certain favors by giving her a choice: "I told her 'fuck or walk,'" the
boy recounted. Leaping to his feet, my grandfather announced that he

was confiscating the boy's bursar's card and turning it in to the dean "for conduct unbecoming of a Harvard student."

My grandfather's constitution was less French than Greek; he made himself into a legendary stoic. At a conference outside New York City, he suffered a heart attack. His response was to excuse himself, hurry upstairs to take a cold shower, and rush back to the meeting room. Everything he did, even his pleasures, he took on with concentrated ferocity. During assorted vacations and long weekends he taught himself Swedish, Norwegian, and Danish so he could read writers he loved—August Strindberg, Knut Hamsun, Hans Christian Andersen— in their native languages and also, perhaps, so that when people asked him what he'd done over the summer he could shrug and say, "Oh, I learned Swedish." He enjoyed solving chess problems and could be spotted crossing busy city streets against the light with a portable set in his hands, his face buried in the rooks and pawns. Once he strode into a Harvard seminar room packed with poetry experts and, like Art Tatum at an after-hours-joint cutting contest, he stayed on until he'd out-quoted them all.

Sometimes two people would offer conflicting versions of the same Gerschenkron story. Often my grandfather turned out to be the source for both of them. When asked about his childhood, he might say that his father worked as a plant manager for a factory owner in Russia. Other times he would explain that his old man had operated an inherited family business—a huge bordello in Russia with six thousand women. It was a truly grand operation, the biggest bawdyhouse in Europe. This brothel had many different departments, including one for intellectuals where all the women knew Ovid's *Art of Loving* by heart. They'd read the book in the original Latin and knew how to apply it in translation.

When the Bolshevik revolution came, my grandfather was said to have fled by swimming an icy river with his father and then walking for hundreds of miles from Russia, through Romania, all the way to Vienna. He lived in the Austrian capital for eighteen years, until the Nazi soldiers arrived from Germany. I heard various accounts of how he got out of the country. One claimed that he sped through a snowy pine forest into Switzerland on a BMW motorcycle under a hail of bullets with my grandmother hunkered down behind him on the bike, my infant mother in her arms. Another had him disguising himself as a Saint Bernard and trotting slowly past a row of Nazi sentries.

His next port was America, where his life remained colorful. Eventually he became the rare Harvard professor to be offered chairs in three disciplines—economics, Slavic studies, and Italian literature—and the only economics professor to lecture to undergraduates on great Russian novels. Not only that—he was said to have played chess with Marcel Duchamp, corresponded with Simone de Beauvoir, maintained the close friendship with Ted Williams, and charmed one of the world's most beautiful women on an airplane. "He was going from New York to Boston," Franco Modigliani told me. "He was reading a book in German. All of a sudden he had the feeling that there was someone very female sitting next to him. He didn't look up. Then a long, black, leather glove reaches under his nose with a box of chocolates. Still without looking up he said 'No thank you.'

"A deep feminine voice said, 'Did your mother tell you never to accept candy from a stranger?'

"He said, 'No, my father.'

"She laughed and said, 'You must be a professor.'

"He turned from his book and looked at her. 'Yes,' he said, 'I am.'

"'What is your university, Professor?' she wanted to know.

"'I teach at Harvard,' he said.

"She looked down at his book and then intensely up at him and asked, 'Wissen sie nicht wer ich bin?' (Don't you know me, Professor?)

"He said, 'I am sorry. I am very absentminded.'

"Then she said, 'But Professor,' and leaned toward his ear.

"He sat back and looked her over carefully. 'So you are!' he said at last. And they had a wonderful conversation in German all the way to Boston. An awfully good time, they had. 'Franco,' he told me later, 'she's a very intelligent woman.'"

When he got home, he said, "Erica! On the airplane I met someone who grew up in Berlin. She wrote her name down for me." Then he handed his wife the piece of paper and watched her see that Marlene Dietrich had slipped him her telephone number.

*   *   *

A WOMAN WHO WORKED WITH MY GRANDFATHER TOLD ME, "YOUR grandfather was a very religious man."

"What was his religion?" I asked her.

"I don't know," she said.

There were similar confusions about his name. After hearing several people call my grandfather Shura, Robert Dorfman did the same and was brought up short by my grandfather, who told him that he disliked being called Shura. Please call him Alex. André Weil, on the other hand, was always encouraged to call him Sasha. To Holland Hunter, my grandfather was his patronymic—Alexander Pavlovich. A cast of affable men sat across lunch tables with "Good Old Gerschenkron." To my grandfather's unending pleasure, Nancy Nimitz, who'd seen him type, opted for "Three Fingers Gerschenkron." (He called her "Contemptible Nancy.") An economist named Donald Hodgman finally threw up his hands and asked, "What do I call you?" Purring with nonchalance, my grandfather replied, "You can call me Professor Gerschenkron, or Gerschenkron, or Alexander, or Alex, or Aleksasha, or Sasha, or Sashura, or Shura, or anything else you like."

It was often this way. My grandfather offered an abundance of provocative details about himself but managed to obscure the actual facts of his life in a cloud of rumor, mystery, speculation, and conjecture. His students, who revered him, were endlessly curious about his background. Many of them wondered if he had something to hide. He let them wonder, and they weren't the only ones up in the air. Among his most cherished friends was his fellow Russian, the Oxford philosopher and polymath, Sir Isaiah Berlin. Sir Isaiah and my grandfather knew each other for more than thirty years, but what did Sir Isaiah really know? "He never told me about his past," Sir Isaiah said to me. "It didn't come up in conversation. I didn't ask him and he didn't bring it up. He wasn't a man who encouraged delving into his past."

"But you were close friends," I said.

"I don't think your grandfather had close friends," he replied.

He had one sister, my great-aunt Lydia. When she wrote to me about him, she confessed that she "hardly knew" her brother and went on to say, "Nicky, I do honestly believe you must have known him a great deal more closely than I did."

Not many people recognize my grandfather's name. When I meet someone who does—an economist, a history professor, a graduate student, a businessman, someone in government—they always get excited. "He was your grandfather?" they'll say, often taking my hand again as they begin talking, and it's as though my grandfather was Joseph Mankiewicz or Dan Quisenberry or Louis Kahn or Charles Ives—a completely unusual man who went about his game in a way that nobody else did. More than twenty years after his death, my grandfather's work retains its interest—in 1995 *The Times* of London and the American Academy of Arts and Sciences included his *Economic Backwardness in Historical Perspective* on a list of the one hundred most influential books written since 1945—but it is his personality that really stays with them. He intrigued people and he impressed them. Sir Isaiah Berlin told me that my grandfather "had a very clear view of life's values, what is good, what is bad, what is wrong, what is right. It was all very clear to him. I don't think he ever had dilemmas. He never was tormented. No 'Should I do this, or should I do that?' He always knew."

My grandfather's life spanned the first three-quarters of what he referred to as "our unhappy century." By the time he was a middle-aged man he had survived as a political and religious refugee from two of the most sinister regimes in history. Watching the events unfold in Russia and Austria cost him something. A man cannot flee two countries without regrets; my grandfather had plenty, a dark side that he seemed to do his best to damp down. He was not always successful.

My grandfather's anger increased his internal complication; his humanity grounded him and made him more morally certain. Over the years he had seen a lot of powerful men with different ideas about the way people ought to live: Lenin, Otto Bauer, Hitler, Franklin Roosevelt, George Marshall, Joseph McCarthy, Richard Nixon. They helped him to arrive at his own sense of life's values—what he called decency. As he grew older it became increasingly important to him that he exist as a model of decency for his community—his peers, his students, his grandson. He thought a lot about how to do this. As with every other problem in his life, he found the solution on his bookshelf. If there was a single thing his reading taught him, it was that people remember great characters. Such was his passion for writers like Tolstoy and Dickens and Pasternak, I feel sure that if he could have, my grandfather would have invented a great literary character, a Levin, a Copperfield, a Zhivago. But this kind of writing was not his talent, and so he improvised. My grandfather made up such a character all right, but he didn't put him into fiction. He lived him. His life became his stories, and his stories were his life.

ONE

SHOWING OFF
IN ODESSA

They talk in Western Europe of our duplicity and
wily cunning; they mistake the desire to show off
and swagger a bit for the desire to deceive.

Alexander Herzen, *Memoirs*

T HE RUSSIA ALEXANDER GERSCHENKRON WAS BORN INTO
in 1904 was a vast and varied country of people who had been
so frequently abused by tyrants that out of all the misery came
a commonality of spirit shared even by Europeanized Russians like the
Gerschenkrons. It was with enormous pride that all his life Alexander,
known to his family by the nickname Shura (pronounced *Shoo*-rah, with
the *r* rolled soft), referred to himself as "typically Russian." Typically
Russian behavior was a matter of both style and attitude, a rough-hewn,
zestfully counterintuitive approach to living that was evident in many
aspects of comportment, from the wordless sounds only Russians made
to express their appreciation for something—such as a just-downed
glass of vodka—to the uniquely Russian shudder that came over people
experiencing strong emotion. It was typically Russian to sleep in stuffy
rooms with the windows closed, to enjoy breathing in the air on dusty
roads, to insist there was no finer music than the murmur of the
samovar, to have political arguments in which you were quietly modify-
ing your position all the time while loudly refusing to concede anything, and typically Russian to look at the schoolboy warning you to
rub snow on your nose because it was nearly blue with frostbite and
inform him that you preferred it that way. After you had sent the

schoolboy packing, it was also typically Russian to think you had spited your nose for the good of a not-yet-typical child.

At its essence, to be typically Russian was to be "more so." Though Russians, for instance, were not always energetic—were, in fact, famed for their abilities as sleepers—in his fleeting moments of vigor a typical Russian was more vigorous than anybody. In this way, Russians were "more so" about everything. As a Russian saw it, a Frenchman might be ardent when it came to France—or a Frenchwoman—but he never truly lost his head about anything except a Frenchwoman. (Usually it was someone else's Frenchwoman.) Germans were even worse. They were so rigidly organized that they never lost their heads at all. Russians, however, believed in losing their heads and aspired to do so. Russians made outrageous claims, traveled to absurd lengths, pushed the limit, and exceeded expectations. Always they wanted to be more loyal, more devoted, more steadfast, more stoic, and—when circumstances called for it—more long-suffering. That was a lot to live up to, and to meet the perpetual challenge typical Russians spent spectacular amounts of time lying around dreaming up magnificent feats for themselves to accomplish. In other words, it was a nation of show-offs.

In Shura's view, this behavior was rooted in the populist intelligentsia's long-standing tradition of appropriating and preserving rural values. Russia was slow to industrialize, and into the early twentieth century many social mores still came from the provinces—from the peasantry. Even townspeople like the Gerschenkrons were familiar with tales of peasant heroics: the heavy sacks of grain this *mujik* had hoisted; the broad fields of ripe wheat that one had cut to the ground by himself in a single day with his scythe. Many of these stories featured men who had allowed so much work to accumulate that everyone said this time, truly, it was just impossible: no man could finish such a job in such a limited time. Whereupon the peasant went out and completed the task in a remarkable lather of activity. Sometimes these frenzied finishes were pyrrhic victories. Among other things, they led to an epidemic of Russian hernias.

Nobody but the afflicted worried too much about that. Far from earning any kind of censure, the reckless approach was prized in Russia, and peasants who betrayed too disciplined an attitude toward their work were scorned as "acting German." Even in Soviet times, factory workers were notorious for lazing about until the end of a planning period and then compensating with the *shturmovshchina*—a storm of activity. As a city boy Shura was not obligated to do any physical labor, and he readily admitted that his own heroic displays were "not functional." Still, he said of his youth that "you were called upon at all times to surprise the world by unusual achievements," and added that "it was natural to indulge in it, since it was all around us." That is to say, Alexander Gerschenkron was a moral and a dignified person, but he did not despise a show-off. Indeed, he was one himself.

THE YEARS OF SHURA'S YOUTH WERE SPENT IN THE BLACK SEA PORT city of Odessa. Every August the nearby coast became crowded with men unloading boatloads of watermelons freshly harvested from the Ukrainian steppe. Shura never really thought about this until the winter of 1918, when he was fourteen and happened to read a book which described how difficult it was to be a mover of watermelons. Not only were the smallish fruits heavier than they appeared, but they were slick against a man's hand and had an oblong shape that the book said made them cumbersome even for veteran stevedores. Shura decided that when the late summer came he would show those watermelons.

Early in August, he walked down to the water and came upon an energetic scene. Moored in the shallow surf were a number of skiffs piled high with Russian melons of the darkest green. Parked above the beach on the shore road were an equal number of fruit wagons. Between the boats and the wagons stood the watermelon movers. They worked bucket-brigade style in groups of five, tossing the melons up the line to the drayman, who settled them into his wagon. Noticing a team that had only four men, Shura stepped forward, offered his services to the foreman, and was waved into formation.

The watermelons turned out to be as unwieldy as advertised, and in no time Shura had allowed two of them to slip through his grasp and smash at his feet. Immediately he was set upon by the foreman, who marinated him in a thick stream of invective that concluded, "You drop another one and you are out, but before you go, I'll mend that dirty running nose of yours." In a rage Shura directed a series of murderous threats of his own back at the foreman, concluding with a guarantee of "utter destruction." Then he bent his back. He didn't drop another melon all morning.

At lunchtime he was not required to make good on his vows of mayhem; instead he was given his first short snort of vodka and was otherwise treated with great affection by his new colleagues, including the foreman, who, after inquiring if Shura would like some help changing his diapers, quivered with laughter and announced that he was not such a bad kid after all. Then the foreman proceeded to teach him what Shura remembered as a dazzling multitude of unsurpassable blasphemies. More melons were fumbled that afternoon, but not by Shura, who received his pay and hurried home to fulfill his real purpose in the whole enterprise—telling everyone in the family all about it.

All the Gerschenkrons enjoyed the tales of little Shura leaping across broad ditches or charging through rushing currents yelling *"Dvum smertiam nye by vat, I odnoi nye mino vat"* (Two deaths cannot happen to one person and one death cannot be avoided). From the time he was four, his parents had him standing up on chairs in front of the company, reciting little poems he'd memorized. As he grew older much of the inspiration for his "achievements" came from the conventional source, the peasants he met while the family was summering in the countryside outside Odessa.

Many educated Russians had sentimental feelings about rural life. That was because in the sweltering summer heat, Russian cities became oppressive places. The air reeked with the stench of sewage and disease, the streets were strewn with garbage, rats and flies moved in bold swarms, and cultivated families packed their trunks and got out of town. They built small houses in clearings, glades, and meadows and took up residence in these dachas for a few short weeks—just long enough for many of them to romanticize the bucolic life.

Shura's father, Paul Gerschenkron, owned two such properties. There was the dacha that he bought in a moment of prosperity to please his wife Sophie. But Sophie was a particular woman and did not like the cottage. She preferred the family's *pomiestie* (small rural estate) eight miles outside the city limits in a forest close to the Black Sea. It was easy to see why. The estate was a charming place. Besides the rustic wooden farmhouse surrounded by a veranda, there were meadows dappled with red and blue wildflowers, walnut trees, tall hedges, livestock, vegetable patches, cherry orchards, a strawberry field, and a garden where the samovar murmured on the table in expectation of the friends and family who were always dropping by for afternoon visits. One day a traveling peasant woman stopped in to ask for some food. While a hamper was prepared for her, she remarked upon the dozens of ghosts she'd seen the night before swirling around in the local graveyard. As soon as Shura heard this, he informed his father that he wasn't afraid of that graveyard and, furthermore, he would be glad to prove it. His father took him up on the offer, inviting Shura to walk through the cemetery by himself at midnight. After Shura returned home triumphant, his father nodded thoughtfully: "Now you know there are no such things as ghosts," he said. Shura adored having a father like that. Not only was Paul affectionate; he was always one step ahead of his oldest child, an endless source of incentive.

Shura and his friends were all strong swimmers, well trained in the Russian sailor's breaststroke, a regional style that involved raising your cupped hand high above your head and crashing it down into the water like a paddle wheel. One aquatic competition involved seeing who dared to swim the farthest distance out into the harbor before turning back. (Shura won, but had to be rescued.) Another stunt they dreamed up required participants to run at top speed alongside a barbed wire fence. Whoever bled the most was the champion. Afterward they followed the old peasant practice of stanching all wounds with cobwebs, a remedy that anticipated the discovery of penicillin, but on these occasions led their French governesses to shake their heads and mutter, *"Oh! Ces russes!"*

As an adult, Shura rarely spoke of his youth except to tell what were, in effect, more watermelon stories. That is also the way he wrote about it. Late in his life Shura set down some of his boyhood recollections and fashioned them into a memoir he called "The Uses of Adversity." Shura's descriptions of his adventures are often vivid, but what is most striking about the work is how much it doesn't explain. This is the rare childhood memoir in which the author neglects to name his parents.

He is, if possible, even more discreet about his two siblings, and there is scarcely any mention at all of his other relatives or his friends. The family's religion, political leanings, quirks of character, and peccadillos are all elided. There is no portrait of what Odessa looked like—he never even refers to his hometown by name, identifying it only as "the city"— nor are there descriptions of life around the neighborhood, the house the Gerschenkrons inhabited, their possessions or quotidian activities. Shura is a future historian living through the twilight of imperial Russia, and he never really lets on how he feels about the Revolution. There are shards of him in many of his stories, but few of his dimensions beyond the swagger. In the end, perhaps it is not surprising that a boy who amused himself by proving his firm indifference to hunger, exhaustion, fear, and pain would grow into a man who kept his past to himself. The way it is with show-offs, even the best of them, is that they spend their time letting people know how enterprising and capable they are. It doesn't do for them to speak of the things that make them unhappy.

ODESSA WAS CONCEIVED AS A TOWN FULL OF SAILORS. THE UKRAINE was long the breadbasket of Russia, but through the eighteenth century exports lagged well behind potential because the region had no natural deep-water harbor. In 1794 Catherine the Great spent 26,000 rubles to construct Odessa harbor on the northern coast of the Black Sea. Soon, out across the horizon went thousands of hulls packed full of wheat grown in the rich black soil of the steppe. Back came the world. Joining the salts and swabs who went shouldering their way up and down Richelieu Street were entrepreneurs, speculators, and merchants from Turkey, Greece, Italy, France, Germany, Arabia, Romania, Hungary, Armenia, England, Spain, Austria, and dozens of other places. With their forty-nine languages and ten religions, the foreign businessmen very quickly made Odessa Russia's most cosmopolitan city. They settled on the limestone bluff two hundred feet above the waterfront and began to trade. By the mid-nineteenth century, many of them were prospering.

What made Odessa so much more than a commercial boomtown

was the exotic artistic culture that developed there. Odessa was geo-graphically at such a remove from the Russian political and population centers that nonconformist sensibilities could thrive. Pushkin wrote portions of *Eugene Onegin* in an apartment on Italian Street. Trotsky attended an Odessa grammar school. The Moldavanka slum district was Isaac Babel's childhood home and the inspiration for his edgy tales of urban life, *The Odessa Stories*. Odessa became a depot on the musical main line, a destination for Liszt, Tchaikovsky, and Rachmaninoff, and home to so many esteemed violinists that a boy like Shura who didn't study the instrument became the exception; every petty bourgeois set of parents wanted to discover that they had bred the next Jascha Heifetz. Tsarist Russia was a brutally repressive place, but many people in Odessa lived freely and pursued their happiness liberally, as Mark Twain noticed when he came through in 1869. "We saw only America," wrote Twain. "There was not one thing to remind us that we were in Russia."

What Odessa had most in common with the United States was the feeling it inspired among European émigrés that they could live there the way they'd wanted to live at home. The settlers tried to imbue the city with the most attractive features of what they'd left behind, and they succeeded so well that Odessa acquired flattering and far-flung nicknames—the Pearl of Russia, Little Venice, Little Vienna, Little Paris. Glistening up on the heights, Odessa became not a distillation of Middle Europe but a sophisticated and notably secular city, with people of many nationalities and religions living together in closer proximity than they did even in New York. The city's wide boulevards were lined with French and Italian cafes, lavish Beaux-Arts town houses painted in soft yellows, mochas, and blues, and the acacia trees that warded off strong sea breezes. Architects commissioned from St. Petersburg and cities across Europe designed a baroque opera house, a Wedgwood blue-and-white English club, the stock exchange, the famous *Potemkin* stairway, and also a large downtown synagogue. For tolerant Odessa had many tens of thousands of Jews. One of them was Shura's father.

Paul Gerschenkron was a Russian businessman and a true Micaw-ber—the lifelong victim of pecuniary liabilities to which he was unable to respond. His father was a lawyer, a kindly, witty man who suffered from tuberculosis and often spent time away from his family, "taking the cure" in Finland. As a child, Paul often did without. His fortunes turned when a wealthy Odessa industrialist named Samuel Gourary took an interest in him. Gourary's great beak of a nose and overgrown beard made the deep-set eyes behind them look like twinkling seeds. Sweet-natured and very fond of children, Gourary was also religious enough that, during a period when he manufactured railroad ties, he consulted "the rebbe" before making bids on lumber contracts. Paul became his protégé. Gourary considered Paul to be such a courtly and intelligent person that after Paul completed the university in Odessa, Gourary sponsored his graduate schooling at the Sorbonne and the London School of Economics, and then made him a junior director of his business at age twenty-four. The boss asked Paul to conduct many of his foreign negotiations. That made sense: besides Russian and Ukrainian, Paul spoke Arabic, Hebrew, Turkish, Romanian, Polish, German, French, Italian, and English. He learned new languages so quickly that people said he could reach out and pluck them from the air like balloons on strings.

Paul also had a common touch. He ran a strict shop, but he did not subscribe to old Russian industrial theories linking steady production with the infliction of steady beatings. He got to know the laborers and treated them with sympathy and respect, giving his own money freely to workers' funds and to individuals who came to him with long faces and sad stories. He was a popular boss.

Paul may have been born a Jew, but religion carried little importance for him. He married a Russian Orthodox Christian woman—Shura claimed his father converted to do so, his sister Lydia says not—made donations to the Quakers, and told his children that he didn't care what they believed in as long as they treated other people with respect. Shura was out one day with his father when a man with whiskey breath and gaunt cheeks stopped Paul outside a tavern and told him that his wife had a fever in her liver. Paul handed him fifty kopeks, "for tea," he said lightly. "At its best," Paul liked to ask, "what is religion but good manners?"

Once Paul had money, he wanted to own fine things, and the large salaries he earned as the manager of tobacco and match companies in

Odessa, Kirov, and Moscow flowed out of his hands. He became a familiar figure in the smart shops along Daribosov Street, Odessa's Champs-Élysées. Paul was always commissioning accessories: a solid gold box to hold his cigarettes, a tooled leather case for his hairbrushes, and one of the city's first showers so that he could more easily be the rare Russian who washed every day. (Even in the cold months it was a notoriously noisome country.) No Savile Row swell had anything sartorial on Shura's father. He wore brushed felt bowler hats, kidskin spats, pince-nez, silk cravates, collars cut at the most fashionable angles, and he dressed this way even when all he was doing was sitting at home in the evening, smoking a cigar and reading a blue novel.

From his father Shura inherited his gift for languages and his gift for enemies. Paul Gerschenkron was someone who looked forward to confrontations and then resolved them with a theatrical stubbornness that could have been expected from the opera buff he was. A customs man tried to cadge too a high a tariff for the four bottles of excellent French perfume Paul was bringing back to Russia from Paris as a gift for his wife. The official may have been anticipating a counteroffer, but Paul did not negotiate with scoundrels. Squinting steadily at him from behind the pince-nez, Paul poured each bottle out onto the floor of the customs house. If the tailor gave him a date to pick up an order and the clothes weren't ready, Paul rapped his cane on the counter demanding the suit "*as it is.*" He had no truck with shoddy railway conductors or theater ushers either. When Paul was led to a seat on a train or to a box in the opera house and then touched on the shoulder a few minutes later and told that, regrettably, there had been a mix-up, he always refused to move. If, however, he arrived to find his seat taken, he was wildly indignant and might grab the intruder bodily while howling, "To the gendarme! To the gendarme!" Paul was a frequent visitor to Bucharest, where the best restaurants all had house string quartets. It was common in these establishments for the first violins to step forward and serenade pretty women. Paul was married to a very pretty woman. "If you don't go away at once, I'll break your violin over your head," was his way with fiddlers.

Sophie Gerschenkron, slender and pink, always knew just how to respond to her husband's displays: "You handled that so nicely," she would say to Paul. She was an intelligent woman and understood that his obstinate streak was born of his feeling that the surrounding world was highly insecure and essentially hostile. To give in was to be destroyed by the inimical forces. It's also true that in his hopelessly Russian way, Paul lived to inspire Sophie's awe.

So did her eldest son, so she had two of them out there working full-time to impress her. Shura went to great lengths to one-up his father, not easy, given that Paul was prone to grand gestures, coming home, for instance, to tell his wife that he'd had a good run lately and so he'd bought her a little dacha out in the country. Shura countered with elaborate displays, and sometimes these schemes were too effective. Once he enlisted his younger brother Tolia's help in staging a hanging. Nooses were cinched, red liquid was splashed about the room, loud cries resounded, and chairs were kicked over. Sophie hurried into the room, looked at her two dangling children, and collapsed on the spot.

It was hopeless; Sophie Kardon was a fainter. She was the child of a brief liaison between a French governess at the imperial court and one of the tsar's economic advisers. (Shura had economics in his bones.) Both of Sophie's parents died when she was an infant, leaving her to be raised in a Bessarabian convent. She came to Odessa to study medicine, but was forced to switch to history and mathematics because she kept passing out during postmortems. Sophie was a tiny woman with a beautiful singing voice and piles of lush brown hair to go with her creamy complexion. Her husband loved that hair. When she decided in middle age to cut it off, Paul staggered about in a daze for weeks. His responses to her pregnancies were similarly distraught, and Sophie was much praised for the consideration she showed him as she went about the business of bringing forth their three babies. Shura, Tolia, and Lydia were born six years apart, and always on the weekend, giving Paul maximum recovery time from his traumas of childbirth.

Although she spent her childhood among the nuns, Sophie shared Paul's religious skepticism. "Don't have anything to do with the clergyman," she cautioned her children. "Thugs, the lot of them." Paul's older sisters were observing Jews, and in deference to them Sophie allowed each of her two sons to be circumcised and bar mitzvahed. Sophie's own system of beliefs had more to do with the occult. She was an extremely superstitious woman who feared broken mirrors, grew queasy at the sight of a dinner table set for thirteen, and counseled her children never to refuse coins to a beggar because he might be a saint. Shortly after Shura was born, an elderly friend of Sophie's warned her that it would be bad luck not to raise her firstborn under the eyes of the Lord. So Shura was the only Gerschenkron child with a true religious upbringing, albeit one that would confuse anybody. He was brought up as a Russian Orthodox Christian by a pair of freethinkers who packed him off to the synagogue whenever his pious Jewish aunts came for a visit.

Many people who have been exposed to a number of religions come to feel that the grain of all faiths amounts to the same thing—treating others with the kindness you would like them to extend to you. That was how the Gerschenkrons thought. They were enlightened humanists, far ahead of their time in tsarist Russia, a notably bigoted country where artificial biological distinctions between the "white" bones of the aristocrats and the "black" bones of serfs were contrived by the ruling class to reinforce the fiction of inherent superiority. To a very real degree, Shura was raised on an ecumenical creed with tenets best expressed by Pushkin in his poem "I Built a Monument Not Made With Hands"—the last verse in particular:

> Long will be remembered by the nation
> That of the good in men's hearts I did speak—
> That I praised freedom in this age of deprivation
> And called for mercy for the frail and the weak

Those lines were quoted so frequently in the family that all the Gerschenkron children knew them from memory, none better than Shura. "This poem Shura worshiped," says Lydia. What the entire family admired was both the nerve of the rebel poet standing up to tyranny wherever he saw it, and his belief in a moral and compassionate life. Paul and Sophie Gerschenkron were the unusual wealthy Russians of that time who were truly liberal, who sympathized with the workers and the oppressed, dispatched their children to prisons to read to "the little unfortunates," as Sophie called them, and made genuine friendships with people from lower social classes such as Sophie's dressmaker.

Their personal ethics were also progressive. Many upper-class Russian boys in their midteens had their first sexual experiences with a young peasant house girl who'd been hired by the boy's parents more on the basis of, in Shura's inimitable words, her "well-formed rear" than any domestic skills. The parental thinking was that it was safest to get it all over with at home with someone "clean." If the girl got pregnant she was sent back to her village with a small bag of coins and a lot of big talk about the depraved morals of people who seduce innocent little boys. In his memoir Shura says that his parents considered this practice "grotesque" and "tragic."

WHEN SHURA WAS SIX, SOPHIE GAVE BIRTH TO HER SECOND CHILD, Shura's brother Anatole—Tolia. There followed a long postpartem stretch when Sophie lost interest in everything but her baby. Her neglected firstborn was left to run wild. He shied eggs against windows, filled the sugar bowl with salt, and put obstacles on paths he'd lead people down, then widened his eyes when they stumbled. He also became an accomplished spitter. This last talent he owed to the combination of his taste for eating sunflower seeds and his strict adherence to two local superstitions. Every time he saw a nun he sent three gobs over his own left shoulder; whenever he encountered a gendarme, he followed the old Russian thieves' policy by hawking up a quick one over his right. During the winter, which he spent in the frigid north near the Ural Mountains, it pleased Shura to discover that when you spat, the saliva froze into a ball in midair and rolled when it hit the ground. It was in the Urals that his hands swelled with frostbite. They never returned to normal, and for the rest of his life people would catch themselves staring too long at his puffy fingers.

There was a lot that could be told about the Gerschenkron boys from their eyes. The enthusiastic Tolia's were always huge and bright. Shura's were heavy-lidded and wary, narrow doorways to what as an adult he sometimes called "my dark Russian soul." He was moody and

prone to worry. A persistent source of agitation was his father's libertine habits. Paul's preoccupation with his wardrobe was regarded by Shura as a daily reminder of the extravagant ways that were always plunging the family into difficulties. Shura registered his disapproval by being perpetually disheveled himself. In good years Paul bought each of his sons a custom-tailored suit on his birthday; Shura left all of his in the closet. Instead he appeared for breakfast every day in a Russian sailor's shirt.

That Paul was attractive to all sorts of women, some of whom he failed to discourage, was something Shura found deeply unsettling. And although Sophie was far less inclined than her husband to engage in "betrayals," Shura was aware that she too had extramarital affairs. He knew because Sophie took him with her to the park, where she rendezvoused with men who seemed most disappointed that she'd brought her son along this time. "Sex," she explained to Lydia, "is just an appetite, like eating and drinking. If you go over the top, it won't do you any good." Broad-minded and cosmopolitan though she was, at some things Sophie drew the line. She agreed with Paul that her children should be citizens of the world who spoke many languages, but she also knew her husband well. One of Sophie's requirements for the mademoiselles she hired to teach her children French was that they had to be older than she was.

In response, from an early age Shura lurched between ribaldry and prudishness. As a little boy he was already very interested in sex. He picked the locks that guarded Paul's shelf of pornographic books and listened avidly to anything "French" the older boys in his school had to say about women. He developed a risqué conversational technique— the deliberate sexual misunderstanding. Sitting at dinner, Paul might mention a nephew of his in Kiev who was operating a hotel. "What did you say?" Shura would inquire in a loud voice. "He's running a house of ill-repute? Was that it? So, we have a relative in the brothel business. Well, well. Do relations get a discount?" In the end, however, all Shura did was talk about it. He could always make exceptionally suggestive remarks, but, wanting to lead a different life than his parents had, Shura suppressed his sensual instincts. The dismay he felt at his parents' behavior was never expressed directly. Instead, he acted out his frustrations with mischief.

One Sunday he lured a well-dressed youth to the pump and thoroughly doused him. Animals were treated no more gently. Out for a stroll, Shura noticed a bowl of freshly stewed fruit someone had set out on the windowsill to cool. Next to the fruit was a sleeping cat. Without breaking stride Shura scooped up the cat, dropped it into the fruit, and kept going. On the beach he encountered a boy who wouldn't play with him. This was little Jascha Heifetz, who had to protect his hands, even on vacation. Unable to distinguish a child prodigy from a sniveling fiddler, Shura rewarded Heifetz with a sound thrashing for his caution.

FOR SIX YEARS SHURA ATTENDED THE *GYMNASIUM,* THE MOST ELITE institution in the country's educational hierarchy, and recalled it as "a place where one wasted time in a dull and resentful coma." School days began with the singing of "God Save the Tsar" and continued through hours of tedium and anxiety as the students waited to prove that they'd memorized the assigned pages of several different textbooks. When they were called, they walked to the front of the room, clicked their heels, bowed from the waist and recited in a frantic, racehorse mono-

tone. After they were finished their teacher made a surreptitious notation in his grade book. Although these marks were of crucial importance
for advancing from level to level, teachers never told anyone how well
they'd done on anything until final grades were posted at the end of the
year. Everybody was, of course, curious about his standing, but they
learned quickly not to ask; petty cruelty at the slightest provocation
seemed endemic to *gymnasium* teachers.

Most of the men who taught Shura were fearsome martinets to those
below them and callow bootlickers with the authorities above. They
owed their jobs to their mastery of grammar, syntax, penmanship—"A
fine hand is at least as important as a clever head," Shura was told—and
their slavish devotion to the curriculum set out by the Education Min-
istry bureaucracy in St. Petersburg. Shura's teachers did not require
students to analyze material and absolutely forbade them from offering
their opinions or observations. Anyone who questioned the system was
subject to harsh punishment. Shura was once locked in a dark closet for
six hours for making a quick comment to a friend. The year his penmanship was judged substandard he was forced to spend several hours a
day all summer long filling a huge cloth-covered copybook with Old
Church Slavonic script, writing out the same sentences hundreds of
times a day. (All his life he took a certain pleasure in his illegible scrawl.)

Shura did not enjoy being treated like a parrot, and he felt entitled to
abandon his own scruples and fight back. All his friends did the same.
Clad in uniform shirts modeled after Russian sailor's blouses, they seldom allowed a day to pass without some form of mutiny. They cheated
and lied, threw spitballs and larger missiles at the teacher while he
wrote on the blackboard, and, when the teacher was out of the room,
they filled his desk with sparrows, frogs, and firecrackers.

After spending his days at the mercy of a classical Russian education,
Shura went home and found solace in what became the central pleasure
of his life—reading books. He learned to read at four, and by age six
was a regular peruser of the Odessa newspapers. Early twentieth-
century Russian papers were enthusiastic troves of crime, suicides (always
with a romantic background), accidents, fires, and court reports. Shura's
interest in this sort of reportage left him eager to discuss what he'd
read. One day while sitting among the eight ladies who were attending

his mother's weekly tea party, he listened to a woman remark that her young daughter had developed the bad habit of running downstairs into the basement of their apartment house and playing among the winter's store of logs and potato sacks. "Oh," said Shura, thinking about a recent dispatch he'd come across. "Yes, it is very dangerous for her to go into the dark cellar. She could be raped there very easily." The room went quiet. Sophie went purple. The French governess was called. As Shura was led off to the drawing room, Mademoiselle wondered what had happened. When he told her, the governess laughed. Did he know what the word meant? No, he did not. *"Ah, ces russes!"* she said. *"Ils sont trop drôles."*

Between the ages of eleven and fourteen Shura read a lot, and what he read he remembered better than anything he picked up during the rest of his life. When he sat in a soft drawing room chair or in the crotch of a tree out at the rural estate, turning the pages of Balzac or Ibsen or Dickens or, more discretely, *Anna Karenina*—forbidden by his parents because of "the betrayal"—he said he felt "this is life."

Most of the books from early childhood that meant a lot to him then were by well-regarded writers—Jules Verne, Mark Twain, Jack London, Hans Christian Andersen. An exception is Talbot Baines Reed's *The Willoughby Captains*, a brittle tale of English schoolboy life in which a school briefly falls into chaos and then recovers because the misdemeanors of the moment are no match for the moral stability of the institution. "Our childhood was dominated by that book," Shura's sister Lydia says. "Part of it was the attraction to all Russians in that time of all things English. But perhaps it was more the old precepts of fair play, decency and honor were still a beacon for us in a darkening world."

The forms of showing off among Shura and his friends became more cerebral as they grew older. Book learning was the central daily activity for city boys, and in the neat application of rural values to urban life, they began devising gladiatorial displays of intellectual dexterity. Soon they were reading at violent speeds and reaping prodigious literary harvests—spectacular efforts predictable in their purpose: they wanted to impress girls. You could arrive at the home of a gray-eyed object of your admiration and inspire her affections by embellishing your conversation with long quotations from Sir Walter Scott. (Since nonchalance was recognized as the handmaiden of dominance, this had to be done casually.) Then you might dazzle her father with offhand speculations on Scott's debt to Cervantes. If a rival appeared, you could unsettle him with a slight raising of your eyebrows when he confessed he hadn't read any Sir Walter Scott besides *Ivanhoe*. And finally you devastated your entire circle by maintaining a page-turning pace through all of *Waverley* that nobody else could match. It was typically Russian to read a favorite author's entire oeuvre. It was typically Gerschenkron to tell people that he was trying to read *every* author's entire oeuvre.

Shura and his friends were also reading for each other. Some days after school, instead of playing soccer—Shura was a scrappy right forward—they gathered for discussions of their reading. For these conversations they prepared with athletic intensity. Shura filled notebooks with book summaries, references to ancillary reading, quotations to be memorized, and his own speculations. During the discussions, positions shifted constantly, the japes, jibes, and bons mots flew thick, ground frequently shifted but was never given, and, before they knew it, they'd been going for seven hours on whether the soul was immortal.

Fifty years later Shura was still at it. One evening in Cambridge, a Harvard graduate student named Abbott Gleason encountered him at a small dinner party. Gleason happened to mention how much he admired the novels of Vladimir Nabokov. Shura, who regarded Nabokov as a pretentious and vastly overrated writer with precious little to say, told Gleason exactly that. Gleason pressed on, arguing that Nabokov was certainly a more important novelist than any number of the great Europeans—Sir Walter Scott, for instance. Shura's eyes glinted and, says Gleason, "I was then annihilated. I couldn't believe how much he knew about Sir Walter Scott. He cited criticism of Scott. He made reference to assorted works of Scott. He quoted from Scott. It was a torrent, an absolute avalanche of Sir Walter Scott. I got the feeling he could also do this with Daniel Defoe, with George Eliot, with Victor Hugo, with various Scandinavians, with an untold number of writers, really. I'll never forget how he rubbed my nose in the mashed potatoes."

The one area where Shura and his friends were unanimous was the superiority of Russian writers to all others. Turgenev, Dostoyevsky,

Gogol, Goncharov, Chekhov, Lermontov, Blok, and especially Tolstoy and Pushkin were their heroes and pop icons, for they agreed with Lermontov that "the story of a man's soul, however trivial, can be more interesting than the story of a whole nation." The defining literary question of Shura's youth was whether you preferred Tolstoy or Dostoyevsky. He was a Tolstoy man. He read *War and Peace* more times than he remembered, and sometimes turned from the last page right back to the first and started over again, so unwilling was he to leave the world of the book. Dostoyevsky, he argued, was "a cruel talent" who wrote clumsy Russian. In the face of a particularly spirited defense by a Dostoyevsky lover, he would defer a little. "It is true that the cruel talent improves in translation."

Sometimes there was the impulse to see in real life what he had read on a page. Shura had owned a rifle since age nine, and when he and his friends went off into the woods with their guns, they were reenacting scenes from Turgenev's "Sketches From a Hunter's Album." After they read *Oliver Twist*, they formed a pickpockets' school. The Bavarian writer Ludwig Thoma's *The Stories of a Naughty Boy* improved their skills at egg throwing. It was especially gratifying to egg a window in the winter, counseled Thoma, because frozen yolk was so difficult to clean off cold glass. When winter came, Shura tested the theory; then every day for weeks he could see for himself that Thoma was right.

At fourteen he nearly ran away to sea. Growing up by the Black Sea made him curious about life on the decks, and, when he began reading naval adventure stories, the lure of the tar and rigging became overpowering. Without informing his parents Shura sat for—and passed—a merchant marine exam. Afterward he came home and casually announced he was quitting the *gymnasium* to become a sailor. His father nodded just as casually and returned to his newspaper. It was early summer. For months, Shura moved with a rolling gait, spoke in a slight brogue, and watched intently to see if his father was flinching. Paul wasn't. Fall came and Shura quietly went back to school. He always said that Paul had handled the situation brilliantly. If he'd been challenged, Shura explained, his honor would have forced him to go.

At sixteen Shura went off and found himself a summer job working as the assistant to an impoverished net fisherman. Shura slept on the beach, or under an overturned rowboat when it rained, ate seafood three times a day, and passed his waking hours on the trawler, waist-deep in squirming fish. By summer's end he had cured himself forever of the lust for water. His happiest hours were spent on dry land, at the market, bargaining with a usurious old woman fishmonger. His boss couldn't get a decent price from the woman because he owed her money. She had once lent him enough for a new boat and then had set her interest rates so high that the fisherman could never hope to pay her back and was forever dependent upon her—very limited—mercy. Shura had no such constraints. Frowning at the woman, he told her he was poised to buy the fisherman out and would then be sure to do all his business with her competitors if she didn't treat him well. "She used to sneer at me and ask who would be wiping my nose while I was out fishing, and advise me to wait until the mother's milk would dry on my lips," he remembered. "But at the same time she half believed me." Not only did he succeed in coaxing a higher rate for the day's catch out of her, but he got his boss's debt reduced too.

The fishing job sapped all of his energy—after one especially strenuous stretch of work he didn't come out from under the overturned rowboat for seventeen hours—and he didn't have time to do anything else all summer. It got back to his friends that Shura wasn't reading. This they regarded as grounds for indictment, and they showed up on the beach to accuse him of "intellectual decline." Shura irritably waved them off, but he was gratified. Keeping up with your reading was only the start of it; Shura and his friends had an entire system of protocol. Among their rules was never to make a profit off a friend. Nor did you gossip about friends, for "if you can denounce Volodya to me, you will next denounce me to Volodya." Nothing was lower than an ingratiator except for a tattletale. You were more generous with a friend than you were with yourself, and when you gave a friend a gift you tried to choose something you knew he wanted but was too modest to buy for himself. Instant reciprocation was discouraged. This diminished the first gift, making it seem more like a transaction than a pure gesture.

Shura and his friends were intensely devoted to each other and would undoubtedly have known one another through life had politics not intervened. In 1917 Russia's roof blew off.

*   *   *

THE RUSSIAN REVOLUTION TOOK THE FORM OF SO MANY REBELLIONS, beginning as an outraged response to a corrupt and decadent regime and then, as it achieved success and power, losing its early idealism as its leaders became far worse than the venal old shufflers they had overthrown.

Like much of the guilt-ridden liberal intelligentsia, the Gerschenkrons were initially sympathetic to the Bolsheviks. Although Paul was a consummate capitalist, he and Sophie knew well that this henpecked tsar, who had submitted so meekly to his wife's effusions over the charlatan savant Rasputin, was a hapless despot who did little for the starving peasantry. Anyone who protested joined the multitudes rotting in Russian prisons. Years of gradual decay had left the Russian countryside populated by illiterate, often syphilitic people clothed in rags, living in vermin-infested hovels where they watched their babies starve to death. Then the defeats of the First World War made a shambles of the entire country. Millions of Russian soldiers were massacred abroad, while famine and typhus devastated the cities at home. Life in Odessa was miserable. From 1914 to 1918 the port was blockaded, causing grave shortages of meat, bread, and fuel. There were long bread lines and citywide blackouts every night. Outbreaks of looting were common. The five Gerschenkrons spent one cold winter living together in a single room that Paul heated by filling the fireplace with chairs and tables he took from the rest of the house and splintered with his hatchet.

Shura was not terribly interested in politics as a boy. In a burst of political enthusiasm he and his friends did all sign up to be Mensheviks (a democratic faction of Marxist Socialists), but it is also true that they were turned down for "political ignorance" and "extreme youth." Once the stirrings of revolution came, however, Shura took notice. He never said that he agreed with his father about the early potential of the Bolsheviks. The way he implied such feelings was by describing, in his autobiography, the martyring of his friend Pashka Toporov.

During the Russo-Japanese war, Pashka's father had done a brave service on the battlefield for the director of a margarine factory. After the war he went to work in the factory, where he died in an explosion, leaving Pashka to grow up alone with his mother in a filthy slum. The still-grateful factory director learned of this and assumed the burden of educating Pashka, paying his *gymnasium* tuition. That was how Pashka became the only working-class pupil in Shura's grade at school. Pashka wasn't much of a student, but he was loved and admired by his peers for his personal qualities: he was hardworking, tough, brave, loyal, and a talented fund of profanity. When older boys picked on Shura or his friends, Pashka defended them. Then he took them on tours of the factory yards near his home, where they could climb on piles of rusting machinery.

One day at school, the reading lesson in French class involved a story called "All That Glitters Is Not Gold." It told of a poor boy who envies the rich boy living across the street until he learns that the child of prosperity has a pair of paralyzed legs. It wasn't much as literature, but this was a feast compared with the gruel they were usually served, and Shura was musing to himself about how pleasant it was to live in a just world where the rich have their problems too, when suddenly Pashka Toporov blurted out, "What business does he have to be paralyzed?" Shura was astonished. He had never before heard a student make an unbidden comment in a Russian school. The teacher was just as surprised and asked Pashka to repeat what he'd said. He did and was immediately called to the front of the classroom, forced to make a deep bow from his waist to the teacher, and then asked to explain himself. "Rich boys are not paralyzed," Pashka said. He was clearly very upset. "In our house water keeps running down the wall. My sister is sick. She cannot walk. This is not just my family. There are millions of families like that all over Russia. I have read all about it." He pulled out a Bolshevik pamphlet. "Here it is," he cried, and began to read aloud. He didn't get far. The teacher cut him off and led him out of the room and down to the administration offices, where he was instantly expelled and given a "wolf's certificate" banning him from all schools in Russia. He was not even allowed to return to claim his possessions. The janitor brought them out to him and Pashka was sent off with a warning never to cross the school's threshold again.

This probably happened in 1917. By 1920 the tsar had been shot and the Bolsheviks had taken Odessa twice, lost it back to the White Russian army both times, and now were once again converging upon the city. The machine-gun and rifle fire was so intense in the Gerschenkrons' neighborhood that nobody left the house for three days. Finally things quieted down with the Bolsheviks apparently back in power, and people began to make their way furtively out into the light. Shura was looking through the main courtyard gate when a Bolshevik horseman pranced up. He had on a bright red coat and a carbine was slung over his shoulder. A red cockade blazed above his handsome face. It was easy to tell how happy he was because he was singing a gleeful song of victory at the top of his lungs.

"Pashka!" Shura exclaimed.

"Oh, that's you," said Pashka Toporov. "I see you keep yourself hidden behind a gate. You didn't use to be such a yellow coward. Do you realize that we have thrown those Whites into the sea?" At that moment, a couple of White soldiers turned the corner. One of them dropped to his knee, took aim, and before Pashka could reach for his gun he was shot off his horse. Shura helped carry him into a neighbor's kitchen and ran out to find a surgeon. But there was no helping Pashka. The Bolsheviks gave him a hero's funeral and buried him in a "brotherly grave." Pashka Toporov is the only person identified by first and last name in "The Uses of Adversity."

THE RUSSIAN CIVIL WAR LASTED FROM 1918 TO 1920 IN ODESSA. Peaceful lulls would give way without warning to pitched and bloody battles. Bands of liquored-up peasants roamed the countryside looting cows, pigs, and horses, requisitioning crops and treating farmers like crows, shooing them off their own property. The chaotic nature of the violence made it difficult for normal citizens to gauge when it was safe to move around. One moment Shura was growing blisters on his hand as he pumped water for the fire crews who were keeping the city from burning down; the next he was running for his life. You never knew when a light armored car would come careering round the corner to spray the block with bullets. It was a traumatic moment in history—the country was being cleaved to pieces— but in his memoir Shura implies that his reaction was similar to that of the young Vera Brittain, who said that when the Great War began, "It came to me not as a superlative tragedy, but as an interruption of the most exasperating kind to my personal plans." In other words, the Revolution was simply a less auspicious time for showing off.

The Bolsheviks turned out to be just as corrupt as the Romanovs and much crueler. In 1919 Maxim Gorky told Victor Serge that they were "drunk with authority," cramping the violent, spontaneous anarchy of the Russian people and "starting bloody despotism all over again." In Odessa the Reds stirred up crowds of people into frenzied mobs that set fires, looted shops, and killed with random appetite. Every dictatorial regime seems to have a highly organized instrument of repression with a malevolent nickname, and in Bolshevik Russia the Extraordinary Commission for Struggle Against Counterrevolution, Sabotage and Speculation was known as the Cheka. Each day this ruthless secret police force rounded up entire city blocks of people and herded them down to the railway station where they were tortured and shot. Everyone came to dread the sound of truck engines revved up high—the Cheka technique for drowning out the screams and the gunfire. One day there was a change in policy; the Cheka decided it would be even more intimidating to switch off the motors. They also took to pasting up posters of the bloodiest corpses on walls all over town. Among their many insidious stratagems was the creation of the Day of Peaceful Uprising. This was a flexible new holiday. It could be declared any time a cadre of local officials and Cheka men chose to arrive at your door and announce that they were claiming your possessions for the People. The Cheka men were talented confiscators. Redistribution, however, proved a more elusive skill for them.

By the winter of 1920, with it now illegal to earn a profit, a great exodus of merchants, foreigners, and political and religious undesirables began leaving Odessa for Western Europe and America. Paul didn't want to go, refused even to consider the prospect, and instead became willfully optimistic. When word came that the Reds had been ousted from Kiev, Paul rejoiced and bought a new cow for the small country estate eight miles outside town, declaring that he wanted things to be up and running properly before the family went out there for the summer. Then, over Sophie's objections, Paul asked Shura to deliver the cow to the estate.

Shura was terrified—people were starving and bandits stalked the edges of the city—but he wasn't going to have his father think he was gutless. Dressed in his school uniform blouse, plodding an open road beside a fat, handsome cow in a starving country, he could not have felt more exposed. Yet after six hours he was able to turn the animal over unscathed to Grigori, the estate gardener. Shura was always pleased to see Grigori, who knew an astounding number of vulgar poems, all of which he attributed to famous poets. While Shura ate a piece of brown bread "steeped" with salt given to him by Grigori's wife, Grigori wondered if he'd like to hear a little Pushkin. Shura said "Why not?" and was treated to a shrill rendition of an obscene verse poem. "Some Lermontov?" asked the gardener. "Absolutely!" said Shura, and he heard the story of a priest's wife who endures a violent sexual assault. At the conclusion of the narrative, Grigori's wife crossed herself, and Shura said he had to head home. Grigori invited him to spend the night. Shura demurred. There was school the next day, he explained, and he owed a paper on Ivan the Terrible. "Ivan the Terrible," Grigori smirked. "You should pay attention to the Ivans of our day who are much more terrible." The two shook hands, Grigori's wife crossed herself, and Shura set off for the city.

Shura liked to sing, but he was aware that he had no ear for music, so he never sang unless he was alone. This long walk seemed like a propitious time. Unfortunately he had miscalculated. His mauling of a song about the beauties of "Mother Kiev" attracted the attention of a Bolshevik marine. Not even Lenin himself would have said that this was a particularly bright marine. That Shura was wearing a Russian sailor's blouse but did not otherwise appear to be a Russian sailor seemed suspicious to the marine. "Are you a sailor?" the marine asked. Shura said he was a *gymnast*. Why, then, was he wearing a sailor's blouse? The explanation was unsatisfactory, and he was arrested for "impersonating a sailor" and taken to a nearby artillery battery, where the marine announced that he'd caught "a spy." Shura lost his temper. "That's a dirty lie," he said. A great many marines then spent hours trying to make him confess. "You know," one of them told Shura, "a year ago when the Bolsheviks had to abandon the city, it was boys your age who shot at our backs. I, for one, will not be deceived by baby talk." Shura admitted nothing.

Finally a compromise was reached. A report of the incident was prepared in which it was set down that Shura had dishonored the Red fleet by wearing a Russian sailor's blouse without being a Russian sailor. Shura refused to sign the report. There was a moment of confusion. Then a marine said, "In that case *we* will sign it," and they all did. Next they confiscated his blouse, and when Shura pointed out that he needed to go out in public wearing something above his shorts, he was sent back to Odessa in a genuine blue-and-white-striped Russian sailor's T-shirt. On the way home it occurred to him that, if he were a spy, he would now know everything about that Bolshevik artillery battery.

EVENTUALLY, EVEN PAUL HAD TO ADMIT THAT THE GERschenkrons' future in Russia was unpromising. For quite some time he had been operating Samuel Gourary's tobacco factory on his own. The Old Man had taken one look at the Bolsheviks and declared to anyone who would listen that they were nothing but hoodlums and opportunists, a bravura display that forced him into hiding. Through the war the factory continued to be productive, partly because the workers remained devoted to Paul. That was the case even among the Bolshevik sympathizers, who did not blame him when they groused that there was not a drop of vodka to be found anymore in the whole damned country.

After the Old Man disappeared, Paul received periodic visits from Cheka representatives looking for him. Paul always told them that Samuel Gourary had done a lot for him and he would never betray him. Once a pistol was put to Paul's head. He smiled and said, "Listen, boys, if I were that scared of you, I'd be sitting under the desk, not at it." They laughed and slapped him on the back and told him, "You're okay, comrade." It helped that one of Paul and Sophie's old classmates from Odessa University was the local Cheka chief.

Then arose a problem so serious that it trumped powerful connections. The factory was a joint stock operation, and, while most of the shares were owned by the Gourary family, there were also minor share-holders who were entitled to dividends on factory profits. Over the war years Paul had maintained a policy of blowing with the political winds. While the Bolsheviks were in charge, Paul suspended the dividends. When the Whites regained power, he resumed paying them. In December 1920 the Bolsheviks seized the factory office files; the auditors could see that Paul had been "giving away the state's profits," and they were not amused. "Permit me to congratulate you on making the acquaintance of the Cheka," one of them said.

Word was passed to Paul—possibly by the Cheka chief, possibly by a female Bolshevik admirer of Paul's at the factory—that he'd been black-listed and had better get out of the country fast or it would be the back of the railway station for him. A family meeting was held that night after supper. Paul was calm. He said that the house had to be abandoned immediately and that it would be best for him to flee. The logical destination was Paris, where he had many business connections and friends from his years at the Sorbonne. It was decided that he would take Shura and the others would follow after Paul had found a job and got settled. Until then, Sophie, Lydia, and Tolia could stay with Sophie's dressmaker, who was generously making her attic available for as long as Sophie needed it. The Cheka chief offered to get Sophie new papers printed up in her maiden name. By the next morning Sophie and the little children were installed at the dressmaker's, while Shura and his father took temporary refuge at another friend's home, where Paul planned their escape. Getting out of Russia forced all of the Gerschenkrons to rely on a large number of people for shelter and discretion. Nobody ever failed them.

Two weeks later Paul and Shura set out for the Romanian border. Their entire complement of luggage was a single flour sack stuffed with Paul's elegant dress clothes for Paris, bills in various currencies, and false papers that some of the Bolshevik workers in the factory had signed and stamped for Paul. These papers said that the bearer was going to Romania to purchase raw materials for the factory. Paul hoped he would not have to do much walking on the trip; Sophie had sewn a number of Swiss gold francs into his underwear and they were heavy.

Shura placed two books in the flour sack, a small volume of poems by Alfred de Musset and a political history of nineteenth-century Europe. The rest of his library he left on the shelves.

A hired cabman drove them in his buggy across the vast gray steppe toward a town on the Dniestr River—then the Romanian border—where Paul had a friend. Once Odessa's grain elevators were out of sight, they saw nothing but bleak tundra. That made it disturbing when they came upon a cart loaded full of cabbages parked in the middle of the empty road. The cart driver was cursing as they drove up, and he appeared to have been in a foul mood for quite some time. It turned out that before dawn he had set out for the vegetable market. Then someone warned him of roadblocks manned by Bolsheviks who were confiscating everything. So he turned around. Then someone else came by and told him, "Why, no! The road is clear." This had been going on all day. He was reversing directions every hour. What a quandary! He swore mightily. After they left the cabbage man, Shura looked back and saw him preparing to make another try at the market. "A triste pendulum marking the uncertainty of the times," he thought.

At dusk they stopped in a small farming village and slept fully clothed on narrow wooden benches. The next day they reached the frontier, where Paul's friend welcomed them with kisses and Shura blushed at the sight of his very pretty youngest daughter. Paul's friend said it was not yet safe for them to be smuggled across the river, so he installed them in a nearby house. After a few hours of waiting, Shura no longer felt like being a fugitive, so he opened the door, went out, found a public library, and withdrew a book. That night Paul's friend reported that a local Bolshevik commissar, an old pal of his, was going to help them. They soon met the commissar, a plump, friendly sort who said that yes, indeed, a peasant from a nearby village owed him a favor and he would be so pleased to spend it on these good friends of his good friend, a man who had such a very pretty youngest daughter. He gave her a smile. She smiled back at him. The commissar said that a nearby village would be a much safer place for the Gerschenkrons to make their crossing, and he promised he would ask the peasant to help them do it. They just had to be patient.

Days passed. Paul grew increasingly uneasy. One afternoon he visited a teahouse where he met a man who offered to sell him some Polish money. "I have no use for Polish currency," Paul said, but he worried that this had been an informer trying to trap him into revealing his plans.

The next day, a group of officials and their Cheka escorts arrived at Paul's friend's house and declared the Day of Peaceful Uprising. The officials spent many hours making careful inventory of the friend's possessions. When finally they were gone, the friend's very pretty youngest daughter played Chopin's "Funeral March" on the doomed piano, and everyone cheered up.

In the morning Shura proposed that before the house they were staying in was visited by the officials, they should transfer the flour sack to the friend's house, which had already been searched. This was done. Unfortunately, Paul had just draped his custom-tailored *visitka* (morning coat and striped trousers) over the back of a chair when some of the officials returned to clarify a detail. They saw the chair and looked at Paul's friend as though he'd been holding out on them.

"Ah, a *visitka*—is it yours?" the lead official asked Paul's friend.

"No, it is mine," Paul said.

"*Documents!*" cried another man in a gray fur cap. He was the Cheka representative. Paul produced them and the Cheka man read through them twice. "Why do you need a *visitka* for such a business trip?" he asked, looking up.

"As you know well, Odessa is starving," Paul said. "I took these clothes along in the hopes of bartering them for some food."

The first official was examining the coat's label. "The curious thing is that this coat was bought in Bucharest, in Romania," he announced with a meaningful glance.

"Yes," Paul admitted. "I bought it there in 1915, when I visited Polish Russian ambassador on business for our firm."

"That was the tsarist ambassador, was it not?

"Yes," said Paul. "There were no others then."

"Yes," the Cheka man repeated after a heavy silence. "There were no others then. But now you can go talk to the authorities and nobody will give a damn how you are dressed. You don't need your *visitka* anymore."

"You deprive me of the possibility to bring a sack of potatoes back to my family," said Paul.

"I hope you'll get your raw materials," the Cheka man said smoothly. "You should stop mixing official business with pleasures." After they left, Paul got a kiss from his friend's wife and a compliment from the very pretty youngest daughter: "You can really lie!" she said.

It took a full two weeks before the commissar finally sent word that a horse and buggy would be there that night to take the two Gerschenkrons to a little riverside village from which they could make their crossing. The buggy driver arrived in a very nervous state. He feared roving bands of highwaymen that, he said, "are everywhere in this tortured country." It turned out that they saw nobody. When they got to the little village and found the commissar's peasant friend waiting for them, Paul pulled out a thick wad of Soviet rubles and presented them all to the buggy driver. The value of the Soviet ruble was depreciating nearly by the hour, so this was mostly a gesture. The driver responded with a majestic oath, one that managed to embrace, in a single protracted sentence of considerable syntactic complexity, his life and his trade, the hardships of the times, Trotsky's mother, the perils of the return trip, the scarcity of oats, and the Day of Peaceful Uprising. He was mourning, in particular, he confided, the recent confiscation of his prized fox fur shortcoat.

The peasant left them in a hut telling them to wait there until he came back. Sitting in the hut was an old, toothless woman who drank cup after cup of rancid carrot tea while declaiming against the Lord God for what he'd done to Russia. At two in the morning, the peasant finally leaned his head inside the door and said they could go. Paul was nightblind, so Shura took his father by the arm as the peasant led them through backyards and orchards. At one point, a figure suddenly appeared a few yards in front of them. The peasant raised his pistol, then lowered it and went to investigate. He came back a few minutes later looking relieved. "Nothing to be concerned about," he said. "It is only the village thief. He has to work at night."

When they got to the Dniestr, the land along the river was flat on the Russian bank but rose up in a tall bluff on the Romanian side. At the crossing, the guard, who had already been bribed, now demanded more money. Paul had only a few rubles left, but this was no time for empty-ing cologne bottles. He took them out, tucked them into his gold ciga-rette case and said, "Will this be enough?" It was. The peasant walked them halfway across the frozen river, kissed their cheeks, made the sign of the cross and turned back. A distant shot rang out as they scrambled up the steep slope, but only one shot, and it came nowhere near them.

They hoisted themselves over the bluff, tumbled down the other side, and landed in a road. Brushing themselves off, they began walk-ing. Their destination was Kishniev, where Paul had another friend. Soon enough, a man with a wagon full of hogs came along and offered them a ride. Paul sat up front with the man. Shura crouched behind them with the hogs, who treated him as an equal. The man wondered where they were going, and Paul named a town where the Kishniev train stopped. The man said good luck to that. Anyone who walked through that town's gates had to show Romanian papers. Only people in carriages were waved on past. He hoped Paul had Romanian papers. Paul had none. Soon enough, however, a lady in a carriage came by, and Paul hailed her and asked for a ride to town. The woman inquired where they were from.

"Kishniev," said Paul.

"What is the price of milk in Kishniev?" asked the woman.

"*Le même prix,*" said Paul laconically. The woman looked over the nicely curving eyebrows of this man who spoke such charmingly accented French and said she would be pleased to offer him and his "young friend" a ride into town.

They took a train to Kishniev, trusting that again nobody would ask them for papers. Nobody did. "One must believe in one's own star," Paul said to Shura when they were walking through the Kishniev ter-minus. From there they went on to Bucharest, bought an Austrian visa, and boarded a three-day train for Vienna. Paul hoped to rest there for a week before pushing on to Paris. Their train car was full of people laughing and telling what seemed to Shura to be wonderfully com-pelling things. He couldn't be sure of this, because he didn't understand any German.

Back in Odessa, neither of them could have known that this would happen, nor could they fully realize what they were leaving behind until years later. Sophie, Lydia, and Tolia had moved into the dressmaker's attic where things were hard. There was no milk in Odessa, and hideous ulcers appeared around four-year-old Lydia's eyes. Sophie went to Paul's brother, who was a doctor, and he gave her some drops, but the left eye never completely healed. One day they all visited Paul's father, who was very ill with tuberculosis. Lydia thought she could tell that the frail man missed Paul as much as she did, and she tried to cheer him with a few clumsy ballet steps. "Bravo, Lidochka," he quavered. A few days later he died.

PAUL AND SHURA NEVER SAW RUSSIA AGAIN. LEAVING RUSSIA SAVED Shura's life, but the Revolution cost him plenty. He was sixteen when he fled Odessa and already into that time when a young man forms his expectations of what life will be like. In the classic adolescent pattern, he had ventured out, taken risks, tried his limits, unsettled a little dust, and was developing a confident sense of who he was. It had been, in many ways, an idyllic Russian childhood. Then, suddenly, the society around him collapsed. For a boy who had known his homeland as such a cultured and interesting place, watching it plunge into a chaos of burning and killing made him feel the way the writer Ivan Bunin did when he asked, "What have they done to our country?"

Whatever of his that wouldn't fit in a grain sack to be carried out of Odessa disappeared, along with most of his relatives. Whether it was Russian firing squads or Nazi death camps or the far-flung diaspora or just the daily hardship of life in the Soviet Union, by 1942 there weren't any more Gerschenkrons in Russia. Lost to him were his home, his language, his community, and his future. A person who grows up in a stable place has a broad time horizon, a long view of where his life is going. Shura no longer knew where he'd be next Wednesday. That uncertainty took from him some of the pleasure of possibility, and after he left Russia the latches to his inner life were more tightly fastened than before. Shura had thick brown hair, and at about this time he stopped cutting it short, creating a remarkable contrast in photographs between the waves rolling freely across the top of his head and the clenched expression below them. The experience of living through the

Russian Revolution exaggerated Shura's natural reserve, and his own accounts of the time are sparse and unrevealing. He was prematurely seasoned in disappointment, an ebullient person made watchful when he was still a boy. "After the Revolution he was very careful as to whom he was speaking," his sister Lydia remembered. "He opened up to our father, but he would not let other people know what his thoughts and opinions were. He was very cautious, and he didn't talk about how he felt."

THE BIG TEST

How salty tastes the bread abroad and how difficult
to mount and descend foreign staircases.

Dante

WHEN THEIR TRAIN FROM BUCHAREST PULLED INTO
Vienna, Shura and his father entered a country whose
ropes had been cut. Only six years before, in 1914, the
Austrian emperor Franz Joseph had ruled at the center of the prosperous Austro-Hungarian empire. Then began what Paul Gerschenkron
told his children was the cruelest, most abysmal waste of human beings
he'd ever seen. The First World War was a brutal slaughter that
brought credit to no country, but Austria may well have got the worst of
it. Austro-Hungary's soldiers were so badly beaten that the historian
Richard Rickett describes this as "perhaps the only instance in history
of an army that went off to war and never came back." The Habsburg
empire was hacked into separate Polish, Slav, Czech, and Hungarian
pieces, with Austria yielding its proprietary access to Bohemian potatoes, sugar, and textiles, Hungarian grain, Silesian coal, Galician oil,
and the entire lush Southern Tyrol, pocketed at the surrender table by
Italy. The Treaty of St. Germain also demanded that Austria pay war
reparations to the Allies, but that was just piling on. Austria had been
stripped of its resources and its markets and had less to give than anyone. All that remained was a humiliated little rump of a country
crowded with starving refugees, homeless young people, and derelict

former Habsburg cavalry officers who went trudging about every day in their tattered blue tunics because they had nothing else to wear.

If Austria couldn't have its empire anymore, it would have liked an *Anschluss*—an annexation—by Germany, but the Allies weren't about to permit a new Teutonic empire. So Austria became that strangest of phenomena: a country given its independence that did not want it—a republic without republicans.

Shura must have seen some of those dolorous images—the magnificent Schönbrunn Palace transformed into a welfare center; the emaciated women waiting in bread lines; the newspapers describing Austrian politicians traveling across Europe begging for flour to feed their starving people—but he never mentioned them except, in a passing way, as elements of his adventures.

THE FIRST THING THOSE FRESH-OFF-THE-TRAIN IMMIGRANTS Paul and Shura did when they arrived in Vienna was go to a cafe for a big lunch. All that was on the menu was eggs and sausages. When they asked for some bread as well, the waiter brought over two rolls, and instead of placing them on the table, he slid them into their laps. It turned out that during the grain shortages, Austrian restaurants got their bread through the black market, something they preferred not to flaunt. Since the whole town was dining out on illegal bread, nobody was worried about being arrested. The discretion was a way of maintaining a code of civilized behavior during a time when hardship forced people to make small ethical compromises. As was his nature, from the moment Shura set foot in Austria he was formulating notions of "typically Austrian" behavior. He thought of those rolls arriving under his napkin as his introduction to the distinctively light Austrian touch.

When it came to privations, illicit bread was the least of it. The food shortages were acute enough that people took to mixing sawdust in with their cooking and eating their pets. Men couldn't find jobs, and fuel was so scarce that families burned the wooden crosses they removed from cemeteries and wore overcoats and gloves indoors. Nobody but foreigners could buy anything because the currency was worthless, so worthless that in Vienna the phrase "inflation story" came to mean something astonishing, incredible, not to be believed—and possibly also true. Among the inflation stories in wide circulation was the one about the woman who wallpapered her house in large bank bills, another about the schoolchildren who did their homework on schilling notes (there was hardly any paper), and one about the man who used a wheelbarrow as his wallet.

With Vienna overburdened by refugees and returning soldiers, there were also housing shortages. The best Paul could find was a bed for himself in a friend's apartment and one for Shura at the Hotel Royal. A friend of a friend had a room there and was willing to share it for the week until the Gerschenkrons journeyed on to Paris. Shura's new roommate was a well-dressed flaneur, and he looked Shura over carefully as the introductions were made. It was six o'clock, but the long flight from Russia had exhausted Shura. He got into bed and slept for fourteen hours.

The roommate wasn't there when Shura finally awoke the next morning. Shura got dressed and spent the day wandering around Vienna by himself. Russian steeples were all covered with crosses, and as he looked up at the stone eagle perched on the spire atop St. Stephan's cathedral, Shura told himself, "This is Europe!"

At the end of the afternoon, when Shura got back to the hotel, he found a housemaid, a clerk, and a handyman all gathered with his roommate in the hallway outside his room. There seemed to be some consternation. "Here he is!" shouted the roommate who began upbraiding Shura. "Why did you not open the door for me last night?" he demanded. "Do you realize that I had to spend the night sleeping in a bathtub? I woke up the whole floor knocking on the door." Shura began to apologize. The roommate was just getting started. Could Shura not at least have left the key with the porter? Didn't he know that metal was so scarce in Austria that no hotel had duplicate or master keys?

The roommate was still going strong, holding forth on Shura's general rudeness and lack of brains, when Paul arrived. He had paid a visit to someone he knew—Samuel Gourary's son Jules, and Jules had been very pleased to see him. Jules knew all about how Paul had protected his father, the Old Man, from the Odessa Cheka. Jules was grateful, and he promptly offered Paul a position running his turbine factory in the little town of Stockerau, northwest of Vienna. This was a good job, and who could say what Paul's old friends from the Sorbonne would turn up for him in Paris? Maybe nothing. He hadn't been to France in a long time. So he had accepted Jules's offer. Paul was optimistic. The collapse of the Habsburgs and the militarism that had gone with them was, he said, "a good thing," because Austria could have "a new start." His businessman's instincts told him that although Austria looked devastated now, there would soon be wonderful opportunities for investment as the country began to rebuild. Shura had been looking forward to trying out his French in Paris. He asked his father what he was going to do in a country where he couldn't speak the language. "You will have to learn it," Paul said. The roommate smirked. "That will take him a long time, I'm sure," he said.

Shura had to agree with the man. On the train ride out to Stockerau, Paul wanted to read the newspaper. He asked Shura to tell him the name of the stations they passed so he'd know when to get off. "Dienstraum," announced Shura at the first stop. Paul nodded. "Dienstraum," he announced at the second. Most perplexing, the next stop was also Dienstraum. How was Shura supposed to know that these were the signs for the station master's office?

There was a housing shortage in Stockerau too, especially where foreigners were concerned, and all Paul turned up was a single room for himself. Shura said that was fine with him. He wanted to go to Paris, as originally planned. "Now, Shura," said Paul, and then he began to speak very seriously on the ways that learning a new language gave a person a fresh view of the world. Paul argued with the help of a torrent of quotations from Lessing, Goethe, Schiller, Herder, Kant, and Schopenhauer. Shura had read these writers in Russian translation, but Paul said that now their true powers would be revealed to him. Shura was intrigued. Then Paul shifted his argument. He understood the task wouldn't be easy, not for anyone, but he wanted Shura to show courage. That kind of remark was bound to find resonance with the old conquerer of graveyards, and it did. In a solemn voice, Shura promised he would try.

There was still the issue of locating shelter for him, a problem that was resolved only when Paul began to look outside Stockerau. Someone suggested that he try the summer resorts where it was off season and the hotel owners could probably use a little income. Sure enough, in the spa town of Baden, a drafty room was found in an almost deserted establishment belonging to the vice-mayor of the town. Baden was a more than three-hour trip from Stockerau, so, while Paul worked, Shura spent the week on his own. Soon he discovered that there was another Russian guest at the hotel, the painter Peter Nilus. Nilus had once been commissioned to paint Chekhov's portrait. The idea that he was talking with someone who had known Chekhov left Shura, as he put it, "in perfect rapture." And then Nilus told him something about Chekhov's personality that could have been known to very few people, making Shura feel that he had privileged insight into his hero. The contradiction between Chekhov's lighthearted disposition and the melancholy atmosphere of his plays was often remarked upon, but Nilus clarified that impression, saying that he had known a man whose gregarious spirits came well cut with dolor. Chekhov suffered from chronic consumption, and after his coughing fits, the writer would spit whatever had come up into a dainty glass bottle he carried around for the purpose. Then Chekhov would apologize with a wistful little joke or pun. Eventually Chekhov grew too ill to pose, and Nilus never finished the portrait.

Shura spent the rest of his time that first week reading French novels, listening through his wall at night as an energetic young couple exercised their bedsprings, and noticing some of the differences between Russians and Austrians. A Russian would never go anywhere "simple-haired," but the Austrians did not bother with hats. They also seemed to bathe constantly, with the result that in February half the people you encountered outdoors had a corona of ice on top of their heads. (Because Russians bathed once a week at the most, Russian men bought their wives cologne more frequently than Austrian husbands did.) Austrians did their drinking differently too. Where Russian men always finished off their vodka in a single gulp and then chased it with a complex grunt expressing both triumph and pleasure, Austrians took a sip of wine, swished it over their palates while engaging in ecstatic contemplation, and then finally, gently, swallowed it. Russians were defiant, informal, and approximate, while these bareheaded Austrians were cool, precise, and punctual. They were a map-loving people and carried them wherever they went. Russians did not have maps to carry because most of Russia had not yet been mapped.

When the week was up, Paul came to Baden and took Shura to see the principal of the local *gymnasium*. Before the meeting Paul instructed Shura not to say anything to the principal—Shura pointed out that there really wasn't any other option. He then sat quietly as the principal rolled small sips of his white wine *Spritzer* around in his mouth and tilted his head slightly while Paul explained that his son had completed his certificate from the *gymnasium* in Russia and would like to continue his education in Austria. The principal asked a few questions about Shura's previous studies, looked increasingly horrified by Paul's replies—those Russians didn't teach Greek?—and finally closed his eyes. Mr. Gerschenkron would have to understand that an Austrian education seemed to be significantly more demanding than what was required in Russia. However, he too would like to see the boy educated, so what he could do was look at Shura's certificates and then perhaps something could be worked out. Paul explained that the certificates had been left in Russia and could not be retrieved because the Communists had closed off postal connections with the rest of the world. The principal grew very grave. "In that case," he said, "all we could do would be to admit him to the first level."

"With the nine- and ten-year-olds?" Paul asked.

The principal acknowleged that such a situation would be difficult for a boy of sixteen. "But," he said, nodding at Shura, "perhaps he could do it. He seems to be a very modest and shy chap. Seems too bashful even to speak."

"His German is not quite yet where it should be," Paul said hastily. Then he changed course. In his most reasonable tone, he asked whether Shura could be admitted to the seventh year if he passed an examination.

The principal said this was possible only in theory: "He would have to be examined for two days in every subject covered in the *gymnasium* curriculum over the preceding six years. There are strict regulations about that. It would be a tremendous task to prepare for such an examination." He held out his hands. "It's really quite hopeless."

Afterward Paul told Shura what had happened. "I suppose you'll have to go to France," he said sadly. "Things would be simpler there." To pass the test Shura needed first to teach himself the German language. Then in German he would be obligated to master material ranging from the laws of thermodynamics to botanical classifications to the sixty major trigonometric formulas. That was not to mention catching up on all the Austrian history and geography Austrian students had been learning since childhood. And then there was the matter of using German to learn Latin when he didn't know any German or Latin. The job was just overwhelming enough to persuade Shura. With a little of the old nonchalance, he sketched an impromptu schedule for his father. It would take him three months, he estimated, to read enough German to start with the textbooks. Then, if he really applied himself, he could be ready for the exam four months later. After all, a lot of the material was already up in his head in Russian and presumably could be converted into German without much difficulty. It would be nice to be able to say that a Russian could learn in seven months what took Austrians seven years.

The next day he went to work. There was a little table in his room, and he got to know it well that winter as he crammed sixteen hours a day, seven days a week. After eight weeks of vocabulary lists, grammar books, and volumes of poetry, he could get through a German novel, although when he spoke nobody—particularly barbers—could understand what "that Russian boy with the extremely short hair" was saying. His articulation was the problem. Russian does not use the *h* sound that is such a fundament of spoken German, and Shura struggled to say it for weeks. Once he finally could, he overcompensated by enthusiastically applying *h*'s everywhere, and this led to predictable disasters. When he said *uhren* (watch), for instance, it came out *huren* (whore). The presence of such a fellow living in a once-exclusive accommodation where haughty aristocratic ladies still came for their Sunday afternoon dinner could not have improved the matrons' freely voiced opinion that this new Austrian republic was a hopelessly heathen place.

In a nearly empty hotel in a nearly empty little Austrian resort town, Shura might have begun to brood about what had happened to his life. Instead, at this time he developed what amounted to a personal philosophy about human adversity that was more nuanced than the stoic Russian belief in enduring through suffering. Russian stoicism signaled bravery, but for all the expenditure of emotion, ultimately it was passive, and Shura wanted to act. He had come to view hardship in pragmatic terms, as a fillip for moving on in life. His intuition told him that there could be advantages to being placed in backward circumstances. A person just had to be shrewd enough to discover them. Left by himself in a foreign country with unfamiliar customs and a language he couldn't speak, Shura chose to regard the situation as his greatest opportunity for showing off. He would make it in Austria, and faster than anyone expected him to.

Education became his diversion and his source of hope. The task he had set himself was so ambitious that to have any thought of succeeding at it he had to shut out everything else. In his accounts of the time, Shura never mentioned missing his father in Stockerau, missing his mother, or missing his Russian friends. What he told were stories about the staggering amounts of information that he was packing into his brain. The task had become his reason for being, and he gave himself over to it completely. He worked so hard that it took something on the order of the hotel's blond cook appearing half-naked at the window across the way to distract him. When she saw him gaping at her, she shook her finger and giggled.

By May, Paul was making such a fine impression in Stockerau that suddenly a whole apartment became available for him to rent. Shura rejoined his father. Life in Stockerau consisted of days neatly divided between the hours he spent at his desk and his daily sessions with five *Hofmeister*, the private tutors who coached him in descriptive geometry, trigonometry, Latin, drawing, and the four Austrian subsets of natural history—botany, zoology, mineralogy, and somatology (the study of the human form). These tutors were an interesting collection of people ranging from the Latin expert, an excessively proper Austrian named Opitz who bent his head so that Shura could appreciate the "genuine Silesian form of my skull," to the trigonometry mentor, a warmhearted young man who, as he reviewed Shura's homework, would check off the answers, saying "correct, correct, *conspicuously* correct!" After the tutors were finished with him, on his own Shura reviewed algebra, French, physics, chemistry, geography, and German literature. It was now the summer of 1921. The school year would begin in September, and he was planning to enroll.

If you were going to take on such an intensive project, Stockerau was a good place to do it. While the surroundings were attractive, with views of old castles and distant Alpine peaks, Stockerau itself was a notoriously provincial town. The Austrian playwright Johann Nestroy immortalized it in "Tales of the Theater: Love, Intrigue, Money and Stupidity." A young actress speaking with a local dialect challenges a snooty young thespian to explain his lack of interest in her. "Amour did not come from Stockerau," he replies.

There was a Sunday afternoon that summer when Shura left Stockerau and went over to a nearby beach on the Danube where he dusted off his Russian sailor's breaststroke. He'd never thought much about why Russians crashed their arms into the water so inefficiently as they swam, but the stir he created along the shore now made it clear to him: the point was to call attention to the swimmer's remarkable aquatic prowess. More remarkable was that from May until September that lone Sunday was the only day Shura did not study from dawn until well past nightfall.

On a sunny mid-September morning, seven months after arriving in Austria, Shura took the 6:20 a.m. train to Vienna for the *gymnasium* admissions examination. His father escorted him to the station, offered him the Spartan battle exhortation, "Well, with the shield!" and hurriedly departed, leaving Shura "in a state of confusion and turmoil." It was one of those trips that went by in a moment and was also endless. Formulas, laws, classifications, tenses, dates, tributaries, properties, and conal projections swirled through his head. Frowning Teutonic professors besieged him with unanswerable questions. Then he was entering the schoolhouse, and a little bit of a real nightmare took shape. He stood in a hallway with the other students and noticed that, while the Austrians all carried sleek briefcases, his own attempt at a bookbag was no more than a dumpy little suitcase. Were these Austrians finding amusement in his inferior portmanteau? He was still pondering the possibility when he noticed that everyone else had drifted away and he was alone in the hallway. A diminutive fat man came by, spotted Shura, and asked him what he was doing. When Shura told him, the fat man grew indignant. The examinations had begun fifteen minutes ago. It was too late now. He would have to go home. Shura looked so traumatized by this development that the fat man took pity and sent him into a classroom where twenty others were already frantically scribbling compositions about the historic significance of German classicism.

In the face of that, Shura suddenly felt calm. Even if he hadn't been through Lessing and Schiller and Goethe yet in German, he had read them long ago in Russian, and it somehow gave him reassurance to fall back on the reading experiences of his past. He knew exactly what he wanted to say; the only problem concerned the limitations of his German vocabulary. He was busily flipping through his Russian-German dictionary when the proctor sidled up. "I have never seen anyone using a Russian dictionary to write a German composition," he observed. "This is most irregular." The proctor moved along to the next desk and Shura went right on using his dictionary. Afterward he was given an oral exam in which he was asked about the contents of an epic poem. He had memorized a four-page textbook description of the poem and this he proceeded to disgorge with a measured exactitude that would have made his Russian teachers proud. Then he watched the grader read his German classicism essay. "An intelligent piece," Shura was told. "But you must work on your spelling and punctuation. They are outrageous." With that he was told he had passed the German examination.

Shura lingered in the room, trying to think up some way of conveying to the grader how recently he had not spoken a single word of the language. Then he was late for the drawing test and had to race to a classroom where the instructor was waiting to ask him to copy Dante's profile. An hour's struggle somehow produced not a faithful likeness at all, but a mocking caricature. The instructor's assistant appeared at his side for a look. "Did you do it on purpose?" he asked. Shura was speechless. The assistant picked up the pencil and with a few quick strokes sketched a respectable Dante. Then he walked away, and the instructor ambled over, glanced briefly at the assistant's drawing, wrote "fair" beside it, and sent Shura on to history and geography, where he was peppered with questions about Austrian battles and reigns. Shura submitted for a while, but after he was asked about the Treaty of Verdun, he thought he might shift matters to more familiar terrain. He announced that Verdun reminded him of a similar agreement brokered by the eleventh-century Russian prince, Jaroslav the Wise. "When I wish to hear about Jaroslav the Wise, I will tell you," snapped the teacher, and rewarded him by demanding an inventory of India's rivers. Afterward Shura asked how he'd done. "Be a man and leave curiosity to girls," he was told. An hour of French and another of mathematics finished the day.

He got home after 8:00 p.m., famished. His father's housekeeper looked him over as he bolted down his supper. "During the Great War there was a point to death," she said. "Men died for Austria. But here you are killing yourself for nothing."

Next morning he was back on the 6:20. The second day began with the various quarters of natural history. While Shura attended to somatology by diagramming the human circulatory system on the chalkboard, a tiny professor with a brilliant red beard crept up behind him and put a rock under his nose. "What's that?" he bellowed.

Shura was terrified. "Gneiss," he guessed.

The professor returned to his desk, where his voice dropped to barely above a whisper. "You think natural history is not important," he murmured. "And you are right. It is neither like mathematics nor Latin. It is a secondary subject." Then he asked Shura a question about potatoes. Shura answered. As Shura spoke, the professor was wincing. He wondered if Shura had passed the German exam. Shura said that naturally he had. Looking positively forlorn, the professor said that if they passed such a boy in German, a boy who couldn't say potato, he had no choice but to pass him too. Then he began to shout again. "You may go," he thundered. "But it was not gneiss. It was *not* gneiss."

Next came oral exams in chemistry and physics. Each time Shura was sent away with a curt *"Mit Nachsicht der Taxen"* (The quality of mercy is not strained). The descriptive geometry problems he was given, however, were beyond him. Translating German into Latin went just as badly. The instructor noticed his Russian-German dictionary, called him "impudent," and confiscated the reference. Without it Shura was marooned.

Afterward, the principal explained to him that because he had failed geometry and Latin he could not be admitted to the seventh level. The man was kind, told Shura "Do not throw your rifle into the rye," and encouraged him to take the examination again at the end of the school year in June. Shura maintained his dignity until he was outside the gates. Then he staggered to a nearby park and sat down on a bench, so dazed that he neglected his little suitcase long enough for a thief to make off with it.

By the turn of the year 1922, Sophie, Tolia, and Lydia had spent more than a year in the dressmaker's attic as Odessa grew increasingly unstable. Lydia came home one day in great distress because she'd seen a soldier shoot a mother and her baby. After that, Sophie got a letter through to Paul telling him that she was leaving. She collected money for the trip by selling the little dacha Paul had bought for her. She had never liked that dacha herself, but at a time when the Bolsheviks had outlawed the ownership of property, she knew how to make it irresistible to someone else. "These Bolsheviks," Sophie had said, standing close to the buyer and giving him a warm smile. "They are a passing fad. And then they will be gone, and because I had to follow my husband you will have my wonderful dacha with the orchard full of fruit trees."

They came by hay wagon, by train, and finally on foot through the forest to the Polish border, where Tolia filled a little bag with Russian soil as Sophie negotiated terms with the Soviet soldier who was going to smuggle them across. The soldier was of two minds. "I'm letting down the Revolution," he would mutter. Then he'd take a giant draft from his vodka bottle and remonstrate with himself: "But everybody needs money." Once they were safely in Poland, Sophie gave the soldier a stack of bills. The soldier handed half of them back to her, saying "That's enough." Looking her in the eyes he added, "Anyway, you're so pretty it's almost a pleasure to risk one's life for you."

Paul met them in Warsaw and escorted his family home to the large apartment he now rented. Shura was waiting there to greet them. Lydia was struck by how somber he was.

The examination failure had sent him into a malaise that lasted for many weeks. All he knew of Austria was his desk, and now these Austrians had looked him over and decided they didn't want him. He felt he had wasted almost a year of his life. The sound of children's laughter outside his window only increased his anomie; he had made no Austrian friends. A year ago he had been a young man of promise in a glamorous Russian city, and here he was, a failure residing in an Austrian backwater where the most exciting event of the day came when the farmers chopped off chicken heads in the town square. A traveling troupe of classical Russian actors passed through Vienna, and Shura attended all of their performances. He did not enjoy them. The sound of Russian voices speaking the familiar words of Chekhov left him nostalgic and resentful.

He wasn't the only one feeling embittered. One afternoon while passing through the working-class suburbs in the outskirts of Vienna, he encountered a crowd of laborers who were marching toward the city center. There was an Austrian tradition of workingmen's public demonstrations. Usually they were festive events organized by the liberal Social Democratic political party, with many of the marchers walking shirtless, carrying their tools and bouquets of flowers in their arms and singing folk songs. Shura followed to see what would happen. On this day the workers wielded sticks and crowbars and bawled out obscenities protesting the grotesque rate of Austrian inflation, which was soaring so fast that the price of a streetcar fare sometimes rose during the course of a single ride. They cursed the slick young merchants and finance men who traded on the margins while the workers' salaries shrank to nothing. They cursed the foreign tourists who'd swooped into Vienna with their overvalued dollars and pounds and were living the high life, crowding the city's antique shops, hotels, and restaurants. (In Vienna everyone could afford the high life except Austrians.) They cursed their squalid living conditions. And they cursed the new republic which rewarded foreign profiteers while honest laborers couldn't support their children. At the gates of every factory they passed, the workers would yell "Come out, boys!" and more men and women would join them. By the time they reached Vienna they were a mob. At the sight of the city's fashionable shops and brokerage firms they began screaming, breaking windows, and bashing in store fronts. Shura watched, fascinated by the passion of poor men smashing windows full of objects they could never own while the shopkeepers struggled to get their shutters closed. He returned home that evening more excited than he'd been in months.

The next morning he awoke feeling disgusted with his own lack of purpose. No examination was going to defeat him. He would try again in June. "I knew you'd come around," Paul told his son.

All was well until shortly before the new test day when Shura suffered a vexation. Upon arrival in Stockerau, ten-year-old Tolia had been placed into the fourth grade of the local grammar school. For two weeks he could only express himself with hand movements. Then, without any visible effort, he began to speak German, first with short phrases, soon in full sentences, and then in complete and compelling paragraphs. After only three months in Austria, Tolia effortlessly passed the entrance exam for the first level of the *gymnasium*.

"It is ever so much easier for a kid of ten," Shura told his mother.

"He has a real talent for languages," she replied.

In June, Shura retook the test for the seventh level and this time strained nobody's mercy. "There is little glory in having remedied a shameful failure," he thought to himself on the train back from Vienna. If he had been in Russia, he would have been entering the university. Now he had condemned himself to associating with mere boys one and two years younger than he was. He returned home, left word that all had gone well, and crawled into bed. A moment later his door opened and Tolia strolled in wearing his long nighty. "If you had flunked it again, my own glory would have been greater," he announced. "But I don't mind." He patted Shura on the head, laughed, and padded back to his own room.

Tolia was a scamp, a sunny, lighthearted, smiling little boy, full of fun and adored by everyone. Sophie was right: Tolia did have an extraordinary gift for languages—and for many other things. He was a brilliant mimic, a witty raconteur, a talented enough writer to begin publishing parodies and satires in the leading Vienna papers as a teenager, and a magnificent chess player. Twenty boards were once set up, twenty serious chess enthusiasts were brought in to play at them, and, simultaneously, Tolia beat them all. When he sat down behind his pieces, he got a peaceful feeling in his head and all the right moves came to him, lined up one after the next across his mind like a succession of streetlamps. Eventually he became the Austrian national champion. With his cupped ears and angular features, Tolia looked like a baby starling—but his face resonated with brains and personality, and women were crazy about him. From the time he was twelve he was bringing crowds of them home to meet his mother.

Tolia was Shura's unspoken nemesis. Shura was nonplussed as much by the ease with which his brother walked through the world as he was by Tolia's competence. In Shura's autobiography Tolia appears just three times, portrayed always as the upstart "kid brother." They learned to play chess on the same board, but after Tolia began to win their matches easily, the games between them stopped. Tolia was no brat. He was charming, eloquent, and gifted, and his older brother knew it—knew it too well. He had a way of making Tolia seem so impressive that if you weren't careful, Shura might have you forgetting what a substantial person he was himself.

Years later Shura would confide to a friend, "I was driven by my brother's abilities." He thought of Tolia as the family natural and he formed himself in relation to him—as a man who had to push himself to succeed. Not that he was exactly straightforward about it. Shura sometimes enjoyed leaving the impression that he had done something difficult—like learning Swedish—without any exertion. Yet a competing side of him also made it his distinguishing virtue that he could work harder than other people. In 1949, when Henry Rosovsky, one of his students at Harvard, mentioned that he was going to hear a concert that night, Shura wanted to know "What concert?"

"Reginald Kell, the British clarinet player, is performing with the Boston Symphony," answered Rosovsky.

"Ah," Shura said stroking his chin. "You know I haven't been to a concert in thirty-five years. I haven't got the time." At that point in his life he was sleeping only every other night and inviting those who wanted a word with him to stop by his office at six in the morning.

SHURA SPENT THE SUMMER BEFORE HE ENTERED THE AUSTRIAN *gymnasium* wandering alone through the high Alps with a red Old Bulgarian grammar book and a few Old Slavonic texts in his rucksack. He had decided to complement the upcoming *gymnasium* curriculum with an independent study of Slavic languages. In this way he would not be so much a seventh-level *Gymnasiast* repeater as an inconvenienced Slavicist who, in two years, would know vastly more Slavic philology and linguistics than his peers at the Sorbonne.

His Alpine summer began with a train trip through a small town where he would make a connection to the Alps. While waiting for the second train, he walked around the small town and soon had the distinct impression that everyone was laughing at him. It wasn't until he got back to the depot that he realized that the problem was his new pair of Austrian leather hiking shorts. He had neglected to fasten a rectangular frontpiece, leaving it open and flapping most indiscreetly. This mistake so aggrieved Shura that at one point during the second train ride he let out an involuntary groan, prompting the man sitting near him to ask if he was troubled by a toothache. Shura said quickly that indeed he was. But the fib added guilt to his embarrassment. Suddenly he announced that he had no toothache. His companion gave him a suspicious look and turned away.

Solitary mountain climbing became one of his great pleasures. The Alpine forests were cool and light, and above the treeline little streams ran off the snow-capped peaks, watering the meadows into natural gardens of red, purple, blue, and yellow flowers. Sometimes at dusk he'd check into a high-country inn for the night. Thirsty from a day of heavy walking—and heavy Slavic—he liked to go into an inn's public room, order a beer, and practice his German. One evening he discovered a fascinating local custom. A waitress whose skirts could not conceal what Shura (inevitably) evaluated as "a broad but well-formed rear" brought foaming steins to the patrons. After each man paid for his beer, the wait-ress would turn and allow him a generous pinch. Shura couldn't wait to order a refill. When it arrived, he looked up at her. She began chuck-ling. *"Das ist nur für Erwachsene"* (This is for adults only), she said. That produced much high-spirited back-and-forth among the other drinkers, who made overjoyed and clearly hilarious comments: after each one, they all collapsed into laughter and then raised their glasses to Shura. All he could do was lift his in return, while feeling twice cheated because he didn't know their Styrian peasants' dialect.

At the end of the summer he took the two trains down from the mountains to begin school in Vienna. There every block was busy with similar frustrations. Postwar European fashions featured shorter skirts and lower-cut blouses, and Shura was in a constant state as he pondered the smooth legs he saw from the windows of streetcars and the décol-leté that seemed to navigate like proud schooners through the sidewalk traffic. His dreams were active, filled with what he called "voluptious enjoyments." The blond country girls walking arm in arm with their boyfriends around Stockerau also filled him with libidinous yearnings.

That Shura had no experience with women was not how it had to be. Although he was not an imposing figure—from the soles of his size-six feet to the top of his head he measured barely five feet, seven and a half inches—he had become something to see. His body was lean, and there was a delicate and lugubrious quality to his face. He had a mouth that brooded at the corners and deep-set dark eyes traced with worry. The ridge of his nose sloped gracefully away from thick eyebrows that were, in turn, shaded by the prow of brown hair descending from his fore-head. When he grew older his face and trunk broadened and his bear-ing revealed the intimidating force of his personality. In his late teens and early twenties, he was pouty and pretty.

So pretty that one day a film maker stopped him on the street in Vienna and told him, "I want to put you in movies." Shura turned the man down on the spot. The sultry features were deceiving: people found that there was something distant and inhibited about him.

"My father adored women," says Lydia. "He was a great lover of women. It was in Shura's nature to be resistant. He and my father were different in that way. Shura was such a beautiful, beautiful boy when he

was young. Girls tried so hard to be friends with him. He was standoff-ish. Everybody thought it was sweet. The beautiful boy who said 'No.'"

A young woman his age named Fifi Bader who helped him with his German was madly in love with him. He never noticed. It was the same with Lilly Stepanek, who would become a famous Austrian stage actress. She was a Stockerau teenager, a classmate of Tolia's, when she first encountered Shura sitting with Paul on the train to Vienna. "I had gray gloves on," she remembered. "He shook my hand and I totally fell in love with him. I never cleaned the glove or threw it away until even-tually it disappeared. Shura was enchanting."

Shura was holding out for the sort of woman he'd read about. His ideas of love had been formed by literature to such a degree that he dis-missed every woman he'd met because they all failed to inspire him in the way the lovers in his favorite books were inspired by each other. Much of this was Pushkin's fault. In the great historical drama *Boris Godunov*, Boris lies on his deathbed admonishing his son Feodor to seek out a pure, sacred, innocent love, and Shura was sure that Boris was also speaking to him. He was similarly influenced by a couple of French poets and, of course, by Tolstoy. It was Levin, the sensitive idealist in *Anna Karenina*, whose life provided Shura with his romantic model. At one point in the novel Levin vows to forget Kitty, who has rejected him. Then, by chance, he glimpses her driving along the high road in her carriage, and Levin realizes he has been deluding himself: "There were no eyes like those in the world. There was only one creature in the world who could concentrate for him all the brightness and meaning of life. It was she." Shura was sure that he was also meant to feel that way, and just as convinced that to make it happen, he was obligated to avoid any indiscretions. "I wanted no fleeting affairs, no chance encounters," he wrote in his memoir. "I wanted the real thing, the true love, which would last for ever and ever. I was waiting, certain that some day, somehow the great wonder would occur with the ineluctable force of predestination."

SHURA CAME TO THE ALBERT HAMMERLING GYMNASIUM FILLED with dread, and the fears were realized. He couldn't understand his German teacher's German, he couldn't fathom the calculus lesson, and his Latin recitation was so inept that the entire class turned to give him pitying glances. The Latin teacher corrected his many mistakes with increasing disgust before finishing him off with "You don't know any German either." Last came the gym hour and Shura was disgraced at *Volkerball*. He caught balls he was meant to dodge, avoided those he should have caught, and in his panic got so repeatedly tangled up with his teammates that the captain finally requested that for the good of the team he stay out of the way and do nothing. When the team was defeated anyway, Shura felt that everyone was thinking the same thing: "The Russian was to blame."

Arriving home for supper that night, he found Tolia, now eleven, regaling the family with an account of his own first school day. Paul, Sophie, and Lydia were all listening as Tolia detailed the well-buttered praises he earned from his Latin teacher and the clever Russian nick-names he had thought up for his flock of new friends. Sitting there at the table, Shura seethed. Then and there he decided none of them would ever hear anything about his school days. And they never did, a vow Shura kept by forging his father's signature on his report cards and on all school-related notes, statements, and permissions. "This" he says in the autobiography, "had the markings of being grown up."

Mark Twain had taken one glance around a *gymnasium* in 1880 and declared, "Foreign youth stay clear of the gymnasium, its rules are too severe." Forty-two years later it was as rigid as any Russian would have predicted for a German system of education—an endless procession of useless facts that needed to be memorized for the *Matura* university admission examination at the end of the eighth year.

Remembering his own miserable years in the *gymnasium*, the great Austrian novelist Stefan Zweig said it was "more than too much . . . the entire period of my schooling was nothing other than a constant and a worrisome boredom." Shura was an immigrant boy still learning German, and he later said that the *gymnasium* experience frequently left him "in a state of near prostration." The other students—none of whom had ever heard of Pushkin—were always good for comments about people from places that were "centuries behind in their cutural development." Then there were the teachers. The young French instructor, for instance, was a Viennese butcher's son who spoke almost no French, had a drinking problem, and made clever puns at the expense of Shura's German. Shura considered him to be just about the best of the lot and when the bottle put the teacher in his grave a few years later, Shura went to the funeral.

Latin came so easily to Tolia that he soon was earning money as a tutor. Shura couldn't compete. He grew so frustrated trying to translate the Latin he was learning into the German he was learning that he stopped doing his homework. Instead, every afternoon he brought his Slavic texts to the University of Vienna library reading room, where he sat among the college students and told himself it didn't matter that he was failing German, Latin, and math because his Old Bulgarian was coming along so well that he really would astound them at the Sorbonne. There was a morning when his Latin teacher asked him a question and Shura responded curtly that there had been no time to prepare for the lesson because he'd been reviewing his Old Bulgarian until very late.

"Did you say Old Bulgarian?" asked the teacher.

"Yes," said Shura.

"I see," said the teacher, and called on someone else.

A GROUP OF BOYS AT SHURA'S SCHOOL SPENT THEIR FREE TIME HAVING serious discussions. They talked about the newest works of Sigmund Freud in relation to their own dreams, and they collected copies of *Die Fackel* (The Torch), a dazzling satirical publication entirely written by the poet, playwright, and feuilletonist Karl Kraus. These boys reminded Shura of his old circle of Russian friends, and he wanted to join them. He tried reading Kraus, but this was a recondite stylist who liked to boast that "language is the common prostitute I turned into a virgin," and Shura could make nothing of the highwire wordplay, the sweeping array of allusions, and the multiple threads of meaning. He also bought a volume of Freud, and one day he approached the boys while they were talking and told them that he had dreamed about the caves along the Black Sea coast. They laughed at him and then, full of oleaginous concern, they told him that clearly he needed to visit his girlfriend. Shura lost his temper and said that this talk about wish fulfillment was self-indulgent. What a man accomplished out in the world was the important thing. The boys replied that this was the kind of limited thinking you could expect from a Russian.

By February Shura was so disaffected that he was scarcely doing any schoolwork at all and was well on his way to flunking out. Love is what saved him.

Before the formation of the republic, girls in Austria had not gone to the *gymnasium*. After finishing grade school, they stayed at home, where they learned to become ladies, studying French, taking drawing lessons, practicing their piano playing, and learning to cook Austrian dishes. Following the collapse of the monarchy, a few very liberal families began sending their daughters on for a higher education. One of those young women was the only girl in Shura's class, and it was she with whom he had been assigned to share a desk. Through his life he never tired of telling other people those qualities he first noticed about Erica Matschnigg: her low voice, her quiet dignity, her fierce independence, and what a sensational Latin scholar she was—much better than

Tolia. He observed that Erica's blond braids were worn in the style of Goethe's Gretchen. (He had, by now, added *Faust* to his romantic archive.) His loyalty to the gray eyes of Russian girls was strong, but soon enough the Austrian blue had won the field.

Erica wanted nothing to do with him. When he got up enough nerve to try out a couple of the witty expressions he'd heard employed by the swains of Stockerau, they turned out to be the coarse phrases of country boys, and she winced while another student standing nearby gasped and said, "Did you hear what he said to the girl? Those Russians have no manners at all." While Erica ignored him, Shura watched with loyal indignation as the teachers found ways of communicating their aversion to coeducation. Some of them shamelessly undergraded her, and the Latin instructor, noticing she was absent one day, said cheerfully, "Since she is not here, we need not omit the obscene passages in the dialogue."

One morning toward the end of the year they both arrived early for school and Shura found himself alone with her in the classroom. To his surprise, Erica asked him when he planned to teach her some Russian folk songs. Mindful that he had the musical ear of an artilleryman, he was searching for a clever means of postponing when she added, "The time is getting short." He asked what she meant. "Didn't you fail in the main subjects?" she said with stunning casualness. "I have never heard of anyone failing three subjects at mid-term and not having to repeat the class. You won't be with us next year."

Somehow it hadn't occurred to him that if he flunked out he wouldn't see Erica anymore. A frenzy of study ensued. By the end of the year he had salvaged his grades and also made some progress on other fronts. After one too many digs about "Russian dogs," he grabbed a boy who'd insulted him and gave him the Heifetz treatment. Afterward he was praised by one of his hopelessly feudal classmates for having acted "well and correctly." It also helped that he had emerged as a crackerjack *Volkerball* player. Suddenly he was being called "Russ" and receiving invitations to join the others at the theater. He went, and was fascinated when two men in the audience got into an argument. One told the other he was "stupid" and in return was called "neurotic," the cutting-edge insult in Vienna, circa 1923.

That summer he traveled alone through Germany. In Bremen, he swam in salt water for the first time since leaving Russia, and the North Sea, so dull and green, made him miss the sparkling blue waters of the Black Sea all the more. There were happier moments. A German wait-ress asked him if he came from Austria. "I can always tell," she said proudly. He was becoming an excellent German speaker.

Susi Schneider, the daughter of one of Shura's Austrian friends, says that "all his life he spoke to us in very clear *Hochdeutsch*, the high Ger-man equivalent of the King's English—BBC English, *Pygmalion* En-glish. You know, someone says to Eliza that she has to be Hungarian because no English person speaks English so beautifully. That's how Shura spoke German. But I never knew he wasn't Austrian until much later. He *was* Austrian! He was uniquely Austrian! He was like everyone I knew. They spoke perfect German, they were witty and intelligent. All the guys who came back after the war were like that. Witty and sensitive."

Back in Vienna, on the first day of the last year of *gymnasium*, came the great romantic revelation he'd been holding out for. This is the way he described it himself: "When the girl with blond braids came in and took her wonted place in my bench and I saw again the blue eyes in the face tanned by the Alpine sun of the summer and heard her soft voice, I knew that I was in love, desperately and irretrievably, for the first and last time." All year he did his best to conceal his feelings. Around Erica he was either dumbstruck or too loud. Away from her he pined. He imagined her lover and fantasized about different methods of killing him. One day, without a word on the subject from her, he got it into his head that she would be at a certain park, and so he went there and spent the afternoon aimlessly wandering around. When she didn't turn up, he felt rejected. Her reserved manner convinced him that she didn't care for him at all. This had a certain romantic appeal. She could spurn him, and he would remain forever devoted.

Deciding that with love—even unrequited love—came responsibili-ties, he told his parents that he was moving out on his own. His father, going through a wealthy phase, offered him money. Shura declined, explaining that a grown man of almost eighteen should not live off his parents. He rented a room in Vienna and paid for it by translating Ger-man books into Russian. Until he completed his first job he had so little money that for two months he ate nothing but peanuts three meals a day. When he received his first check, he saw that he had discovered a means of supporting himself that paid much better than peanuts. The next time he saw Tolia, he was not brief with the details.

Erica was harder to impress. She seemed not to notice his progress as a student, as an athlete, and as a street fighter, and so obvious was her distaste for showing off that he could not alert her to his triumphs. Nor could he find out very much about her. One thing he knew was that her stepfather was a politician and a leader in the national temperance movement. This prompted Shura to give up beer. He wanted to tell her he'd become a teetotaler for her but feared that this would somehow have the wrong effect.

He went through a chess craze. Not only did he enjoy playing, he liked the stylized ambiance of the game: the Cartesian system for identifying piece movements; the green-covered Austrian chess magazines; "the consequences of alternative decisions with all their ramifications," which he considered "a beautiful exercise in casuistic thinking." In the classroom he was studying the Aristotelian syllogisms, but it was chess, rather than his yawning philosophy teacher, that taught him lessons about logic that held.

At the end of the year the whole class took the *Matura* exam and everyone passed, some with the aid of stolen solutions to the math problems, which had been expertly concealed in the washroom. In conversation afterward with "those Austrians," Shura was able to slip in that the *Matura* was much easier than the admissions examination given to foreigners.

The delight he felt at finally putting the *gymnasium* behind him was nothing compared to the euphoria he experienced as he, incredibly, found himself strolling through Vienna beside Erica, escorting her home. He remembered every detail of this "walk of indescribable beauty." A street organ played Strauss's "Blue Danube" waltz. A tall blade gamboled by. The air smelled of freshly mown hay. Erica was slim and composed. She noticed that a new building looked like an ocean liner. How poetic were her observations! How attractive were the rays of the sun on her shining golden hair! How creamy was the neck below it! Far too quickly they were at her gate. They shook hands.

She was off to spend the summer at her family's little house in the mountains west of Salzburg.

Back at home in Stockerau he couldn't stand it any longer. At his desk he composed an "irate confession of love" and posted it to the mountains. A few days later a letter came to him in a slim white envelope. She had hoped they were becoming good friends. She wished him luck at the Sorbonne.

Brokenhearted, he went to the Alps and walked alone for weeks. One night, sitting beside a moonlit lake, he decided that he would not become a Slavicist. For ten years he had been a minion to grammar and syntax and structure. He couldn't bear any more of it. He wanted to open his mind. In the mountains, where this seemed ever so possible, he felt exultant. Then when he got back to Stockerau he didn't know how to go about it or what to do with himself. He moped about the house. One day he idly pulled a blue economics text from his father's bookshelf. A "Eureka!" moment can take many forms, and this was Shura's. What he was reading was more than interesting—it was a system of thinking that instantly made such profound sense to him that it was as though someone had handed him a prism and said, "Look through this and see the world."

Money and commerce suddenly seemed to him to be at the hub of everything. Wasn't Russia's inability to elevate the population from vast poverty the real cause of the Revolution? Then he was thinking back to the Austrian workers' anti-inflation demonstration he'd seen in 1921, and what the power of economics could do even to something as culturally embedded as what the locals called "the golden Viennese heart." The great cares of the world told themselves in economic terms, and, now that he thought about it, the world's great thinkers were drawn to them. Shura remembered Tolstoy's newly married Levin seated in his library grappling with so many problems—land distribution, communications, railroads, the development of industry and credit, the artificial grafting of foreign ideas on the Russian civilization—as he considered the age-old miseries of the Russian peasants. Shura too could become such a man, a scientific humanist who used his imagination to draw up reforms that became blueprints for human progress. This was his giddy observation: the world was a place willing to accommodate what you wanted to do if you wanted to do it badly enough; you just had to find your opening. That same day he decided he would go to Paris to study economics.

The very next morning a letter was waiting for him. Erica had returned to Vienna. Did he want to visit the museum? Paris was renounced, and in the fall of 1924 Shura enrolled at the University of Vienna's famous school of *Nationalökonomie*.

There Shura's memoir ends. "My decisions were made," he writes. "I knew what I was to do and what I was to wait for in this universe. What lay ahead were serene years of young manhood; they were crowned by great felicity. But the annals of a man's happiness are short and simple, much more difficult to talk about and much less memorable than the joys of childhood and the confusion and heartache of adolescence."

THREE

A FAMOUSLY
CIVILIZED CITY

To know so much, to have seen so much, and to
say nothing, just about nothing.

Robert Walser, untitled poem

S HURA RARELY SPOKE ABOUT HIS GROWN-UP LIFE IN AUSTRIA.
The jubilant, crowing pleasure with which he described those
teenage years when he covered himself in glory by triumphing
over both the German language and Erica's reluctance to fall in love
with him was completely absent from his clipped accounts of what
came afterward. "As I see it in retrospect, my sojourn in Austria had
two purposes," he said once. "To get myself a university education, and
to take a wife to myself." That he spent fourteen more years in Vienna
following his graduation and his wedding was almost never mentioned.

Self-concealment came naturally to Shura and was undoubtedly to
his advantage in a Vienna where ten years of hard luck left people spoiling with resentments. Vienna in the 1920s was a city of beautiful stone
buildings, and not nearly enough of them. In workers' districts you
could find three different families sharing an apartment in revolving,
eight-hour shifts. Men slept in wagons and in wooden shanties, men
and women shared their bed with other couples, and people lived in
cellars and on hallways where there was one toilet for over a hundred
tenants. Shura and Erica had it a little better than that, but not much.
They rented a flat on the outskirts of the city that was so cramped

Shura could stand in the middle, stretch out his arms, and run his fingers down opposite walls. Books were stashed into every corner. After their daughter Susi was born, for the next nine years there were three of them keeping out of each other's way in a tiny room not much grander than a tool shed. Every night Shura and Erica strung up a curtain and went to bed with their child lying so close to them that they could hear her breathing as she slept. The lack of privacy made them crave space of their own; devoted as they always were to each other, later in their lives, when Shura and Erica had a little money, they used it to rent a house with separate bedrooms for themselves.

Because the housing shortage forced people to spend so much time outside their homes, more than most cultural centers, Vienna was a city of public talkers. In the most popular refuges, the coffeehouses that occupied every corner, a man was judged by the quality of his conversation—how nimble was his repartee, what kind of a raconteur he was. During the late twenties and thirties, that culture of public wit evolved into a culture of public scrutiny, a downside to the Freudian spirit of personal investigation, in which a man's most private thoughts and feelings could be rooted out and used against him to bring him harm. It was a nasty shift in public temperament, and Shura, who had witnessed a more abrupt version of the same phenomenon in Russia, probably sensed what was happening. Descriptions of his conversation by people who knew him then—clever, amusing, gregarious, in the moment—make it clear that another of his abilities as a talker was that he knew how to protect himself. His drollery seems to have had a diverting effect, because beyond the pleasure of being with him, people remember few specifics of what Shura was doing with himself. He was an obscure young man who left behind faint traces.

His skill at resisting observation then has made it difficult to observe him now. There are only fragments, and fitting them together isn't easy. What is certain is that his young manhood was not, as he claimed at the end of his memoir, crowned by great felicity. He didn't much talk about the period from 1924 to 1938 because that was for him a period of growing frustration and disappointment that culminated in catastrophe.

*   *   *

SHURA BEGAN HIS FIRST SEMESTER AT THE UNIVERSITY OF VIENNA by taking a seat in the political scientist Hans Kelsen's lecture hall. Kelsen was the author of the republic's new constitution, and Shura expected to find a graying eminence wearing a *Gehrock*—the old-fashioned academic frock coat. What appeared instead was a lean, youthful man in a dapper bowtie. Kelsen's subject was the concept of the nation-state, and for weeks Shura had no idea what he was talking about. Then suddenly he had the feeling that it was all opening up to him "like a flower," and the course became "a momentous intellectual experience."

It was also a thoroughly atypical experience. Shura found the University of Vienna to be as oppressive as the Viennese *gymnasium*, but in completely the opposite way. It asked nothing of him. There were no class discussions, no required readings, no papers to write, no professorial office hours. All you had to do was memorize your lecture notes and you were assured of a degree. Most of the lecturers were, Shura said once, so "horribly poor" that nobody attended their offerings except a few wily entrepreneurs who took careful notes and then sold them for steep prices at exam time.

The disappointment of going to a university like that was a bruise that never lost its color, because Shura's expectations had been so high. And well they might have been; up past the turn of the century, the University of Vienna was the great imperial university of the Habsburgs, the nave of liberal higher learning in a famously civilized city. The physicians at the University of Vienna's school of medicine trained the best doctors in the world—the skilled Viennese practitioner became a staple Hollywood character—and the standard was just about as high for legal theory, art history, philosophy, and economics. Yet what made Vienna special was not that it had more educated citizens than other large cities; it was that the Viennese were so intensely educated. At the university, where the ideal was a mind both supple and broad, mere expertise was pedestrian. "Viennese lecturers were very haughty," says Gusti Kollman, whose husband was a classmate of Shura's. "They

thought they knew it all. They did!" The typical professors were genuine liberal artists who remembered their Goethe, Heine, and Schiller
well enough for reciting, read in Latin and Greek, spoke several
Romance languages, and maintained professional interests that might,
as Franz Brentano's did, travel from ethics to philosophy to psychology
to epistemology to literature to devising metaphysical puzzles ("The
mind can think about things that do not actually exist" was one). The
most original of these scholars could glean inspiration from the dust of
other men's ideas. They looked across the many things they had studied
and extracted the bricks for that most exciting intellectual construction—a new system, a new field.

There was, for instance, Sigmund Freud. Of Freud's many teachers,
the one for whom he claimed "the highest esteem" was the University
of Vienna physiologist Ernst Brücke. Another of Brücke's students, the
future playwright Arthur Schnitzler, wrote that Brücke was "usually
feared." A slight man with a huge skull, Brücke had blue eyes of such
level intensity that Freud reported seeing them in his dreams. (Some
people look at photographs of Freud's face and see Brücke's eyes.) From
1876 to 1882, in the foul-smelling old gun factory that was Brücke's
laboratory, the professor supervised Freud's copious studies of nerve
cells in fish. According to the historian Erna Lesky, Brücke was a man
who "considered himself not only a teacher of physiology, but the
representative of a general cultural idea," and he may have provided
important guidance to Freud as a scientist whose expertise ranged
widely into what Freud called "human concerns." Brücke wrote with
authority on thermodynamics, optics, German poetry, drinking water,
Hindi, and Italian painting and sculpture. He sketched well, and even
created one of the world's first phonetic alphabets. Brücke encouraged
Freud's inclination to pursue diverse subjects relating more to human
than animal nature—literature, philosophy (Freud took several courses
with Franz Brentano, whom he called "a damned clever fellow"), foreign languages (Freud made a translation of John Stuart Mill), and aesthetics. In the end Freud found a way to integrate all of it into nothing
less than a reinterpretation of the human mind. "The poets and philosophers before me discovered the unconscious," he said on his seventieth

birthday. "What I discovered was the scientific method by which the unconscious can be studied." Freud had many teachers, but it was Brücke for whom he named his son Ernst.

Fifty years after Freud's student days, when Shura entered the university in 1924 to study *Staatswissenschaft* (political science and economy), there were still plenty of men like Franz Brentano and Ernst Brücke in Vienna. Shura was a freshman the same year that a genial physicist-turned-philosophy professor named Moritz Schlick formed the Vienna Circle. This was a group of disciples of the Austrian physicist and empiricist philosopher Ernst Mach, who gathered every Thursday evening behind a small door on the Boltzmanngasse for an ongoing meditation on physics, mathematics, logic, and philosophy. Mach had been a man of such inspiring intelligence that when William James met him he later told his wife: "I don't think anyone ever gave me so strong an impression of pure intellectual genius." Schlick, Rudolf Carnap, Otto Neurath—the astonishing polymath who invented the pictogram—and Einstein's close friend the physicist Philipp Frank were Mach's worthy heirs. The discussions began with science and philosophy and traveled through psychology, semantics, economics, social planning, and so many other fields that the talks came to seem like great piano improvisations, offering a stream of arrhythmic flourishes, tonal improbabilities, and whorling tremolos. Word of what was taking place on the Boltzmanngasse spread, and the scientists were sometimes joined by well-known Viennese like the jurist Felix Kaufmann and the methodologist Karl Popper, as well as by students who boarded trains and ships from ports of call clear across Europe and—in the case of Willard Van Orman Quine—from America, so they could sit in on what amounted to an intellectual backroom jam session. Backroom, because as early as 1925 there were swastikas hanging in the halls of the university.

SHURA SPENT HIS COLLEGE YEARS WATCHING HIS UNIVERSITY SUC-cumb to religious and political fanaticism. From the first he had understood that Vienna was an insular place. "One could not help finding out that for better or worse the Middle Ages was something that was very close to the people," he observed on one of his first days in the city. He was, of course, thinking about more than the architecture. The peeling church bells, the crowds of little girls in white bridal gowns at confirmation time, the way people said hello to each other on the street—*Grüss Gott!* (I greet God)—were habiliments of the Catholicism that over the centuries had worked itself deep into the Austrian grain. In a country of white faces that worshiped Christ, Jews were the most obviously different people, and they had long been a repository for every kind of hostility and resentment, an excuse for shortcomings and a means of explanation for turns of fate that were otherwise inexplicable. That many Jews were studious, not a small number were rich, and some few were sly fed the cant that Jews were grasping outsiders ever on the alert to cheat simple, God-fearing Austrians. In 1419, the theological elders at the University of Vienna detected a conspiracy between Jews and Hussites on the basis of "the luxurious style of living ... of a large number of Jews and their damnable books." Two years later, hundreds of Jews who refused conversion were burned alive at the stake.

When Shura arrived in the country, there had been sixty years of relative racial comity and also much assimilation, for which the great engine was the University of Vienna. In 1867, after the Austrian government passed the seminal equal rights legislation that colloquially became known as the "emancipation of the Jews," Jewish students began attending the University of Vienna in numbers vastly out of proportion to their slender share of the population. Then they went off into the larger campus of the city and made outsized successes of themselves. Although Vienna was 90 percent Catholic and never even 9 percent Jewish, as late as 1936 Jews accounted for more than 60 percent of the city's lawyers, over 90 percent of its advertising executives, almost half of its doctors, 123 of 174 newspaper editors, as well as large numbers of merchants, department store owners, manufacturers, bankers, financiers, artists, and writers. Some of them became famous. Many of them, like Paul Gerschenkron, became wealthy.

That Jews and foreigners were flourishing in Vienna had quickly provoked the city's old impulses. As early as 1882, a German-Austrian Student Fraternities resolution declared, "Every son of a Jewish mother, every being with Jewish blood in its veins, is born without honor and must therefore lack in every decent human feeling." Student political movements often anticipate national political movements. In 1897, a hypnotic speaker named Karl Lueger was elected mayor of Vienna. For the next thirteen years, until his death in 1910, he was Austria's most popular statesman. Throngs of small shopkeepers and low-level businessmen shuddered with pleasure each time "Beautiful Karl" set new lyrics to his most familiar theme: "I do not care whether the Jews are hanged or shot." (A notable thrill went through the city after Lueger's aide de camp Hermann Bielohlawek proclaimed, "When I see a book I want to puke.") Lueger always contended that this was all so much rhetoric, that he actually admired the Jews, but his speeches had a conditioning effect on the city, and his legacy was the assurance that, more than ever, Jews and liberal, educated people became the usual suspects.

After the First World War, with Austria reduced to an impoverished beggar state, the organized bigotry swelled into organized violence, and the University of Vienna was the site for most of it. In the early 1920s the frustration of living in a waxwork country of dim futures and empty purses grew so intense among the young Catholics studying at the university that, according to historian John Haag, "the vast majority of the students were now embittered reactionaries and racists." A familiar sight during Shura's college years was the armed upperclassmen in matching fraternity caps moving in packs across the courtyards, searching for Jewish scapegoats.

The Catholic student fraternities were clubs that had occupied generations of Austrians through their university years with beer drinking, song singing, and the dueling with sabers that left many student leaders with "scars of honor" on their faces. To these traditional activities were now added more modern rituals. The fraternity boys, along with the thugs they sometimes hired from the Vienna Technical University to do their brawling for them, disrupted classrooms where "Jewish" subjects like psychology and philosophy were being taught. They beat up Jewish and "Slavic" students, setting upon them even as they sat taking their examinations. It wasn't always easy to know who was Jewish. Some victims were chosen because of their large noses. Others had their trousers ripped down to see if they had been circumcised.

One reason all this was possible was that Austria's feudal university regulations concerning "academic freedom" forbade policemen from setting foot on university property. It became routine in the mid-twenties to see drunken hoodlums chasing down "those foreign flat-footed parasites who exploit us," slashing at them with metal bars and truncheons and then throwing them down off the main ramp of the University of Vienna where the police stood helpless below. Not that most people found the situation terribly troubling. "There were always riots at the university," one of Shura's contemporaries says. "The city recognized it with a cynical smile." It wasn't war—these attacks were sporadic—but the lurking threat that violence could happen anywhere, even on a university campus, stayed with a man, especially one with a Jewish father, a liberal mind, and a Russian accent.

Shura had an Austrian girlfriend, traveled in a cosmopolitan circle of friends, and considered himself to be Christian, but he made no secret of his political beliefs. He enrolled in classes taught by famous liberal professors like Hans Kelsen; Max Adler, an Olympian intellectual with an assortment of specialties that included legal theory, Kant, and Ibsen; and the philosopher Heinrich Gomperz, whose lectures on Plato were enlivened by the dramatic progressions of a beard sprouting like ragweed below the knot of his necktie. No conservative student would ever have sat before any of these men. A liberal like Shura found it just as easy to avoid the right-wing socioeconomist Othmar Spann, whose protofascist theory of "Universalism" rejected the use of empirical evidence in favor of "intuition and inspiration"—ideas that the Austrian political scientist Karl Müller says dryly "found no response abroad." The university's extremist overseers counted the essential criteria in making appointments to be religion and politics, leading them to present a coveted chair to Spann, who dominated the University of Vienna's economics faculty during Shura's years in Vienna. In 1970 Shura received a letter from a professor who proposed to write an intellectual critique of Spann. Shura refused to help him on the grounds that "intellectual is a strong term when applied to Spann. Since I fail to see the purpose of rescuing this particular corpse from its well-deserved oblivion, I should not like to contribute to the labor of exhumation."

Among other things, he knew that the presence of men like Spann at the University of Vienna had cost him. The study of economics was on the decline in Austria of the 1920s. Eugen von Böhm-Bawerk, Friedrich von Wieser, Carl von Menger, and most of the other liberal thinkers who had made the Austrian school of *Nationalökonomie* world-famous were aging or dead, and that pretty well described their approach. Economics was a changing field, gradually evolving from a historical-cultural discipline into a mathematical science, and the University of Vienna wasn't even trying to keep up. The practical result of Shura's college years was that he received an inferior education. "It was his tragedy that the economics he learned in Vienna from 1920 to 1935 was unbelievably primitive," Paul Samuelson would write after Shura's death.

The larger unbelievability was how primitive one of the world's most intellectual universities had become. In 1926, when a visiting professor from England used the occasion of Sigmund Freud's seventieth birthday to stand in a University of Vienna lecture hall and praise Freud as an Austrian national treasure, his remarks were received in wintry silence. Freud worked for seventeen years as a *privat Dozent* until he used personal connections to gain a full professorship. This was at least in part because he was Jewish, the same reason that Hans Kelsen was fired by the university in 1929, the year after Shura graduated. Kelsen soon left Austria for an academic position in the West, as did Rudolf Carnap, Otto Neurath, Philipp Frank, Max Adler, Heinrich Gomperz, and Sigmund Freud. Moritz Schlick's was a far bleaker fate. One June day in 1936, as Schlick climbed up the University of Vienna's main interior staircase, a crazed student came rushing down toward him, held out a pistol and pulled the trigger at point-blank range, leaving Schlick crumpled on the marble steps. Out in the streets the murder met with not a little rejoicing. "The chairs of philosophy at the University of Vienna in German-Christian philosophy belong to Christian philosophers!" approved the Catholic weekly newspaper *Schönere Zukunft*. Schlick's murderer pled "political motives" and served only two years in prison before the government granted him a full pardon.

*   *   *

IN A MOMENT OF STRONG EMOTION LATE IN HIS LIFE, SHURA WROTE that "only someone who was put through the mill of a continental university in Europe can fully appreciate the freedoms of Harvard." Although he didn't elaborate about his Continental experience, in this slim sentence Shura does something extremely rare for him: he uses a cliché. The problem with stock phrases is that they obfuscate meaning by generalizing experience. Shura felt so much that way that he was not above a little semantic showmanship at a cliché's expense. (A typical Gerschenkron retooling is "a train of thought without a logical derailment.") This was a man who used language with exacting precision, someone consummately in control of what he was saying, especially when he was talking about that most guarded subject, his own past. And so when he reflects on his college days and writes that he had been "put through the mill" at the University of Vienna, it's worth pressing his words a little, because he is revealing the extent to which the University of Vienna disappointed him and, in turn, something subtle about the way his mind worked.

Shura was someone for whom the word "mill" had real resonance. Not only was he a student of economics who became an expert on industrial development, he was the son of a factory manager. Shura knew all about mills, and especially the postindustrial version, the factory mill. As a metaphor, the phrase "put through the mill" refers to the pulverizing of grain into flour or meal and implies either an oppressive force that pounds away at a person's spirit or the diminished thing the person becomes as a result of that ordeal. But to Shura, any form of self-pity was anathema; he was someone who never wanted to be seen as a victim. Instead, he preferred to bear grudges, and he thoroughly enjoyed the authority of contempt.

When Shura used the image of a mill to describe his college years, he was expressing, in the most concentrated way, his disdain for the University of Vienna as a vapid place of crushing dullness, a large plant in which students were processed like batches of textiles instead of being truly educated. What he wanted to say about this university that did not care about the imagination, placed no value on inspiring people, and allowed flagrant intimidation to compromise the free flow of ideas was that he had no respect for it. But it never would have occurred to Shura that the university could have diminished him. It diminished itself much in the way, as it happens, a cliché does.

As late as 1934, Vienna was a city with seventeen daily newspapers and three stoplights. It had dozens of women's literary salons where, says Peter Gay, "small talk was frowned upon." It had libraries of every sort—the Gerschenkrons were habitués of the Russian and the French—and a bookstore on every second block. Shura spent a lot of his life in Vienna climbing up and down bookshop ladders, taking what he wanted from the high shelves, settling into a leather chair, reading a whole volume straight through, and then climbing back up the ladder to replace it—a common and accepted practice. When the walls got too close, he dropped in on friends like Adolph Meier, who lived in a flat with his wife Thea on the Luxemburgerstrasse. If Adolph wasn't in, Shura sat down to wait right on the curb and opened up his book. He was wearing wire-rimmed glasses by this time, a style associated with the composer Franz Schubert. When Adolph got home, the housekeeper would sometimes have a message for him: "The man with Schubert glasses sat in the gutter and read for two hours."

Many afternoons he visited the Kunsthistorisches Museum to stand in the room entirely filled with Bruegel paintings. He liked Bruegel for the same reason he liked Dickens—the crowd of vivid characters created in service of a picaresque story. Pieter Bruegel's paintings are filled with ambiguity—is *The Tower of Babel* about human folly or human ingenuity?—and the drama of suggestion: darting looks, furtive glances, light fingers, lecherous gazes, and strange little tortures. Some of them, like *Children's Games* and the various peasant wedding paintings, are filled with so much activity that he could look at them for many minutes and not begin to notice everything that was going on. Shura spent the bulk of his time, however, in a place where most educated Viennese could be found day and night in those years, a coffeehouse.

The seventeenth-century Turkish invaders had left coffee behind as their legacy in Vienna, and over time the Viennese perfected the setting in which to drink it. Typically this was a tatty, well-worn room with velvet-upholstered benches, marble-topped cafe tables, crystal lamps, and the odd painting on the wall, often the work of an artist who was behind on his bill. Coffeehouses had high ceilings painted in dark shades to absorb the clouds of tobacco smoke, terraced pastry trays stacked with jam cakes, creamy tortes, and wild strawberries in the spring, and a supply of newspapers and periodicals in several different European languages. The coffee itself was delivered on a silver tray along with a spoon that was balanced on top of a glass of water. Every half an hour your waiter would refill your water glass. Ordering even one cup of coffee upon arrival bought you the right to sit unbothered for as long as you liked. If you stayed ten hours, the waiters would simply refill your water glass twenty times, never with a glint of reproach. (A satire by Karl Kraus features a man who walks into his old coffeehouse for the first time in twenty years, where he is greeted by the waiter and handed his favorite newspaper.) The coffeehouse was light and warm. It smelled of mocha, cigars, perfume, sugar, and chocolate. The same faces came every day.

People wrote letters and picked up their mail at coffeehouses, they cut deals, met eyes in the large mirrors that ran along the walls, took naps, read books, recited poetry, did schoolwork, had rendezvous, played chess, played bridge—during the bridge craze in the late 1920s, many coffeehouses retained a lady bridge "expert"—and they talked. "This coffeehouse is not a place; it is a way of life" was what passed for an ice-breaker in Shura's Vienna, and inevitably things were soon thawed well beyond that. Talk was both sport and science, and people prepared by poring over books and newspapers because, as Stefan Zweig said, "it was a mark of inferiority not to know some exciting thing that was familiar to someone else." Much more than the university, it was the coffeehouses in the twenties that stimulated the desire to accumulate and display broad knowledge. Each little group had its special table—its *Stammtisch*—where all day and night the bons mots, puns, and putdowns flew. So much one-upmanship went on in these places that most proprietors kept an encyclopedia on hand to resolve disputes. Shura, who knew a thing or two about showing off, fit right in. He became known as "a real character at the coffeehouse."

There were coffeehouses favored by orchestral composers and coffeehouses popular with operetta composers, there were coffeehouses for pianists and coffeehouses for stamp collectors. Other coffeehouses became famous for who went there. Gustav Mahler had a *Stammtisch* at the Cafe Imperial close to the Musikverein concert hall. Leon Trotsky played chess in the domed back room at the Cafe Central, a classic institution near the center of the Ring where the novelist Robert Musil and Social Democratic political party leaders like Otto Bauer and Karl Renner were also customers. (Trotsky had contempt for these labor politicians as "well-educated people [who] . . . represented the type that was farthest from that of the revolutionary.") Karl Kraus was a regular at the Central too, until the constant fawning attentions of his fans chased him elsewhere. Shura, a lifelong student of chess, liked to stop by the Central to observe the Viennese *Grossmeister* trying out new stratagems. (Some of these were the creations of Tolia, who published a book on chess openings.) On occasion Shura would sit in for a game himself. The Central was a sleek locale. A more nondescript coffeehouse on Langegasse in the eighth district—nobody seems to remember its name—was Shura's usual destination.

He was a regular. Public establishments provide opportunities for close association without the obligations of intimate friendship. You can be as much of yourself as you please. Shura enjoyed the give-and-take of serious conversation, and there are many photographs taken through his life of him with an arm thrust over a comrade's shoulder, but even in this uninhibited city, he never wanted to talk openly about himself or about other people he knew. On the Langegasse he didn't have to. What people were passionate about at that coffeehouse was politics—socialist politics. Many of the customers were Social Democratic party activists, and Shura became one too.

IN SHURA'S AUSTRIA IT WAS COMMONLY BELIEVED THAT ALL WORKers were foul-smelling. Workers had no voting rights, no guarantees of free speech or free assembly. In one Austrian city, an ordinance prohibited laborers from using the sidewalk on their way home from work. Viennese workers were banned from the city's better parks, restaurants, and hotels, and they were routinely harassed by the police and the courts. The workers themselves came to internalize their inferior position; Shura noticed that they always chose seats in the trailing second or third cars of streetcar trains, never in the first. As Shura once explained it, an instinctive Austrian aversion to industry coupled with rigid class stratifications and reflexive xenophobia displayed toward the foreigners who came to Austria to find factory jobs had produced a culture of blatant discrimination against labor.

Social democracy emerged as a powerful force in Austrian politics in 1889, in response to these atrocious living and working conditions. The Social Democrats were progressive insurgents. To fight discrimination they employed some of the same nonviolent methods of political persuasion that would later be used by blacks in the American civil rights movement—sit-ins, marches, boycotts, and work stoppages. As elected statesmen, their enthusiasm for social programs made them an Austrian analogue to the American New Deal Democrats. For a time they were very effective.

By 1914, the Austrian workers had achieved general manhood suffrage and a variety of other improvements. Successful efforts were made to plow under the sprawling working-class ghettos and sow them fresh with high-quality public housing projects. Between 1919 and 1934 nearly 64,000 new houses were constructed, many of them in white concrete apartment blocks built in a style that could be called functional-monumental. (They looked like Bauhaus fortresses and were named for men like Marx and Goethe.) Among the Social Democrats' other concerns were literacy, adult education, hygiene—there are panoramic photographs in the party archives of lines of workers' children with toothbrushes in their mouths—ecology, mental health, and physical fitness. They organized industrial athletic leagues, workers' singing and dramatic societies, workers' weekend excursions, and workers' libraries. As Shura arrived in Austria, the party was lobbying for higher wages, shorter workdays, access to insurance, pensions, collective bargaining, and child labor laws.

The most committed Social Democrats neither smoked tobacco nor drank alcohol, and their hatred for the Catholic church's domination of Austrian politics made them radical secularists—militant egalitarians who considered all citizens to be "souls." Shura was enraptured. Here was a political philosophy that seemed to come straight out of "I Built a Monument Not Made With Hands," the Pushkin poem that had been at the ethical center of his childhood. Here were a group of people who truly "praised freedom in this age of deprivation / And called for mercy for the frail and the weak."

One day Shura came home for a meal at his parents' house and announced to the family that he no longer believed in religon. "He denied God," says Lydia. "I was very young at the time. I had a medal somebody gave me. It said 'God Protect You.' He tore it off my neck and said, 'You shouldn't wear things like that.' He acted as though he were swallowing it. He was very young, you know." He also finally renounced all alcohol, began dressing like a worker "out of solidarity," as he later told a friend, and he succumbed completely to the many charms of the undisputed great man of the Social Democratic party, Otto Bauer.

Son of Philipp Bauer, a Viennese manufacturer who exploited his workers, and brother to Ida Bauer, better known as "Dora," the troubled young woman Freud describes in his portrait of a hysteric, the bluff, burly Bauer was a lawyer and scholar who had made a careful study of Darwin, Marx, Kant, Hegel, and Goethe. As a young man Bauer consulted Freud about his career prospects, and Freud advised him that he was better suited to teaching than politics: "Do not try and make men happy; they do not wish happiness," is what the doctor is supposed to have ordered. But Bauer went ahead and became Austrian foreign minister and then the leader of the Austrian liberals. Rising to his feet in Parliament, Bauer's voice carried above insults like "Jew pig" flung at him by his rivals as he described his desire to live in a country where "our" farmers read Goethe, "our" factory workers know Kant, "our" manual laborers learn Marx. That was the sort of abstract and vaguely condescending talk that made Trostky cringe, but others were impressed. "When I think of the young Marx," said the Czech socialist Karl Kautsky, "I see him as Otto Bauer." Shura regarded Bauer as the living embodiment of his literary hero, Tolstoy's Levin. The difference was that Levin's aspirations to improve the lives of the serfs remained only daydreams; Bauer really seemed to be fulfilling them.

Friends of Paul's reported that "your son has become *ardent* in his political beliefs," and they described him as idolizing Otto Bauer. This was no news to Paul. At the spirited weekend dinners around the Gerschenkron dining table they discussed little else. "We talked about politics and literature, literature and politics," says Lydia. "We grew up eating politics and literature." Paul was a liberal and compassionate man who, after all, had raised his children on Pushkin, but he was also a capitalist businessman with accounts at posh tailors and haberdashers. The situation created tension between father and son that was painful for both of them. "My father didn't like it," says Lydia. "My brother had become a bit too left for my father's taste, and he didn't like what he called 'parading one's beliefs.' My father was very liberal, but my brother went beyond. That was youthful exuberance." Nobody in the family exactly blamed Shura. The way they saw it, the fault was all with that high-hat little socialist he was so taken with—Erica.

ERICA'S FATHER DIED BEFORE SHE WAS BORN AND TEN YEARS LATER her mother, Maria Matschnigg, married a man named Michael Schacherl. Schacherl was the son of a widowed Jewish laundress. He drank too much in his youth and then reformed to become a lifelong opponent of liquor. Trained as a doctor, he soon took the concept of curing people well beyond his infirmary, creating a dual career for himself in public service as a labor advocate. There followed a succession of jobs in Social Democratic politics, culminating in his election to the Austrian Parliament, where he became one of Austria's most respected statesmen, the good-hearted politician who fought for the health of the average man. He also published the leading workers' paper *Arbeiter Zeitung* and worked for the rights of children.

Maria was Michael's second wife, a Lutheran-turned-unbeliever, and in her Michael had found someone as liberal as he was. Maria had blond, Alpine milkmaid good looks, she had studied French, she could boil a succulent tafelspitz, she played the later, more difficult Beethoven piano sonatas with skill, and she was an excellent weaver.

She taught her daughter none of these things. Instead, Erica was sent off to school with the boys. Her friends were the children of liberal intellectuals and politicians, like Gretl Afritsch, the daughter of Anton Afritsch, a Social Democrat well known in Austria for working with slum children. Even as a girl, Erica was enthusiastic about Egon Schiele, Arthur Schnitzler, and Paul Hindemith, but she was pointedly raised not to know how to cook, clean, wash, or iron. She was brought up to be a professional woman, with the result that she was a feminist before the term existed.

As a stepparent, Michael's were flaws of overcompensation. Erica adored him and Michael felt the same way about Erica, favoring her over his own five children from his first marriage. The little game Michael and Maria played with Erica was that they had to court her approbation—the grown-ups had to prove themselves to the child. Maria and Michael were both well pleased when Erica was dismissive of them, which she soon knew very well how to be. At the *gymnasium*, Shura had only been getting the usual treatment from her.

For the most part, her aloof attitude didn't go over so well in the world outside her stepfather's house. Erica was an intelligent, highly educated woman, but nobody ever called her amiable. "Peck, peck, peck, peck— Erica was always so sharp," one of Shura and Erica's old friends from Vienna says. She had been brought up to believe that because she was so interesting other people would make unusual efforts on her behalf, and when they didn't, she tended to scowl. Everyone who knew her remembers that scowl, a grimace of keen displeasure you still see today in Vienna fixed on the faces of the audience at a classical concert while they are enduring a piece by a twentieth-century composer that has been slipped into the program between works of Mozart and Brahms. Susi Schneider, Gretl Afritsch's daughter, says that Erica "always looked so severe. She was critical of almost everybody including my mother."

All sorts of people, including his parents and siblings, wondered how it was that Shura, whose propensities were often so joyful, was taken with such a prickly woman. "He could have had a lovely girlfriend in Stockerau, Fifi Bader, who helped him with his German at exam time," says Lydia. "Fifi was beautiful, kind, and sweet. But in the end Erica won. Why or how no one will ever know. After that he adhered to her views, her opinions. It took some of the shine off him, that free spirit of boyish gaiety."

The Gerschenkrons had been right to suspect that Shura liked Erica's Social Democratic pedigree. Michael Schacherl's standards of how to live were positively puritanical in contrast to the bourgeois Paul Gerschenkron, and that appealed to Shura, who'd always been offended by his father's occasional lapses with women and money. Shura quickly became devoted to Erica's family and was hugely impressed by Erica's dazzling circle of politically progressive, socially high-minded friends. Part of it also may have been that for a man who liked challenges, Erica posed a suitable degree of difficulty. She was hard to get in the beginning, and continued to be across their lifetime. Over and over again he had to win her favor. Thirty years after his wedding day, Shura wrote to one of his children describing a guest lecture he'd given in Milan: "Mama was there and she watched me, which was a little bit frightening, but she approved."

They seem to have shared the same dynamic in private. Both Shura and Erica enjoyed Wilhelm Busch's comic adventures of the two young tricksters, Max and Moritz, and one day Shura composed a Shura-and-Erica pastiche. He entitled his little sketch "A Story of Violence and Love in Pictures." The first cartoon panel finds Shura creeping toward "the quiet chamber where a girl is resting." This girl is Erica. "With expectation in her expression she lies in her bed, nice and round and pretty fat. As soon as she sees Shura she says 'Away from here barbarian. I only like the Viennese and the Russian I don't want.'" Matters progress through a series of panels, with Shura about to slink off in despair, when he notices his Viennese friend Adolph Meier on his way to the bedroom. Enraged, Shura throws Meier into a swamp. This impresses Erica and, in Shura's caption, "her responding love is awakened because of this proof of Shura's power." The last drawing shows them *in flagrante delicto*.

Shura had a fixed idea of what his wife would be like before he met her, and in Erica he found someone who fulfilled the image. Once he chose Erica, from then on he was committed to the idea that she was what he'd wanted her to be—a kind of intellectual fairy queen. To him she embodied the most romantic passages in Shakespeare and Tolstoy.

Not that he wasn't capable of expressing his feelings for himself. Throughout his life, his letters and stories unfurled the golden narrative of "Erica and I," with her efforts to kill bees, grow a garden, climb a hill, or entertain guests all described by him in heroic terms. After forty-five years of marriage to Erica, Shura's lone complaint was that she hadn't fallen for him sooner. In a letter to an old friend from Austria he wrote, "I always was for early marriage and if Erica hadn't been so stubborn and unable to appreciate my high qualities we would have married immediately after high school and been living in sin before that."

In 1928 Shura graduated from the University of Vienna. His thesis "The Crisis of Democracy and the Party System," an attempt to predict Austria's political future as a Marxist democracy, was praised by Adolph Menzel as "a busy and on the basis of an extensive knowledge of the literature, well written piece." It was written, of course, in German, and awarded a "good," one level below "excellent." After his graduation Paul and Sophie gave a luncheon in Shura's honor at a superb restaurant on the Kobenzel, a hill of several serpentine rounds in the middle of Vienna. Tolia, Lydia, and eighteen of Shura's friends attended. It was a memorable occasion. The restaurant had tall glass windows on all four sides, giving a dazzling panoramic view of Vienna. Diners sat down at place settings that included damask napkins with a fresh rose on top for the ladies. In a niche along one wall sat an orchestra playing tunes from Lehar's operettas. At the end of the meal, Shura thanked his family with a speech couched in a parody of Pushkin that contained enough erotic banter that it could not be explained to Lydia. Not long after the party ended, without telling anyone his plans, Shura went off and married his girlfriend.

Shura and Erica traveled alone together to a Secular Registry Office in Vienna to exchange their vows. They stood before a public official who took them through a civil ceremony. When it came time for him to express the customary hopes "for a fruitful union," the official paused. As Shura proudly recounted, the man "cast his eyes upon the blushing bride's bulging front and tactfully swallowed the rest of his sentence." Erica was pregnant.

*   *   *

EARLY IN 1929, SUSI WAS BORN. AFTER ERICA WENT INTO LABOR, Shura walked through the streets of Vienna all night long. Actual fatherhood made less successful claims on his attention. Some men feel an instant rapport with their babies. Not so Gerschenkron. He said that newborn children did not interest him because they could not keep up their end of a conversation.

With a family to support Shura needed a job, so he took a position with a Belgian motorcycle firm representing its interests in Austria and the Balkans. With the widespread joblessness in Austria, he felt lucky to have it. And despite the fact that he himself did not know how to drive, he did well at the work. Later it would give him pleasure to say that he was the only member of the Harvard economics department who had ever met a payroll.

Shura might have been earning good money, but most Austrians weren't. In 1929 the worldwide Depression slammed into the country's fragile economy like bad weather. Within two years, the Austrian National Bank had lost a third of its holdings. There had been 32,000 unemployed Austrians in the dreary year of 1921. By 1933, the total had grown to 406,000—more than a quarter of the labor force. There were food shortages and power shortages. Families sold off everything they had.

Austria was a meek country, but the days of imperial glory had gone so recently that most Austrians remembered them with longing. If ever a city was living in the past, it was Vienna. Naturally that made the Viennese vulnerable to assertions that the grandeur of the empire could quickly be restored, and plenty of sanguine types—and plenty of scoundrels—were more than willing to sport them. Almost inevitably, the means proposed was the old dream of *Anschluss* with Germany. Since the war there had always been assorted factions in Austria calling for a German annexation, and now that Germany's new chancellor, a failed Austrian painter and architect named Hitler, had the German economy humming with new factories, the support in Austria for *Anschluss* swelled. As the Austrian Richard von Warton wrote in his private memoirs from the time, "The worse the living conditions and the unemployment, the more people joined the Nazis."

The Germans, meanwhile, were doing everything they could to

encourage Austrian demoralization by undermining the chancellor Engelbert Dollfuss's Christian Nationalist government. In the mid-1930s, Vienna was full of German spies and arms smugglers, and there were so many Nazi bombs exploding in the streets of Vienna that merchants put swastikas in their windows to protect the glass. "Danger in the air, uncertainty!" wrote Richard von Warton's wife Rosario in her diary. "Wild reports, arrests, further explosions, demonstrations . . . soldiers, gendarmes. Groups of intent people, talking quietly so as not to be overheard." Dollfuss was a prim, tiny man—recalling the great Austrian diplomat Prince Metternich, Viennese pundits referred to him as Millimetternich—but he was brave. In 1933 he disbanded Parliament and outlawed the Nazi party in Austria. A dictatorship was necessary, he said, to keep the country independent. Nobody was more disgusted than a third political interest, the Social Democrats, who began to consider a physical protest. They had arsenals of secret weapons and a private workers' militia, the Schutzbund. By this time they also had Shura.

IN 1931, DESPITE A WELL-SATISFIED EMPLOYER AND COMPETING job offers from the Italian magnate Adriano Olivetti, Shura had put aside the four-in-hand life of a businessman and gone into politics. He was with the Social Democrats for the next three years. Over this time, his distance from his father grew to the point where he insulted one of Paul's colleagues, who happened to pass by during a political demonstration. It wasn't hard for Paul to take something like that personally, and he did. Shura worked in many capacities for the party as everything from an accountant to a carpenter's assistant to a polemicist for *Der Kampf*, the leading theoretical journal of Austrian Marxism, to a contributor to *Arbeiter Zeitung*, his father-in-law's Social Democratic newspaper. For a time he wrote a short column on economics, which he signed "Alex." In the 1930s, many left-wing Austrian journalists refrained from using their full byline or substituted a false one. Shura earned next to nothing for his efforts. Why did he do it with a wife and baby at home? "Gerschenkron got a bad salary," Adolph Meier said, "but that was no matter for him. He lived for his ideas and imaginations." Shura's life now seemed to be all about the cause.

Things had not been going well for the Social Democrats. In 1927 a peaceful workers' march had been interrupted by gunfire from the window of an inn that killed a crippled war veteran and a child. After two soldiers from the Christian Nationalist paramilitary force (the Heimwehr) were acquitted of the murders, workers demonstrated outside the Palace of Justice in Vienna. When police tried to disperse them, the workers rioted, and by the time the day was done, eighty-nine people were dead and the Palace of Justice had been set on fire. With fire engines unable to get through the angry mob, the building burned. Otto Bauer spoke poignantly over the coffins of the martyrs, but his party's prestige was never again the same. The Social Democrats had been goaded into forsaking their principles of nonviolence; this gave credence to their critics, who complained that the Social Democrats were provocateurs so concerned about the workers that they were sacrificing the safety and economic well-being of the country as a whole. Otto Bauer, they said, was a bellicose and intractable man who had failed as a leader in a moment of crisis.

By early February 1934, the workers' disgust with their abysmal living conditions, their hatred for the Dollfuss dictatorship and for the Heimwehr soldiers backing him led them to prepare for violence in the name of democracy. A massive national strike was planned that would shut down electricity, water, and the railroads. Despite the reluctance of leaders like Otto Bauer, hidden caches of weapons were retrieved in case the government responded with force. Just before noon on February 12, the electrical workers cut off the current in Vienna. Streetcar trams coasted to a stop. Lights flickered and went out. Some party members hurried to their Schutzbund command posts, but many did not. Trotsky and other critics of the Social Democrats had, in some ways, been right. For all of their admirable ideals, the Social Democrats were too distanced from the people whose lives they wanted to improve. Now, when solidarity was crucial to their mission, they did not have it. The results were swift and lethal.

A friend pounded on Karl Kraus's door and burst into his room yelling, "They're firing on women and children." Kraus rushed off to join an ambulance brigade. Heimwehr strikebreakers had descended upon the working-class neighborhoods where Social Democratic sympathizers were barricaded in party clubs and housing projects. Field howitzers and mortars lobbed shells into the huge white apartment buildings, ripping enormous gashes in the walls. Sporadic bursts of machine-gun fire cut through courtyards. The fighting lasted for three days. In all, between 1,500 and 2,000 workers were killed, and many more were wounded. One of them was Shura. He arrived at his parents' door from the second civil war of his life bleeding from both arms. They took him inside, his mother bandaged his wounds, and he was kept out of sight.

Dollfuss declared martial law. He made the Social Democratic party illegal, confiscated its assets and property, abolished its publications, and sent his soldiers searching house to house for "incurables" who'd taken up arms against the government. Some Social Democrats hid in the sewers. Others, like Otto Bauer, eluded the checkpoints the Heimwehr had set up all around the city and escaped into foreign exile. And then there were those who didn't get away. Eleven socialists were strung up on ropes and hanged from trees and lampposts in Vienna. Thousands of others—including many of Shura's and Erica's dearest friends—were rounded up and sent to concentration camps. Progressive labor in Austria was dead and everyone knew it.

Soon enough it was also the end for Dollfuss. Nazi agents murdered him in July, leaving him to bleed to death on a sofa, pleading for a priest. The Nazi coup failed, and Kurt von Schuschnigg took Dollfuss's place in the chancellery, vowing to continue the effort to keep Austria Austrian. In Vienna, Karl Kraus gave one of his celebrated public readings, and instead of his own prose he chose act 4, scenes 2 and 3 from Shakespeare's *Macbeth* ("Bleed, bleed, poor country . . . O nation miserable"). Meanwhile in Berlin, Adolph Hitler began amusing himself by sketching out the architectural improvements he intended to make along the Vienna Ringstrasse.

Shura must have felt devastated watching the end of a movement that had meant so much to him. The boyish optimism that even the Russian Revolution hadn't compromised now seems to have retreated into equivocation. "Shura was always slightly pessimistic by nature," says a friend who met him several years later. At a certain point Shura elided his time in the Social Democratic party from the narrative of his life. In 1969, a year after the assassination of Martin Luther King, Jr., he gave a sermon at the morning prayer service in the Harvard University chapel in which he compared the Austrian struggle to King's. He went into some detail and yet managed to sound as though it was all just Austrian history to him; there was not the slightest clue that he'd been personally involved. He was even circumspect with people like his friend Walter Fischer, who had participated in the movement with him.

Fischer was a doctor married to Magda, one of Erica's stepsisters. He had devoted himself to caring for poor workers, and after the revolt spent a year in prison before the Austrian government released him. By then Walter and Magda were disillusioned with the Social Democrats, who, they felt, had "betrayed the cause by not fighting and by allowing armed right wingers to overrun the country." They left Austria and settled in Russia. Years later, when Walter was back in Vienna, Shura came to visit and Walter tried to discuss what had happened with his old friend Gerschenkron. "Let's not talk about it," Shura told him. With Walter's daughter Ruth, he went to see the high school where he had met Erica and passed his *Matura*. "He was happy to go to see his old *gymnasium* with me," Ruth says. "He had very strong feelings about his old school. But mostly—emotionally—it was clear to me that he'd locked away his past after that."

FROM 1934 TO 1938 SHURA HELD DOWN A NUMBER OF DIFFERENT jobs. He assisted an old friend, Victor Schimmerling, with his rawhides business. He taught at adult education centers, and he tutored younger students in foreign languages. None of this earned him much of an income. When he needed a suit, Adolph Meier bought him one. Living for your ideals was fine, but Shura also believed that a fundamental obligation of manhood was to make your own way in the world and to support those you brought into it. Every time he put on that coat the wool fabric weighed on him like a freshly hurt feeling. And there was an even greater humiliation. He began accepting financial help from his father, "a very generous allowance," according to Lydia.

Through all of this time, he had very little sense of being what he was, a professional economist, and he wasn't alone. A second generation of exceptional Austrian economists emerged during the interwar years. They were highly creative, liberal of mind if not always liberal-minded, and some of them were Jewish—all reasons for which Friedrich von Hayek, Oskar Morgenstern, Gerhard Tintner, Gottfried von Haberler, Paul Rosenstein-Rodan, Fritz Machlup, and Karl Schlesinger, among others, were, like Shura, consigned to the intellectual penumbra. This being Vienna, however, persecution begat inspiration. The liberal Austrian economists met informally in coffeehouses and office spaces around the city, and the most dynamic of these small groups—Ludwig von Mises's Society for Political Economy, Karl Menger's Mathematical Colloquium, and Hayek's Institute for Business Cycles Research—became the economics equivalents to the Vienna Circle. The country's perpetual economic miseries alone gave them plenty to talk about. But since these were highly cultured men in the Austrian scholarly tradition, on any given day their conversation might drift from capital theory to general equilibrium theory to John Maynard Keynes to the novels of Thomas Mann to game theory to the symphonies of Schumann. In 1937 Shura became a member of the Institute for Business Cycles Research. No doubt he would have reveled in such a stimulating setting, but once again politics intervened.

Paul moved for a time in the early 1930s to Salzburg, the city of Mozart's birth, two hundred miles from Vienna. On her way to school in Salzburg every day, Lydia passed a Jewish-owned sweet shop where she and her friends bought chocolate. One morning as she drew near the shop she encountered a crowd of excited local schoolboys swarming outside the front door. Next she noticed that they were all wearing white kneesocks below their leather shorts and bluebells in their buttonholes—the trappings of Austrian Nazis. Then she saw that the sweet shop windows were broken, and that blood was smeared on the floor and walls. Finally her eyes fell on the proprietor and his wife. They were lying there on the floor, blood pooling around their dead bodies. Lydia kept walking, turned the corner, and threw up.

Lydia says that everybody in the family knew at a certain point that "Vienna was a doomed city. My father talked about it at dinner with us. 'The Germans are at it again,' he said. With the rise of Hitler, Vienna was always suspended, waiting for the ax to fall. People were thinking 'We ought to move, we ought to flee.' Then they'd laugh and say,

'Well, it hasn't happened after all.' Austrians were famous for shrugging off problems." In the Viennese vernacular of the time, things were said to be "desperate but not serious." That phrase, so exquisitely embroidered in contradiction, said more about the Austrian capacity for self-deception than the Nazi menace. Freud himself was not immune. Even as he compared himself to a man staring at the ceiling in his hotel room waiting for the other shoe to drop, Freud was adamantly refusing his friends' entreaties to leave Vienna. The Germans, he said, would never dare to occupy Austria. Some Jews and intellectuals did emigrate, but many more stayed on, dismissing the Nazis as blithely as Shura had once heard Russians shrugging off the Bolsheviks.

Karl Kraus wasn't one of them. In 1936 Kraus told a friend that since Hitler had come to power in Germany, the trees in Austria weren't as green anymore. Kraus's health declined rapidly that year, and he died in the summer. As Karl Mark later said to his children, "If you wanted to know what was going to happen, you knew."

Paul left Austria in late 1934, taking Sophie and Lydia with him to Letchworth, England, where the Gourary family owned the Anglia Match Company. He urged his sons to leave as well. Tolia was immersed in the dissident political opposition and he wanted to stay. Shura wouldn't go either.

Part of it was his wife. Erica detested what was happening to Austria. When Susi came home from her public school one day and reported that the teachers were trying to find out who the non-Catholics were by asking all of their students whether or not they had gone to confession, Erica immediately removed her from the school. And yet Erica was "wed to Austria in every way," in Lydia's words. She was devoted to old friends like Gretl Afritsch and the child psychologist Bruno Bettelheim's wife Gina. (Gina was a kindergarten teacher who taught Susi to harmonize during a summer vacation they took together.) Erica loved Austria and she hated Austria, and like so many Austrians, she couldn't think of leaving.

Shura understood how she felt. By now he had developed his own attachments to Vienna and felt reluctant to pick up his life again and move it a second time. Being forced to run away from home is a wrenching and, among many other things, a shabby and undignified experience. Both his daughter and his sister say that Shura claimed he could foresee no benefit to starting over somewhere else. Sometimes a person whose existence has become static doesn't realize that this has happened. He doesn't know how else life could be, and he moves along in the familiar pattern as time passes. Then something unexpected jars him into awareness, and he looks back and realizes how desperate he's been all along.

In early 1937 Shura got his big break. One day a librarian from the University of Vienna reached him at the Institute for Business Cycles Research and told him that an American economics professor from the University of California was in town and needed help from somebody local with training in economics. Shura went to see Charles Gulick, who told "this shy and pleasant young man" that he was writing a work of political and economic history entitled *Austria from Habsburg to Hitler.* Gulick was looking for an assistant to help him gather material on a variety of subjects, including the history of the Social Democratic party. Shura knew where the party archives had been hidden after the party was outlawed. He soon became indispensable to Gulick, who would recall the project as "the hardest work I ever did." When Lydia came from England to Vienna for a visit, she found Shura absolutely buried in paper and struggling with his English. Lydia had learned the language so well that she would soon become a radio correspondent for the BBC. She and Shura sat in coffeehouses working all day together. She says that his English improved "miraculously," so quickly that after Gulick went home to the United States in May, Shura became his one-man Vienna bureau.

That October, Shura and Erica's second daughter was born. They named her Maria Renate but she was always called Heidi. Gretl Afritsch stayed by Erica's side in the hospital. She was an ideal companion. Like her father Anton, the famous Social Democrat, Gretl had wanted to work with children, so she became a pediatric nurse. She and Erica spent a lot of time talking about Gretl's boyfriend Charly. Erica thought Charly was a good-for-nothing. Yes, said Gretl, but such a handsome good-for-nothing.

Heidi was born into a city with its shoulders tensed for a collision. The Austrian Nazis, ever more boldy assertive, made up lists of "prob-

lematic" names and addresses. Gangs of boys in brown shirts challenged people on the street to return their "Heil Hitler" greetings and
beat up those who tried to get by with a *Grüss Gott*. Jewish cemeteries
were vandalized. Lilly Stepanek says that what made it all so insidious
was that "people everywhere were suddenly turning into Nazis. It was a
kind of dusk where you couldn't tell a dog from a wolf." One day while
Shura was hurrying down a crowded street, a young Nazi reached out
and banged him on the head with a cudgel.

Beyond the physical terror they inflicted, the open drain of propaganda emptying into Vienna revealed a parallel Nazi gift for emotional
intimidation. Hitler's views about blood reduced Shura's existence to a
basic issue: was he what he thought he was? Before renouncing religion, all his religious life he had lived and worshiped as a Christian. To
the Nazis, that made him even worse than a mere Jew. As the Russian-
born son of a Jewish father, Shura was not only a *Judenfresser*, a devour-
ing Jew, but he was also stateless, a *Staatenloser*, in the pitiless German.
After all the years of immersing himself in the culture of his second
country, there was nothing legitimately Austrian about him. He was no
more than a wandering Russian Jew, and, for implying otherwise, a
charlatan. Heidi says that living within an atmosphere of accusation
that claimed he was hiding his true self provoked moments of self-
doubt in her father, the fear that he was in some way misrepresenting
himself. He also felt guilty on another score. To qualify as an Austrian
citizen under Nazi law, a person had to own a certificate of his own
Christian baptism as well as that of both his parents and all four of his
grandparents. Shura's children were in danger because of him.

In early 1938 he knew he would have to leave Austria. He submitted
an application for travel papers and went every day to the emigration
office to check the progress of his request. A woman who worked there
took a liking to him and always chatted a bit after she'd told him "not
today, perhaps tomorrow." Meanwhile, Shura began to make contin-
gency plans for smuggling the children out of Vienna.

In early March, after he received an urgent telephone call from his
father in England, Tolia and his girlfriend Vivian got on a train to Paris.
On March the 12th, the German invasion came. The Vienna sky went
dark with clouds of warplanes. Tanks and foot soldiers rumbled across

the border and toward the capital. When the German troops entered this city where there had been nothing to celebrate in more than thirty years, there was such primal ecstasy in the streets that a young Vienna resident named George Clare thought Vienna "behaved like an aroused woman, vibrating, writhing, moaning." With the pleasure came an animal desire to inflict pain. Jewish doctors were handed buckets full of acid and made to scrub the cobblestoned Vienna streets on their knees while boys pissed on them from behind. Old men were ordered to do hundreds of knee bends. When they collapsed, they were kicked. Jewish stores were looted. Jews were ordered out of their homes by Christian neighbors who moved right in. "Everybody saw," Lilly Stepanek says. "The Jews were forced to wash the streets with toothbrushes. No day passes when an additional detail doesn't come to me of the horrible things that happened at that time. They stood there and cheered."

Suicides had been more common in Austria over the past few years than anywhere in the world. Now they became epidemic. Nobody knows how many hundreds or even thousands killed themselves in the first few days of the occupation.

In the photographs of this event, one can see Hitler's open car trolling along the Ringstrasse between stiff twin rows of storm troopers. Hitler is standing with his back to a Burgtheater already draped in swastikas, revealing how efficiently the redecorators worked—how fast something became something else. There are pictures of Jews being harassed by the ordinary people they used to pass on the street, and then there is a photograph of the enormous crowd of faces that massed in the Heldenplatz to see Hitler speak from the balcony of the Neue Hofburg. There in the crowd one of those tiny white dots in the photograph listening to Hitler announce "my homeland's entrance into the German Reich" is Shura. When the people around Shura raised their arms in the Nazi salute and screamed *Sieg Heil*, he raised his arm too. If he hadn't, they would have killed him; he was sure of it. He told Lydia it was the single worst experience of his life and he said that later he got sick in the street. Since the same thing had happened to Lydia in Salzburg, this became their shared memory of different traumatic events.

The next morning, as usual, Shura went to check the progress of his emigration papers. The friendly woman had a strange look in her eye. Quietly she said, "Actually, it looks pretty bad." He understood immediately that this was a warning, similar to the one his father had received from the workers at the factory in Odessa. When he got home, as Paul had done in Odessa, Shura planned his family's immediate escape from Vienna.

A WOMAN NAMED RENZ, A CHILDHOOD FRIEND OF ERICA'S, HAD A daughter named Susi roughly Susi Gerschenkron's age. Frau Renz offered to put Susi Gerschenkron's photograph on Susi Renz's passport and go with Susi Gerschenkron on the train to Zurich. Erica and Shura accepted. Leaving Heidi with Shura, Erica boarded the same Zurich train and sat in the next car from Susi and Frau Renz. She spent the trip praying that her nine-year-old daughter wouldn't say anything that would give them all away to the conductor. Susi behaved beautifully, betraying no fear, and lying like a card player each time people asked her questions. When the train arrived at Zurich, some Gerschenkron cousins who had long ago emigrated to Switzerland were at the station to meet them.

Back in Vienna, the Gestapo was out in force, going from house to house, rounding up Jewish men. Alone with his five-month-old baby daughter whom he did not know how to care for, Shura did not want to chance another night at home. He took Heidi to her great-aunt Hedwig's for the night. Meanwhile, in Rotterdam, the husband of another childhood friend of Erica's, a Dutch minister named Melle Visser, was on a Vienna-bound train. The next day, Great-aunt Hedwig and Shura met Visser at a discreet location near the railroad station and handed Heidi over to him. In his pocket Visser was carrying his own infant daughter's Dutch passport. He was guessing that no Nazis he encountered would question a man wearing a clerical collar, and would in any case agree with Shura's view that all babies looked alike. Visser brought Heidi back to Rotterdam, where his wife took care of her for months. As the train rolled out of Vienna, Great-aunt Hedwig said, "There goes the baby," and was overcome.

With his wife and children on their way, Shura went to see Gretl

Afritsch. "He was very worried," Susi Schneider, Gretl's daughter, says. "He said to my mother, 'I'm leaving tomorrow. I have been told there will be a Gestapo raid tonight. I don't want to sleep at home. Can I stay at your apartment?'" Gretl and Shura had been friends for fourteen years. "Of course," she said. "Come and stay."

Shura's plan was to sleep at Gretl's, catch a Salzburg train in the morning, and then hike and ski through the mountains. Traveling with him would be a friend from his class at the *gymnasium*. The friend had become a Nazi, but he told Shura that their friendship was more important than politics. The friend was familiar with all the trails through the Alps and knew which ones were patrolled by Nazi guards. He agreed with Shura that if anyone asked, they would claim to be old school friends out for an annual vacation ramble. That the Germans had taken over the country would be news to them.

Shura went back home to get his things. In a light rucksack, he packed a few hiking clothes. He also took the passport given to him by the mother of a friend of his who'd been shot by the Nazis. "I hope this will keep you alive," she'd told him. For a moment he looked around at the apartment where he'd lived for so long, at his photographs, at his book collection, and at all the little objects acquired in the course of seventeen years in Austria. Then he walked out, shut the door, and put it all behind him. In the hallway, wanting to appear casual, he stopped in to greet some neighbors and forced himself to chat for a moment. Then he set off down the street, making sure not to rush.

Gretl meanwhile met up with her boyfriend Charly and her brother Pepo, a young politician. When she told them about Shura, the men looked uneasy. "You're endangering your family," Pepo said to Gretl. It took a while, but eventually Charly and Pepo made Gretl see things their way. It was after dark when Charly went to Gretl's apartment and told Shura to leave. "Hitler had just marched in," says Susi Schneider. "The mood must have been so eerie. In that atmosphere it was like a boot to the face." The streets were empty of everybody but the Gestapo patrols. Shura boarded the trolley and rode seven miles back to his apartment. He stayed there for the night. Nobody came for him.

In the morning Shura joined his friend and they went to the train station. Gretl knew what train they were taking to the mountains and was waiting for Shura at the station. She ran beside him as he walked along the platform, but he, who from boyhood had been a connoisseur of dazzling feats of courage, looked straight ahead. Finally he said simply, "Your father should know about this."

Shura and his friend made it through the mountains without incident, arriving at a border town on the Rhine River. There was a salt mine near the town. Every day migrant Swiss miners rode a trolley across the river span to cut salt out of the hills. At night the workers went home to Switzerland. Shura's plan was to meet up with a Swiss miner who was friendly with one of Shura's cousins in Switzerland. The Swiss miner would have a "companion" trolley pass. The man and Shura would ride the trolley out of Austria on its evening trip back across the Rhine to Switzerland.

The man with the pass was to meet Shura at a beer hall in the border town. The first beer hall Shura walked into turned out to be packed with drunken Nazis. Eventually he found the Swiss. The two men went to a place where Shura could put on a miner's outfit and rub dust all over himself. Then they walked to the trolley. Shura's companion pass was displayed for the sentry. The sentry was drunk. "What's this companion?" he wanted to know. "I'm tired of these damned companion passes. That companion could be a dog as well as a man. It could be a Saint Bernard. A Saint Bernard is a large dog, you know." He went on for some time. Shura said nothing. Finally the sentry made up his mind. "This one time I'm going to let you through," he said. "But at the other end you'd better tell them to make things clear. If it's a dog, say dog. If it's a man, say man."

In the trolley, the Swiss miners covered for Shura. They told jokes, laughed, poked him in the ribs, and slapped him on the back. There was an armed Nazi guard in the car, and Shura thought it best not to seem as though he was avoiding him. So he crossed the river standing next to a Nazi guard, laughing, jostling, and being jostled.

Erica met his train in Zurich. She hadn't known when to expect him and had been going to the station day after day to meet a husband who didn't appear. When he did get to Zurich—which was full of Germans—the three of them left right away and made their way to England.

Years later Susi and her parents went to a movie together called *The Last Chance*. It was the story of a mountain escape from Nazi Germany. As they walked out of the theater, Erica noticed that Shura and Susi were bathed in sweat. That surprised her because they had handled their real escapes with absolute composure and no sign of anxiety.

As soon as Shura arrived at his parents' house in Letchworth, he found that Charles Gulick had sent him an invitation. After reading in American newspapers that Vienna had been occupied, Gulick wrote to Paul to find out what had become of Shura. Shura made contact with Gulick, who urged him to come to Berkeley and resume work on the book. Gulick offered him the coveted "Affidavit of Support." It meant that if Shura proved unemployable, Gulick accepted all responsibility for him. Shura bought Erica a manual of English for foreign students, inscribed it with a quotation from Heine—"For grammar I used the face of my loved woman"—and said farewell to everyone. He couldn't kiss Heidi goodbye. She was still in Holland. When Heidi was finally brought to Letchworth, months later, Erica noticed that during the time of separation the baby had forgotten how to smile.

On board ship to the United States Shura distracted himself from his anxieties by rereading Arthur Conan Doyle's Sherlock Holmes stories. When he got to California, he moved in with the Gulicks and worked, as Gulick later said, "Ungodly hours. Twenty of them at a stretch. He helped me in a way that is impossible to exaggerate." Gulick also praised Shura's "incredible" memory, his "wide range of knowledge," the rapid pace at which he got things done, and his excellent analytical abilities. Gulick had a few criticisms too. He said that when it came to describing the history of the Social Democrats, Shura was "prone to exaggeration. A Socialist victory in an election was always 'overwhelming.'"

For twelve months Shura was as good as Gulick's indentured servant. He lived in the guest room, took all his meals at Gulick's table, and worked for him seven days a week, helping to write a book that relived some of the killing disappointments of his life. Gulick recalled that

Shura's moods fluctuated, lurching between joviality and depression. "He was super-sensitive and suspicious," Gulick said. At one point someone told Shura that Gulick was going to throw him out. "He was in a black mood for a week until I found out what the matter was," Gulick said. "I told him he was a damn fool." It was an awkward situation. Gulick was Shura's benefactor, yet Shura bristled at being the poor foreigner forced always to defer to the mighty American, particularly someone he thought wasn't especially intelligent.

Many people who met Gulick weren't overly impressed by him as a thinker. *Austria from Habsburg to Hitler*, however, turned out to be a very impressive book. Published in 1948 in two volumes that together were 1,900 pages long, it is a magisterial work of scholarship, one that is still considered the defining contribution to the field. Here was something of a paradox, this brilliant book by this less-than-brilliant man. Some people wondered about it.

One of them was the labor economist Walter Galenson. He was a young colleague of Gulick's at Berkeley when *Austria from Habsburg to Hitler* was published. "It was a very good book," Galenson said. "I knew Gulick. Gulick was no better able to write that book than the man on the moon. Impossible! It had all the earmarks of Shura's work."

In Berkeley Shura would come to know another talented European refugee intellectual, the political and economic historian Albert Hirschman. Hirschman met Shura in the early 1940s, but it wasn't until one day in the early 1970s that "Shura told me something I think he hadn't told anybody else. He took from his shelf the book by Gulick and said that actually it was written in a large part by him. He's mentioned as a faithful research assistant, but he wrote it and made Gulick famous. It was a book everybody concerned with Austria *had* to read. He was a little unhappy about it."

Gulick died in 1984, and today there is no certain way to tell how much of his prose was actually set down by Shura. The language and tone of the book betray many similarities to the Gerschenkron style— "mother's milk," for instance, was a favorite simile, and Shura frequently began his sentences with the word "naturally." The book's reflections on the nature of dictatorship and the development of backward economies contain the germ of the signature Gerschenkron themes Shura would explore throughout his professional career. And yet there are also the undeniable facts that the book was Gulick's idea and that he devoted years of his life to it. Perhaps what Shura felt was that Gulick could not have completed *Austria from Habsburg to Hitler* without him, while he certainly could have done it all without Gulick.

Shura's expressed feelings about the collaboration evolved. In the 1940s and 1950s, Shura would tell family members that he was glad to have found a way to come to America, glad to have had a chance to do real scholarship, and that it was worth it to have ghostwritten a book to get English and the United States in exchange. "A book for a passport was a good deal," he would conclude. Yet by the mid-1970s, when the Oakland Athletics played in the World Series, Shura rooted against the Athletics because, as he told Walter Galenson with a sardonic grin, "Gulick will be rooting for them." Gulick had met Shura at a time when he was desperate and Gulick had helped him. For that Shura always said he was grateful, but he did not stop at leaving people with the impression that on balance he appreciated what Gulick had done for him. Instead, when somebody talked about Charles Gulick with Alexander Gerschenkron, they walked away thinking that there are few things more unseemly than doing a man in danger a good turn and then feeling free to take advantage of him.

The year with the Gulicks in California was an emotionally fragile time for Shura. "Shura was not scarred by his experience getting out of Russia," his sister believes. "He was young and felt protected. Leaving Austria did affect his nerves. He didn't say it was a hard time for him. He wouldn't admit to it. But you could tell." Shura was now thirty-five. Lydia said that she herself found that "your thirties [are] the best time. For it's only in the thirties that you realize truly what makes you tick as a person." But all Shura was doing with himself was starting over again. He had nothing besides his work. He was an ocean away from his family, there was no clear future, and the world he had left was imploding.

This was his news from Europe: In Salzburg, where they were burning books in public bonfires, the Gestapo came to the home of one of Lydia's best friends and took her brother away in the night. Two weeks later the boy's mother received a package containing her son's bloodstained clothing and a bill for funeral expenses. Fifi Bader, the girl who'd helped Shura with his German in Stockerau, was arrested and taken with her parents to a concentration camp where she was killed. Erica's half-brother Wolfie had disappeared into Australia. She wouldn't see him again for ten years. Shura's conspicuously correct tutor from Stockerau had gone into politics and become the mayor of his small hometown. When the Nazis arrived there, he and his vice-mayor were each given a pail and forced to walk along the main street behind a horse-drawn cart. In the cart was a barrel of liquid manure. The two men had to keep filling their pails from the barrel and dumping them out over one another's heads. When the barrel was empty, they were taken to a concentration camp and put to death. Sigmund Freud was now in England where he was slowly dying of cancer. Otto Bauer was sick too; he died in Paris in October 1938. Also in Paris was Tolia. While getting there from Vienna he had caught a chill and came down with pleurisy. Shura's little brother was only twenty-eight years old in November when the fever infection overwhelmed him. He died in a Paris hospital with his bride Vivian by his side.

Paul and Sophie took Lydia to Paris for the funeral. "It nearly killed my parents," Lydia said. "As for me, a light went out. My brother Tolia was brilliant. A brilliant linguist, a brilliant mimic, a brilliant writer, a brilliant poet. A warm, loving, loyal, humorous, caring and tolerant person. He was my friend, teacher, playmate and confidant. Even now I can't talk about it without a flood of tears." Shura's solution was never to mention Tolia at all.

IN JUNE, AT THE END OF THE 1939 ACADEMIC YEAR, SHURA WENT back to England and found his whole family waiting to greet the boat. At the sight of them all standing there on the dock he began weeping for his dead brother. Through the summer he fought hard to keep control of his emotions. To Lydia and the others he seemed tired but composed. "I never discussed Tolia with Shura except to remember his *mots justes*," Lydia said. Only to Erica did he confess how upset he was. He let her know in an unusual way. Erica was beginning to learn English, and to help her along Shura began making her presents of English and

American novels. On the flyleaf of each of these books Shura wrote his wife inscriptions. They were always in German. One book he chose for her was Margaret Mitchell's *Gone with the Wind*. Inside the cover he wrote:

> *Für Erika**
>
> *Im Wind verweht, se stecht's geschrieben,*
> *Damit Du eines nicht vergisst.*
> *So mancher der in Wien geblieben*
> *Hat doch Die Heimart eingebüsst.*
>
> *Sommer 1939*

> Gone with the wind, that's how it is written,
> So don't you forget one thing:
> Some of those who remained in Vienna
> Have also lost their fatherland.

Another of his gifts was H. G. Wells's *The Holy Terror,* the story of a villain's rise to power. Here Shura's inscription was much longer:

> *Der Erika*
>
> *Wir haben die Welt voll Hoffnung gekannt,*
> *Voll Hoffnung auf Liebe und Glück;*
> *Der Traum ist entschwunden, verflossen im Sand,*
> *Wir schauen nicht mehr zurück,*
>
> *Noch chauen wir verbairts. Wir schen Wien,*
> *Das Wien des Feber und Märzen;*
> *Was immer der kommenden Tage sinn;*
> *Es rührt nicht unsere Herzen.*
>
> *Die Herzen sind tot und der Körper lebt*
> *Er lebt gestaltese Tage,*

---

*Erika changed her name to Erica when she became a U.S. citizen.

Die weil das rasende zünglein bebt
An der Menschheit Schicksalwege.

Gewesene Menschen, wir leben fort,
Wir schlafen, trinken, und essen,
Wir schleppen uns müder von Ort zu Ort:
Man hat uns zu töten vergessen.

S.

18.6. 40

We have known the world full of hope,
Full of hope for love and happiness.
The dream is gone, disappeared in the sand.
We do not look back anymore.

Nor do we look forward. We saw Vienna.
That Vienna of February and March.
Whatever the meaning of the coming days
It does not touch our hearts.

The hearts are dead and the body lives.
It lives shapeless days.
The little tong on the scales of human fate trembles.
We are former beings, we live happily.

We sleep, drink, and eat.
We drag ourselves tiredly from place to place.
They have forgotten to kill us.

In September, with war declared across Europe, it was clear that the family would not be going back to Austria anytime soon. So Shura bought Erica, Susi, and Heidi tickets on the *Aquitania* and they all sailed for America. The North Sea and the Atlantic Ocean were heavily mined, and the two grown-ups alternated sleeping shifts so that if necessary someone would always be ready to hurry the children to a lifeboat. They arrived safely in New York and took the train across the country to California.

Shura would not see Austria again for eleven years. When he finally returned in July 1950, he refused to go to Vienna. Instead he went to Ramseiden, the little Alpine village full of flowers of every color where Gretl Afritsch was now summering with the well-known leftist politician Karl Mark, the man she had married after breaking up with Charly. Karl and Gretl had two children, Susi and Toni.

Toni and Gretl were sitting on a bench in front of their little wooden house when Toni saw her mother freeze. Down the road a man was approaching. Gretl stared at the man. Then she got up to her feet and began running toward him. He began running too and they met in an embrace. They kissed and held each other, hugging and burying their heads in one another's shoulders for many minutes. Gretl could not stop sobbing.

Shura finally released her and immediately began smiling and joking. He was introduced to Toni, looked her over, and called her "L.P.," short for *Landpomerantchen* (little country bumpkin). He had made a new home by then, in America. He had a promising future. His family was safe and healthy. Erica, of course, sent her greetings. He stayed for weeks, and they had a wonderful time in the little mountain town full of flowers. Never once did Shura or Gretl talk about the night after the *Anschluss*. It was simply understood that he had forgiven her.

FOUR

THE IMMIGRANT
AND THE EXILE

As his wife grew more irritable and exacting and Ivan
Ilych transferred the center of gravity of his life more
and more to his official work, so did he like his work
better and become more ambitious than before.

Leo Tolstoy, "The Death of Ivan Ilych"

I N CALIFORNIA SHURA BEGAN LIFE FOR THE THIRD TIME. DUR-
ing his years at Berkeley he was part of a group of recent European
immigrants who were paid a pittance to help the senior members
of the economics department write their books. Although they were
called research associates, the men were really no more than glorified
graduate students. They spent their days behind heavy gray metal desks
working side by side in a common space at Berkeley's Doe Library. That
proximity should have enabled them to get to know one another very
well, and mostly they did. Shura was the exception. His response to his
latest cycle of escape, flight, and arrival was similar enough to the way
he'd started over in Austria that it was nearly a reprise. He took on the
present with a grim intensity that served somehow to shed whatever
skin he'd worn prior to America. Whom you see, he seemed to be saying, is all I am. Not that the other young men at the gray metal desks
didn't try to learn what he'd been before.

One of the desks belonged to Albert Hirschman. Hirschman was a
German-born Jewish socialist and a delicately built man with a soft way
of speaking, but he was sturdy enough. In 1939 he had been living in
Paris, working as an economist, when the war began. Hirschman joined
the French Resistance. There he encountered the American Nazi fighter

Varian Fry and joined on sabotage missions until, with France occupied, Fry helped Hirschman escape out of Marseilles. He crossed the Pyrenees on foot and, with the aid of some friendly cowherds, made his way through fascist Spain into Portugal, and then went on to California. In time Hirschman would become famous within the American academy as a distinguished scholar whose theories of social change and economic development were informed by a deep and esoteric knowledge of Western thought. He was in his mid-twenties when he arrived at Berkeley, and the moment he met Shura he immediately sized him up as someone who shared not only his interests, but also his experiences. Hirschman did his best to become intimate with Shura; indeed, he spent a lifetime courting him, but the friendship never quite came off.

"In Berkeley I was full of stories," Hirschman says. "I had a few picaresque stories to tell about my problems leaving France. Shura never reciprocated. It was frustrating. He was very secretive in many ways. It was never easy to find out, for instance, even what he was working on. He wouldn't tell you or show you. He'd surprise the world with his new things." Something that intrigued Hirschman was that Shura, who came from Vienna, was always disparaging Freud. He seemed to have only imprecations for the idea of people spending their time thinking about human psychology.

None of this put Hirschman off. He liked Shura. All of the young men at the Doe Library did. "I never found him not gregarious," says Alexander "Sandy" Stevenson, a cheerful Scot who breakfasted with Shura many mornings and also sometimes joined him for a lunch of Swedish meatballs at a hash house on Telegraph Avenue. Shura would come bursting into the restaurant, slide into his side of the booth, and begin describing the latest Jack London novel he'd picked up. Reading American writers, he said, made the country feel more accessible to him. The two men also had conversations about the great Scottish economist Adam Smith, and they discussed problems of language. Shura was taking all opportunities to add to his collection of American idioms and phrases—he loved to say "hold the hail" when ordering orange juice without ice—and he was overjoyed when Stevenson told him that the words to a bawdy Berkeley fraternity house song were actually

adapted from an even bawdier Scottish ballad. Stevenson had a dense Scottish brogue, and Shura would coax him into repeating over and over particularly vulgar lines like "The minister's wifey she was there and she was awful fu (drunk) / They tied her to the barn door and bulled her like a cow." But if questions of Shura's life in Europe came up, Stevenson could feel a heavy curtain dropping. "Shura was a very, very private man," he says. "If he was unhappy about something you'd never know it, you'd never be told. He never told us stories of his life, never discussed his past. He was looking forward."

Shura once explained this reluctance in a letter written in 1954, from Marburg, Germany, where he was spending the summer doing research, to his friend the economist Abram Bergson. "It is very quiet," he wrote Bergson. "People are pleasant and it is almost inconceivable to think that only a few years ago a horrible hurricane went through the land, that unspeakable crimes were committed and everything worth living for was trampled down. One can of course understand these things in a general way, but not really, not humanly. So I suppose there is not much point in talking about them." And he didn't talk about them. The

Dutch-born Harvard economist Hendrick Houthakker once began to describe for Shura what it was like to be in Holland during the Nazi occupation. "I was a prisoner of the Gestapo during World War II for some time because of my Jewish origin," Houthakker said. "I was about to tell Gerschenkron about an incident in which I more or less intimidated a sadistic sergeant, and Gerschenkron made it clear he didn't want to pursue that. He got off the conversation. It was odd. He didn't want to talk about anything that happened in the war." When Shura was asked directly about his own experiences with the Nazis, he would say, "Let's not talk about it," using a tone that could not have been more final.

When Shura came to Berkeley, even if he'd been so inclined, he would not have spent time assessing the past, because his present was too rutted with anxieties. He had gone from a precocious boy to a man now fallen behind in life. There were strands of gray in his hair, he had lived nearly half his allotment of years and yet he was no more than a humble clerk, spinning in his professional place while much younger men gamboled past him. As a newcomer making an unplanned arrival in California, the circumstances that had set him back when he first got to Austria as a refugee were against him once again. Shura didn't have any friends in America, the customs and language of the country were unfamiliar, and his immigration status seemed very precarious. At one point early on he was forced to leave the United States and wait out several weeks in Canada while his petition to extend his American visa was considered. To feed himself he swept the floors in a Montreal factory. He worried about money, worried about his wife and children, worried about his career. All that and his brother was dead less than a year. It could have broken him. Instead, he fenced off his memories. "Shura didn't have a nervous breakdown, or become hysterical," Lydia says. "That wasn't his style. He always gave the impression of being on top. His remoteness was intentional. It kept people from pestering him. He wanted to be left alone."

His feelings about the recent past were what anyone would have guessed them to be. He was angry, but he remained by instinct and by nature the Russian stoic. There was a quality within him that thrived on all the opposition because it could be bested. Creating small disadvantages for himself was something he did habitually, and as he prevailed over them, the little successes gave him confidence that he could survive larger setbacks. When reading books, for instance, he positioned himself flat on his back with his book on his chest and nothing supporting his uplifted head, "because it strengthens the neck." There was a certain amount of satisfaction in denying himself some of the pleasures he now began to renounce, like meals and nights of sleep. He liked tests of the will and he believed—as Job did—that hardships gave a man the opportunity to persevere and prove his virtue, his goodness, and his strength of character. To Shura, the experience of overcoming was itself a reward, and one that also earned the promise of future recompense if you simply kept on. Somewhere along the way religion had reentered his life, and for him stoicism became imbued with Christian moral qualities. He thought that God tested and God kept count. How else was Shura to explain, for instance, that he was alive in America when so many people, including members of his own family, had been shot or gassed? All that is why, when he got to California, Shura did not dwell on his disappointments. He put his head down and threw himself into his work with everything he had in him.

Among the Berkeley faculty, word of Charles Gulick's helpful young man spread quickly, and Gulick began to receive inquiries from people like the zoologist Charles Kofoid, who had "heard that you have a very efficient translator." Soon, besides helping Gulick move along with *Austria from Habsburg to Hitler,* Shura was assisting Howard Ellis on a book called *Exchange Control in Central Europe* and Jack Condliffe with his investigation of state trading monopolies. One of the countries whose trade regulation policies were particularly interesting was Norway, and so Shura taught himself to read Norwegian. While he sometimes looked weary to his Doe Library colleagues, it was only when the United States entered the war that they discovered just how hard he was working. To save energy, a nightly electrical blackout was imposed on the Berkeley campus. Late one evening, the police officers patrolling the university spotted a faint lamp glowing behind a drawn shade in Doe Library. They made their way into the building, opened the door, and turned up Shura, stealing time at his gray metal desk.

After that he set up a card table in the living room and spent his nights working at home. It was a snug apartment where there were plenty of distractions—a wife, two young children, a frisky puppy—but his concentration was formidable. He could be talking with Susi or Heidi, and after a little while, even as he looked them in the eye, they could see his mind straying to his work. "Daddy! Daddy!" they'd yell. "Come back!" Once Heidi, failing to get his attention, crawled under the table and began barking and scratching at her father's feet. Lost in thought, he patted her head and mumbled, "Good dog."

Eventually, Erica and the girls went off to bed, and the house would be still except for the scratching of Shura's pencil. Not only was he helping three different men finish their books, but he was also writing one of his own. He divided his time this way: he gave his days to his employers' books; the nights belonged to him.

At 224 pages, *Bread and Democracy in Germany* is his longest single piece of published writing. Like everything he wrote, it is much less a comprehensive study than an essay. Shura chose big topics—in this case the rise of German fascism—and mastered them with muscular reading and archival research. Then, when it was time to write, he did so with a lathe, turning his ideas over and over as he honed them into lean meditations.

Published in 1943, when Shura was thirty-nine, *Bread and Democracy* has served him as an elegant calling card among other scholars ever since. Martin Peretz picked it up as a Harvard graduate student in the 1960s and says, "I read it twice—I couldn't believe how good it was." Writing in the *New Yorker* in 1991, Patrick Smith praised Shura's book at length as a "classic of economic history." In truth, *Bread and Democracy* is really a classic of Austrian scholarship, a book whose eclectic intellectual pedigree makes it as much a work of political science and sociology as anything economic. The book's subject is the Junkers, the powerful Prussian planter aristocrats who owned the sprawling wheat, oat, barley, and rye fields east of the Elbe River. The Junker landowners' influence with the German government was such that in modern times they wrested a medieval privilege for themselves—the right to supply all of Germany with bread grains. The grain monopoly enabled the Junker estate owners to charge wildly inflated amounts for their crops, meaning that the German population was paying double the market price for bread. *Bread and Democracy* argues that the tolerance of such blatant government protectionism was symptomatic of an anti-democratic sensibility in German politics that left the country vulnerable to fascism. Hitler made shrewd use of the situation. The public welcomed the dictator partly because he seemed likely to stand up to the abuses of the monied establishment. And the Nazis did spend a lot of time loudly denouncing the Junkers. Then they slipped into back rooms and cut deals with them, an insidious pattern that led Shura, writing in 1943, to conclude that "if the grain of the Junkers grows, the grain of German democracy will wither and perish from the earth." That wasn't a bad sentence for someone with less than five years of English. It was also the closest the author would come to suggesting that the Nazis were anything more to him personally than garden variety villains.

Just before the book was finished, Berkeley promoted Shura to lecturer, and he began to teach courses in economic history and international trade. But his writing and teaching did not give him much reason to feel his life was really going anywhere at Berkeley. He was always badly paid and was never offered any possibility of becoming a professor. Shura did, however, find a summer job that brought him immense satisfaction. As soon as the United States fully joined the war in Europe in 1942, he tried to enlist. Told he was too old for the service, he began making regular blood donations and soon had given away so many pints that he made himself ill. Gratifying as this was, that kind of bloodletting did little to quench his desire to put his full physical self into the fight against Germany. So he went down to the piers in Richmond, on the bay north of Berkeley, and signed up to help build the large cargo vessels that were known as Liberty ships.

Every morning Shura laced on a pair of heavy boots, jammed a cloth cap on his head, collected his hardhat and his lunchbox, and climbed into his car pool driver's Model A Ford for the thirty-minute ride to the entranceway, where the sign said "Through These Gates Go the World's Best Shipbuilders." They were undeniably the world's fastest. Henry Kaiser was the Eli Whitney of shipbuilding, quickening production by devising ways to prefabricate increasingly large sections of each boat instead of putting them together piece by piece. Spurred by loudspeakers urging them to do their part in keeping the country from losing the "Battle of Supply," the Richmond workers assembled Liberty ships at such a clip that only four and a half days after construction was begun on the *Robert E. Peary*, a champagne bottle was smashed against its bow and away it went, plunging into the Pacific.

Shura filled several positions in the shipyards. At various times he was a shipfitter, using a blueprint to chalk out markings showing the crane operator where the metal beams and brackets were to be placed on a given sheet of steel; a flanger, pounding the beams into postion with a sledgehammer after the crane had set them down; a welder, joining the beams to the steel with a blowtorch; and an expediter—a traffic policeman of sorts—directing the flow of parts and materials between the storage shacks and the work stations. At least in his memory, shifting from job to job did not bother him, and neither did Northern California's summer chill—especially when dressed in his welder's leathers—or the incredible din of heavy machinery. He had grown up in a port and liked the rough ambiance of the piers. Becoming a member of a union, the International Brotherhood of Boilermakers, Iron Ship Builders and Helpers of America, was a badge for his old socialist sensibilities, and he got so used to the physical exertion that, missing it later during the academic year, he took up boxing and lifting barbells.

Laborers in the wartime United States made good pay. Kaiser began him at $62 a week, a rate far higher than his $1,300 first-year salary at Berkeley, and enough money for him to discover what workers all over the country were discovering: that in America you didn't have to be rich to own the latest models. One day he came whistling up the front steps of his house with a large box in his hands. He was carrying the family's first radio, a brand new 1942 Philco tabletop. That was a real concession to please Erica and Susi. While he was interested in current events, he did not like broadcast entertainment, considering it a household intrusion and the enemy of a thinking person. When Shura was reading or writing at home, Erica was never allowed to listen to classical music. In later years he was equally severe with his grandaughter and her flute. "No, no, I can't have this," he would say. "Play it when I am away."

The best part of the shipyards for Shura was working in the company of American men. The plump wages the shipyards were paying had created a kind of industrial gold rush, drawing thousands of workers from all over the country to fill Richmond's round-the-clock production shifts. There were the Okies who'd driven west in listing sedans, sharecroppers up from Louisiana, Texas, and Arkansas, roughnecks from the Montana copper fields, vacuum cleaner salesmen out of Nebraska, hillbilly tobacco farmers, miners from the Eastern coal belt, Middlewestern farm boys, immigrant Chinese, and slicks who boarded westbound buses in New York or Philly, all of them with their different talks and walks and food in their lunchboxes. To Shura, it was the long span of his new country compressed down to size right in front of him.

Not everything was new. What Shura heard on the job was familiar to him as both a former mover of Russian watermelons and a past consorter with foul-mouthed Russian peasants. The shipyard workers behaved the way physical men do when a group of them are thrown together, and Shura reveled in the comraderie: the bluff affections, the jokes, the japes, the blasphemy, the profanity, and the obscenity; especially the profanity, because the deft application of a crude intensifier— "What do you do all day?" "We wait for the fucking *crane*!"—told other men that you were a regular guy both clever and genuine. Once, during his lunch break, Shura pulled out his pouch of Half & Half pipe tobacco and a passing wit cracked, "Yeah, Professor, half crap and half shit!" That man and Shura were fast friends. Another day the foreman swaggered up and allowed, "There's nothing like a good shit." Shura never forgot him for it. At Harvard, when another professor stopped by the office for a visit, sometimes Shura would look serenely out across the desk cluttered with books in various languages, scholarly journals, and seminar papers, and he would muse, "You know, I've been thinking about something my old foreman in the California shipyards used to say, and I believe he was quite right. There really is nothing like a good shit." It broke the ivory tower boys up every time.

As the war progressed, the shipyards began hiring increasing numbers of women, and Shura observed among his peers much energetic door holding and cap lifting, along with a corresponding linguistic elevation: "What do you do all day?" "Well, Ma'am, we do our level best to stay out of trouble." Shura was thoroughly charmed. He believed the sight of a woman ought to transform a roomful of men, and with chivalry, as with profanity, he considered excess to be a virtue.

In later years, when he thought back on all the hardhat days and nights, there was always one moment that stood out. Early in his stretch as a welder, Shura began to doubt his skills, had recurring nightmares in which rows of rivets popped out one after the other like buttons down a shirtfront, and boatloads of young men went to the bottom because Gerschenkron didn't know how to handle a blowtorch. Eventually he asked the foreman to come and inspect his technique. The next day the foreman called together the unit and praised Shura, saying, "We're here to do the job well, so don't be ashamed to speak up if you have any concerns about anything you're doing. We're all in this together."

Right there in Richmond Shura became a hopelessly besotted American patriot—fell into an American swoon that would last a lifetime. He was terribly, deeply grateful to the United States in the outsize way that people who have endured much turbulence in their lives are overcome with appreciation when they finally come upon something stable. In 1946, when the FBI sent out field agents to see if Shura had participated in "activities . . . considered inimical to the welfare of the United States," what they assembled was a confidential file packed with descriptions of "a man of loyalty and integrity." If anything, the file only understated. No man ever loved a country more. Shura reminded people of the Irishman arriving in New York Harbor on the Fourth of July under an evening sky filled with fireworks. Standing beside him on deck is an Englishman. "What's all the noise about?" the Englishman asks, looking around. "That," the Irishman replies, "is for the day we licked you."

Shura extrapolated what he saw in the shipyard into an idealized conception of America that was the antithesis of what he'd seen in Vienna. He became something of a flag waver, a man prone to sweeping national generalizations like "Americans are happy people," as he took to saying. His United States was a warm, tough, egalitarian, assimilated place where everyone worked as one, getting the boats out on time for a national cause they all believed in. These people in their overalls and hardhats had seen the darkest days of the Depression. Now they were rejuvenated as the country was rejuvenated, united behind their spirited president, who had given the ordinary man a New Deal, united in what for them was a war of principle and faith against enemies so evil that if you hadn't actually stood and watched them in a public square in Berlin or Rome or Vienna they seemed to be outlandish caricatures of cruelty. In Shura's America, nobody cared who your father was or what your accent sounded like. They cared about what kind of a fellow you were. Once the other workers got to know "the Professor," they invited him home for meals and took him to parties. The feeling was the same as it had been hanging out in coffeehouses with the Vienna socialists. He was a regular again.

It took a sly Harvard professor to calculate just how much the shipyards meant to Shura. In his time, the labor negotiator John Dunlop had settled some of the most contentious disputes in American industrial history, taking on rooms with embittered steel workers on one side and their management on the other, and wearing both sides down with blunt reason. When all the cerebral appeasements failed, Dunlop had been known to reach for rawer tactics—his whiskey bottle. His strategy was to drink everyone under the bargaining table, send them off to bed, wait for a couple of hours, and then haul them back into negotiations. According to Dunlop, this usually worked.

Dunlop was the chairman of the Harvard economics department during much of the 1960s, when Shura was probably its most irascible member—someone, says Dunlop, who "had very strong views about everything and not much sense of mediation." One day as Dunlop thought about how to handle Shura, it occurred to him that "the only thing he ever told me about his life in detail was the shipyards." He had noticed the enthusiasm with which Shura spoke about the shipyards, the obvious affection he had for the people who'd worked there, and Shura's sense that they had appreciated him too when nobody at Berkeley really had. So when Dunlop wanted Shura to go along with him on some sticky departmental matter, he would invite him into his office and get him talking about the shipyards for a while before putting his request to him. The shipyards, Dunlop says, worked every time.

*   *   *

ERICA, MEANWHILE, WAS MISERABLE FROM THE MOMENT SHE SET foot in America. Standing there on the pier in New York Harbor amid the commotion of parcels, ropes, luggage, sailors, taxi and hotel touts, the businessmen rushing off to West Side bars, the couples hurrying to their hotels to freshen up for the theater, the reunited lovers and the stray tourist or two, she began to laugh and couldn't stop. She laughed and laughed and laughed until suddenly she was sobbing hysterically.

Once she got to California, while Shura hurled himself into his future, all Erica thought about was Austria. For a brief time she took a job in a factory washing bottles. It did not go well. She was a highly educated Viennese lady and the idea of herself as a scrubwoman agitated her so much that soon she was almost frantic. After a few weeks she quit and thereafter stayed home, where her *Heimweh* (homesickness) became so severe that her body ached and hurt. She worked herself into distress with existential thoughts—why had all this happened to her? why had it happened to Austria?—until finally she gave up and became listless. For all of her education and intelligence, there were few jobs availble to her because she didn't speak English. Nor did she try to. Instead, Erica became a depressed housewife. Even during the worst years in Vienna, domestic labor was so shamefully cheap that there had always been a young servant girl around to help her out. Now she had to do the baking, laundry, and cleaning herself. Increasingly she leaned on Susi to interpret, fold the sheets, dust the bookcases, scour the bathroom, and take care of her baby sister. Erica didn't want to learn English, didn't want to buy hamburger meat or balance a checkbook.

She didn't want to explore the Marin Highlands or Sonoma County either. A brief train ride over the bridge from Berkeley was San Francisco, a beautiful and cultured seaside city, proud of its library and the opera house designed by Arthur Brown, Jr., a place full of luxurious movie palaces and charming cafes. But to Erica San Francisco was the last outpost, a quaint little frontier town so laughably unsophisticated that she thought it gauche. San Francisco had an opera house? Vienna *was* opera. Berkeley seemed no more to her than a bland hamlet with a lot of flowers and students with large jaws and big white teeth who didn't speak her language. "There is nothing for me here," she thought. All she wanted was for the war to end so she could go home.

Erica knew that Austria had been complicit in terrible things, but she did not like to think of the Austria that embraced the Nazis as the real Austria. Her country had been victimized by Hitler as she had been victimized by Hitler, and now that she was far away, it was easy for her to remember things as she wished to. Out in public she clung proudly to Austrian culture. Oblivious to the hostile stares that came to someone who insisted upon speaking the language of the enemy, she dressed Heidi and Susi in dirndls, and at the movies she made them cringe by loudly pointing out the large numbers of Teutonic cognates that appeared in the dialogue. (She was right; the big studios were hiring so many Austrian refugee writers and directors that people began referring to Hollywood as "Little Vienna.") Wherever she went, she was prone to asking people if they spoke German.

Some of the Berkeley faculty wives tried to befriend her. They were scorned. "She was miserable in Berkeley," says Walter Galenson's wife Marjorie. "She missed her mother. She was unyielding, hostile, and rejected friendships which she considered patronizing. When she did have something to do with you, she imposed. She didn't drive, so she asked for help marketing and carrying bundles even when I had a bad back. Then I once drove her when she had a bad back, and she berated me every time we passed over a bump." That Erica had not been brought up to function as a practical woman in the world was costing her. It was wartime, everyone had troubles, one had to adapt, and she couldn't.

Shura knew that his wife wasn't learning English because she expected to go home soon. Around him Erica never criticized the new country— he would not have stood for it—and she did not tell their children they were "stupid" or "ugly" the way she now sometimes did when he was away. In turn he was just as careful never to say anything against her. He ate what she cooked for him, and he did not judge her as a mother. Although he encouraged her to improve her English, he always spoke with her in German. He filled the home with company, bringing home the radio, the puppy, and also a cat he named Katinka for her to put in her lap and stroke as she sat in the backyard under an apricot tree. Yet he was too immersed in his work to provide much of what Erica really wanted, his companionship.

Everyone in the family missed that. The house was a notably more pleasant place with him around. Susi came down with laryngitis, so he boiled a big pot of water on the stove and then, when Susi was afraid of all the steam, he stood under a towel inhaling with her, cheek to cheek. He had to make particular efforts with Heidi. Before she arrived in Berkeley, Heidi had spent most of her first two years living apart from her father in Holland and England. The first men she got to know were Melle Visser, the Dutch minister who had rescued her from Vienna, and Paul, her grandfather. When she was taken away from Paul and brought to California, she missed her grandfather and regarded her father with suspicion. Gradually Shura won Heidi over. Part of it was that he was so much fun. (If they had to get somewhere by a certain time in the morning, he might propose a dressing race.) Part of it was his obvious concern for her well-being.

THROUGH SMALL, UNSPOKEN ADJUSTMENTS OF PERSONALITY, PEOPLE like his children came to see that even if Shura didn't want to talk about his life in Europe, the past remained vivid in his memory. He grew wary, always needing to understand how things would be, and, since life permits that kind of foresight to no man, Shura became more easily anxious and a little less spontaneous. As he grew older, the surfaces of his life might at various times have looked unkempt, but that was by design; he always knew where everything was. His friends the Galensons, along with their eight-year-old daughter Emily, were once out with Shura and Erica for an evening stroll, and they were taken aback when Shura, a man in his fifties, suddenly stopped in front of a high parapet they were passing and proposed something to Emily: "Would you like to see me get up there?" he asked. She said she would. The Galensons begged him not to do it. "You'll kill yourself," Walter told him. Shura went ahead and scaled it. As her husband stood there looking down on them all from the ramparts, Erica shrugged and said, "He always does these things." What Shura didn't happen to mention to his friends was that this wasn't an impromptu stunt. He'd inspected the parapet on a previous walk and plotted out his ascent.

One likely reason Shura never revealed much about himself, that he gladly talked business or politics or baseball but stayed away from discussing his family, his doubts, and his discontents, was that he sensed the power of these emotions and wanted to take no chances with setting them free. Albert Hirschman was mistaken; Shura had read a lot of Freud, praised him for the beauty of his prose, and could quote freely from his works. Yet much as he was stimulated by Freud as a writer and thinker, Shura never gave any indication that he allowed those ideas access to his own emotional life. To the contrary; he seems to have worked hard to keep them out. Shura's daughters Heidi and Susi—who became a psychologist—thought a lot about their father's reactions to psychology and decided that lurking in his dismissiveness was the fear of what he might find if he began searching within himself. There is no way to know, of course, what a person keeps to himself about himself, but this much is clear: the longer Shura lived in America, the more private he became.

Shura remained a bright and curious person, yet now there was a forlorn side to him too, a hatred of having anything he liked go away, even temporarily. Through his life, when he saw any of the few people he allowed to become dear to him, he always spent the first part of the visit bargaining to make it last longer. If you'd come to see him for two hours, he begged for four. If you'd planned a stay of a week, he didn't understand why you couldn't make it two. "Don't go home," he would plead with Heidi when she came to see her father with her family. "You don't have to stay with us. I'll put you up in a fine room at the Commander Hotel and then I'll come and take you out to tea." He was awful at farewells. After the most cheerful visits, as his guests made their way out, he'd stand waving from the doorway and his shoulders would slump, his chin would drop toward his chest, and his clothes—already rumpled—would seem to droop a little more at the wrists and ankles until he seemed thoroughly attenuated. Losing so much when he was young made him worried that once something he loved left his sight, he'd never see it again.

*   *   *

HEIDI WAS SIX YEARS OLD IN 1944 WHEN A COUPLE OF BERKELEY professors recommended Shura to the Federal Reserve Board. He was invited to Washington and subsequently offered a job as a European economic analyst at the Fed. Listening to him on the phone as he called home with the news, Heidi could hear how excited he was. He felt that Washington would put him right at the pulse of things, working for the government, working for Roosevelt, fighting the good fight not just with a sledge or a torch but with his mind. He took the job, came home, and then went back to Washington saying he would send for the family once he'd found a place to live. For the time being he rented a room by the week in a boardinghouse, where he did his best to ignore the city's sweltering summer heat. Two of the other residents didn't make this easy: the reclusive cheese hoarder who owned no icebox (the stench was blinding) and the brazen hall pacer who preferred to do his wandering without any robe on. Eventually the hall pacer traded one affront for another. When undressed he kept behind the closed doors of his room, which he now cooled with the fan he'd stolen from Shura.

After a few weeks of keeping such company, Shura rented a rambling house on South Dakota Avenue and got it ready for the family. Susi didn't want to go. She felt hustled into yet another move and spent much of the trip east sobbing in her Pullman berth for her high school friends. But leaving Berkeley wasn't hard for Shura. Years later he would tell one of his students, "Don't go to California. It's too beautiful to get anything done. You'd just play chess all day there and stare out at the sea."

WASHINGTON IN THE MID-1940S WAS A SMALLER PLACE THAN THE capital is today, and yet in its way the city was also more cosmopolitan. With the United States fighting a world war, federal agencies were hiring not only international specialists from the best American universities and research institutes, but also large numbers of educated immigrants and refugees to provide expertise on the places they'd left. People liked to say that the large white marble Federal Reserve building on Constitution Avenue was a university in exile, an economics department with no students. At meal times, the Fed's top floor cafeteria was packed with tweedy professors from Yale, Princeton, the University of Chicago, and, it seemed some days, half the Harvard economics department, all of them avidly discussing the subtleties of fiscal policy with men whose speech bore thick traces of Hungary, Greece, Spain, Germany, and England (John Maynard Keynes and Sir John Hicks both made appearances at the Fed). After lunch, anybody calling the elevator might have his patience tested while down on the first floor two Viennese gentlemen, Fritz Machlup and Gottfried Haberler, and a Russian with impeccable Viennese breeding, Shura Gerschenkron, were each determined to be the one to usher the others out of the door. Around the Fed the joke went that Gerschenkron's manners were so good they were holding up the war effort.

In Vienna Shura's interest in liberal politics had been passionate, and in Washington he quickly became just as absorbed in the daily drama of American government. As far back as anybody can remember, Shura hated Republicans. These were feelings he believed himself to have come upon naturally. Like a person's foot speed or his sense of humor or the color of his eyes or his taste for garlic or his capacity for worry, his politics were not a matter of decision, but a part of what he was. They were also an expression of who he was—a part of his character.

The first Republicans Shura encountered were the men President Roosevelt dubbed "economic royalists." Shura identified these wealthy businessmen as jellyroll tycoons, the sort of ungracious elite he had despised in Europe, and to find them thriving in America gave him no joy. Many Republicans seemed to him to have a lot and appeared primarily interested in a status quo government that helped them hold on to as much of it as possible. Take his Cambridge landlord. The man was a staunch Republican who turned every discussion about leaf-clogged roof gutters into a lament about what Roosevelt and Truman had done to impoverish property owners, so that—much as he'd like to—the landlord simply could not afford to keep his buildings maintained. If Republicans were self-made men, they tended to think that because they had succeeded, everyone else ought to succeed too. They might recall their humble origins when it was politically expedient to do so, but the truth according to Shura was that these Republicans had contempt for poverty, contempt for their former selves. "Nixon Republicans" is what Shura began calling such people after the 1952 Checkers speech.

Most of all, Shura disliked the increasing propensity through the late 1940s and 1950s among Republican politicians to describe those who disagreed with them in terms of who was a better or more loyal American. The flag-waving Hearst newspapers, the fervid congressional committees, and the indignant men narrowing their eyes and demanding "Who lost China?" appeared to him to be more in the business of ruining people than protecting them. Even Dwight Eisenhower, whom Shura had grudging hopes for, quickly disappointed him. "He considered Eisenhower to be a reasonable and distinguished man who unfortunately happened to be a Republican," says Heidi. "Then Eisenhower chose a vice president who turned out to be Nixon and my father said the general was just like the rest of them." Shura did have a few friends who voted Republican, and he always felt that he was excusing them, the way he might forgive an adulterer or a drunkard. A man could possess many salutary qualities, but if he was a Republican, Shura knew he was morally flawed.

He was quite serious about this. Like many immigrants, he was attracted to talking about what ordinary Americans talked about because it made him feel like one of them. Also, freely offering his opinions on the process of government reaffirmed the quotidian pleasures of living in a democracy. For him, talking politics was a trope for talking principle, a moral debate with the nation at stake. He loved the rancor of it all, and yet when things did not go the Democrats' way, he found it very upsetting. In the late 1960s Shura declaimed bitterly against the less-than-populist policies of the new governor of California. As a mark of his disdain, Shura began intentionally mispronouncing the man's name. *Reegan*, he called him.

In wartime Washington he did not yet have these problems. Raymond Gram Swing was, with Edmund R. Morrow, a leading liberal political radio commentator of the day, and whenever he came on the Philco in the evening, Shura would get excited. "Shsh! Shsh! Swing! Swing!" he would cry, and everybody in the house would listen. Shura was someone who wanted to believe in politicians, and he believed in Franklin Delano Roosevelt as he'd once believed in Otto Bauer. Like Bauer, Roosevelt was a scion of great wealth and privilege whose social views strayed far to the left of his class—"an aristocratic radical" with "old world manners and new world conviction," as Sir Isaiah Berlin put it. Berlin met Shura at Harvard in 1948, and a number of their early conversations were about Roosevelt. To émigrés like them who had grown up watching the thudding political failures of the Russian and Middle European intelligentsia, Roosevelt's success at creating economic opportunities for underprivileged Americans was a revelation. So was the experience of watching Roosevelt send some of those Americans to the shores of France, Italy, and Africa to defend not their own country, but their country's principles. Roosevelt had, as Berlin wrote, "all the character and energy and skill of the dictators, and he was on our side . . . he really did desire a better life for mankind."

Shura admired so much about the president. For certain, Roosevelt had his troubles. The man wore heavy braces on his polio-wasted legs, he was despised by powerful enemies in both business and politics, and fighting the long and bloody foreign war enervated him. Yet nobody could have said that any of it thwarted his spirit. Roosevelt brought against adversity all the many attributes that Shura, Isaiah Berlin, and other admirers saw in him: his brains, his pluck and good cheer, his compassion, his stoicism, his charm, his cunning, and his guts. Roosevelt could play rough, and yet because his ethical lapses were ultimately in service of what Shura considered such righteous causes, the president remained in Shura's mind a thoroughly moral leader, the most conspicuously decent public figure of his lifetime.

To share not only a country but also a city with such a man buoyed Shura. His Washington was an oddly accessible place, where an ordinary and recent citizen like Shura walked the streets side by side with the powerful. Long before most people considered Harry Truman anything more than a political hack, his local reputation in the capital as a genial sidewalk time passer had endeared him to Shura. Shura used to drink coffee and eat doughnuts in the Mayflower Hotel coffee shop because members of the the president's cabinet like Harold Ickes went there. Shura never approached Truman or Ickes, but these Roosevelt men circulating amid the people they represented matched his conception of truly democratic leadership.

As 1944 became 1945, Shura's admiration for and physical proximity to the president led him to feel increasingly close to Roosevelt, to achieve a love for him. When he heard the news of Roosevelt's death in April, he went white and was, says Heidi, "absolutely stricken. We all were. We grieved at home for days." Through all the years of crisis, the president had been a reassuring presence for people like Shura, and now at his death there was nobody left to do the reassuring. Roosevelt died just before the Allied victory in Europe was completed. For Shura, losing Roosevelt sapped him of whatever pleasure he might otherwise have felt over the next two weeks as American soldiers crossed the Danube and liberated concentration camps. This was nothing to celebrate, he told the family, sounding just like Paul. It was all just the end of a long, ghastly waste of life.

INITIALLY THE FED WAS INTERESTED IN SHURA BECAUSE OF WHAT he knew about the economies of America's enemies Germany and Austria. But by the time he got to Washington in late 1944, it was pretty clear that Germany was going to be defeated, and Washington policy makers were already looking ahead to the two postwar issues that would dominate American foreign relations in the coming years: how to rebuild Europe and how to contain the Soviet Union. Shura did Western European economic consulting work on the Marshall Plan for the Fed, and he was proud to have made some small contribution to such a progressive political concept. He had seen firsthand the consequences of the humiliating surrender conditions imposed upon Germany and Austria after the First World War, and so the idea of helping the just-vanquished enemies to recover struck him as a miracle of mercy and good sense. How better to preclude future grievances and urge democracy on a country than by treating it better than it had treated itself?

He hoped to apply the same conciliatory sensibility to what very quickly became his chief concern in Washington—what to do about the Soviet Union. Early in 1945, under the aegis of the Committee on International Economic Policy and the Carnegie Endowment for International Peace, Shura published a seventy-three-page study, "Economic Relations with the USSR." He began the essay by describing the disastrous consequences for the rest of the world that had followed the Soviet withdrawal from the world economy after the First World War. Then, with gentle allusion to Santayana, he argued that a fully industrialized and potentially hostile Soviet Union could be soothed through economic incentives: "Bygones are bygones," he wrote, "but past mistakes teach the lessons of today. And one of the most impressive of these lessons is the necessity of Russia's incorporation in the world economy."

When the study was released to the press, Shura was all over the New York newspapers: "Gerschenkron for Multilateral Allocation of Soviet Imports Among Export Nations," headlined the *New York Times*. "Dr. Gerschenkron says the case of Russian trade presents unusual probems, but he does not consider them insoluble," advised the *New York Herald Tribune*. As it turned out, of course, the Soviets could not be mollified, and their relations with America grew increasingly hostile. That only made people who understood Russia more valuable. Suddenly editors at publications like the *Review of Economic Statistics*, the *American Economic Review*, and the *Journal of Economic History* were soliciting Shura's ideas on Soviet industrial production, and so were government agencies. During the summer of 1945 Shura was on loan to the Office of Strategic Services (the OSS), for whom he prepared a classified paper containing his finding that with very little incentive hardline Communist Soviets had been willing to abandon their ideological aversion to cartels. (This led him to posit that, although they claimed to be strict Marxists, their true and thoroughly hypocritical fiscal motivations were similar to those of a profit-driven capitalist firm.) After the OSS interlude came one at the State Department. Back at the Fed, in 1946, he was promoted to chief of the International Section. He was given a secretary, began to travel on expense account, managed subordinates, and received a high salary. The job put him in position to meet all kinds of people, and many were intrigued by Shura's brains, wit, and accent. "I first ran into Alex at the Board, and you wouldn't forget Alex once you met him," says John Dunlop. It was ironic: nobody could have loathed what the Soviets did to Russia more than Shura did, but because of their intransigence in Europe he was a made man in Washington.

THE WAR AND THE YEARS RIGHT AFTERWARD AT THE FED BROUGHT Shura real fulfillment. He thought it a great place to be and it was. The Fed building had colored marble floors, intricate ironwork in the balustrades, gold-plated rest room doors, scalloped moldings, one of the only central air-conditioning systems in Washington, a recreation room, a free in-house barber, even a shoeshine man who came to your desk. That was all pretty swank by wartime standards, and Shura spent increasing amounts of time in "the wonderful environment of that old place on Constitution Avenue." On their way out of the building at the end of the day, his colleagues would often pass him heading back inside after a quick dinner, ready to work through to morning. Sometimes he appeared haggard to the people who worked with him; on other days his reserves of energy could seem limitless. While Sandy Stevenson, also now working at the Fed, worried that "Shura was kind of taking it out of himself," a group of female employees including young Nancy Dorfman thought Shura looked so good that in a lunch-table poll they voted him the most handsome man in the building.

Now that the Soviets were Shura's business, he expected himself to be an authority. For him that meant there shouldn't be anybody who knew more about the subject than he did. That was an impossible standard, but he tried to meet it anyway. He instructed his friend Abram Bergson up at Columbia University's Russian Institute to buy an extra copy of any book Bergson bought for himself and to send it down to Washington with a bill. He also enlisted Bergson to comment on his writing. Acting as the reader for a man as sensitive as Shura was a delicate business. One letter Bergson received began "Let me have your criticism, general and particular, and let me have it promptly"; a postcript added, "Criticisms are to be submitted in the form 'I suggest the following change' never in the form: 'This does not make sense' or similar."

Shura did not usually disclose such vulnerability. He tried hard to seem generous, cheerful, and at ease with himself. At work his door was always open to younger researchers who needed help, and although he wasn't the sort to go out for a beer—he still didn't really drink—he turned out to be a fiend for Ping-Pong in the recreation room. He obviously liked to talk, radiating such conversational warmth that it made people feel they were on intimate terms with him even though he was actually the least forthcoming man they knew. "We were close friends at the Fed," says J. Burke Knapp, who would become the vice president of the World Bank, "but he never confided in me."

It was the same with Chuck Harley. Harley was the only person Shura knew who owned a car. Shura was curious about driving and Harley offered to teach him in the Fed parking lot on weekends. It turned out to be a big commitment. Shura had no facility whatsoever with automobiles. Weeks passed before Harley felt Shura was ready for the city streets, and even after several weeks of the open road, many more practice sessions were required because Shura kept flunking the District of Columbia driving test. That was a lot of hours together in the front seat, but all Harley could remember Shura's telling him about Austria was that "he got out on a dog visa."

On the rare occasions when he drew up the blinds a little, whoever was around for the glimpse never forgot what they saw. One day at the Fed, the economist Randall Hinshaw began humming a German song in Shura's presence. "He got very upset," says Hinshaw. "The war was the one thing he didn't laugh about."

There was something else—his wife. By now Erica had accepted that they weren't going back to Austria. The war had ended, but a razed, partitioned Vienna had even less to offer Shura than before, and meanwhile his life was flourishing in America. He had become in many ways a classic American immigrant success, someone who came from the old country to New York Harbor, took a job for which he was overqualified, worked hard, made his way, and created a better life for himself. Erica, by contrast, saw herself in perpetual exile, a woman who had been chased away from her home and prevented from returning.

She never got over the sorrow of leaving Austria. Thirty years after she moved to the United States she'd sit upstairs in her room with one of her grandchildren, a thick yellow quilt spread across her legs, and tell the child stories. They were all stories of Austria. There was her half-brother Wolfie, a little boy of unpredictable movements who occasionally ended conversations by taking all of his clothes off. And there were the walks she wished she could take again through the forests where she'd spent part of her childhood. These were the wooded foothills outside Graz, and to the grandchildren, the way Erica described them they seemed a lot like the enchanted landscapes in the old German fairy tales she sometimes read aloud. The forest paths were made of soft, tender earth, the breezes were clean and sweet-smelling, the brooks splashed clear water, and the bees—even the bees—buzzed in a way that Erica said sounded friendly. Erica was usually nice to her grandchildren, but up in her room she was expansive and enthusiastic in a way that they rarely saw elsewhere. Since she was so different—so much more muted—downstairs during the day, they thought the warm Grandma had something to do with the bright yellow quilt.

Sometimes the tragedy of losing Austria preoccupied Erica to the point of paralysis. Once, as an older woman in 1970, she asked Heidi to drive her from Cambridge to Toronto to visit a friend. Heidi agreed. It was a long trip for the driver, with Heidi's two young children quarreling in the back seat of the car and Erica up front in a highly critical mood, harping on Heidi for being a lax mother. Finally, somewhere around the Thousand Islands, Heidi looked at her and said "Mom, can't you stop? Can't you see I'm having a hard time?"

"I had a much harder time," said Erica immediately. "I lost my country."

In the early 1940s, everyone in Washington could tell just as well as people had in California how it was with her. The Hirschmans knew Erica in Berkeley, Washington, and later in Cambridge, and their consistent impression was that "she breathed unhappiness." She did prefer Washington to Berkeley, though. The capital was a far larger, more European city, and with so many other foreigners around she found people to talk with in German. She enrolled at George Washington University and began a master's in German literature, later completed at Boston University. Yet she could find nothing professional to do with herself. She might have taught German, except that Washington schools weren't hiring German teachers. There was tremendous hostility to anything German; nobody wanted to learn Hitler's language.

Becoming American was an adjustment for every immigrant. "We all had to strain ourselves to be citizens of the United States," says Valerie Fellner, the wife of Shura's friend the Hungarian-born economist William Fellner. But the Fellners wanted to be Americans. Erica had no desire to assimilate. She continued to live in Austria in her mind, and she continued to try to raise Austrian children. Susi and Heidi were still required to speak German with her at home, and also on the streetcar. Susi, who'd gone to school in Vienna, didn't mind, but Heidi began to answer in English. Erica's response always began *"Bei uns,"* which means "by us" or "in our house," and meant that what goes on elsewhere is immaterial to the way things are done at home. At the Gerschenkron house, things were done the way they were done in Austria, right down to the coffee, which was prepared in pots Erica ordered from Vienna. They were poorly made and kept breaking, so she was always sending off for new ones.

Shura was practical in his response to his wife's terrible unhappiness. He made what amounted to a deal with her. They would stay in America and she would never have to do anything there she didn't want to do. So she began a life of independent study. She read Defoe and Hamsun novels, ancient Greek and modern military history, and books on French and Italian art. She knew about all sorts of arcane subjects from Swedish Easter—rabbits are hunted, not eggs—to the life of the Swedish painter Karl Larssen. Along the way, she learned language after language. Erica was a maven for grammar and syntax. She understood etymology, and she could plot out a perfect translation, but it was years of living in the United States before she would hold up her end of a sophisticated conversation in English.

Outside of her studies, she was limp. Many days she never even got dressed. She became Shura's dependent, someone he protected "like a rare bird," as one friend observed. Other people who knew them thought he treated her like "a princess" and more like a child than his own children. He felt, perhaps rightly, that she did not have his capacity to overcome hardship, and he expected Susi and Heidi to defer to Erica with absolute obedience and never to impose on her. This generated considerable hostility from both sides. Once, when Heidi was ten, a group of girls were over at the house drawing. Erica walked through the room in her bathrobe, looked over what each girl was doing and said, "Everyone's is good except Heidi's." That night when Shura came home, Heidi told him about it. "Complaining about your mother who took care of you when you had measles?" he said. "Stop this at once."

Alone with his children he was more gentle. One weekend when Susi and Erica went to New York together, Shura put Heidi to bed every night by singing her a Russian lullaby—it was the one song he knew— and stroking her hair until she fell asleep. Another day he taught her how to look at a night sky and measure the distances between stars. Within his children's hearing, he liked to repeat stories of their displays of character and personality to other people, complimenting them indirectly. One of his favorites involved both Susi's great presence of mind and her arrogance, which he admired in equal measure. On a pleasant day in Austria, he had taken her for a walk in the countryside outside Vienna where they met up with a little girl who looked to be about Susi's age—seven. "Where are you from?" the girl asked Susi. "I'm from Vienna," said Susi. The little girl didn't know where Vienna was. "Do you know where Austria is?" Susi asked her. The little girl didn't know that either. "Then," said Susi, "unfortunately I can't explain it to you." Heidi he praised for her vivacious outlook. On her seventh birthday she received a bracelet which reduced her to tears because she had hoped for a bicycle or roller skates. "I don't want all this *jewelry*," she moaned, to her father's delight. When she was in fifth grade, she wrote a poem, and Shura loved that poem so much he memorized it and pranced around the house reciting it over and over. He always told Heidi she was original, that with her mind she would do something interesting one day, and she could feel that he meant it.

His hopes for his children's strength of character—and his concerns about their mother's—made Shura something of a taskmaster, a strict European paterfamilias always advocating strength and self-discipline. When he took Heidi out for walks she was urged to be a good companion, to keep in stride, never to say that she was tired. He always presented the walks as special expeditions, and he made them exciting. Some mornings they'd go to watch and wave at trains. Other times they wandered together through Washington, seeing the city. When Heidi went for lengthy distances and didn't complain he was pleased, offered praise, and might end the day at a public stable where horses could be hired for a girl to ride around a ring. Once a cut on Heidi's arm became infected and she was taken to a doctor who cleaned the wound and then told her she had been very brave. To Shura, that was the Croix de Guerre *avec Palme*. He was so enormously proud that he took Heidi straight from the doctor's office to an ice cream parlor. She didn't usually get treats like that. "He liked me to be a stoic," she says.

IN 1946 PAUL TRAVELED FROM ENGLAND TO WASHINGTON FOR AN extended American visit. He was an old man now, gray and stooped, but still the height of urbanity in his custom-tailored suits. It was a long trip for a man nearing seventy, but he was restless in retirement and he missed his son. He and Shura were overjoyed to see each other. "They always just jelled—so close in every way," says Lydia. "Shura was my father's favorite." Paul stayed and stayed. At first he lived with the family on North Dakota Avenue. Then the landlord sold the house, and the new place that Shura found in Kaywood Gardens had no extra room. So Paul moved to a nearby boardinghouse. For a while he spent much of his time looking for a job in Washington. He had no luck, however, so he was often available to help Erica with Heidi. "My grandfather and my father were completely different to me as fathers," she says. "My grandfather didn't require me to be a stoic. He was gallant with me, and bought me dresses. When we went for walks he'd take me to restaurants. He liked the elegant Parisian life, while my father flouted it."

Paul required himself to be clean and groomed and he always took a hot bath, even on the most stifling Washington summer days. One miserably overheated afternoon he soaked in a steaming tub, went back to his room, sat down in an armchair, and had a massive, fatal stroke. Shura had Paul cremated and then he went to England to see his mother. When he arrived in Letchworth, he said he wanted to go to the St. Alban's cathedral. As soon as Lydia heard that, she mischievously reminded him of the day he'd torn the religious medal from her neck and said, "Now you want to go to a service after what you did to my little chain?" He looked embarrassed, but then he said, "A denial of religion reveals a paucity of the mind." Sophie and Lydia discussed it and decided that in his grief after Tolia died Shura must have privately returned to Christianity.

That may be true, although it is equally possible that he never really gave up his faith. A few years later, in the early 1950s, Heidi remembers driving along an empty road from Rome to Ostia Antica with her father. They hadn't seen any other traffic for some time when a black Fiat sports car sped past them in a blur. A minute later, Shura suddenly hit the brakes. There was the Fiat in the middle of the road. It had slammed into a tree and spun around. The driver's door was open and the driver was hanging half out of the car with his head resting on the pavement and his arms stretched past his head. Shura stepped from his car, walked over to the man, and watched him die. Then Shura turned, bowed his head, and made the sign of the cross. Heidi had no idea what it all meant. That night, she said to him, "Daddy, why did you cross yourself?" He asked her what she was talking about. When she told him what she had seen, he said, "I did?" He had suppressed the rituals of his youth, but they remained ingrained.

Paul's death brought out the Russian in Shura, the deep capacity for suffering. True to form, in public he was stoic in bereavement. As he once explained it to Heidi, you resigned yourself to life's miseries, stood up straight before the world, and relied upon your spiritual faith to ease your anguish. Yet he also felt that although you went on because you had to go on, real consolation was never possible. Death was one subject that, in private discussion anyway, softened the hard face he felt he should wear toward the world. To him, the passing of someone beloved was such a terrible and mysterious sadness that he believed it was natural and appropriate to feel helpless emotion.

By the time Paul died, there had been enough death in Shura's life that he knew this one wasn't something he was going to put behind him easily. Nor did he want to. Shura came home from England, set the wooden box holding Paul's ashes in his closet, and grieved for his father as he had never grieved for Tolia or anyone else. "Shura got a lot of love from his family, and he loved all of us, but the closest relationship was with our father," says Lydia. "Maybe it was their togetherness on the flight from Russia, much as Tolia's, my mother's, and mine was in hiding, but they obviously had a tremendous bonding which lasted to the end. They were the truest of friends." Twenty-five years after Paul died Shura was still writing in letters, "Even now I sometimes think about his death and grief overcomes me."

Losing Paul was also a reminder of Shura's own mortality, the diminishing time left to him to get things done. His father was gone, so he was next. Heidi says Shura felt low and pressed. Then came something that picked him up. It was word from Harvard that the economic historian Abbott Payson Usher, the author of *A History of Mechanical Inventions*, was retiring after a long and distinguished career. Would Gerschenkron be interested in a move to Cambridge? When Shura described his reaction many years later to the *New York Times*, he said that he hadn't been sure whether he wanted to leave the Fed, where he was so happy. "You weigh the pros and cons," he told the newspaper, "and then you make an 'oh, hell' decision. Oh, hell, I'll do it. Oh, hell, I won't." After thinking it over for weeks, he said he decided, "Oh, hell, I'll go to Harvard."

What really happened is this. The day the call came to his office at the Fed from Cambridge, he listened, swallowed hard when they mentioned a salary lower than what the Fed paid—he was now sending money to his widowed mother in England—and then he went home. It was a hot day and by the time he walked into the house his clothes were sweat-stained. He took them off. Then, stripped down to his underwear, he walked into the living room, and, with a golden smile spreading across his face, he struck an Atlas pose and announced to his three women, "I'm going to be a Harvard professor!"

Erica was knitting. "That's nice," she said, without looking up from her needles.

MOST MEN WHO RECEIVED OFFERS FROM HARVARD WERE ESTABlished academics. They had years of teaching behind them, had published acclaimed books and papers, and already had a fine reputation in the field. Shura, therefore, was not an obvious candidate. And, indeed, Walt Rostow, then with the United Nations, was the economics faculty's first choice for the job. When he turned it down, the Harvard economists became uncertain. Economic historians were a somewhat scarce commodity in America; there weren't many men in the field at all, and far fewer who had distinguished themselves. As the faculty members discussed the situation, Shura's name kept coming up. Usher himself mentioned how much he admired *Bread and Democracy*, and then a series of professors who'd met Shura in Washington during and after the war began to describe what a fine mind they thought he had, what an unusual person he seemed to be. "It would have taken great skill and charm for him to get to Harvard from where he'd been," said Wassily Leontief, the Russian-born Harvard economist who won a Nobel Prize for his input-output theories. That was exactly what seemed to clinch Shura the position. Sturdy, intelligent American economists like Ed Mason, who'd grown up Clinton, Iowa, and had earned money for college by working in a coal mine, and Alvin Hansen, a farmboy from Biborg, South Dakota, had met him and, like John Dunlop, they never forgot him. With Gottfried Haberler, who had known Shura since Vienna, also arguing for him, it was Harvard that made an oh, hell decision, as in "oh, hell, we'll take Gerschenkron."

That summer, after failing his road test five times—he just couldn't master parallel parking—Shura finally got his driver's license. A few weeks later he bought Chuck Harley's 1940 Ford. Harley was mortified at what he'd done as he watched Shura veer into traffic. At the house, Susi and Heidi helped Shura load up the car and then they all set off for Cambridge. The trip took two days over small, bumpy roads with a near-accident every few miles. All three passengers were completely terrified. At the end of a long first day they arrived in Princeton to spend the night. Trying to park, Shura drove up onto a sidewalk. Then, attempting to correct the situation, he bashed into the tiny Crosley sedan parked behind him and locked bumpers with it. On close inspection Crosleys betrayed certain resemblances to tin cans, and every time Shura touched the gas and turned the wheel, a little more of the Crosley's bumper came with him. The Crosley bumper was crumpled and at a right angle when Heidi announced, "I'm not riding with you ever again," and got out of the Ford.

Shura was contrite but undaunted. He knew he was an incompetent behind the wheel, but he liked driving, both as a lover of speed and as an American. The patriotic element he explained to his Austrian friend

Ruth Scheurer, who wrote to him from Vienna during the early 1970's OPEC oil embargo to say that the gas shortages in America were only poetic justice because Americans had "too darn many too big cars and it wouldn't hurt the world a bit to get a few of them off the roads." Shura wrote her back, addressing the forty-five-year-old Ruth as "Dear Little Girl." First he chided her for her *Schadenfreude*—taking pleasure in someone else's misery. Next he grew ironic. "Don't talk philosophy with me," he said. "I'm not inclined in that direction. When I was a child I fell off a swing on my head and I'm not up to philosophy." Then he told her that "a provincial Austrian girl could not possibly understand how convenient a car is, and how much freedom it gives to working people, the ease and comfort and autonomy it brings to their lives."

The Gerschenkrons did get to Cambridge the next day, not in any comfort, but they made it. Shura, who knew all about the original offer to Walt Rostow, arrived, as one of his new colleagues observed, "loaded for bear." He had decided he was going to show that Harvard.

FIVE

THE GERSCHENKRON
EFFECT

The master economist must possess a rare combination of gifts. He must be mathematician, historian, statesman, philosopher—in some degree. He must understand symbols and speak in words. He must contemplate the particular in terms of the general, touch abstract and concrete in the same flight of thought. He must study the present in light of the past for the purposes of the future. No part of man's nature or his institutions must lie entirely outside his regard. He must be purposeful and disinterested in a simultaneous mood; as aloof and incorruptible as an artist, yet sometimes as near the earth as a politician.

John Maynard Keynes, "Sir Alfred Marshall"

THE SCOTTISH ESSAYIST AND HISTORIAN THOMAS CARLYLE had a genius for making up trenchant occupational descriptions that stuck. Businessmen Carlyle dubbed "captains of industry." Writers he called "a perpetual priesthood." Reporters were "the stupendous fourth estate." Carlyle was not always so laudatory. In the first volume of his celebrated *Latter Day Pamphlets*, he referred to economists as "the respectable professors of the dismal science." It was such an artful turn of phrase that economists have been dismal scientists ever since.

In the popular imagination economists are not thought to be the most excitable men. And mostly they are men—earnest, temperate, technical, masculine tabulators of profit and loss; purveyors of bad news delivered with such seasoned lack of affect that they can reduce even a magnificent financial bust to something as laconic as a well-plotted bar graph. They rely on vocabularies dense with abstruse words and phrases—recession, stagflation, marginal cost, depletion allowance— for conversations that come dressed in gray broadcloth. (The haughty

Keynes considered most economists to be tedious mediocrities.) At the university, the man who spends his days calculating consumption schedules is often quietly regarded by members of other branches of the faculty as a cheerless afternoon, a dull coat of paint.

Noneconomists were always forgiving Shura for his line of work, telling him he was of a different mint "from the typical economist," but he did not share these disdainful views of his peers or anything they implied about his profession. A man who could have been many things, he had chosen in Vienna to become an economist because the job "seemed to bear directly on questions of human happiness and human progress." In other words, he attached inherent moral virtue to his work. As he saw it, an economist was a creative intellectual who did vital practical labor. His mind was his seed plow, his steam shovel, and the decisions he made with it could improve people's lives. Although he might deal in binders, account logs, and columns of numbers, the economist's genius was that he could see into them human faces, human experiences.

Shura had grown up in two economically backward nations, and he had seen the devastating effects of ignorance and poverty upon them. The strong impression lasting from his childhood was that if the people's wants had been better cared for, Russia and Austria would have averted the political crises that wrecked the countries. Economics was a way for Shura to think about the complexities of human needs and desires, to explain strands of human motivation—necessity, passion, greed, ambition—and to parse them into broader systems of behavior. For money is a great measure of man, but not every man acts simply for love of it. Fundamentally, Shura was a heterodox person, and to him economics was a heterodox discipline that required talented practitioners with the ability to examine life from oblique angles. The British political economist William Stanley Jevons called economics "a sort of vague mathematics which celebrates the causes and effects of man's industry," and Shura agreed with him. Economics wasn't mathematics any more than it was science or philosophy or philology. It was all those things. Looking up from reading one of his former Harvard colleague Joseph Schumpeter's books, Shura shook his head and described what he really thought it took to be an economist by paying Schumpeter his highest compliment: "The man knew a hell of a lot," he said.

Shura's view of his profession was intertwined with his approach to it. If economics was the study of man's industry, it followed that the economist should himself be industrious. Shura liked to think of himself as an artisan, a member of a tough and honorable masculine guild of tradesmen. For years he carried a slide rule in his breast pocket and kept an old adding machine and a bulky globe prominently displayed in his office—the tools of his trade. When he organized an economic history research center at Harvard, he named it the Economic History Workshop. It pleased him to regard the students the way Rogier van der Weyden did his young painters, as apprentices toiling over their benches in the workshop of Master Gerschenkron. He was also prone to equating the labors of the economist with those of a farmer, referring frequently to the "rich harvest" of work he'd done, to his mighty "yield," to the exciting prospects of cultivating "untouched soil," and—his favorite expression—to "the roses of research." Describing a summer in New Hampshire, he wrote to a friend of having just completed "seven or eight weeks of intense work and then harvest time. . . . I've been writing day and night like a damned man. I'm terribly hungry. I've made myself a beefsteak and potatoes and tea—a meal for a god."

To him economics was a "hard" science, something that searched for quantitative truth. Accordingly, the Workshop sometimes became a place to conduct empirical experiments. In his preface to the first book of one of his favorite students, Albert Fishlow, Shura made special mention of "the statistical appendixes in which the author offers a full insight into his laboratory and without which no real appreciation of the importance of the study and of the validity of its interpretative results is possible." For all of his appreciation of ingenuity and cleverness, at the core Shura was an academic Calvinist who celebrated the sweat and sore muscles of verification. With his chin out, he demanded proof, as if to say "show me what kind of a man you are." These qualities led the economist Robert Solow to say that Shura "was a very sentimental man, but he was not sentimental in his work."

He was autonomous in these vigorous pursuits and expected others to be the same way. When D. N. McCloskey and the other members of the Economic History Workshop decided, in the mid-1960s, to place a motto above the transom, their choice was "Give us the data and we will finish the job," a boast, McCloskey came to realize, that "would have appalled" Shura. Not only was it risky to rely on another man's handouts, it was downright depraved. Shura regarded people who delegated work to research assistants as frauds and dodgers, in the same way that he had contempt for those who read anything in translation. His distaste for collaboration was so pronounced that when he wrote something, short of pruning a stray conjunction, he did not allow editors to touch his work. To Shura there was honor in an appendix, virtue in a glossary, something noble in a list of sources. He was once overheard reporting in a flush of excitement, "It's not a good book, but never mind that because—oh!—you've never seen such wonderful footnotes."

It all amounted to a moral code of scholarship; he was the economist as truth seeker. Anyone who took the work less seriously than he did outraged him, and the consequences could be very harsh. Once Everett Hagen, the author of *On the Theory of Social Change: How Economic Growth Begins*, a book Shura had reviewed in a most unflattering way, walked up to him and said, "Professor Gerschenkron, I just want to tell you that I'm not angry about your review." Shura managed to look surprised. Then he said, "Angry? Why should you be angry? Ashamed? Yes. Angry? No."

BECAUSE OF HIS RUSSIAN WORK AT THE FED, ONE OF SHURA'S FIRST responsibilities when he got to Harvard was serving as the resident specialist on the Soviet economy. That kept him doing the politically charged economics he'd been working on for the government in Washington. In 1948 the Soviets began to curtain off Eastern Europe by blockading Berlin. That America had a rival superpower was now just as obvious across the prairie as it had been three years before along the Mall, and everyone wanted know, as President Roosevelt had once put it, "what makes the Russians tick."

The problem with understanding anything about the Soviet Union was that for all of Joseph Stalin's supposed interest in creating a "pure society," he was very private about his methods. Unlike Trotsky, whose grand plan for the Revolution was always to export its principles all over the world, Stalin evolved into a leader with little true interest in

ideas. Obsessed with power and control to the point of rampaging paranoia, Stalin turned Russia inward, creating a country that was as much
of a mystery to its own population as it was to outsiders. Russia became
the great hostile void. The Peasant Slayer, as the poet Osip Mandelstam called Stalin, was a particular enemy of casual curiosity. The walls
in Stalin's Russia listened with care, his secret police spies were everywhere sorting out the whispers, and they were known to quiet loose
tongues by cutting them out. Sensible people kept their own counsel
and had a travel bag packed and ready by the door at all times in case
the KGB knocked.

How to learn anything about such a place? Harvard tried an unusual
approach by asking an anthropology professor, Clyde Kluckhohn, to
lead a new Russian Research Center where academics from a variety of
disciplines were deployed as a team of investigators charged with studying the Soviets. Isaiah Berlin was a Center associate in 1948, and found
himself incredulous. "Kluckhohn knew nothing about Russia," Berlin
exclaimed. "His idea was to apply to the Russians the same methods
he'd applied to the Navajo Indians as an anthropologist. There were
people who believed in this, who thought you could find out something
this way." Shura seems to have been just as skeptical. "Research is like
digestion, it's an individual matter," he complained to Harold Berman,
the Center's authority on Russian justice.

Day after day, seated alone in his office in Cambridge, he lit his pipe,
opened the small safe behind his desk, removed the fragments of information American intelligence agents had assembled about the Soviet
economy, spread the documents out in front of him, and gazed at the
columns of numbers with the combination of sustained intensity and
patience familiar to good chess players. As the hours passed he moved
his glasses back and forth from the tip of his nose to the top of his fore-
head and reached without looking into the can of Sir Walter Raleigh
when the pipe bowl was empty, tamping his way through tin after tin.
Finally came the insight. The figures began to add up, bits and pieces
haggling with his intuition until they settled into a fully formed picture,
and there it was. They were cheating, and he knew just how they were
doing it.

*   *   *

THE RUSSIA SHURA FLED IN 1920 WAS A VAST AND THWARTED country. While other large European nations were industrializing in the nineteenth century, Russia's failure to emancipate the serfs condemned generations of ragged people to lives of ignorance and poverty. In 1926 Stalin chose what only a sociopath could have deemed a truly progressive method for pushing the country forward. Every Soviet person would be directed to the single purpose of promoting the greater wealth of the state. The practical features of this conception, forced agricultural collectivization and the Five Year Plans, placed the national energies exclusively in the service of manufacturing quotas set by the central government. The goals were ambitious, but that was the price of making up one hundred years of retarded development in a single decade. Those who failed to produce the requisite tons of nails or sacks of wheat would be swept aside, purged as obstacles to an effective state. There might be terrible hardships at first, but good Soviet comrades would happily endure them, making all necessary sacrifices for the remarkable new world they were building. It was a contemporary version of the old peasant storm of activity, the *shturmovshchina* at warp speed, and from the American perspective, it seemed to be working.

By the end of the first Five Year Plan in the early 1930s, regular as rain word came from the Kremlin that the Soviet economy had achieved phenomenal annual growth. At a time when much of the West was in the nadir of economic depression, and when an advanced Western economy considered 3 to 5 percent growth to be a very good year, the Soviets were making claims for their economy's yearly improvement that were between 15 and 20 percent. That was something truly amazing—the fiscal equivalent of a man running a three-minute mile year after year. In the postwar United States, with relations between America and its wartime ally dramatically cooled, it was also high cause for alarm.

"When I read recent histories of the late 1940s and 1950s I have the feeling that people have a distorted view of the time," Shura's friend, the Russian historian Adam Ulam, said. "These were not the happy, easygoing Eisenhower fifties. We were terribly worried about the tremendous progress the Soviets seemed to be making. We were being told how to hide under our desks if bombs were dropped. How to build bomb shelters. We were quite scared." Because the size of a country's economy determines the size of the military it can sustain, the Soviet economic expansion filled American scholars and government people with dread. The world was busy with rumors about the horrible killing machines the Soviets were developing with their newfound wealth: extremely accurate missiles! deathly silent submarines! a rocket containing one hundred tons of thrust! "It was a pretty emotionally charged time," says the economist Kenneth Arrow. "A lot of Soviet horrors were beginning to be known. Things were creeping out. And those figures made people worry that the Soviets would outgrow us. There was real depression in the U.S.A."

There was also skepticism. The American government had only the official Soviet word on how quickly the Russian economy was growing. It would be years before the U.S. Air Force began providing overhead evaluations of Soviet manufacturing and weapons capabilities, and while there were Americans posted in Russia, they were carefully supervised and had scant access to the kind of information that might confirm the Soviet growth statistics. The Air Force began putting civilian science and technology experts to work on peacetime national security problems. It created Project Rand, short for research and development, a Santa Monica, California, think tank initially attached to Douglas Aircraft. Soon college professors with patches on their jacket elbows sat at conference tables contemplating cold war defense strategies with medal-chested military lifers. The project had moved its offices to the discreet quarters of a Santa Monica basement and become the independent, nonprofit Rand Corporation in 1949, when it got in touch with Shura. Rand wanted him to find out whether the Soviets were as industrious as they said they were. He agreed to try.

One of the best gauges of how quickly the economy is growing in a developing industrial country is the amount of heavy machinery it builds. With this in mind, Shura's first Rand study set out to compare the annual Soviet and American manufacture of heavy machines over a recent ten-year period. This was a difficult task in part because the Soviets had created an economy in a vacuum—one without market prices or market currency. Beyond that, the job also created an index number problem for Shura—a problem of statistical translation. Within the Soviet Union, heavy machines were valued in rubles. American heavy machines were valued in dollars. To establish comparative worth, there had to be a common measure. He decided on a dollar index, meaning that he would assign dollar values to the Soviet products.

Over the next year Shura spent a lot of time thinking about presses, pumps, boilers, and turbines. Looking through the Rand files, he perused official Soviet government publications like the State Plans and the Soviet annual economic handbooks, and he immersed himself in the diagrams, photographs, design specifications, and statistical fragments that had been acquired "through back channels," as Rand people explained to him in the affably cryptic fashion of intelligence men. It soon became clear that the two countries did business in very different ways. Not only were there American and Soviet models of any given product, there were different methods of counting how many of them you'd made. The Soviets, for example, measured the production of power transformers by total voltage capacity, while the Americans added up the number of units built. Dragging values set in one price system across to another was a tricky job, and some of the judgments about what something was worth were beyond Shura's expertise. So he packed his suitcase, bought a sheaf of train tickets, and began traveling the United States, talking with people who thought about tractor-drawn hay mowers, gear-cutting machines, derricks, and gas meters for a living.

In all, he visited the executives and engineers at more than fifty American corporations, and during long nights of conversation they helped him gain a picture of what was really going on inside a Perm or a Stalingrad factory. When the information on a given product was insubstantial, he asked questions—"If you did sell this, what would you charge and why?"—so that he could make interpolations.

He took all the numbers back to Harvard and there began the exacting job of making the thousands of comparative machine price calculations that would become his machinery index. Eventually, the raw data took shape and Shura began to notice patterns. What the Soviets manufactured could be made to look good in a ledger but often made no practical sense. The Plan's quotas were so ambitious that factory managers sometimes resorted to desperate tactics to meet their objective. Nail producers who were expected to produce a given number of tons of nails a year might make only large, heavy nails, with the result that it was difficult to find small nails in the Soviet Union. That was the essence of the entire economy. It made nails, to make more nails, to make more nails; it made steel, to make more steel, to make more steel. This was a peculiar kind of subterfuge. The numbers represented real production, but they didn't always represent real progress. Russia had more. But the more often did not mean anything.

When Shura completed his index he discovered the most important Soviet chicanery—the explanation for the spectacular surges of annual growth. Anti-Soviet Westerners had long contended that the Soviets simply invented their numbers—made them up out of the sky. Shura disagreed. He thought that the raw numbers were credible; it was just that the Soviets had been guilty of cooking them—enlivening them with a rather exotic strain of Baltic spice.

He liked to explain the deception in terms of sickles and tractors. In a preindustrial economy, sickles are common and cheap, while heavy machines like tractors are rare and expensive. As an economy industrializes and industrial facility with technology improves, the mass production of machinery brings the price of tractors down low enough so that most people can afford to replace their sickles. Following the pattern to its extreme, eventually very few sickles are produced and they become vintage items, in the same way that today the mass production of window glass and quartz timepieces has turned hand-blown lead casement windows and hand-wound pocket watches into coveted antiques.

An index measuring any growing modern economy's annual expansion has to account for the declining value of high-technology items as mass production of those items makes them cheaper—has to account, in effect, for quartz watches becoming inexpensive to make and cheap to buy. Economists do this by adjusting the weights on prices. The early stages of an economy's development are measured by using a Laspeyres index, on which values are calculated from a fixed year. Once brisk development sets in, those old values become outdated, and the price structure needs to be adjusted to reflect, in effect, that a tractor is not worth what it used to be. This is accomplished by using a Paasche index, which compensates for the years of growth by replacing the fixed-year prices with an adjusted scale that reflects modern prices. Herein lay the Soviet duplicity. Shura discovered that as late as 1950 the Soviets were still valuing everything in their economy according to the base-weight 1926–1927 preindustrial price structure. In 1950 each tractor was still being valued according to what it had been worth nearly twenty-five years earlier. The systematic upward bias in value allowed the Soviets to continually overstate the economy's actual worth. It was, Shura concluded, "the shameless exploitation for propaganda purposes of an altogether untrue yardstick." The 20 percent growth was a canard. At its highest levels in the 1930s the Soviet economy grew at 12 to 13 percent, and by the 1950s those numbers had sharply diminished. As Marshall Goldman, an economist and the associate director of the Davis Center for Russian Studies at Harvard, says, Shura "had penetrated the Iron Curtain."

Among Soviet policy connoisseurs, *A Dollar Index of Soviet Machinery Output* was the subject of breathless conversation. "For a while, *everyone* was talking about the index number problem," says the economist Stanley Engerman, then a graduate student at Johns Hopkins. Kenneth Arrow read the study and says, "This work put the whole question of Soviet income in a new perspective. The rates were not so high. It deflated a lot of the fears on one side and a lot of the exultation on the other. It was impressive work that changed the whole climate of understanding." People began referring to the statistical insight separating the Soviet walk from the Soviet talk as the Gerschenkron effect, something that had come to Shura's attention one day just as Nancy Nimitz arrived for an appointment with him. She came into his office and found him leaning back in his chair. He pushed his glasses on top of his head, smiled gleefully at her, and said, "I'm an effect!"

EVEN AS HE WAS EVALUATING SOVIET STATISTICS, THROUGH MUCH of the 1950s Shura kept looking for other ways that the Soviet Union might inadvertently be revealing itself. One potential source of information was contemporary literature. Among the most persistent of Shura's sorrows was the Soviet interdiction of creative writers. He wrote down the thrust of these feelings in one of his essays on totalitarianism: "As Stalin's crimes were told and the story of atrocities unfolded, one victim of the dictatorship remained altogether unmentioned: the unprecedented decline of Russian literature; the transformation of a great art stemming from a great tradition into a mechanical process of mass-fabricating products according to patterns prescribed by the dictatorship."

The Stalin era prompted the growth of the Soviet industrial and collective farm novels, books with titles like *Cement, The Smoke of the Fatherland, Steel and Slag*. Written by an unctuous crowd of hacks, sycophants, simpletons, and cynics, it was a body of work remarkable for its dullness. To a man raised on Tolstoy and Turgenev, immersing himself in such unattractive offerings was torture. Shura endured a book like Leonid Leonov's *The Russian Forest* because, as he explained in his essay "Reflections on Soviet Novels," for all of the "unlearned disquisitions on forestry, brazen distortions of the historical truth in supine obedience to the wishes of the dictators, a preposterous search for closets filled with skeletons, and characters drawn with the tritest means . . . [the book] actually reveals the imperfections of Soviet industrialization." When he read about characters who met grain quotas by drawing from secret stores they'd illegally amassed in surplus years, or when he came upon anecdotes featuring wheat farmers who reported their harvest based upon its wet weight in the field rather than what it came to in the grain sack, he knew he was hearing about the real-life schemes of desperate people. It was the same with the portraits of lazy workers and shiftless managers. These men might be cast as villains, but their existence rang true, putting party flacks who made claims about the "conflictless" Soviet society to the lie. Unwittingly, the Soviet novels displayed the economy of tyranny at work.

SHURA AND ISAIAH BERLIN USED TO SIT TOGETHER IN LARGE, COMfortably upholstered chairs in the reading rooms at All Souls College, Oxford, and at the Harvard Faculty Club, arguing about the modern Russia they'd both left as children. Berlin had a voice that murmured out of his chest like a cello as he raced up and down the octaves of a discussion. He believed that the only way to treat the Soviets was by *modus non vivendi*—by avoiding conflict with them.

"No, no, no," Shura would say to him, his Russian full and plangent. "*Modus non vivendi* is simply *modus moriendi* [the way of dying]!"

"No, no, no," Berlin would counter. "It means to live in the same world and avoid each other as much as possible—don't provoke each other."

To Shura that was impossible because everything about the Soviets provoked him. The Soviets were, he said, "carnal, bloody, and unnatural," and that is how they made him feel. These people who had murdered millions of innocent people—his people—and were killing many more of them every year drew up from him a miasma of boiling fury he struggled to control. Sometimes he succeeded. Every year, for instance, he subscribed to *Pravda*, the Soviet state newspaper, so he could keep up with the infidels. Every year, issue after issue would come to his office, and every year he filed all of them away unread because it made him so angry to look at them. There were a few occasions, however, when the rage could not be contained. One of them came during a seminar at the Russian Research Center that had been moving along quite pleasantly until Shura turned it into a massacre.

To Shura there was a simple distinction to be made between a Russian and a Soviet. Russians were long-suffering people of character; Soviets were moral degenerates. Few things irritated him more than scholars at the Center who hadn't met the Cheka, and yet wanted to make claims for "typically Russian" Soviet behavior. One day Shura's narrowed eye fixed on a young political scientist named Leopold Haimson. Haimson had come to the Center from New York, where he'd been working with Margaret Mead at the American Museum of Natural History. One of his projects there was a study of the Soviet style of chess since the beginning of the Second World War. Haimson contended that a distinctive feature of recent Soviet play was the preference for counteroffensive attacks. Soviet players, he observed, preferred to play black. They allowed their opponents to make the first commitment, holding back, luring them in, waiting for the right opening, and then striking. Haimson's was the sort of argument which seemed to have possibilities for broader application—it conformed nicely, for instance, to Napoleon's and Hitler's invasions of Russia—and Clyde Kluckhohn was intrigued. The director asked Haimson to present the paper at the Center. "No sooner did I sit down," Haimson said, "but Gerschenkron like a panther, like a tiger unchained, like a rabid dog pounces on me and ridicules the piece. I was absolutely startled. Nobody'd ever treated me like that. I thought he deliberately misunderstood the paper. It was bullshit. I didn't even try to respond."

"It was a charming and titillating presentation, and most people could have taken it or left it," recalls Alex Inkeles, then a sociologist at the Center. "He described many important chess games, analyzed moves, and made conclusions about the Russian national character. But Haimson did not count on Shura. He was the first commentator and you had to feel sorry for poor Haimson. Shura demolished him, totally destroyed him. He knew every game from memory and could explain each move not in terms of Russian national character but in terms of the personal style of the players involved. It was an intellectually enormous virtuoso demonstration, and it was also a display by a person with little tolerance for anything that wasn't first-rate."

Or for anything that praised the Soviet Union. "His feelings against the Soviet Union were very, very strong," says Paul Samuelson. "He thought 'a plague on all their houses, their best people are no good.'" This the Harvard decision theorist Howard Raiffa learned when he came home from a trip to Europe with stories of the KGB men he'd met there who were "nice to their families and nice to their secretaries." When he put this to Shura, Shura became so enraged that Raiffa "thought he'd have apoplexy. He couldn't imagine that anybody could be so stupid as to think that KGB people could be nice people. He couldn't stand it."

Raiffa Shura eventually could forgive. Dr. Walter Fischer, his friend from the Vienna Social Democrats, he would not. Shura's refusal to talk over the old days with Fischer reflected a reluctance to relive painful memories of the failed Austrian labor movement, but Shura also bore Fischer a grudge. After spending a year in prison for participating in the Austrian civil war, Fischer left Austria in 1935 and lived in Russia for most of the next eleven years. He returned to Vienna in 1946 and served as an official in the central Austrian Communist party until

1968, when the Red Army crackdown against the Prague Spring in Czechoslovakia led him to renounce the Soviets. Fischer was a frail, elderly man, about to be seventy years old in 1973, when he learned that Shura was coming to Vienna. They had not seen one another for forty years. Fischer had been terribly disappointed in 1954 when he learned that Shura had visited Austria and failed even to telephone him. But this time a visit was arranged. For weeks Fischer looked forward to the reunion. Now that so much time had passed, and now that he shared Shura's hatred for the Soviets, Fischer hoped Shura would be more forthcoming with him. Fischer wanted to explain to Shura how he'd evolved politically and to talk over the perversion of European socialism with someone who'd known him when he was young and full of hope. Shura never gave him the chance.

It was a sad meeting. Fischer found Shura cordial but distant, and when Fischer brought up the past, Shura brushed him off firmly, saying, "Let's not discuss it." A few months later Fischer wrote to Shura in Cambridge. "It's too bad we didn't talk about the different paths we chose," he said. "We could have had a reconciliation." Shura wrote back questioning "the validity of talking about this." It was, he thought, "better to avoid the subject because there was the chance we'd regret what we said and be angry about what wasn't said. I feared conflict. . . . Surely we were sensible. This way we had a rendezvous with our youth." He and Fischer never spoke or exchanged letters again.

The difference for Shura between Fischer and a young man named Yuri was that Fischer had chosen the Soviet Union. Yuri was an associate professor at the University of Leningrad who came to Harvard in 1963 as part of an American-Soviet academic exchange program. A gentle, guileless man much interested in Kierkegaard, Yuri soon became popular with Harvard students, especially when it grew obvious that he was a Soviet dissident. Not long after his arrival in Massachusetts, he began talking, in his open way, of his desire to seek asylum. There were three other Soviet students in Cambridge on the program that year, one of whom was almost certainly a KGB *starik* (slang for the older student monitor). The *starik* heard about some of Yuri's remarks and told him not to criticize the Soviet Union. If he did, the *starik* said, word would be sent to his wife in Leningrad that Yuri was consorting with

American women. There are those who say that perhaps the *starik* made stronger threats as well.

In late December 1963, Yuri was told that the Soviet students would be making a trip together to New York, and they were expecting him to join them. A car would pick him up. This news sent the young Russian into a panic. Taking cover inside a Harvard graduate student's apartment, he announced that he wanted to defect. The United States government was duly contacted, and an official arrived at the apartment to interview him. Somehow, things went wrong. During the conversation Yuri suddenly dashed across the room and jumped out of a window. He bounced off a tree and hit a snowbank before sprawling on the ground. At Cambridge City Hospital he was found to have suffered a ruptured spleen and a deep cut in his head. His recuperation took a long time. Eventually he was transferred to Harvard's Stillman Infirmary, where Shura began to pay him visits, as did a number of other professors who spoke Russian, including Edward Keenan and Marshall Shulman.

Shura grew fond of Yuri. "He got to like him," Keenan says. "He didn't usually have any patience with Soviet culture, but he did like Yuri." In addition to his wife, Yuri had a young child at home in Leningrad, and increasingly he feared for his family's safety. Marshall Shulman says that after a few days in the infirmary Yuri was thoroughly distraught. "He wasn't just ambivalent, he was terrified," says Shulman. "He didn't know what to do. He'd say 'I want to go back. I don't want to go back. I don't dare go back.' It went on like that." One day Shura came by for a visit, and Yuri begged to be taken outside. He was going mad in his room, he said. He needed some fresh air. Shura agreed to escort him on a stroll. They were walking along together when Yuri suddenly bolted and began running away through the streets of Cambridge. Shura had suffered several heart attacks by this time and was twenty-five years older than Yuri, but he didn't hesitate to give chase. Yuri headed for the Harvard Square subway station. Down the stairs he flew, Shura in frantic pursuit. "That man is going to kill himself!" he yelled. He caught up with Yuri on the platform, and with the help of a good Samaritan graduate student he managed to grab and restrain Yuri as the train pulled into the station. Yuri was taken to a local mental hospital and placed in a narrow cell. Soon enough he went home to the Soviet Union.

Shura was too ill to teach for a while after that. His eyes bulged unnaturally because he had trouble with his thyroid gland, overactivated, possibly, by the exertions of the chase. Around Cambridge he became something of a hero as the old man who risked his health to rescue a young person, but Heidi says the whole episode mostly made him glum. "He was discouraged," she says. "He badly wanted that man to become an American. He loathed the Soviet Union. It had ruined his country. He wanted better for the poor Russian people who were trapped there."

Gradually Shura became even more extreme in his anti-Sovietism. In the 1950s he could be cajoled into meeting with visiting Soviet economists when they passed through Cambridge, and, although he exploded in anger at them once or twice, he generally made an effort to be civil. A decade later, as he confessed to Jack Condliffe, he could no longer abide "sitting down with [Soviet officials] peacably around a table or even within the same four walls." During the 1969 meeting of the Economic History Association at Brandeis, he stood up and urged his peers to boycott the upcoming International Economic History Association meetings in Leningrad, saying it would be wrong to do anything that encouraged an authoritarian regime which stifled freedom of expression. It was a long and impassioned speech, and after a while the future Nobel Prize–winner Douglass North of the University of Washington, scheduled to make a presentation, became annoyed. When Shura finally sat down, North remarked, "We're better at being scholars than politicians." Shura leaped to his feet and demanded an apology. North refused. The two men did not speak for two years. Finally, in 1971, North was in Cambridge and Shura invited him into his office for an 11:00 a.m. glass of cognac and they made up. "'Well, Doug,' he told me," says North, "'you know I felt so strongly at Brandeis because of my childhood.' He implied that the scars were very vivid."

THAT WAS A RARE MOMENT OF DISCLOSURE. MOST OF THE TIME Shura's Russian past was off limits and out of view, even for men he felt close to like Isaiah Berlin and Adam Ulam, both Russian-speaking immigrants. When a conversation went that way, a frown would trace his brow, and anyone could tell that it was prudent to stay away. Berlin would have liked to have a serious talk with Shura about Odessa, but even with Berlin, Russian-born and a friend to Pasternak and Anna Akhmatova, Shura would not do it. It was the same with his daughters. "He never talked about his feelings about Russia," says Heidi. "There was never anything about leaving or longing for that country."

It wasn't a happy tension, investing so much energy in work dealing with a country that had been ruined in a way he didn't want to think about anymore. There was also the frustrating question of how much good any of it was doing. The insights into the Soviet economy were considered important discoveries at home, but, after all the congratulations, the sad fact of the matter was that they didn't change anything for the average *mujik*. "He disliked the regime," says Edward Brunner, with whom Shura worked at Rand, "but he had a great love for the Russian people."

At a certain point Shura left the Soviet Union to others. He still thought about Russia, of course, and even expressed his thoughts on the politics of paranoia by writing a pair of essays on dictatorship. There he argued that it was in a dictator's interest for his country to seem perpetually endangered by powerful foreign enemies because, under those extreme circumstances, ordinary citizens, who would otherwise not be so willing to overlook the dictator's abuses of power, would tolerate him as their source of protection against the supposedly even more threatening invaders. That, Shura said, explained the Soviet penchant for cultivating hostile international relationships with countries like South Korea, China, and the United States. But aside from such occasional meditations, Shura "did not follow the USSR very closely," says the Harvard Russian historian Richard Pipes. Pipes could understand that. "For many of us the USSR was such a sordid subject," he said.

By the late 1950s Shura became more or less exclusively an economic historian. Instead of trying to learn what the Soviets were doing in the moment, he wanted go back and explain the nineteenth-century Russian economic disasters that had led to the twentieth-century Soviet political disaster. The policies that led to the rise of Communism were an important, provocative subject, and Shura could have profitably concentrated on it for a long time. Certainly that was his firm intention. But he never quite did so, and the reason was that his personality kept getting in the way. Shura simply knew too much about the world to think for long about any one part of it. What began with old Russia ended with a broad and beautiful new idea.

SIX

THE ADVANTAGES OF
BACKWARDNESS

The fox knows many things, but the hedgehog
knows one big thing.

Archilochus, fragment 201

Tolstoy was by nature a fox, but believed in being a
hedgehog.

Isaiah Berlin, "The Hedgehog and the Fox"

THE NOBEL PRIZE–WINNING M.I.T. ECONOMIST ROBERT
Solow once met Shura on the street in Cambridge. They
exchanged greetings and Shura noticed that Solow had a book
in his hand. "Bob, what are you reading?" he asked. "A better historian
than you, Alex," Solow replied. "His face clouded up," Solow remembered. "He bristled and looked as if he was going to say something
nasty. So I showed him my copy of Tacitus. 'That's okay,' he said." One
reason it was okay was that Shura had something on Tacitus. Tacitus was
merely a historian. Shura was a historian who was also an economist.

Shura's desire to be superior led him to develop standards of superiority that placed him at favorable advantage. One of them held that
exception was the coefficient of superiority. In other words, there was
virtue in being unlike the other people in your line of work. "The thing
he liked most was to be the odd man, to be different," says one of Shura's
former students, the economic historian Gianni Toniolo.

A number of variables helped Shura to set himself apart from other
scholars: the extraordinary range of his learning, the sheer strength of
his personality, and also the power of his imagination—he loved ideas
and had the ability to conceive new ones, to think differently. Circumstances also played a role. By the time Shura got to Harvard, the field of

economics was changing in such fundamental ways that he could not keep up. What Shura decided was that not only did this not matter, but that there might even be advantages to falling behind. By staying his own course—by not branding his cows when everybody else was hurrying to heat their irons—in the world of American social scientists Gerschenkron became sui generis.

In 1941 Paul Samuelson completed his Harvard doctoral economics dissertation, "The Operational Significance of Economic Theory," a piece of writing so technically advanced that some of Samuelson's teachers had trouble following it. After the Second World War ended the thesis was published as the pathbreaking book *Foundations of Economic Analysis*. By restating the principles of economics in mathematical form, "the Samuelson math" became the scaffolding for modern mainstream economics. Where an economist's discussion of a phenomenon like consumer behavior had once consisted of facts and stories, it now featured two-sector general equilibrium models and basic discussions of price and income that looked like this:

$$\sum_{1}^{n} \sum_{1}^{n} \left(\frac{\partial x_i}{\partial p_j} + x_j \frac{\partial x_i}{\partial I} \right) dp_i \, dp_j \leq 0$$

Economists no longer aspired to resemble Keynes's cosmopolitan intellectuals. They were numbers men, applied scientists practicing a theoretical discipline which relied on mathematical models to solve the riddles of production, distribution, and consumption. Looking back on things in 1976, Samuelson himself happily admitted that by the mid-1930s "it had become easier for a camel to pass through the eye of a needle than for a nonmathematical genius to enter into the pantheon of original theorists."

Shura and Samuelson grew to be such close friends that in Shura's last year, Samuelson visited Shura's house at least once a week. Samuelson says that Shura "could have handled the math" if he'd been taught it as a student. "He was so bright, with such a good memory and such good analytical skills." Samuelson says he thought it was "tragic" that Shura's "active scholarly years came at a time when economics and economic history, for better or for worse, had moved to a different plane. No one speaks a new language without accent after age fifteen, and few after age thirty-five can move to the frontier of mathematical mainstream economics."

Mathematics interested Shura the way everything interested him, but it neither inhibited him personally nor especially excited him generally. Shura took the long view. Economics was going through a phase. A powerful new tool had been developed, one that economists could install in their laboratories for use in achieving important insights. In a speech he gave in 1967, Shura went so far as to scold economic historians whose fears about their "inadequate comprehension" of high-level quantitative techniques might lead them to "interfere with the work and dim its promise." But as much as he admired men like Samuelson—and he admired him immensely—Shura did not share the contemporary reverence for the modern methodology and thought it was foolish to believe that economics had somehow become math. Shura felt unthreatened by the new math because, ultimately, it was an advanced method of research—a modern kind of slide rule, but still only a slide rule. To Shura, the real cachet lay in the imagination. The economist who could work up his facts into some broad observation about the human condition, there was Shura's true aristocrat. Not coincidentally, there was Shura.

Shura's premise was that while people across time have appeared and acted very differently, in economics, as in every other form of human behavior, there exists an essential shared nature. Having studied the economic history of nineteenth-century Europe more thoroughly, perhaps, than anybody ever had, Shura could look around him and declare with authority that "modern discussion of economic developments, vast as it is, has raised few problems that were not raised in one way or another in the course of European industrialization of the nineteenth century." For that reason, as Shura observed in a letter to the economist Wolfgang Stolper, "I feel it is very important to utilize the accumulated historical experience for the better understanding of the current problems of economic development."

That the past is always present was a familiar philosophical and historical homily—"Life can only be understood backwards; but it must be lived forwards" was Kierkegaard's variation—and it's true that Shura was offering it yet again, but he was also saying a little more. For all that accumulated experience to be of any use, it had to be made accessible. You needed a way to gaze over time's shoulder, across all the many mornings of history, and see in them not a sequence of determined events, but unique stitches that fit a timeless pattern. Within that apparent contradiction was the insight that Shura believed made him truly unusual. He not only had more stitches than anybody else, but he had the pattern to order them by.

DURING THE YEARS SHURA WAS AT WORK ON THE SOVIET INDEX number problem, he was simultaneously thinking hard about the Russian past. The spectacle of Soviet leaders turning the country into a mass grave made him ask himself again and again how it could have come to this. The terse answer that he settled upon was at the core of his view of the world. "The Soviet government," he wrote in 1952, "can properly be described as a product of the country's economic backwardness." Had Catherine the Great, Alexander I, or Nicholas I abolished the tyrannical practice of serfdom, "the peasant discontent, the driving force and the earnest success of the Russian Revolution, would never have assumed disastrous proportions, while the economic development of the country would have proceeded in a much more gradual fashion." In other words, had Russian social policies been more enlightened, the natural consequence would have been a flourishing modern economy, and, in turn, political moderation.

Instead of enlightenment, Russia got Stalin. Stalin resolved to yank Russia forward, and in so doing he exterminated with impunity. Russia's submission to this sort of leader was often explained in terms of popular fear of Stalin's secret police and his windowless eastbound trains. Shura thought differently. Linking his ideas about dictatorship to his analysis of Russian economic history, he wrote that "such a government, can maintain itself in power only if it succeeds in making people believe that it performs an important social function which could not be discharged in its absence. Industrialization provided such a function for the Soviet government." Two demoralizing centuries of backwardness had left "Russia, my beggarly Russia," as Alexander Blok called the Russian people, so desperate for prosperity that they tolerated Stalin's prison camps as the price of economic hope.

Russia was Shura's porthole into the subject of backwardness, but he had also lived in Vienna in the 1920s and 1930s, a time when no educated person could have escaped a central contention of psychologists like Freud that childhood traumas shape adult personalities. The same observation could be made about youthful economies. The more Shura thought about it, the more generally he became intrigued by the position of the struggling state. "If the Soviet experience teaches anything," he wrote, "it is that it demonstrates *ad oculus* the formidable dangers in our time in the existence of economic backwardness." A country that smoothly accelerated through the course of modern development was to be admired. Yet there was more narrative complexity in the plight of the economic stepchild. The Dickens novels he read and reread told of unfortunates like David Copperfield, Pip Pirrip, and Nicholas Nickleby and their efforts to come up in life. That was the essential dramatic tension for a backward country: how to get from rags to riches. The country that sat slumped in the foyer of economic backwardness as other nations swept past into the airy drawing rooms of industrial progress was vulnerable and volatile in a way that Shura found intensely provocative.

This was not surprising. Twice he had fled backward countries and come to places where the languages and the bread were strange. In each case it had required a magnificent effort for him to catch up. He *had* caught up, and the fact that he could do so gave him a sense of optimism about other people's chances. Yet, as he knew well, things could go the other way. While he had overcome adversity, the countries he left behind both yielded to dictators. Walking around Cambridge thinking about the state of the world, Shura felt that he had come upon an area of inquiry rich enough that it might offer diagnostic insight into explaining both the forces that kept people back and some of the conditions that could help them move forward. The economist taking on backwardness could prevent much real suffering. He could also look into human experience in a way that nobody else ever had.

Shura was more than fully engaged, he was roused. People were expecting him to explain Russia. What he would give them instead was all of Europe. He was going to try to explicate the collective modern European economic experience by looking at it through the lens of backwardness. It was an enormous intellectual undertaking. The years of copious reading he'd done in Vienna gave him the bricks for his project, and now he began to look for the mortar to stack them with. What people who know a lot know best is how little they know, and Shura's notebooks make it clear that he read his way through entire sections of Harvard libraries, leveling one shelf after the next. The history of plowing led him to the history of planting and that took him to the distribution of labor in small communities. (Russian and German farmers, it turned out, shared similarly collegial neighborly instincts.) He swerved across Europe, from English factories to German blast furnaces to French investment banks to Bulgarian flour mills, and then he made his way north where there were Norwegian trade and Danish mercantilism to reckon with. He read journals, biographies, and autobiographies. With such a sweeping topic, everything related to everything; you had to know what people thought and felt to understand why they did what they did.

The sheer bulk of the task never discouraged him. From time to time he made trips, taking up brief residence in German university towns and Italian cities, where he sifted through the files of Roman corporations. Sometimes he taught himself new languages, achievements useful to his work—and to his conception of himself as an economist apart. (Samuelson didn't know Swedish.) Sweden was of strong interest to Shura because the country had risen dramatically from abject backwardness to the most advanced economy in the region. That was reason enough to acquire a Swedish grammar and to subscribe to *Dagens Nyheter*, the leading Stockholm daily. The book he wanted to read right away was Eli Heckscher's massive four-volume *Economic History of Sweden*. (The full quartet placed side by side measures a foot and a half across.) Heckscher also published a condensed single-volume version of his *History*, known as Heckscher's "little book," but Shura's policy in any language was never to read a little book when there was a big one available.

Shura was always an easily tempted reader, and Swedish proved to be typically distracting. There were brief flings with modern novelists like

Stig Dagerman and Agnes von Krusenstjerna, and the chance to read Strindberg in the original he could not resist. Eventually he took up Heckscher and became truly infatuated. Here was "a scholar in action," a "great figure." That such a man was largely unknown in America Shura judged nothing short of heresy. He realized that not everyone would do the upstanding thing and learn Swedish in order to read Heckscher the way he had. After all, they hadn't. So he took matters into his own hands, dragooning one of his graduate students, a Swede named Goran Ohlin, into helping him translate Heckscher's "little book" into English. They met each morning at six in Shura's office. "There would be lots of snow, just awful, not a soul around but us," Ohlin recalled. "Gerschenkron, he was a very early riser."

SHURA SET DOWN HIS FIRST THOUGHTS ON BACKWARDNESS IN 1951. All the hundreds of thousands of pages he'd read prompted not a book at all, but a brief twenty-five-page monograph called "Economic Backwardness in Historical Perspective." Shura first presented the essay at a conference at the University of Chicago. (Subsequently he published it as the lead entry in a collection entitled *The Progress of Underdeveloped Countries.*) Albert Hirschman was in Chicago that day and remembers leaving the conference hall elated. "I want to make it quite clear," he said. "The contribution of Gerschenkron is fundamental."

Like most big ideas, Shura's is simple in the abstract and draws from an established intellectual tradition even as it sets itself apart. His initial fillip was Marx's comment in the preface to *Das Kapital* that "the industrially developed country presents to the less developed country a picture of the latter's future." Thorstein Veblen offered a means to that future in *Imperial Germany and the Industrial Revolution* by observing that backward countries had the opportunity to develop quickly by borrowing technology from the industrialized world. Shura collected Marx and Veblen into a theorem which stated that backwardness was not necessarily all bad; it had its benefits. The advantages of backwardness became the centerpiece of what he liked to call "my approach," the first historical synthesis of modern economic development.

The industrial revolution began in mid-eighteenth-century England, a nation of farmers and shopkeepers whose prosperity was born of ready and longstanding facility with new technologies for farmland trade. That mature, preindustrial history made the shift from local cottage industries to urban textile mills smooth enough that it seemed inevitable—an evolutionary transition. The fast and efficient English manufacturing techniques drew notice from other Western countries who sought the abundances of large-scale production for themselves. Some of them had brisk success. By the 1820s the United States, Belgium, and Switzerland were industrializing, and within the next fifty years France, Germany, Austria, and Sweden all had flourishing advanced economies as well. Russia and Italy, however, were hapless by comparison, tentative economic travelers who took nearly until the end of the nineteenth century before they set sail for the shores of modern development. To all appearances they were the great industrial laggards, nations to be scorned as paradigms of backwardness.

As Shura looked across Europe, he noticed that the region's backward countries had consistently found the most inspired solutions to the problems of development. The degree of backwardness so neatly corresponded to the degree of ingenuity used to overcome it that he constructed a postulate: "The more backward a country," he concluded, "the more complex and exciting its industrial history." Now he was twice endeared. Not only were backward countries the most sympathetic, they were also the most interesting. That backward countries did not do what other countries did was precisely what made them special. They were the improvisers of development.

That Shura had a theory of development is not to say that he ever drew up a formal blueprint for industrialization, as his archrival from M.I.T., Walt Rostow, did in his book *The Stages of Economic Growth*. Shura thought of Rostow's checklist of prerequisites as "beautiful exercises in logic" which had "been defeated by history." The varied paths men took to improve their means defied precise itineraries, were too alive with possibilities to adhere to any map. Shura wanted an approach to development that was dynamic enough to encompass the full range of human behavior, yet not so elastic that it failed to explain anything. In this spirit, he produced a pliable series of general axioms which explained features of a country's developmental experience based on economic conditions in that country at the time it began to industrialize. Shura thought of backwardness as his "orchard," and so his axioms became a grove of freestanding observations all rooted in a single theme, a choice basket of fruits from his orchard.

He began by explaining that backward countries would have to overcome significant impediments to industrialization. Many of these constraints were biases against development embedded in either national psychology or ideology. Cases in point were the German burghers who feared change, the contented small-scale Belgian artisans who saw no need for it, and the tradition-minded French farmers who felt fierce antipathy for any form of newfangled machinery. Another, related axiom held that the creation of a disciplined modern workforce would be one of the most stubborn obstacles to successful industrialization. In the so-called Gerschenkron paradox, while people might assume that in a relatively backward country labor is cheap and capital expensive, the reverse usually turns out to be true. Shura found that when rural workers are suddenly thrust into a manufacturing milieu, they are often unable or unwilling to adapt. People want change, but they don't like change.

Beyond overcoming such grassroots resistance, there were also bound to be broader institutional hindrances to development like the serfdom that held Russia back, or the governmental instability that plagued Germany until the political unification of the late 1860s. Once these barriers were all removed and a country was poised for development, then came the question of what would fuel the economic growth. Industry depends upon investment, and the proven way to raise capital is by putting limits on consumption. Yet asking any society to embrace a period of austerity for what amounted to an act of faith that their standard of living would some day improve was a considerable request, and Shura could find no nation where the nature of the people inclined them readily to make such sacrifices. But envy is a powerful thing, and the mounting anxiety a backward country experienced as it watched advanced countries living the good life would help it over the rough roads leading toward development. "There are," Shura said, "no four lane highways through the parks of industrial progress."

Shura viewed economic revolutions in somewhat the same way that the historian of science Thomas Kuhn interpreted scientific revolutions.

The industrial moment in a previously backward country was a historical discontinuity, a sudden, spectacular period of social change. Hesita-
tion capitulated to desire and the industrial transition began, always in a
surge. Another of Shura's axioms held that big changes begin with big
efforts. The more backward a country was, the more substantial that
initial effort had to be. The phrase Shura invented to describe this initial burst of industrial activity was "the great spurt."

The great spurt was the canvas on which the real artists of development displayed their powers of invention. Great spurts could take many
forms. Where the wealthy British had relied upon moderate-sized private enterprises to finance their industrial moment, poorer countries
frequently required help from the government. The initial French spurt,
for instance, was fed by the Crédit Mobilier, an innovative noncom-
mercial bank specifically designed to raise and distribute investment capital. Germany achieved its great spurt after established commercial banks
diversified by taking up entrepreneurial investment and sponsoring a
number of heavy industrial ventures. In strapped imperial Russia, where
there was not enough private wealth accumulated for banks to sponsor
industrial investment, the driving wheel of the first concerted industrial
push was the state itself. The massive government-sponsored railroad
building project of the 1880s was completed using hordes of Russian
contractors and laborers.

Backward countries took something besides inspiration from the
nations that had industrialized before them—their diaries. The obvious
advantage that a backward country derived from its latecomer status
was that it could sift through the experiences of other countries and
learn from them. Just as the pioneers' mistakes—and many of their
heavy expenditures—could thus be avoided, their successes might be
exploited. Yet, contrary to what Marx said, the shrewd backward country did not look at the industrial pioneer and glimpse its own mature
self. It was instead motivated to make its own unique industrial future.
Backward countries tended to employ only the latest, most up-to-date
technology. (Following the Gerschenkron paradox, Russian factories
were more reliant on cutting-edge modern equipment than manpower-
intensive British industry had been.) Indeed, one of the ironies of Shura's
approach to economic history is that, in his view, it is the backward

country which offers the most modern displays of development. In the process of overcoming its late start, the backward country showcased the virtues of industry by being quicker and more efficient than those that came before. Backward became forward.

The concept of the advantages of backwardness was born of Shura's democratic faith in the potential of all people to accomplish unusual things. Backwardness was an argument for complexity, for surprises, for the imagination. Advanced mathematics, computers, game theory—all the many clever mechanisms humankind developed to grapple with its world—could not really compete with what Shura considered humanity's most absorbing and elusive invention: history. "In its very nature what is truly new in history cannot be predicted, although it could be explained *post festum*," he wrote. His approach was ultimately appreciative; it required people to know and rewarded those who knew the most because they could recognize what was truly new and could prize it.

MANY PEOPLE DIFFER WITH THE GERSCHENKRON APPROACH. "THE resounding theses of Gerschenkron tell the size and shape and weave of the stockings the family hangs out on Christmas eve, but say nothing of when or why Santa Claus comes down the chimney," complains William Parker. That is, backwardness is a heuristic framework, not a predictive or testable theory. It has been argued that Shura is too dismissive of the role agriculture can play in a developing economy. There has been concern that he overestimates the importance of banks and government, that—more generally—he places too much of an emphasis on "bigness" and that he exaggerates the difficulty of training an industrial workforce. Others have observed that in poorer countries, like China, late development often coincides with the promotion of authoritarian structures. Shura, of course, knew that an authoritarian regime that imposes a sudden catch-up may be compromising an organic economic development with a more stable future, but he has been faulted for not really grappling with how backward countries can spurt great and free. Critics have called him vague, Whiggish, short on statistics, and too long on irrelevancies.

There are a flock of other objections, mutterings, and demurrals besides, and what they have in common is that Shura responded poorly to every one of them. "That man is against me!" he would cry if someone's name was mentioned who had been even gently critical. Once Shura decided that his honor—or the honor of scholarship in general—had been questioned, he rushed to the challenge. "He took a 'here's my card, my second will call' you attitude to criticism," says the economist James Duesenberry. Heidi remembers her father coming home and describing his arguments with professional rivals as swashbuckling duels. "Academic battles appealed to his zest for romantic adventure," she says. "He was never happier than when he was surprising academic castles, swinging on intellectual ropes, and winning with gorgeous verbal swordplay." Susi's husband Anthony Wiener says that "Shura made me think of D'Artagnan in *The Three Musketeers*, always ready to draw his sword and defend his honor. He wanted to remain the unquestioned expert, and so he answered people in ways that crushed them."

Shura never came to blows with an academic rival, but this was not for lack of trying. He frequently complained of the "extreme rudeness" with which his ideas had been treated and responded to all such tormentors with extreme insolence. At a certain point he began to find the English vocabulary lacking in insults, and so he resorted to put-downs of his own invention. ("First-rate second-raters" was his favorite. "Flathead" was Gerschenkron for coxcomb.) His correspondence is lively with accusations of "arrogance," "ignorance," and "incompetence," and there is the occasional crowing admission that "I personally had to win a shouting match . . . winning is much better than losing." What made Shura such a fierce opponent is that beyond his absolute willingness to parry slander and spleen with bile and derision, he fought smart and, when necessary, he fought mean. "He was an armed man," says D. N. McCloskey. "He knew how to hurt you."

Shura always preferred excellence in his opponents. Having no use for flatterers or weaklings, he did not often waste his energy on them, and his greatest bouts came against his most formidable rivals. For years Shura tried to interest Walt Rostow in a debate, but Rostow always declined, so Shura contented himself with harassing Rostow's *Stages of*

Economic Growth with periodic sorties. "Rostow deals generously with the whole world," he told the *New York Times*. "I cannot deal with the whole world. I am much more modest."

"He was shadowboxing," says Rostow. "That was his style. It wasn't mine. So he fought. I didn't."

The distinguished Cambridge don E. H. Carr was less peaceable. Shura encountered Carr in the late 1960s when Cambridge invited him to England to give the university's four Ellen McArthur lectures. A large, shambling man who published a large, shambling history of Soviet Russia, Carr shared Shura's interest in Russian belles lettres—he wrote studies of both Dostoyevsky and Herzen—and also his enthusiasm for broad theoretical inquiry—he caused an intellectual sensation in England with his book *What Is History?* He and Shura had one more thing in common: "I love writing polemics," Carr told Ved Mehta.

Shura had already given three of his Ellen McArthur lectures and had prepared the fourth one when he happened to pick up an essay of Carr's entitled "Some Random Reflexions on Soviet Industrialization." As Shura read the piece, it rapidly became plain to him that what Carr was reflecting upon was Gerschenkron, and that most of what Carr had to say was less than flattering. Early on he accused Shura of "romantic nostalgia" for the English industrial revolution. Russia's industrial development, Carr explained, was actually much more advanced than Britain's. Then Carr offered Shura a little scolding: "Nostalgia for the past seldom makes good history," he wrote.

Shura was seething. The whole point of the Gerschenkron approach was that backward countries like Russia did not simply imitate industrial forerunners like Britain, but compensated for their slow start by devising sophisticated new means of development. It was as though Carr had asked to borrow Shura's walking stick and bashed him over the head with it. Shura still had the one lecture to deliver. Storming back to his rooms, he sat down and wrote out a new fourth lecture. It was time for Carr's economics lesson.

On the appointed day, Shura stood at the lectern and alerted his audience that he had "stumbled across" a "vicious" critique that "distorts and perverts the nature of a historical interpretation." Then, staring out at the audience like a defamed foreign nobleman come across the Atlantic to reclaim his good name, he declared that "the confusion that has been created at Cambridge must be clarified at Cambridge."

With his audience wondering just what this man was so angry about, Shura proceeded carefully to outline his theory, indulging himself in a few jabs at the absent chin of Walt Rostow along the way. Then he turned to Carr. Operating under the principle that the best way to inflame an Englishman is to compare him unfavorably with a Frenchman, he described Henri Monnier's "wonderful" classic, *Les Mémoires de Joseph Prudhomme*, where there appears a painter sitting on the embankment of the Seine and offering to paint portraits of the passersby. He has a price list attached to his easel. It reads:

Resemblance Parfaite	25 francs
Demi-Resemblance	15 francs
Air de Famille	5 francs

"I doubt that Professor Carr's portrayal of my approach, in which even the family looks blurred, would rate five francs," Shura sneered. Then he was on to Carr's "shallow depth psychology" and a confession of just how "tired" he was of this man who "goes around" telling everyone what history is. Carr was accused of a dozen varieties of malice—of having things "up his sleeve," of having "suppressed" and "appropriated" ideas, of "infringement," of "juggling," of "abuse of the printing press," of "perversion." Carr was, Shura concluded, nothing but an ignoramus and a schemer.

After the lecture there was a public seminar led by Shura, and Carr attended. Shura was hugely disappointed when Carr kept quiet and made no effort to publicly defend himself. Shura soon returned to Massachusetts, where he received a conciliatory note from his antagonist. In a letter of reply to Carr, Shura wrote, "I had hoped we would have a battle royal with [another professor], in the end pouring soothing ointments on the mutually inflicted wounds." Then he made an admission. "I do enjoy controversies," he wrote.

So did David Landes, and he had none of Carr's restraint. When Landes and Shura met in 1949, Landes was a junior fellow of the Harvard Society of Fellows finishing his thesis at the Research Center for

Entrepreneurial History, an economic hothouse dominated by the ideas of Harvard's first famous Austrian émigré economist, Joseph Schumpeter. Schumpeter conceived of innovative entrepreneurs as the heroic agents of economic progress. Shura, with his emphasis on large institutions sparking change through capital and investment, thought Schumpeter had vastly overstated the impact individuals could have on development, and he gave all the appearances of regarding the Center as a building that was only slightly less reprehensible than a Republican social club. As proof, he pointed to the affiliation of the junior Harvard economic historian, John Sawyer, a man Shura not-so-privately regarded as "an intellectual lightweight."

Nobody would have said such a thing about Landes, who, in any case, would not have stood for it. "I have a rule," Landes says. "You never say 'I won't say this because I don't want to hurt somebody's feelings.'" A brash controversialist, Landes heeled to no man, including Shura, with whom he now began to engage in vigorous public debates well soaked in contumely. That anyone, let alone a graduate student, wanted to take on Shura astonished other people. "I was scared stiff of Alex," says the economist Frank Holzman, a Gerschenkron graduate student at the time. "I couldn't believe this guy was fighting with him." To Shura, raised in hierarchical Vienna, this bumptious lack of deference to an older professor was monstrously disrespectful behavior, and he could not let it pass unpunished.

He went about the task methodically. Landes had accepted a job at Columbia and gone off to New York by October 1953, when Shura published a fourteen-and-a-half-page paper in the journal *Explorations in Entrepreneurial History* tearing at both Landes and Sawyer and their sociological approach to economic history. Landes had argued that the French aversion to risk had slowed the country's development. Shura derided this as a "one-sided," sweeping generalization, and told Landes to look at Germany, where the preindustrial social traditions were more conservative than in France but the rate of growth was still high. Landes was also referred to a passage in Somerset Maugham's notebooks where the novelist "justly claimed that to know one foreign country one must know at least one other foreign country and then added that

'Arnold Bennett has never ceased to believe in a peculiar distinction of the French to breakfast off coffee and rolls.'" Shura concluded with five pages of footnotes.

In the next issue of the journal, Landes responded to Shura with a fiery and sometimes sarcastic fifteen-page rebuttal in which he accused him of misunderstandings, inaccuracies, and irrelevance. To his delight he had discovered that one of Shura's statistical computations contained an error. It related only to a peripheral figure mentioned in a footnote, but Landes seized on the miscalculation at triumphant and protracted length before concluding with a patronizing caveat on the "tricky" and "dangerous" nature of statistics "because of their power to impress." Shura was also upbraided—probably for the only time in his life—for the "excessive brevity" of his footnotes. Landes's own notes section extended across a full fourteen pages.

Sawyer, who by this time had moved on to Yale, sent from New Haven defenses of his own, a somewhat mellow litany in which he rebuked Shura for creating the impression "abroad" that there was "group bias" at the Center and asked him to "settle down."

That was like urging calm on a long-tailed cat in a room full of rocking chairs. "Landes and Gerschenkron did not settle down," says Henry Rosovsky. A series of slashing rejoinders followed. "I am sure the Center will survive my criticism," Shura forecasted in one of them, "and I am even willing to predict that it will also happily survive Professor Sawyer's defense which, of course, is a somewhat more difficult proposition."

As for Landes, he picked up the next issue of *Explorations* and was surprised to learn from Shura that "Professor Landes's critical tone quite unnecessarily conceals his agreement with me." Landes, Shura explained, had obviously not read his Gerschenkron with enough care. Perhaps, Shura mused, this was because Shura's article was "too long." The statistical error was "regrettable" but not of "any real significance for the point I was trying to make."

The weary journal editor permitted a final response from Landes, who used the space only to purr. "I'd won the argument," he recently confessed with a shrug. "You go to court with tainted evidence and you're done." He was referring to the statistical mistake, which, it turned out, had been committed by another scholar. That was the moment when Shura commenced his lifelong aversion to research assistants.

In 1964 the Harvard history department made a job offer to Landes. Shura could have raised objections to the appointment. He did not, and for the next twenty years the two men were, says Shura's former student, the economic historian Paul David, "united in acrimony." Time passed, each man published books expanding his ideas, and, says Landes, "in a strange way we came to develop great respect for each other. Even if I didn't agree with his details, I thought the work he did with backwardness was absolutely seminal, an illumination. In a way I've become an ambassador for Gerschenkron because I agree with him that backwardness matters. To a great extent, the difference between us was the difference between a historian and an economist."

One of Shura's pleasures was to welcome people into his economics department office at all hours of the day for brandy and conversation. Just about every senior Harvard social scientist was invited to come by sooner or later, but never once David Landes. Yet late in Shura's life, when he fell too ill to finish teaching his course, the person he asked to fill in for him was Landes. Afterward he sent Landes a gift, a rare and precious 1820 edition of Jean-Antoine Chaptal's book on early nineteenth-century economic growth. When Landes opened the little leather-bound volume, on the flyleaf he found an inscription from Shura. It read "to mine enemy to whom I am much beloved." "Gerschenkron," says Landes, "did have very rare lapses in grammar."

ONE REASON SHURA FOUGHT SO HARD AGAINST PEOPLE LIKE LANDES, Rostow, and Carr is that he saw his historical synthesis of industrial development as the great proof of his scholarly supremacy. Nobody else had such an approach to economic history. Intellectually it made Shura his own man. He was not a Marxist or a Keynesian, nor was he obviously indebted to John Stuart Mill or Max Weber. He was the advantages of backwardness. You reckoned with Gerschenkron purely in terms of his idea. Who else could say that? "He felt superior," says Henry Rosovsky, "because he had a theory."

Shura admitted as much in that polemical fourth lecture at Cambridge. "Someone," he said, "may be able to succeed where Professor Carr has failed and construct an operational and more specific model of European industrial history . . . but this, I am presumptuous enough to believe, will not necessarily detract from my approach to European industrialization."

Fifty years after *Economic Backwardness in Historical Perspective* was published, there is no new model, and scholars are still tilting at Shura's. The idea continues to absorb so much attention because it is deep, provocative, and functions on many levels—an economic model that offers a worldly outlook. The underlying intrigue in the concept is that Shura conceived an economic sensibility neatly paralleling his own personal sensibility. Shura's view of life held that a successful person was someone limber enough to understand that each event in life can prepare you for the next event if you know how to let it. He was thinking particularly about adversity. Adversity forced its opponent to find new and creative ways of moving forward. Sometimes the setbacks it administered were stinging, but with effort and understanding they could always be overcome.

Yet some people do not possess Shura's extraordinary combination of cleverness and willpower, and some countries don't either. In the end, perhaps the most obvious general weakness with Shura's theory is that not everybody is Shura.

SEVEN

DR. GERSCHIZHEVSKY

I hope you will soon be playing well enough for me
to beat you.

> Vladimir Nabokov's response when Edmund
> Wilson told him that he had taken up chess

FOR MOST PEOPLE, THE GAME OF LAWN CROQUET IS A WAY OF
passing tranquil summer afternoons in the garden. To Shura, it
was a sport of the gods, an epic contest of strategy and tactics.
He played croquet with great ceremony, offering authoritative analysis
of other people's shots, praising aspects of their form that even they
were unaware of, drawing attention to every motion and gesture. All
along, however, his ultimate motives were clear. He wanted to win,
which, inevitably, he did. That was because he cheated. "He was always
cheating," says Gianni Toniolo. "Anytime somebody got ahead of him,
he'd say 'I forgot to tell you,' and he'd make up a new rule. He told very
few rules at the beginning and then they'd be invented as the game
went along. He was continually making up new ones." After the game
was over, with Gerschenkron victorious yet again, it was "cocktail hour."
There were, however, days when an opponent was playing so well—or
Shura was handling his mallet so poorly—that he could dream up no
amendment that would help nudge his ball into the lead. On such afternoons there would always come a point when he suddenly realized that
it was "cocktail hour," and the game would be abruptly called off unfinished, the undefeated record intact.

Shura's desire to be superior went well beyond promoting and defending his theory of backwardness. "He was very competitive about every-thing," Lydia says. "It was terribly important to him to be the best." A bit like his beloved Tolstoy, who was always challenging the acclaimed novelists of his day to duels, Shura took all sorts of opportunities to prove himself superior to other intellectuals. Isaiah Berlin was once in the hospital and Shura paid him a visit. "He came to see me with a bot-tle of some kind of brandy and a book or two in German by Raimund, an Austrian dramatist of the 1820s and 30s," Berlin remembered. "I don't read German very well. Maybe that's why he brought me that. He loved one-upmanship, he did."

He thought up unexpected means of expressing unexpected superi-orities. In 1955 Shura spent some time working in Rome, where he shared an office with an M.I.T. economist, Richard Eckaus. Every morn-ing when Eckaus arrived for work, Shura was already at his desk. Eck-aus began to want to get there first. One day he awakened two hours early, came into the office, and, as he opened the door, Shura said, "Good morning, Dick." The next day Eckaus shaved another hour off his sleep and again Gerschenkron was there to greet him. This pattern was repeated a few more times until Eckaus decided upon extreme measures. He roused himself well before dawn, hurried through a stilled city and burst through the office door. "Oh," said Shura, looking up. "It must be time for breakfast." He reached into his pocket, produced a sweet roll, and took a bite. "Best put-down I ever saw," says Eckaus.

Raised as a boy to be a show-off, the adult Shura became a cogno-scente of the art. One of his favorite displays came while driving along an Italian road with the economist Milton Friedman. Friedman was at the wheel and Shura beside him in the passenger seat when a police-man pulled them over for speeding. Shura watched while Friedman attempted—in notably halting Italian—to reason with the notably unresponsive policeman. Then Shura took over. Using phrases deliv-ered with vivid Roman inflection, he quickly persuaded "*il caro poliziotto*" to let them go. "The cop was going to throw the book at Friedman," Shura said when he told the story. "But, you know, Friedman, he one-upped me because he said, 'Well, Alex, you could only do that because you were raised in a police state.'"

That was a delicious little kicker and one that Friedman has no memory of delivering. When people heard the story, somehow they sensed that Shura had made it up, and somehow they knew why. Part of it must have been that he couldn't resist a good line, even if he had to put it in someone else's mouth. But there was also the matter of decorum. One-upmanship as Shura practiced it was an art of indirection in which it was more than acceptable to make a fool of a worthy opponent. Unless the opponent insulted you first, however, it was never acceptable to say he was a fool. After you'd scored against someone, you always lavished praises upon him. That made you look both clever and gracious.

MOST PEOPLE WHO KNEW SHURA WOULD SAY THAT ONE-UPMANSHIP was for him less an incentive for knowing things than an enormously gratifying dividend. The primary motivation that led him to accumulate and display broad knowledge seems to have come from within. He had demanding expectations of himself that were complemented by a churning curiosity. There were so many things to know, and he was compelled to know them all—felt he should know them all. "He just knew vastly more than the rest of us," says the economic historian H. R. Habakkuk of Oxford. "Therefore he could make links the rest of us couldn't make because we weren't as bright as all that and also because we didn't have the range of information in our minds." D. N. McCloskey concurs, saying that "even other people who knew everything were impressed by Gerschenkron." One such person, Isaiah Berlin, said, "Shura was a jack of many trades and a master of many trades. He liked me for that reason."

Shura was the sort of man who sat down and wrote the U.S. Weather Bureau because he wanted to know why low-pressure systems travel in a northeasterly direction on the East Coast and blow southwesterly on the West Coast. (The Coriolis Effect explains that the east–west movement of the earth makes rotational patterns in higher latitudes go clockwise in the northern hemisphere and counterclockwise in the southern.) When it occurred to him that nearly every famous nineteenth-century Russian novel has an unhappy ending, with pith helmet on head and flashlight in hand Shura searched hard for an explanation. He taught himself calculus and he taught himself Icelandic—topics of minimal use for a European economic historian. "Alex wasn't practical," the economist Evsey Domar said. "He wanted to know things for their own sake, not because he needed a footnote."

Shura was an unsystematic learner. "He could be interested in anything," says his former student Gregory Grossman, now a professor at Berkeley. "He'd look out the window, see a man pushing a cart, and he'd be fascinated, want to know all about what the man was doing, maybe even decide to write an article about him." Out for an afternoon drive near the house he was renting one summer in New Hampshire, Shura noticed a ball bearings factory. What was that doing there in the middle of the New England countryside, he wondered, and he turned off the road into the parking lot. Soon enough he was delivering a paper at Cambridge's Joint Center of Urban Studies in which he explained why New Hampshire's "little towns . . . and smaller villages" could support "factories representing the last word in modern technology."

His curiosities became his pastimes. Some men take golf lessons on their weekends. Shura got his friend Harvey Leibenstein to teach him Yiddish so he could read Isaac Bashevis Singer's short stories. Others spend their vacations abroad. Shura went to Schoenhof's Foreign Bookstore in Cambridge, where he bought the latest works of Moravia and Calvino. After he'd read them he'd contrive to meet up with his Italian friends Franco and Serena Modigliani. "He'd ask, 'Have you read this?'" says Franco, who usually hadn't. If the Modiglianis weren't around, perhaps his graduate student from Italy, Gianni Toniolo, was. "He'd invite me into the office and then he'd quote rather obscure Italian poets and make me guess who that was," Toniolo says. "Then he'd laugh at me and say, 'What kind of an education have you got?'"

Shura devoted some time to collecting, but instead of stamps or coins or model ships, he stockpiled Russian, English, and Venetian versions of the same proverb. When he wanted to relax by doing something with his hands, Shura did not whittle or tinker with engines. He pulled out his dog-eared edition of Wordsworth, took up a pencil, and translated a few stanzas into German.

He was fascinated with the relationships between different languages and enjoyed translating poetry. His study held all the chisels and pliers of poetic conversion. Stacked along his bookshelf were old French and Latin dictionaries, guides to English usage, anthologies of American slang, Romanian grammars, Gaelic primers, Italian translations of Russian poems, Polish translations of German poems, and so on around the globe. He was always supplementing this collection of references with regular orders posted to antiquarian book dealers in Oxford, Paris, Rome, and Vienna with whom he'd been doing business for years. The centerpiece of his living room was a handsome stand holding the thickest dictionary Webster's sold.

Translation for Shura required not only a feeling for vocabulary, style, and syntax, it also called for a knowledge of cultural history. An entire letter in the occasional correspondence he maintained with Simone de Beauvoir was about a detail in Alexander Blok's 1908 poem "I would forget about valor, deeds and glory on this mournful earth," in which a lady wraps herself "sadly in a blue cape." Noting the "very large body of literature on that blue cape," Shura said that while "it is usually connected with the mystical role which the color blue played in Russian symbolist poetry," he proposed "a simpler and more earthly interpretation." The poem, he knew, had been written under the strain of Blok's collapsing marriage: "I seem to remember hearing that in some region of France (Normandie?) the peasants have a saying: 'S'envelopper d'une cape bleue' referring to the wife's act of deserting the marital home." Since Blok was familiar with Normandy and Brittany, could the "Dear Lady" tell Shura whether there was a regional or dialectal French idiom that supported his theory?

Erica was, without a doubt, the only woman Shura ever met who could stay with and continually challenge him intellectually, and sometimes she participated in what Shura called "my literary escapades." All their life together they hurled themselves into passionate intellectual debates, to the great satisfaction and elation of both. Paul Samuelson thought of Shura and Erica as a kind of intellectual cartel, which he referred to as "Gerschenkron Inc." "They were intellectual companions for each other, and they complemented each other perfectly," says Heidi. "She had a mind that was razor-sharp and analytical. He was imaginative, full of original ideas—a dreamer. He valued her judgment enormously. With her he could talk about all his ideas. They found each other absolutely thrilling."

This was the sort of couple whose idea of fun was reading aloud to each other in Middle English (Chaucer's ribald "Wife of Bath's Tale" was a favorite). They learned Dutch together, translated A. E. Housman into German together, and talked economics together. In the Vienna literary salon–style discussion group Erica organized for Harvard professors' wives, the theme for one year's reading was the European economy as portrayed in great fiction. Erica selected the books and assigned copies in English translation for everyone else. She herself read everything in the original. There were times—Erica's happiest times—when she and Shura were so mutually involved in the world of thought, so immersed in each other's minds, that weeks passed when all they really noticed was one another. There were dynamic quarrels, dynamic reconciliations, and one particularly dynamic collaboration.

A linguistic conundrum they frequently discussed together was translation's potential for distorting meaning. Was there ever such a thing as an accurate translation? Wasn't even an author's own translation of his work bound to distort the original? In the summer of 1965 they pursued these questions in a formal way through what Shura described as "a pleasant extracurricular enterprise." Among their best-loved pieces of Shakespeare's verse was Hamlet's tender quatrain in his letter to Ophelia:

> Doubt thou the stars are fire;
> Doubt that the sun doth move;
> Doubt truth to be a liar;
> But never doubt I love.

Together Shura and Erica traveled to libraries up and down the Eastern Seaboard and amassed one hundred different attempts at translating the passage. This cache of quatrains contained works ranging across four centuries in sixteen of the more than twenty languages they knew. Included among them was Schlegel in German, Pasternak in Russian, Hugo, Dumas, and Gide in French, Antoni Bubbena e Tosell in Catalan, Carlo Rusconi in Italian, L. A. J. Bugersdijk in Dutch, Krystyn Ostrowski in Polish, Milan Bogdanovic in Croatian, Adolph Stern in Romanian, V. Osterberg in Danish, and, in Icelandic, the writer of that country's national anthem, Matthias Jochumsson. All one hundred entries were evaluated. Then Shura and Erica wrote down their conclusions in an article they called "The Illogical Hamlet: A Note on Translatability."

This was the only time Shura co-authored a manuscript with anyone and it was a contentious experience. He and Erica quarreled so much, according to him, "that it almost broke up the marriage." (His wife was one person who was never afraid of him.) What they finally produced is a lively essay, full of rigorous scrutiny of English iambs that became German trochees, floating triphthongs "congealed into hard feminine rhymes," sundry cases of "rhyme sacrificed to reason and reason to rhyme," and revelations of assorted violences inflicted upon cadence and rhythmic structure. Then came their ominous conclusion: "Hamlet's quatrain is untranslatable."

ERICA AND SHURA'S SHARED PAST LIFE WAS AUSTRIA AND IT remained very much a part of their present. They always spoke together in German, always ate Austrian dishes, always hung Austrian prints on the walls of their homes. The lacuna for them was Russia. Erica hadn't lived there, and aside from buying her husband caviar, she never was much interested in the country or the culture. One language she never learned to read was Russian.

It was left to a perceptive friend like Isaiah Berlin to sense that the anger with which Shura talked about the Soviets was contrapuntal to a great despair. One way Berlin could tell this was that the Soviets' stifling of free Russian literary expression affected Shura like an estranged friendship—every time it crossed his mind he felt miserable and helpless. To him, the censorship of all writers except those who served the state was as emblematic of the depths of the Soviet evil as the purges themselves. For a man who believed that in written words lay mankind's most enduring expressions of humanity, the death of Russia's books was the death of Russia.

In 1957, however, came a small stirring, a momentary beam of warm light from the East. The great Russian poet Boris Pasternak's novel, *Doctor Zhivago*, which had been suppressed in the USSR, was smuggled into Italy and published there. After reading the book, Shura was euphoric. He considered *Doctor Zhivago* to be no less than a miraculous revival of the great Russian literary tradition so long dormant under the Soviets, a mournful work of deep human feeling that existed as an elegy to his doomed country. He was aware that *Doctor Zhivago* had its flaws—stilted dialogue, sections that seemed crudely patched together, contrived plot devices—but he didn't care. The Russian! It communicated such powerful emotion that Shura was moved to write "Notes on *Doctor Zhivago*," an essay he published in *Modern Philology*. Here, he said, was "the old Russian language in all its pristine glory, emerging unreduced and unweakened from the long years of its bewitched sleep." Pasternak's novel, he continued, "will live on as a monument to an art that, turning its back on 'les muses d'État,' refused to be made 'tongue-tied by authority' and fearlessly proclaimed the eternal truth that creative genius and freedom are as inseparable as human life and human breath." Isaiah Berlin read the essay and considered it "the best review of *Doctor Zhivago* by anyone—a masterpiece."

In 1967 Robert Manning, the editor at the *Atlantic Monthly*, sent Shura an advance copy of an *Atlantic* article written by Stalin's dissident daughter Svetlana Alliluyeva. Svetlana had been granted political asylum in the West, and just after she reached Italy she was presented with a copy of *Doctor Zhivago*. Overwhelmed by "a quite unexpected encounter with Russia at a moment when I had just left her," Svetlana set down her thoughts in the form of an open letter to Pasternak. Like Shura and so many other Russian émigrés, Svetlana saw both her Russia and herself in Pasternak's wild beauty, Lara, and the three men who want in some way to possess her. Shura read Svetlana's letter and immediately wrote to Manning. "These pages do hit you where you live," he said.

> I have never fully grasped what this novel—the true Easter Sunday of Russian literature—can mean, does mean to someone who has lived and suffered in Russia. As one hearkens to this outcry, one would like to comfort her, to tell her

in the words of Chekhov, whom she loves, that the time will come when "all the evil of this world, all our sufferings will be drowned in the flood of mercy that will fill the earth. . . ." I suppose the wounds are too deep and words, even Chekhov's words, are of no avail. And I wish I could myself believe that Pasternak's resurrection of the Russian language and literature is certain to be followed by a resurrection of freedom in Russia so that the pleasures of human intercourse and contemplation and creation of beauty will become more important than empty slogans and mechanics of power exercise.

ANOTHER WRITER WHO WAS BOUND TO ATTRACT SHURA'S ATTENtion was the leading American literary novelist of the 1950s and 1960s, his fellow Russian émigré Vladimir Nabokov. Shura and Nabokov don't seem to have known each other, but they had much in common. Both were the highly educated children of wealthy members of the Russian intelligentsia—the Nabokovs were St. Petersburg aristocrats living in a house with fifty servants—who fled the Revolution to the sound of gunfire. The Nabokov family resettled in Germany and then fled the Nazis in 1937. Nabokov ended up in America, where he and Shura became members of Ivy League faculties in the same year, 1948 (Nabokov taught at Cornell). Each hated the Soviet Union and suffered from what Nabokov called "the pangs of exile." Nabokov enjoyed the adventure novels of Jules Verne and Arthur Conan Doyle just as Shura did, and anyone who read *The Gift* could sense the passion he felt for Russian writers like Gogol, Chekhov, and Pushkin, and the disdain he reserved for Dostoyevsky. ("Bedlam turned back into Bethlehem," sneers the poor poet Godunov-Cherdyntsev.) They shared similarities of personality as well. Nabokov was a dazzling talker, charming, proud, high-strung, combative, and a notorious show-off.

Shura was not a fan. For one thing, he didn't like Nabokov's style. Nabokov was the consummate modernist, a Picasso of literary artifice and semantic legerdemain whose own literature had little to do with the socially and morally grounded aesthetic of nineteenth-century Russian writers like Tolstoy, Turgenev, Goncharov, and Lermontov. Shura was someone who looked for real life in novels, who relied on them for spiritual solace—a practice that Nabokov thought was fatal. The publication of *Doctor Zhivago* emphasized these differences.

Nabokov hated it. Scornful of the book's traditional structure—and perhaps resentful that it nudged past *Lolita* on the best-seller list—he ridiculed Pasternak as a muddled and sentimental novelist who should have stuck to poetry. Shura was appalled. He thought that Nabokov's response was "uncomprehending and invidious," the case of a talented man who "should have known better" behaving like a peacock. And there it all might have stayed, as a strongly held private disaffection, had Nabokov not moved on to translating Pushkin's *Eugene Onegin*, Shura's single favorite work of poetry.

Shura was hardly unusual when he said that he had most of *Onegin* "indelibly impressed upon my memory." For Russians of Shura's generation, Pushkin was much more than the author of triste and witty romantic verse. Russia's great writers used their works to declare their love and feeling for the Russian people and to express all of the greater guilt and frustration of a Russian intelligentsia unable to raise the average Russian from misery. The power of the great Russian books was that people of imagination could immerse themselves in the beauty and profundity of the writing and, by living in those pages, could lift themselves above the miserable squalor of the daily reality.

Pushkin was considered the founder of the nineteenth-century Russian poetic language, the little father of the golden century of Russian writers. Because of his irresistible verses, and because he died a young and unnecessary death, he became an angelic figure for a tormented place—something sacrosanct in a country denied even its religion. "Pushkin *is* our poetry," says Shura's sister Lydia.

The Soviets did worse than bury Pushkin; they defiled him in memory. The very government that busied itself killing off writers and banning books—including Nabokov's—shamelessly appropriated Pushkin for propaganda purposes as an early martyred hero of the Revolution. This produced agonized reactions from Russian intellectuals within Russia like the Mandelstams and Anna Akhmatova, and also among émigrés like Isaiah Berlin and Shura. While the enormity of purging millions of people was so vast a horror as to defy understanding, this defiling of

Pushkin's memory was a specific, symbolic crime that Russian intellectuals fastened upon to vent all of their horror and helplessness. As they defended Pushkin, they attacked the government.

Nabokov's feelings for Pushkin were strong too. He revered Pushkin as "the gold reserve of our literature," and considered him the world's greatest poet after Shakespeare. In *The Gift*, he has Godunov-Cherdyntsev sternly warn Koncheyev to "leave Pushkin alone." And yet Nabokov could not do so himself. He took on the job of translating *Eugene Onegin*.

Nabokov sacrificed much in completing his four-volume, 1,850-page English study of Pushkin's shambling romantic verse novel. He began working on it in 1952, and it was three of his own novels and twelve years later before the *Onegin* was finally published in 1964. Along with the text itself, Nabokov provided readers with two volumes of commentary, a mammoth index, and such other heroic morsels as a sixty-page study of Pushkin's African ancestor. *Onegin* had, of course, been translated many times before, but Nabokov's version was something different—an event. Not only was there the inherent drama of the most brilliant modern Russian refugee novelist taking on the most brilliant Russian poet, but Nabokov's approach to translation was as iconoclastic as his prose.

Nabokov aspired to create a literal translation, a crib, a pony that eschewed, as he said, "every formal element save the iambic rhythm. . . . In fact to my ideal of literalism I sacrificed everything (elegance, euphony, clarity, good taste, modern usage, and even grammar) that the dainty mimic prizes higher than truth." Shura's view, published in *Modern Philology*, was that "what Nabokov sacrifices so lightheartedly and disdainfully is not his own elegance and clarity and euphony, but Pushkin's."

Many people did not admire Nabokov's *Onegin*, but none liked it less than Edmund Wilson. Wilson was a powerful—and powerfully cultivated—American man of letters, an erudite essayist and swashbuckling critic who counted Russian literature and Russian politics among his specialties. Early in Nabokov's career, Wilson had served as his energetic patron, championing his talent, if not exactly his kinetic brand of fiction. The two were fast friends. Yet, as Nabokov became an eminence

himself, fissures formed in the relationship. Wilson had enjoyed playing the benefactor. He was not as happy to share the head of the table.
Nabokov's biographer Brian Boyd says that when Nabokov showed
Wilson *Lolita*, Wilson "recoiled" in repulsion. Soon he was even more
alienated by the irrepressible bursts of Nabokov personality. The practical jokes, the incessant wordplay, the lightning repartee, the soaring
bursts of ego that Wilson had once tolerated, now struck him, the way
they struck Shura from afar, as the unseemly self-indulgences of a con-
ceited poseur.

The friendship broke apart for good in 1965 over Nabokov's *Onegin*,
when Wilson wrote a review of the translation in the *New York Review of
Books* that seemed calculated not just to reproach the writer's work but
to hurt him personally. Nabokov responded by defending himself with
what was, under the circumstances, a fairly restrained letter to the editor. As the weight of Wilson's betrayal of their friendship settled and
the pricks of other censorious reviews aggravated his mood, Nabokov
set discretion aside and sent a long, sometimes jeering, sometimes mor-
dant "Reply to My Critics" to the British magazine *Encounter*. Most of
these insults he spewed toward Wilson, who was derided as a ludicrous
pseudo-scholarly simpleton.

Shura and Wilson got to know one another around Cambridge—
both were friends of Harvard's famous Shakespeare critic Harry Levin
(as was Nabokov)—and they socialized from time to time. Paul Samuelson remembers going to one dinner at the Gerschenkrons' where he
fell in step with "this bald-headed man coming up the walk. We were
never introduced. It turned out this bald-headed man was the Pope. He
pronounced with authority on everything." That was Edmund Wilson,
and for all of the sympathetic feelings Shura shared with him concerning Nabokov, he had some of the same reservations about Wilson as
Nabokov did. Harry Levin's Russian-born wife Elena says that "Shura
objected to the vanity in both men." When Shura wrote about *Onegin*
for *Modern Philology* he wasn't doing Wilson any favors. More possibly
he was feeling territorial.

Shura wouldn't have been Shura if he didn't feel instinctively competitive with Nabokov. Nabokov was, he once said, "interesting and
important," but he was also "a great stickler for irrelevancies," not to

mention "silly and exasperating." Shura's reaction to Nabokov's *Onegin* is, perhaps, an example of what happens when a man like Shura meets up with someone who is even more witty and successful than he is. Here, after all, was Nabokov, an acclaimed novelist, an acclaimed talker, and an acclaimed Russian, who was now producing an instantly famous work of scholarship. That, and Nabokov told even better jokes than Shura did. Shura's first word on Nabokov's translation was to label it "a labor of love and a work of hate." Yet, if envy was a component in Shura's reponse, it didn't dictate it. Shura wrote because he simply could not bear to see harm done to Pushkin.

His twenty-page review, "A Manufactured Monument?," is no simple polemic. Nabokov is praised for the great pains he took to maintain precise etymological fidelity to every berry, tree, and animal in the poem. And yet for all of those strenuous efforts toward literal fidelity, Shura's intimate knowledge of the Gallicisms, the peasant dialects, the esoteric lexicon, and the folksy turns of phrase that are such dominant features in Pushkin's Russian led him to conclude that Nabokov had created a most inaccurate translation. Pushkin's lightness, his clarity, and his nuance had all been scrapped in favor of just the right word, except that Nabokov didn't always deliver that either. His desire to brandish his ornate vocabulary resulted in a number of jarring "mistranslations." In the end, Nabokov had created something that Shura thought "should be studied" but "cannot be read." He considered *Onegin* to be as untranslatable as *Hamlet*, but he did believe that a translator could provide a sense of what Pushkin's poem "is really like." From Nabokov, however, he got only what it was "all about." As for Nabokov's scholarship in the commentary, Shura read it as truly brilliant work distorted by "unrestrained egotism."

When the piece appeared, Nabokov's good friend the prestigious scholar of Russian belles lettres, Gleb Struve, wrote Shura to say that "I'm ready to sign on to your every word." Isaiah Berlin thought that "a terrible, just abominable" translation had got what it deserved. Edmund Wilson, naturally, was enthusiastic too. "It is the best thing, the only really thoroughgoing study," he wrote Shura. "I tried to do something about it, but, on the Russian end, was not so well equipped as you. I wonder whether Nabokov has seen it. He was furious about my piece.

Like all people who play practical jokes and like to make other people ridiculous, he's always either aggrieved or indignant when anybody tries anything of the kind on him."

Nabokov had made a point of answering and rebutting every last critic of the translation that had taken so many years of his life, but in Shura's case he did not reply. "Nabokov took issue with every one of them, even the minor critics in the most obscure journals, but he never mentioned Gerschenkron's name," recalls Alexander Dolinin, a professor of Slavic studies at the University of Wisconsin and a Nabokov specialist. "What I noticed is that all the objections and notions of Gerschenkron were so correct that Nabokov quietly made all of Gerschenkron's corrections when he put out his second edition of *Eugene Onegin*."

Yet it was not in Nabokov's nature to miss completely an opportunity to retaliate against a dissenter, even one he respected, and he did find a way to avenge himself against Shura. In 1969 Nabokov published *Ada, or Ardor*, his first novel since the *Onegin* controversy. Nabokov had a penchant for imbedding external meaning in names. Midway through the book there is a snide reference to the "reverent" and "chippy" lexicographer Dr. Gerschizhevsky. Gerschizhevsky was a Joycean portmanteau melding Gerschenkron and Dmitry Cizevsky, another Russian-born Harvard Slavic scholar who had once written a commentary on *Onegin* that Nabokov despised. The *New York Times* asked Shura how he felt about this little lampoon, and the response was brief: "A small man's revenge."

EIGHT

"MR. UNHARVARD"

Man is such a wondrous being that it is never possible to count up all his merits at once. The more you study him, the more new particulars appear, and their description would be endless.

Nikolai Gogol, "Nevsky Prospect"

B Y NATURE AND BY INCLINATION SHURA WAS ALWAYS A LOYalist. Allegiances brought him great pleasure, and he sought out all manner of them. Then, once Shura linked himself to something, he was sure it was the best.

The first two countries Shura lived in had been only modestly successful homes for a man prone to steadfast attachments. Things were different after he got to Cambridge, Massachusetts, in 1948. Cambridge suited Shura so well that during his first extended time away he wrote to a friend, "I don't know what Cambridge without me is like, but I do know that I without Cambridge is nothing." From the moment Shura arrived at Harvard in 1948 until he died thirty years later, he always lived within the city limits. At first he rented the second floor of a house on Whittier Street, a triple-decker stuffed to the shingles with young professors and their families. In 1952 he began leasing a three-story, ochre-colored, stucco house at 8 Shady Hill Square, a five-minute drive from his office and a short walk from the homes of some of his favorite colleagues, John Kenneth Galbraith, Simon Kuznets, Gottfried Haberler, and Harry Levin. To him Cambridge was the true American community of scholars. The bustling squares and quiet side streets with an institute on every other corner had everything he wanted. Not long after he arrived, he began treating it as the old neighborhood.

In Cambridge he grew more expansive than ever in his loyalties. It wasn't long before the full routine of his days was limned with an astonishing number of staunch associations. Everywhere you looked with Shura there were people, places, ideas, institutions, and corner stores whose superiority he would defend with all the passion of a Lancelot.

In the morning, without fail, he made his way across Harvard Square to Albiani cafeteria for coffee and doughnuts. The only times he would breakfast anywhere else were on the days he had no class to teach and decided to awaken at 3:30 in the morning and get out of town—to a seafood shack at the end of a pier in Swampscott. There he would write and read and drink coffee and eat doughnuts and look out at the sea as the sun came up. Under the circumstances he celebrated the Atlantic Ocean, but privately favored the Black Sea above all other large bodies of water.

Coffee and doughnuts were only two of his many vices. For a while he smoked cigarettes (Luckys), until his doctor (he had *a* doctor) persuaded him to switch full-time to a pipe. When it came to tobacco he always made his purchases at a shop called Leavitt and Pierce. It is true that when it came to the leaf he was a pluralist. If his trusted old brand, Half & Half, was not in stock, he was willing to take home cans of Sir Walter Raleigh. (He was pleased to associate with Raleigh, that most scholarly of Elizabethan courtiers who once wrote a history of the entire world.) Pastry always came from a local Viennese bakery called the Window Shop. He was similarly parochial about chicken sandwiches, chasing forty minutes out to Bedford where there was a restaurant that "makes the finest chicken sandwich you can buy." Nobody in the family ever learned the name of this establishment. It was known to all Gerschenkrons as Chicken Sandwiches.

Shura had a party (the Democrats); a team (the Red Sox); a player (Ted Williams); a board game (chess); a breed of dog (Labrador retriever); a flower (pink rose); a lower body haberdasher (he sent to a Vienna tennis shop for white linen trousers); an upper body haberdasher (he ordered his wool plaid lumberjackets and matching caps from a hunting supply outfit in Maine); a brandy; a chocolate bar; an aspirin; a bullet; a pencil;

a shaving soap; a foreign bookstore; a domestic bookstore; a barber; a newsstand (he would go miles out of his way to buy his periodicals from Sheldon Cohen at Out Of Town News); and a weekly news magazine (*L'Espresso*).

L'Espresso was published in Italy and could be described as a more rigorous version of *Time*. The Harvard Renaissance scholar Walter Kaiser says that as soon as his friend Shura discovered it,

> he became passionate about *L'Espresso*. He decided it was the best magazine in the world. Whenever I saw him he had to tell me about "This fascinating article in the new *L'Espresso*." So one day I saw him and he told me, "There's a fascinating article in this week's *L'Espresso*." I said, "Oh?" He said, "It's about the Boston police department." I said, "What does it say?" He said, "Well, among other things it says that 75 percent of the Boston police department is Swedish." I said, "No, no. It must be Irish." His response was "No, no Walter. And when you think about it," he said, "almost every Boston policemen you meet is Swedish." I thought this was so interesting that he was so convinced that if it was in *L'Espresso*, it was true. Alex was not a credulous or a gullible person, but he so admired that publication that he gave it complete credibility.

Shura also had a school. Most people never find a setting perfectly suited to themselves, but that is exactly what Shura discovered at Harvard. He loved Harvard and revered Harvard as a passionate man will love and revere an instition that values what he values. Because for all of its many faces—traditional, ritualistic, ceremonial, exclusive—at its core Harvard did stand for what its motto proclaimed: *Veritas*—learning as a means of pursuing truth. Shura's affection for tradition, ritual, and ceremony was as pronounced as his intellectual elitism. He loved Harvard, not least because it was the rare institution that could perfectly accommodate his personality. In a way it made his personality possible. Being a professor at Harvard enabled Shura to become fully himself, allowed him to decide who he wanted to be and to fashion himself into that man. It was both a realization of personality and a reconstruction. The university became the center of his personal holy trinity of institutional loyalty: the United States was the greatest country in the world; the finest thing in the United States was Harvard; and the best thing at Harvard was the economics department.

HARVARD WAS NOTORIOUS AS A PLACE THAT THOUGHT HIGHLY OF itself. The university expressed its extravagant self-regard by taking extravagant pains not to express self-regard, a conspicuous indifference that was nowhere more in evidence than at Harvard's Society of Fellows, where members maintained a practice of never offering a toast at meals except when one of them won a Nobel Prize. Yet even Harvard would have been hard pressed to regard Harvard as well as Shura regarded Harvard. Henry Rosovsky once remarked that Shura "had a real Harvard thing," which is a bit like saying that Karl Marx had a real working-class thing. Shura displayed his partiality without restraint. When Wassily Leontief was awarded the Nobel Prize in economics in 1973, Shura sidled up to Paul Samuelson at the celebration party and said proudly, "We're ahead of you now, Paul."

"What do you mean?" asked Samuelson.

"Harvard is ahead of M.I.T. in Nobels," Shura replied.

"Grown-ups don't talk that way," said Samuelson.

At Harvard economics department hiring meetings, Shura became a one-man customs house, such a strict "guardian of quality," in the terse words of the economist Dale Jorgenson, that it was a wonder anyone was ever offered a job. When young Dwight Perkins was nominated in 1966 for a new chair in Chinese economics, Shura fought the nomination on principle, arguing that "Harvard ought only to have the world's greatest economists without bothering much about their specific interests." Perkins was given the appointment anyway. Three years later he completed a historical book on the Chinese economy. Soon after *Agricultural Development in China 1368–1968* was published, Shura walked into Perkins's office, looking grave. "Dwight," he said. "I want to apologize to you." "What for?" Perkins asked. "You know," Shura said. "I opposed your appointment." Perkins said that there were probably a lot of good reasons to have done so. "No, no," said Shura. "I was wrong and I have to get it off my conscience. I have read your book and I liked it very much."

"We talked a moment," says Perkins, "and then he left. It was a very serious statement to him. It took me a while to register how serious. I couldn't imagine what he was apologizing for."

"Shura was very proud of Harvard, more so than he should have been," says Robert Solow. "He was not cynical about it at all." In Shura's mind, one of the most elitist institutions in the United States became a paradigm for democracy because, he said, its elitism was grounded in merit. Shura wanted to hear nothing about quotas or wealthy old boys, and he did not wish to be told that Harvard in the 1950s looked and thought and prayed a lot like Ike. To him, Harvard had become the exception because it was the ideal. Which made at least symmetrical sense, for that is what Harvard thought of him. He was Harvard's eccentric exception who became Harvard's intellectual ideal.

Through the years, most of Harvard's great men, from William James, George Santayana, Oliver Wendell Holmes, Jr., and F. O. Mathiessen to Joseph Schumpeter, Arthur Schlesinger, Jr., John Kenneth Galbraith, and James Watson, could be said to have done their work out in the world and therefore brought credit upon Harvard. Shura, by contrast, became revered not so much for what he'd done but for who he was.

The rumpled, lumberjacket-and-nylon-shirt-clad Shura did not look like anybody's notion of a Harvard man. With his thick accent, he didn't sound like one either. He was from Odessa and Vienna, not Beacon Hill and Groton. He was not prosperous or clubbable or Protestant. The Head of the Charles, the Hasty Pudding, the fate of the eleven—they all meant nothing to him. And yet Abbott Gleason, now a historian at Brown, remembers that "when I was a graduate student at Harvard in the early 1960s, he was a venerated and intimidating figure. He was in a class by himself at Harvard. He was the person around the place everybody respected. Even the people who'd look right through you took off their hats and tugged their forelocks when Alex Gerschenkron came around."

It was a situation profoundly to be wished for. Simply by becoming completely himself, by exerting the force of his own personality upon those around him, Shura gained what he most wanted out of life: he was loved, he was respected, he was feared, and finally, late in his forties, he had a permanent home.

SHURA WAS A MAN ABOUT CAMBRIDGE, BUT NOT AN ORDINARY ONE. He did not inquire about the family, shoot the breeze, pass the time, or chew the fat. When he met up unexpectedly with people he knew outside the post office or in the waiting area at the barbershop, he always gave the impression that the encounter was fortuitous because there were things he'd been impatient to discuss with them. His friend the psychology professor Jerome Bruner says that he remembers his spontaneous exchanges with Gerschenkron both because they were provocative and because Shura talked in the vividly erudite way people think all Harvard professors talk, although they rarely do. Bruner would come upon Shura crossing Harvard Yard, and right away Shura would be expressing his doubts about whether a broad psychological theory like Freud's had any real status. "We're always building models to deal with odd, chaotic human behavior," he said one day. "We construct these models according to a theory or concept. Then we behave in imitation of these models, so life imitates art and it imitates models."

Shura's local haunt was the Harvard Faculty Club. For him, a man whose life had been shot through with so much impermanence, the Faculty Club's staid aura of duration was relaxing and reassuring. The food at the club neither excited nor discouraged an appetite: horse steak was a prized delicacy; Indian pudding with ice cream more controversial, at least among the historians who insisted that the Indians didn't have ice cream. The real specialty of the house was the talk, and over the years Shura used it as other men use their favorite lunch counter, taking his meals and bantering with the regulars.

On most days he could be found at the Long Table. This was literally a long, thin, dark wooden table that could comfortably seat more than twenty men. At 1:00 p.m. every weekday, stray professors began wandering in and taking whatever chair was free. The Long Table attracted an intellectually heterogeneous crowd. On any given day you could be dining next to a chemist who'd helped design the first atomic bomb, a man who knew all about tribes in the jungles of Borneo, or a specialist in Jacobean drama. The Nobel Prize–winning scientist Konrad Bloch ate there frequently, as did Jerome Bruner, and Morton White from the Department of Philosophy. There were always quite a few historians on hand—Arthur Schlesinger, Jr., Oscar Handlin, and Donald Fleming were three—and also a goodly collection of social scientists like Sam Beer, Adam Ulam, John Kenneth Galbraith, and Gottfried Haberler.

Conversation ranged from the differences between East and West to the bowing technique of the Russian-born cello virtuoso Gregor Piatigorsky. One day when the Oxford classicist Maurice Bowra was visiting, the Table discussed historiography—what counted as raw data—until Bowra, "the greatest English wit of his day," according to Isaiah Berlin, and something of a postmodernist classicist as well, dismissed the subject by saying that life was all fragments anyway and history was only how each generation chose to interpret whatever fragments it happened to discover. There was no history per se—no certain truth waiting there to be found out. Then Bowra flashed an enigmatic smile. "Everything's interpretive," he said, and the conversation came to an abrupt halt because nobody could tell whether he was being serious or ironic or blithely witty in an especially English way.

The badinage, the barbs, and the ripostes were so routinely entertaining that the Long Table held a certain sightseeing attraction for junior faculty. Shura appears to have been a primary draw for such tourists. "At no table in the world will you encounter a more erudite bunch than at the Harvard Faculty Club," Paul Samuelson says. "But wherever Gerschenkron sat, there was recognizably the head of the table."

Describing what it was like to lunch with Shura at the Long Table, an Oxford don who visited at Harvard found him to be "tremendously clever, while at the same time modest and quiet. I remember one of my colleagues summing him up appositely by saying, 'he's just like a Rolls Royce. You don't know whether the engine is running unless you lift the bonnet.'" A political scientist thought that Shura was "intimidating because you never want a discussion to end with a final and devastating sentence; you want it to peter out so discussion can continue. But Gerschenkron would suddenly say something that encompassed almost every point that had been touched upon, and then he would finish with such a definitive comment that nobody could offer a response." There was also a professor who extended a compliment that had originally been presented to Samuel Johnson: "He was born to grapple with whole libraries!"

Alas, Shura had no Boswell. The Johnsonian could reproduce no lettered fireworks, the political scientist failed to supply even a single Gerschenkron truncation, and the other regulars were all similarly dry of anecdote and allusion. The lapses in recall come as no surprise to John Kenneth Galbraith, who has long forgotten all the day-winning lines as well. "Since this was recreational, a pleasant pause in the academic day, the substance was never something that you remembered," he says.

Yet if the full flavor of Shura's talk disappeared with the moment, traces of it remain. There was the dramatic accent, much influenced by French, German, and English, but still unmistakably Russian with its hard *r*'s rolled into thick-tongued *th*'s—"out-*thrage*-ous"; soft *i*'s spoken as hard *e*'s—"*een*defen*see*ble"; and paired *o*'s transformed into deep *u*'s—"Haf you thread zat buke?" He drew upon a verbal warehouse well stocked with cognates, colloquialisms, and distinctive phrases of his own creation. "That's honey in my ear" was his usual response to a compliment. He pondered by nodding and saying, "Iz zat so?" and pled ignorance by spreading his arms and allowing, "Only God knows, and since He isn't talking, nobody knows." He liked coining bons mots. "There is nothing wrong with turncoats so long as they rotate in the right direction," he might insist, if only for the sake of the inversion. (The truth was that he could never stomach even an abstract traitor.) One thing people found bracing about him was his willingness to denounce people as barbarians or flatheads. He praised just as adeptly. "Your common sense is so uncommonly good that there is nothing common about it" was a typical valentine.

All this he used in support of the most distinctive quality that he brought to the Long Table, which was his learning. The same enormous erudition, the knowledge of languages, history, classical and modern literature, politics, philosophy, and geography that won him the admiration of economists, also impressed people in outlying fields. He did not accidentally use a phrase like "the fleeting years"; he was drawing it from Horace, a poet he knew well enough to hold his own in a discussion with the octogenarian Horace expert he encountered one day at luncheon. It was the same with the scores of other poetic and philosophical epigrams that he liked to feather into the midst of his sentences. Who else but Gerschenkron could put in that "I happen to be a great admirer of Hölderlin and know many of his poems by heart."

The result was that not long after Shura started lunching at the Long Table, he began to be deferred to as the adjudicator for factual disagreements. People would approach him with shards of quotation and he would supply them with the reference.

Abe Bergson: "Shura, where in his writings does Karl Marx talk of reformulating the Hegelian dialectic by standing Hegel on his head?"

Shura: "Abe, postcript to the second edition of *Das Kapital*, Vol. I (1873), third paragraph from the end."

Harry Levin: "Alex, where did Lenin say that after the Revolution the latrines in Russia would be made of solid gold?"

Shura: "Harry, V. I. Lenin, *Polnoye sobranie*, fifth edition, Vol. 44, pp 225–226."

The sort of argument Shura got into on a daily basis was over who had the breech-loading and who had the muzzle-loading rifle in the Franco-German War of 1870–1871. (After that disagreement, finding himself vaguely deficient in his ordnance expertise, he quickly read a four-volume treatise on the history of warfare and armed the tip of his tongue with two hundred years of munitions.) As it was with guns, so it was with plowshares. "I'd done Anglo-Saxon history and I knew a little about the plow, but he knew *everything* about the plow," says the political scientist Sam Beer.

Despite his voracious desire to know things, Shura did not strike his dining companions as an arbitrary hoarder of facts. People noticed that he liked best the small details that reflect the larger patterns of culture. During a discussion of how rigidly stratified class had become in Great Britain, he said that all levels of society were complicit and cited the different ways Englishmen learned to use silence as a way of expressing their superiority or deference. When the subject was how social customs came to be, he could explain that even the strangest of them generally originated as rational responses to the conditions of their time.

Medieval English cooks, Shura said, repeated bizarre ritual chants over their steaming kettles because the clock had not yet been invented and they needed a means of timing their recipes. He did devastate people, and he did, as Sam Beer says, "like to correct you," yet usually he softened his blows with suavity. Of a determinist professor of philosophy Shura once asked, "How do I know what I would know if I knew?"

Then, too, he could be obnoxious and overbearing. When Monroe Engel was a young English instructor, Shura wondered what Engel was doing with himself.

"I'm writing a book on Dickens," Engel replied.

"Oh," Shura said, getting excited. "When I was a boy I read Dickens in Russian and French. Then I read him in German. Then in Italian. Then I read him in English. Since we've been here in America, I've only read all of him two or three times."

"Okay Alex," Engel said. "You write the book."

"He laughed," Engel recalls. "He had an appetite, such an appetite, for knowledge. I had immediate animal affection for him. He had a jaunty, cocky energy that was wonderful to watch."

That conversation took place at another Cambridge lunchtime gathering Shura frequented, the Friday Senior Common Room Table at Eliot House. "Cambridge turns its back on the world, Harvard turns its back on Cambridge, and Eliot House turns its back on Harvard" went a local aphorism, for Eliot was the most socially exclusive of the eight Harvard houses. The houses were the residential colleges within the university where undergraduates lived for their last three years. In Shura's day, the custodian of Eliot's reputation was one of Harvard's great educators—and unabashed snobs—the housemaster John Finley, Jr. A professor of classics irrepressibly given to Greek and Latin exortations, Finley was the sort of man who went out for a walk on a winter afternoon along the Charles River, spotted some ice fishermen, and greeted them by yelling *"Salve Piscatores!"* ("Screw you, Mack," they replied.) Never a productive scholar, Finley was instead a tireless advocate for a broad undergraduate course of study. He had one even greater passion than the curriculum—Eliot House.

Finley wanted only the wittiest and most learned professors as Eliot House affiliates, and he grouped them together with a curator's care.

Over the years Finley's gallery of Senior Fellows included the professor of American history and literature F. O. Mathiessen, the literary critic I. A. Richards, the poet and former librarian of Congress Archibald MacLeish, the philosopher Willard Van Orman Quine, the historian Michael Karpovich, the English professor and literary biographer Walter Jackson Bate, and the Italian-born professor of comparative literature Renato Pagioli, not to mention the likes of Adam Ulam, Harry Levin, and Gottfried Haberler. It was Haberler who went to Finley one day in the early 1950s and told him, "We must get Gerschenkron."

Although affiliated professors had no formal obligations to the house, Shura became devoted to Eliot and made a point of coming by on Friday. That was the day Finley convened his version of a Balliol College high table, the Eliot House Senior Common Room lunch. The professors had a mandate to perform, and perform they did.

While Karpovich was at one end of the table explaining how to interpret Kremlin politics by reading between the lines of *Pravda* articles, Richards sat at the other discoursing on the Platonic ideal of beauty. It was a tough crowd—Sam Beer says that "they all looked down on MacLeish because he wasn't T. S. Eliot." Shura usually sat with Quine or Levin. Peter McClelland, once an Eliot junior associate, says that Quine "is the kind of person people think are at Harvard or Oxford. He's the real goods, and he and Alex used to engage in Olympian intellectual games of tennis. They were the two towering figures of their day, the Borg and McEnroe of the time." Quine was a truly great scientific philosopher, the most famous of the American logicians. He had studied in Vienna in the early 1930s, where he sat in on meetings of the Vienna Circle. Later Quine developed a language-based theory of knowledge. Like Shura, Quine had a reputation for knowing every language that could be spoken and having a similarly athletic grasp of world geography. The result of his hobby of accumulating visits to new countries—he racked up 118 of them—was, according to Monroe Engel, that "the entire globe was imprinted in Quine's head." Also like Shura, Quine was notorious for projecting self-confidence. Around 1930 he replaced the question mark on his typewriter with a mathematical symbol he was using in his graduate dissertation and wrote on the machine for the next seventy years without ever putting it back. When someone asked him how it was to type without a question mark, Quine replied, "Well, you see, I deal in certainties."

Quine and Shura had many discussions. One week they talked about how to translate a German statement of Einstein's one of them had seen engraved on a building at Princeton: *Raffiniert ist der Herrgott, aber boshaft ist er nicht.* "God is slippery but he ain't mean" is what they decided upon. An entire lunch was devoted to paradox. What made a paradox? How many kinds were there? Nothing was too narrow a topic for lengthy examination. An argument about whether or not the letter *p* should ever follow the prefix *in-* in proper English persisted during the week via letters sent back and forth between their offices. Shura insisted that constructions such as "inpour," "input," and "inpatient" were not words at all but jargon: "A concoction like input is incompatible with the genius of the English language, and should not be used by the servants *bonarum litteratum*, except with the feeling of regretful distaste, to be indicated in speech by a slight lowering of the left corner of the mouth," he wrote. Here was a double coup, for not only was this a successful dig at his economics department colleague, the input/output impressario Wassily Leontief, it gave him the last word against Quine, no question mark.

Often that honor went to Levin. Levin was such a brilliant reader of literature that James Joyce once claimed that Levin was the only man who understood him. Levin had an uncanny appreciation for many writers ranging from Shakespeare to Hawthorne to Tolstoy to Stendhal to Mann to his friends T. S. Eliot and Nabokov. Isaiah Berlin didn't like Levin, finding him "a narrow, pedantic, clever, envious man too proud of his insights," but Levin and Shura enjoyed each other. Elena Levin says that Shura was one of the few people her husband permitted to correct him. "They had vivid responses to each other," she says. "It was as though by talking to each other, each felt he made the other brighter." The sight of the elegant and urbane Levin wearing one of his well-tailored suits and Shura in what the Levins called his "New Hampshire clothes" talking intensely about literature made Wassily Leontief and his wife Estelle smile. They thought that both men were "personalities." Levin, they decided, was "Mr. Harvard." Gerschenkron was "Mr. UnHarvard."

People noticed an economist holding his own talking Freud with Jerry Bruner, talking Shakespeare with Harry Levin, and talking logical positivism with Willard Van Orman Quine. Stories began to circulate about "the Great Gerschenkron," who walked into rooms filled with poetry experts and knew more verse than they did, who'd evaluated one hundred translations of *Hamlet* and proved that every one of them was flawed, who'd read the best Russian, Italian, Norwegian, Swedish, and Danish novels in Russian, Italian, Norwegian, Swedish, and Danish. Gerschenkron, it was said, had rigorous literary standards right down to his reading of mysteries; he scorned all but the Dutch ones. Soon Shura was receiving formal requests to hold forth at Harvard on noneconomic subjects.

In the late 1950s, Shura took over the Tolstoy portion of a "Great Authors" undergraduate literature course, nicely complementing the sundry Shakespeare, Keats, Eliot, and Swift lectures given by specialists from the English department. Then John Finley asked him to give a series of lectures on *Doctor Zhivago* as part of his popular course "The Epic and the Novel." Although Shura began by describing himself as "an economist—that is to say a barbarian"—who had no business telling anyone about literature, he gave a complex lecture placing Pasternak as the latest guilt-stricken member of the Russian intelligentsia to take to fiction because he had no tangible way of improving the lives of the Russian people. Around the same time, a noted literary scholar from London was invited by the Russian Research Center to come to Cambridge and give a talk on *Doctor Zhivago*. Twice the scholar postponed his presentation, and when he telephoned from England to explain that he needed to reschedule yet again, Shura became incensed. Clearly, he told his colleagues, this man was never coming. It was time to seek a replacement and he had one in mind: himself.

In time there were new job offers—all of them from Harvard, where Shura already had a job. At one point he seems to have turned down a chair in Italian literature. That wouldn't have been a difficult decision. In 1960 came something more tempting. His friend Roman Jakobson, who'd held the university chair in Slavic studies for many years, announced he was giving up the position, and Shura was asked if he'd like to have it. Among Slavicists the idea did not seem absurd. Victor

Erlich of Yale told people that Gerschenkron "knows more about Russian literature than many professors of Russian literature," while Walter Arndt of Dartmouth, another translator of *Eugene Onegin*, thought of Shura not as an economist but as a fellow Slavicist."I was by far the junior," Arndt said. Jakobson's chair appealed to Shura as a way of certifying his otherness. With the new credential, he would always be something more than the next fellow, an economist among Slavicists, a Slavicist among economists. Nobody could compete with that. Then he consulted his most pragmatic friend, the economist Ed Mason. "Well, Alex," Mason told him. "An economic historian who is offered a Harvard chair in Slavic studies is a terrific thing to be. But it's not as much to be a former economic historian with a chair in Slavic studies who has only written a good review of *Doctor Zhivago*. People may wonder." Shura remained an avocational Slavicist.

A FEW YEARS AFTER THEY GOT TO CAMBRIDGE, SHURA AND ERICA joined up with a group of other professors and their spouses in a play-reading circle. They read Stoppard, Pirandello, Pinter, Molière, Ionesco, Shaw, Chekhov—a different drama every month. Lead roles went often to Shura and he threw himself into them. Nancy Dorfman liked him in comedy. "I can see him sitting over there in that big chair and myself laughing uncontrollably every time he opened his mouth," she says. Perhaps his most impressive thespian moment came as a hardline Communist leader in Sartre's *Les Mains Sales* (Dirty Hands). After watching him declaim against the middle class, Mathilde Holzman says she "was struck that someone who was so anti-Stalinist could put aside those personal feelings, but he did. It was amazing. You would have thought he believed in Communism with everything he had in him, that he was a true Communist believer."

To some people, Shura seemed to be performing all the time. There was about him the element of a man thinking himself up and then playing the part. The Leontiefs felt that he worked at being a personality and "knew of himself that he was very convincing." And yet no man can improvise his most fundamental qualities. What really happened to Shura at Harvard is that for the first time since Odessa he was surrounded by people with whom he felt thoroughly compatible. Shura was a person who was motivated to impress other people at all times, and now he had people he cared about impressing more than any others he'd known. That kind of incentive brought out the fullness of his personality. He wanted to be more than one of those guys who knows everything; he wanted to be that amazing Gerschenkron.

He made a vivid impression on everyone, including the neighbors in the Whittier Street triple-decker as he went bounding down the stairs in the morning and vaulting back up them at night with a stack of books and journals tucked under one arm and an apple cake for Erica cradled in the other. The ragged leather satchel he used as a briefcase dangled from two fingers. If it had been a good day, you could tell because he'd be singing stray fragments of Russian folk songs in a less-than-dulcet baritone as he swept through the front door. In 1951, the year Shura became a full professor, the anthropologist Evon Vogt and his wife Nan had the downstairs apartment. Nan Vogt saw him in front of the house the day of his promotion. Curtsying she said, "Shura, I'm very impressed. A full Harvard professor. I'm so happy for you." Shura took off his hat and bowed deeply to her. "So am I," he said.

The more his stature grew at Harvard, the more playful he became. Heidi says that her father's childhood had been prematurely taken away from him in Russia, and all his life he was making up for it. Over time, puerile pranks, sophisticated devilment, and intentional misunderstandings became well-known Three Fingers Gerschenkron specialties. At parties he would introduce Erica to strangers as "my first wife, Erica," and then watch them with a steady gaze as they thought that one over. When a Harvard professor of sociology named Samuel Stouffer sent him a questionnaire asking for his definition of an intellectual, Shura sent back this entry: "A word of opprobrium. Etymologically, it derives from the Swedish "inte" meaning "not" and the Swedish "lek" meaning "game." Accordingly, the term refers to a person not interested in baseball." For pointed good measure, he added that a pseudo-intellectual was "a person who only pretends not to be interested in baseball."

Shura remembered the period from the mid-1950s to the mid-1960s as "that wonderful decade," and even unpleasant chores did not alter his bonhomie. During the cold months on Whittier Street, he would go down to the cellar in his bathrobe at two in the morning to stoke the furnace, singing, humming, and whistling as he shoveled in the coal. "He attacked that furnace like it was a dragon and he was Saint George," says Anne Lynch, who lived on the first floor at the time with her husband Kevin, a professor of urban planning at M.I.T. Shura seemed to Anne Lynch to be so full of goodwill and pleasure that it expanded him physically. "He was a very large person," she says. "He was neither tall nor fat, but because he was so vigorous he took up a lot of space."

There appeared to be a vast store of energy for everything in his life, including chivalry. No woman ever followed Alexander Gerschenkron through a door. He became a fiend for giving up seats, pulling out chairs, toting grocery bags, and lending his arm in crosswalks. At Shady Hill Square, when Shura at his study window spotted his next-door neighbor Jane Williams outside shoveling snow off the sidewalk, he flung on his gloves, dashed outside shouting, "Emancipation has gone too far!," took the shovel away from her, and finished the job himself.

Not only was he the ardent champion of "French manners," he stressed that they were to be used under all circumstances by everyone, including soldiers and bachelors. (Shipyard workers apparently were an exception.) Sometimes he gave young people conduct quizzes.

Question: When does a man precede a lady?

Answer: When climbing a staircase so that he can avoid glimpsing her "ankles."

Question: What is the first exception to the rule which states that men are always introduced to women?

Answer: Everyone is introduced to a man of the cloth regardless of age or sex.

Shura's enthusiasm for decorum went well beyond following the litanies of formal codes. He believed that for everything in life there was a proper way of doing things, an ineluctable protocol. Take the weather. The more bitterly cold a winter, the more right he felt the world was. Part of it was that an established norm helped him to distinguish himself. He became well known for coming to work in the dead of a Massachusetts January wearing a pair of old-fashioned Austrian leather ski boots and an unbuttoned red plaid lumberjacket. Some days he wore the coat draped over his shoulders as a kind of cape. On others he "forgot" it. "Is it that cold?" he would say when people pointed out the sub-zero temperatures, and then he'd roll down his shirtsleeves.

PEOPLE CAME TO REGARD SHURA AS A MAN OF CRISP CONTRADIC-tions: a quick-witted scamp, a sentimentalist, a frowning moralist, an enthusiast, a loner, a loyalist, and sometimes a considerable pain in the side. It could be said that he was once more a show-off kid, except, of course, that now he'd reached his fifties. So instead, boyishness became one more component of what he really was—not an actor at all, but a character.

Fully established as the scholar among scholars, he began to play against type. Books might be Shura's life, but he did not always like to appear bookish. Gerschenkron without the footnotes was an emphatically active and masculine figure. During meals he made a point of letting people know what a virile eater he was by mentioning his "vitamin-free diet" at every opportunity and loudly declaiming against salad. Into his fifties he remained sinewy and broad-shouldered. (Liking always to seem the natural, he didn't mention that he maintained his triceps with the assistance of dumbbells.) A friend who saw him emerging from the surf after a long ocean swim stared at the supple muscles spread across Shura's torso and thought "he looked like a lumberjack." With his Maine jacket, wool cap, and heavy boots, he created the same impression on dry land. He had a distinctive way of standing, thrusting out his chest and chin like a grenadier. When he walked, he bounced. On a dance floor, women found him surprisingly graceful. He wore poorly ironed white shirts and did not always take great care when fastening his buttons. During moments of leisure he was prone to thinking up dares designed to prove to other people that he could accomplish feats of strength and courage. In one of them, he challenged a man to walk across a mesh net covering an empty swimming pool before doing it himself. Many of the other gauntlets he threw down involved lifting surprisingly heavy objects.

He frequented bad restaurants. Albiani was an over-easy joint, a large, brightly lit cafeteria with weak coffee, a chalkboard full of specials, and

booths crowded not just with university types, but also with working people. You could see places just like this on a thousand corners in a thousand cities and towns. To Shura Albiani was like nowhere else. When he said "Albiani" he always trilled the third syllable, and he got people he was taking there for the first time so excited at the prospects of impending culinary bliss that when they saw that it was *that* Albiani, they sagged for a moment on the sidewalk even as he pulled the door open for them with a flourish. Without fail, his order was coffee and doughnuts, but he always tried to buy other adults ice cream, even at breakfast time. He was not discouraged when they declined and he repeated the offer time after time.

SHURA'S SHADY HILL SQUARE NEIGHBOR JANE WILLIAMS'S HUSBAND was the Harvard linguistics professor Cal Watkins. As he came singing up the driveway at the end of the afternoon, Shura sometimes stopped to discuss typological comparisons of languages with Watkins. Then he'd go inside and get back to work. Night after night through their bedroom window, Williams and Watkins saw Shura's study lamp glowing, his bent head silhouetted against his curtains. With its abundance of dogwoods and wisteria, Shady Hill Square was as pastoral an urban setting as it sounds, and Williams could sometimes hear the murmur of Shura following the Red Sox ballgames on the radio as he worked. She was puzzled that a man so full of song never listened to any music. Donald Fleming thought about this as well. "Schopenhauer said that the virtue of music was that it was the escape from striving," Fleming says. "Music puts all striving to rest. Shura didn't want that rest."

Striving while the world slept brought Shura a gratification that was very nearly sensual. Heidi would come upon him after he'd been up all night at his desk and "he'd just be glowing with satisfaction." He worked in the compulsive way some people exercise, so frantically that after a while it was unclear whether the pleasure of working was the habit or the habit brought the pleasure. His categorical imperative to make use of every minute led him to work in passenger seats, lawn chairs, and hospital beds, and to avoid vacations. In 1954, after being forced by his family to take a seven-day holiday, he confessed in a letter to his friend Abe Bergson that "I don't feel so good about my work right now. We went to Italy for a week and came back last night. As a result I am rather torn out of all my habits and thoughts here and it will take some time before I get back to where I was prior to the departure. For the moment I feel rather blue and have silly fears that the year will pass without my accomplishing anything, etc., etc. But I'll recover, I hope."

Such a moral aversion did Shura have to being away from his study that when he needed to be in Seattle to give a lecture at 10:00 a.m., he booked a flight that got him in at 4:41 a.m. Eating, getting places, life— it was all a distraction. "He had this very strong obligation to make good use of time," says H. R. Habakkuk. "I wonder whether he didn't feel guilty if he was resting. I don't think he liked resting, even at times when it would have been suitable to do so."

Habakkuk was right. Eventually, the striving almost killed Shura, who was never quite as hale as he liked to appear. In Washington he had begun to have problems first with his gallbladder and then with his thyroid gland. Not only did he neglect both conditions, but he made things worse for himself by smoking too much and by ignoring the doctors

who told him to avoid rich foods. Heidi and Erica felt like extermina-
tors hunting down nests of termite colonies as they searched the house
for Shura's cheese stashes. Because of his weakness for smelly Camem-
berts, these sweeps were usually successful. At parties he could not be
so easily deterred and happily gorged himself on ripe Limburger and
rare beef slathered with sour cream. Afterward he'd come home and be
violently sick. Chastened, he might then submit to a few days of tea and
toast until, feeling revived, he'd be at it again with the liverwurst.

And the caffeine. Cup after cup of strong-brewed Brazilian coffee
was one reason Shura could work, as a friend noted in 1958, "like a
house afire with seemingly an inexhaustible store of energy." That was
the year Shura nearly burned himself out.

Shura was fifty-three and spending a triumphant term at Berkeley as
a visiting professor—an invitation he had accepted partly because it
represented an admission from the Californians that they had underestimated him back in the early 1940s. In the spring he flew to New York
to attend a conference at Arden House, the Harriman family estate near
the Hudson River Palisades. During one of the sessions he felt sharp
pains in his arm and chest. At the end of the hour he went to his room
and rested for a few minutes. Then he decided a cold shower was the
thing to revive him. After drying off, he was sure he did feel better, and
he stayed on for the last day of the conference. Then, with a suitcase
filled with books in each hand, he headed for the airline bus terminal at
Forty-second Street, where he felt himself beginning to collapse. Hail-
ing a cab, he instructed the driver to "take me to the nearest hospital."
Down the street at Beth David Hospital, he walked into the emergency
room and said, "I'm having terrible chest pains and I need to catch a
plane. Can you give me a shot?" He never made it back to California.

"When my father got sick, he always wanted people to know that the
real him was strong and vigorous," says Heidi. Diseases were treated as
sparring partners with whom Shura could prove his strength and stam-
ina. Finding himself laid up in a New York hospital bed after a massive
heart attack, once again he was counterpunching fiercely. Erica was
instructed to tell nobody about his condition. Shura refused to use the
term "heart attack" and instead instantly began referring to "my ill-

ness," as though it was something benign and in the past. A few friends at Harvard learned what had happened and came down to New York to visit him. They found Shura full of cheerful bluster about the incompetents caring for him who spoke languages "even I can't understand."

But he was weaker, and, since this was a man who never did anything in reduced fashion, back in Cambridge he became sedentary and had to be dragged out of the house for walks. On doctor's firm orders, he stopped smoking cigarettes and—for a while—put his pipe aside too. To chance upon him in early 1959, with his rheumy eyes, sallow complexion, shuffling walk, and tin pillboxes full of nitroglycerine tablets, was to see a frail middle-aged man with a serious heart condition. That, however, was not the way Shura was going to let people think of him. He decided that a heart attack was really only another setback life was challenging him to overcome. He knew he was changed, but he also knew that he was not visibly damaged and therefore did not necessarily have to *seem* changed. And so, with the crisis at hand, he became tactical, flexing his personality as he had once flaunted his muscles.

A profitable insight Shura had made into strength was that there are many ways to exude it. Someone who behaves in a vigorous way and associates himself with vigorous activities need not be able to swim as far out from shore as he used to. It could all be a matter of aura and implication. And so Shura's interests, his clothing, his conversation, and what he ate and drank all became accessories, aiding him in maintaining a robust persona for himself. More robust, to some degree, than before.

Shura's driving, for instance, had always been poor, but now it became dramatic. With increasing profusion, stories circulated about him backing into rotaries, skidding off roads, and sailing through yield signs, and there were also tales of his wrong-direction forays down one-way streets, his detours onto sidewalks, his natural inclination for running stoplights, his drawerful of unanswered tickets, and his propensity for absentmindedly shifting his distance glasses onto his forehead at eighty miles an hour. Far from denying such accounts, Shura promoted them, as he did his theories about the open road. "The difference between European drivers and Boston drivers is that in Europe you cannot assume rationality, while in Boston you can always assume rationality," he said. On the basis of this observation he felt the confidence to make minimal use of his blinkers and mirrors while shifting lanes. He was always having minor accidents about which he would draft confessions to his insurance company. He liked to share selections from these enthusiastic narratives ("I demolished his right parking light") just after someone had accepted his offer of a lift and settled into his passenger seat.

Beyond dressing like a lumberjack, Shura occasionally talked like one. He knew well that with the judicious application of a little off-color language, a gentleman can enliven any discourse while increasing the esteem in which others hold him; people may respect a prude, but they neither love nor enjoy him. Accordingly, he was rarely profane, but often ribald. "Oh, he had a wonderful vulgar touch," says Sam Beer. While explaining to a group of economists that it was unfair to ask one historical interpretation to explain everything, Shura qualified what he meant by adding, "It is as the French say, the most beautiful girl cannot give more than she has got."

When people like Adam Ulam heard about the wanton tongue of Gerschenkron, they snorted. "Victoria" Ulam called him, and that was also true. At a cocktail party Shura once was introduced to the British sexual psychologist Henry Dix.

"Professor Gerschenkron," said Dix, "weren't you born in Russia?"

"Yes," replied Shura.

"Tell me, how did young Russian boys lose their virginity in those days?" Dix asked him.

Shura was speechless. After a few moments he recovered enough to indicate his inability to continue the conversation. For the next week Shura went around Cambridge mumbling about what "that man" had said to him—emphasizing that he'd been so scandalized by the incident that he couldn't remember Dix's name. Then, a few years later, in his memoir, he went ahead and took on at considerable length the subject of teenaged Odessa boys from prosperous families and the well-formed peasant girls their parents procured for them. "He could describe with relish every kind of sordidness and squalor," Heidi says, "but he wanted to live a decent, proper life."

In the years after his heart attack, those contradictory impulses melded with Shura's increasing desire to assert himself, helping him to emerge as a most surprising intellectual, a man's man who to all appearances drove fast, talked tough, knew all about women, drank hard, packed a gun, rooted for the home team, and sipped his warm infusions from a dainty white porcelain teacup decorated with pink roses.

NINE

LOVE THINE ENEMY

"Sir, I am not saying that *you* could live in friendship
with a man from whom you differ ... I am only
saying that *I* could do it."

Samuel Johnson to Oliver Goldsmith,
in Boswell's *Life of Samuel Johnson*

S INCE HIS TEENAGE DAYS IN VIENNA, WHEN HE HAD FOUND
himself "carried away by its richness and beauty," Shura had been
a self-described chess addict. When a real fix—a partner—was
unavailable, he contented himself with solving the chess problems he
clipped from newspapers he didn't read. He would pull a small portable
board from his pocket and work through a new problem anywhere,
even as he made his way along Cambridge sidewalks. One of his students, Henry Broude, remembers him "stopping traffic as he crossed
the streets." Paul Samuelson says that it was "a dramatic moment" in
Shura's life when he discovered he didn't require the board anymore,
and could solve problems in his head. After he learned to do that, even
faculty meetings were not off limits.

Not that they ever had been. In 1954 Robert Solow was a visiting
economics professor at Harvard, and soon enough Shura discovered
Solow knew his way around a chess board. So Shura began bringing a
tiny, wallet-sized set to department meetings, and the two of them sur-
reptitiously passed it back and forth. At one point, early on, Solow's
conscience began to bother him. He felt they were being rude. "We
shouldn't be doing this," he said. "You're right," replied Shura. "I'm the

host. You are the guest. I should allow you to play white." And he turned the little board around.

Shura might have been a marginally better chess player had he practiced more, but what he wanted from chess was the play—the electric thrill of a blood sport acted out on sixty-four squares. He won often, but by no means always. There were, for instance, his matches with Marcel Duchamp.

The French-born Dadaist became, by his own admission, such a "chess maniac" in mid-career that the purpose of his life shifted from his art to his game. It got to the point where one of Duchamp's friends could say that "he needed a good chess game like a baby needs his bottle." Wherever he went, Duchamp searched out chess partners. In the summer of 1956 Duchamp found himself in New Hampshire. Through the MacDowell artists' colony, he requested help in meeting up with a good local chess player. Soon enough he was given the name of Professor Gerschenkron of Harvard, who spoke French, was known in some circles as "the Great Gerschenkron," and was summering in Hancock. That sounded promising. A call was placed and Heidi, home for the summer from college, answered it. "Daddy," she said. "Marcel Duchamp is on the telephone for you." A game was proposed, Shura accepted, the call ended, and Shura hurried off to the Hancock town library to read up on Duchamp.

On the appointed day, Duchamp arrived, and Shura was disappointed to see that he did not look nearly as interesting as the plate of *Nude Descending a Staircase*. He was a short, small man in a light gray suit so ill-fitting that it made him look dumpy. More interesting was a voluptuous woman with bleached blond hair who accompanied him. Everyone was sure this was the artist's Parisian mistress. He was, after all, French. "Hello," she said. Then she sat down without removing her cloth coat. Erica, who was spending the summer in the kitchen reclining on a chaise longue because of a back problem, rose up on an elbow and made a perfunctory offering in French: "*La chaleur est parfois terriblement étouffante*" (The heat can be so oppressive), she said. The mistress did not respond. Erica grunted indifferently and returned to a book she was reading.

Meanwhile, at a little kitchen table, the board was laid out and play began. Erica read, the mistress sat silent, Heidi watched, and Shura never knew what hit him. Duchamp was a good enough player to have entered international competitions and once nearly defeated the French champion. In less than ten minutes the game was over with Duchamp victorious. A blush crossed Shura's cheeks. "*Encore?*" Duchamp asked. "*Naturellement,*" replied Shura. They began again, and this time Shura was trounced in less than eight minutes. At that point the board was put away and Heidi served coffee and cake. Erica continued to read on her chaise, the mistress continued to say nothing, and Shura tested out Duchamp's conversation. Finding that it was not nearly as interesting as *Nude Descending a Staircase*, Duchamp's chess game, or Shura's own conversation, Shura's high spirits revived. As Duchamp stood up to take his leave, he muttered something to the effect that Shura "must have had a poor day" and they should play again. Accordingly, another match was scheduled. "Goodbye," the mistress said.

A few days later, Duchamp arrived for the return engagement. Again he wore a badly fitting gray suit. Again the voluptuous blonde was with him. Again she refrained from conversation. Again Erica remained stretched out on her chaise. And again the chess went badly for Shura. This time he was prepared to take it, and he did. "The Frenchman administered me another thrashing," Shura said, watching Duchamp and the woman depart for good after more coffee and cake. It was later discovered that the woman was Duchamp's wife Teeny, a natural-blond native of Cincinnati whose first husband was Pierre Matisse, the art dealer and son of the painter. For Erica, who loved French painting, squandering an opportunity to talk with a woman like that was as bad as losing so decisively was for Shura. It was a family humiliation. "That," says Heidi, "was not a story my father repeated very often."

IT WAS ALSO DURING THE EARLY 1950S THAT SHURA GOT INTER-ested in baseball. He followed the Boston Red Sox, and, like most fans of the team, he was immediately long-suffering. He never actually attended Red Sox games. He kept up with the team by radio in his office, in the car, and in his study at home, moving his pencil to the cadences of the broadcasters' voices. When something exciting happened he allowed himself to pause and raise the volume for a moment. Up in New Hampshire he worked at a card table out on the lawn with the transistor beside him, and took the radio with him when he went to the lake for a swim or some sun.

Like so many American immigrants, Shura had seized upon baseball as a means of cultural assimilation, as a truly national pastime. He claimed great admiration for "that truly democratic moment, the seventh inning stretch," when, as he described it, all the classes rose in harmony together as their passions cooled. By way of contrast, he pointed out that in Europe, class frustration was often expressed toward the end of soccer games when fights broke out. The summer the son of some Austrian friends came to visit, he sternly instructed the young man to "go to see the Red Sox and learn about baseball or it will be a *Bildungsloch*" (a serious gap in a boy's education).

He liked that baseball had an underlying principle governing every occurrence, he liked that it required quick wits as well as brute force, and he liked the long six-month season that rewarded mettle and dedication—reasons for which many people admire baseball. Shura being Shura, he also found in the game an opportunity for asserting himself.

Take his friendship with Ted Williams. Not only was this the Red Sox' greatest player, but he was a complicated figure who spat at reporters, flew fighters in two wars, and wrote an intelligent book about the science of hitting a baseball. That Shura was prone to repeating the unflattering things Williams told him about men like Arnold Toynbee and Walt Rostow ("powerful hitters, both of them, but they don't always touch all the bases") roused the interest of Walter Galenson's son. "David was beside himself when he learned that you had lunch with Ted Williams without getting his autograph," Walter wrote from California. "Also, you took on new dimensions in his eyes. What was the occasion of this affair? He—and I—are curious."

It was all a complete fabrication—and one that Shura never confessed. He was proud of his apocryphal relationship with "the Splendid Splinter," and possessive of it too. Another Harvard faculty member, an adventurous philosophy instructor named Robert Paul Wolff who taught Marx and was known to have once visited Castro's Cuba, really did meet Williams on a train. When Wolff told this to Shura, he responded with territorial perjury. "Ah, yes, Williams," Shura told Wolff. "I have dinner every so often with Williams. We're great friends." Wolff was impressed. "He positively one-upped me," he says. "Of course I believed him. Why wouldn't I believe that a famous Harvard professor had dinner periodically with Ted Williams?"

Why would Shura, the crusader for truth, perpetuate a blatant falsehood? Heidi says that her father "thought it was funny." Then she adds, "He wanted to have the best story, especially when he was in competition with somebody who liked Communists and anarchists."

SHURA DID HAVE REAL FRIENDS—AFTER A FASHION. HE LIKED TO spend time with intelligent people who, for the most part, were willing to allow him to dominate the conversation. When Simon Kuznets would stop by, they'd talk for hours about economics and Russian literature. It was always "What about this, Young Simon?" (Kuznets was three years older) and "Well, then, Young Simon, and what about that?" Kuznets won a Nobel Prize for his work on economic growth, and Shura respected him deeply, even as he overwhelmed him with expansiveness. Marge Leibenstein once spent a day with the two of them, and she recalls that "Simon chewed on a cigar the whole time and grunted, and Shura talked the whole time."

He could also often be found at Albiani drinking the local version of *Caffe mit Schlagobers* with the Viennese physicist and Vienna Circle philosopher Philipp Frank. After his student days, for almost thirty years Frank was a distinguished professor at the University of Prague, Einstein's hand-picked successor for his chair in theoretical physics. In 1938 he was on a lecture tour of the United States when Germany invaded Czechoslovakia, making him a refugee. Frank found himself forced to accept a half-time lecturing position at Harvard. That Frank was paid next to nothing and had very little status at Harvard meant nothing to him. A warm, smiling little man with an uncanny resemblance to Mr. McGoo, Frank's slight frame was also somewhat brittle because he had twice been run over by buses—the result of his well-known philosophical opposition to looking either left or right as he crossed streets.

Shura adored him. They would sit together in Albiani's exchanging puns and epigrams, launching syllogisms, extending digressions, and fulminating against the increasing American trend toward academic specialization. Shura was doing something about that. He and a couple of other scholars had dreamed up a new undergraduate course of study that was a slightly more inclusive version of the political economy degree program he had followed in Vienna. The Harvard program in Social Studies would be, Shura said, "an exciting experiment," an interdisciplinary concentration that would require students to take courses in history, economics, sociology, political science, and philosophy. They would be assigned to read the greatest writers in these fields, Mill, Nietzsche, Adam Smith, Durkheim, Freud, Weber, Tocqueville, and Marx, and then be expected to discuss their books with other students in an intimate tutorial setting. Shura envisioned Social Studies as an elite program open only to a small group of honors candidates—a way, he said, "to jump-start future scholars" who wanted "to avoid premature specialization." In 1960 Social Studies gained university approval and quickly began drawing so many talented young "Soc Studs" that the department gained a reputation as a rarefied place where new generations of risky thinkers went to get some necessary background on the old masters before going outside the gates of the university to shake up the world a little.

The way Shura was with Kuznets and Frank was the way he was with many others. He liked to be with other people and he had fun with them, exchanging ideas and cleverness and laughter. By lacing his conversation with stories, set pieces, and outright fictions, Shura dazzled people. With his good cheer he charmed them. Many felt deep affection for him and he reciprocated. Yet with none of these friends did he become in any sense intimate. That was because he showed them only so much of himself. A person who filters his conversation for general consumption forecloses the essence of close friendship, which is trust. This discretion was there with everyone. Even the people Shura was most drawn to eventually discovered that Gerschenkron could only give what he had.

*   *   *

DURING SHURA'S LIFE AT HARVARD, THE MOST FAMOUS PROFESSOR was John Kenneth Galbraith. Galbraith served as a high-level economist for various wartime government agencies, including running the Office of Price Control for President Roosevelt. He was a confidant to Presidents Kennedy and Johnson and served for two years as Kennedy's ambassador to India. He was also a pamphleteer, a political activist, and the author of many works, including a trilogy on the modern economy—*The Affluent Society, The New Industrial State,* and *Economics and the Public Purpose*—that are among the best-selling books in the history of the field. Galbraith grew up on a farm in Ontario and maintained at Harvard something of the wily country boy's detached skepticism—he coined the term "the conventional wisdom"—even as he went skiing in Gstaad with Jacqueline Kennedy Onassis and gave an annual commencement day garden party at his rambling pink Cambridge mansion where professors mingled amid clinking champagne glasses with politicians up from Washington and actresses in summer dresses.

Galbraith was hired at Harvard as a tenured economics professor shortly before Shura's appointment in 1948, and they were assigned nearly adjacent offices. Soon Galbraith was dropping by at frequent intervals. By the middle 1950s they were, as Galbraith says, "back and forth to each other's houses," having conversations that were serious and yet filled with good humor and spontaneity. "Alex was one of my best friends in the university," Galbraith recalls.

> I was very much served by his different educational experience coming from Europe as opposed to mine coming from agricultural Canada. It was an intellectual friendship, an exchange of ideas. We shared an interest in the history of economic thought. This was a basis of our friendship. We also shared a close and sometimes amused view of the Harvard community which we'd both discovered from outside, I from Canada, he from Europe. At that time there was very little interest among graduate students in the history of economic thought. There is always a tendency among students

to desert the history of ideas for what seems of contemporary interest. I shared the view with Alex that you can't understand the present without understanding its origins. That brought us closer. Alex was more passionate than I was. That was his nature. When he believed something, you were never left unaware of the fact. Alex was a tutor for us all on matters outside the basic field of economics. He certainly was for me. He offered me a great deal. I don't know what I offered him.

One specific thing Shura provided was immediate censure in the face of such false modesty. He and Galbraith understood each other. Both were highly principled New Deal Democrats with very different approaches to a similar preoccupation: how could less advantaged people improve themselves? "Roosevelt is the sort of topic we'd discuss," says Galbraith. "Alex would be subject to my tendency to enlarge upon my own autobiography. Roosevelt gave me my first major position in government. My life has been downhill ever since. Nothing gave you such a sense of authority as being in charge of all the prices of the Republic." Both Galbraith and Shura were traditional economists resistant to the incursions of theoretical numbers men, which gave them a common outlook. Galbraith had been trained as an agricultural economist, but his heart was not on the farm, and he left it behind to think about urban poverty. By instinct he was a social critic whose political ideas were grounded in an economic orientation. In this way he was unlike any other member of the economics department, and Shura, whose colleagues considered him a maverick too, was attracted to that. At the most basic level, he thought Galbraith was a man with an original mind who also happened to be a lot of fun to talk to.

Beyond the serious discussions, there were the exchanges of what Galbraith calls "casual good humor." Back and forth between their offices went these polished pebbles of one-upmanship. A typical exchange began in November 1965 with a wager. Shura bet Galbraith that Dean Rusk would not resign as secretary of state before the following August. The stakes were two bottles of the "best Burgundy," a classification they agreed to leave to the discretion of the finest vintner in Harvard

Square. The middle of August came and went, Rusk remained in office, and Galbraith did not pay up. In October, he received a dunning notice from Shura observing that since "the current prices of Burgundy are rather high, I have been led to surmise that possibly straitened financial circumstances may have been responsible for your failure to discharge your debt." Shura then offered to forgive it should Galbraith send him "a written statement . . . confessing to a lack of political acumen and ditto foresight." Galbraith wrote back to say that while, indeed, his pockets were light, "where indebtedness of this kind is concerned, I allow nothing, not even imminent insolvency, to stand in the way. The delay has been a result only of my need to ascertain in depth what is in fact the best of all Burgundies." He then appealed to Shura "as a scholar" and "a connoisseur of every considerable facet of the civilized life, [who] would be the first to agree that a mere six weeks is utterly insufficient for such a study." Back came a reproach—in Latin: "*Bis dat qui cito dat; qui munerari tardat nihil dat*" (A quick gift is a double gift; a late gift is no gift at all). Clearly, Shura said, Galbraith had forgotten the terms. The wine shop was responsible for selecting his prize. Then he tweaked the former ambassador: "I cannot help marveling that after you have spent two years at considerable expense to the taxpayers of this country on doing research in the field, you still need additional time to complete your learning processes." Galbraith paid up right away. Shura kept his trophy for so many years that when he finally uncorked it, the wine had spoiled.

They made an unusual pair. Galbraith was more than a foot taller than Shura, a height which he used to maintain his slightly imperious, vaguely ironic distance from other people. He seemed to glide around the periphery, a branch bending into conversations but remaining, somehow, apart from them—and that was at his own cocktail party. With Shura he was unfailingly good-natured, generous, and deferential. When Shura needed a lawyer, Galbraith found him one who would do the work at a steep discount. When Shura was sick, Galbraith was one of the people who searched out what had happened and then hurried to New York to see him. These warm acts of friendship were reciprocated. After one of Galbraith's children was diagnosed with leukemia, Shura gave blood several times. When Galbraith left his post at Harvard to serve in India, Shura begged him not to go, and then, two years later, went to Harvard's president Nathan Pusey—who did not get along with Galbraith—and passionately argued for his friend's (successful) reinstatement.

Galbraith was vain, and Shura, who made a show of not being vain at all, enjoyed deflating his friend. Galbraith would close a letter, "I am, my dear Alex, Faithfully yours"; Shura would inscribe his reply, "To quote an affected colleague of mine, I am, my dear Ken, Faithfully yours." Galbraith was equally attuned to other people's personal foibles and more gentle in response. Noticing how much Shura liked to be praised, Galbraith sent him admiring notes. "Dear Alex, You enlighten, astonish, and delight me," was a typical beginning. How could Shura resist? He became attached to Galbraith and looked forward to only one person's visits to his office with more anticipation.

That was Isaiah Berlin. "Oh, they loved each other, those two," says Shura's sister Lydia. "They sparked each other. Shura would call him as soon as he got to London and they'd speak in Russian. It was very sweet."

Berlin and Shura had many things in common, most obviously the line of their lives. Berlin's father was a Russian Jewish businessman, a timber merchant first in Riga and later in Petrograd. When the Revolution broke out, Mendel Berlin fled Russia and settled in England. Many Berlins—including two of Sir Isaiah's grandparents—stayed in Russia and were exterminated by the Germans in 1941. So both Shura and Berlin were expatriate Russians who'd settled happily elsewhere but retained deep feelings about Russian culture. Berlin cared about Oxford the way Shura did about Harvard, with the outsize affection foreigners have for the instituions in their adopted country that embrace them. They were also similarly constituted. Berlin's friend and biographer, Michael Ignatieff, describes him as a man who valued "character more than intelligence, vitality more than sophistication, and moral substance more than verbal quickness." Berlin, of course, fit both sides of all three equations. What Shura valued most was his conversation. Talking to Berlin felt like standing under a spring rain; the words poured over you, clear and refreshing. Berlin's conversation mixed breadth of learning—favorite topics were Herder, Herzen, Turgenev, liberalism, class, villainy, and the opera—with enchanting wit, youthful enthusiasm, sly digressions, classical epigrams, and an always-fresh supply of very adult gossip. If the mark of a learned talker is the ability to discuss subjects he doesn't enjoy, Berlin could do that too. When Dostoyevsky came up in a conversation with Ramin Jahanbegloo, Berlin said he didn't find "him very sympathetic," and then he explained why: "Dostoyevsky is like a magnifying glass. If you hold a magnifying glass over a piece of paper in the light, it scorches it. The paper becomes distorted. That's what Dostoyevsky does to reality. The light is so strong that it burns." All this was expressed very quickly. Berlin dispensed his thoughts, somebody once calculated, at the astonishing pace of four hundred words a minute.

Shura was interested in the extraordinary people of his time, but he knew Boris Pasternak and Anna Akhmatova the way the world knew them—from a distance. Berlin could tell him something firsthand about them, and, with his superior gift for sizing up accomplished men and women he had known only briefly and making them bigger than they were before, he did so eloquently. He met Shura in 1948, and got him right away too. "We always spoke to each other in Russian," Berlin remembered. "I never read Shura's books. Not my subject. I was interested in philosophy, in the history of ideas, in the history of Russia, in radical ideas, in political theory, in music, in literature. Shura didn't mind." They talked about Russian novels—both thought Tolstoy the world's greatest writer—they talked about history, they talked about the cold war, and they did so with intensity. Even men with remarkable memories recall only fragments of their own forty-year-old conversations. Yet as soon as Berlin began to relate the details of his discussions with Shura, it was an hour (24,000 words) before he slackened. "What Shura believed in most was knowledge," Berlin said. "Above all he believed in learning, scholarship and culture. He liked ingenuity for its own sake and he liked cleverness. He was very much a defender of civilization." The opportunity to be around Berlin was one of the chief reasons Shura was willing to leave Harvard for a year away at Oxford in the 1960s. They did not otherwise have much sustained time together, a situation that inspired one of the few confessions of unreserved personal feeling to be found in Shura's correspondence. Writing to Berlin, he explained that he had "a very impolite purpose of subject. I just felt like talking with you."

Berlin admired and enjoyed Shura, and because of his ability to make penetrating personal observations based on fleeting encounters, he understood Shura. They wrote lively letters back and forth. To Shura in Rome, Berlin reapplied Goethe's famous "land where the lemons grow" description of Italy to Israel: "Certainly I shall come to Rome to see you, quite soon, somewhere about the 25th or 26th, after which I shall fly in a more easterly direction, for which you have so far shown no aptitude, but which may yet cure you of some of your ills if only by making you laugh, far more than any European country is likely to do. Can you conceive what land it is that I refer to? Wo die Zitronen blühen?"

On some deeper level, however, it frustrated Berlin that Shura wouldn't share his life with him. "He never talked to me about Odessa," Berlin told me. "I thought it would have been a bit too intimate to bring it up." Berlin was a committed Zionist, and when he asked Shura about religion, Shura brushed him off with an uncomfortable—and possibly untrue—comment about Paul Gerschenkron being "a baptized Jew." Berlin did get attached to people. He was able to discuss his self-doubts, to worry aloud that the world was overrating him. Berlin could sit down with friends—and a biographer—and share the intimate details of his life. Shura didn't do any of that, not even with Berlin—a man whose life and disappointments had so much in common with his own. And so he figured for Berlin as someone he enjoyed, but not a man Sir Isaiah could feel close to. Shura's name does not once appear in Michael Ignatieff's Isaiah Berlin biography.

It was a similar predicament with John Kenneth Galbraith. "I have no recollection of discussing Alex's past," Galbraith says. "Alex and I were certainly good friends and we enjoyed each other, but I would be reluctant to advance myself as being singled out in any way by Alex."

AT THE FACULTY CLUB, AT ELIOT HOUSE, EVERYWHERE HE WENT at Harvard, Shura's vast erudition and conversational charm made him seem so unusual to people that, quite naturally, they wanted to know more about him. Sometimes he would oblige by preparing vignettes of his life—carefully blended medleys of fact and fiction replete with village thieves, brothels for intellectuals, and border-crossing permits written out for Saint Bernards. "He was in control of those stories," says Shura's former student, the economic historian Barbara Solow (Robert Solow's wife). "He did not like to talk about close personal things, and they were only told as stories—as a great monologue. You could feel the Bolsheviks and the Nazis at his back."

When John Meyer and his friend Alf Conrad were graduate students and then young professors at Harvard, they used to visit Shura's office and his table at Albiani in the hopes of learning about the Gerschenkron past. "He had lots of apocryphal stories," Meyer says. "You had to know how to follow what was true. There were lots of variations of these set pieces. He'd vary and change the tempo. He told me bits and pieces about Odessa that were true, but not very much. You'd pick up a fragment now and then. Alf Conrad used to collect them and try to put it all together. He couldn't."

They never asked Shura anything more about his personal life than he volunteered. They sensed it was dangerous to do so, and they were right. This was a man who joined a conversation about religion at a cocktail party, and then, when someone wondered, "Alex, what is your religion?," responded, "That's the kind of question Hitler would have asked me." He intimidated people to keep them away, and away they kept.

"I was afraid of Shura," says Sarah Hirschman. "He did not let you in. My own father was like that. A Russian Jew. A wonderful man. Everybody adored him. But he never shared his feelings. Never talked about his past except for a few pet stories. He had emotional barriers. When I have a friend I like to pour out my soul. There's a feeling for people like Shura that doing so is not decent. I wondered how he was at home. He was so hermetic. And yet he was very friendly, nice, smiling. All those tales about people dropping by his office and yet he was so private and so careful."

Shura had far more powerful stories to tell in his office at Harvard than set pieces about flirting with a sexy German actress on an airplane, playing chess with a famous artist, or making imaginary friends with a great baseball player. He had lived through the Russian Revolution and the rise of European fascism, and his experiences in Odessa and in Vienna were nothing if not real-life dramatic adventures that revealed the very qualities of strength, toughness, and fortitude that Shura wanted people to see in him. It was a vivid contradiction: a warm person who was close to nobody, a rigorous historian uneasy with the details of his own past.

MUCH MORE THAN ANY OF HIS FRIENDS, SHURA WAS PREOCCUPIED with his competitors. These were his true close companions, in the sense that he carried them with him at all times. They were people whom Shura respected enough that he allowed them to motivate him and therefore to form him. He measured himself against the likes of David Landes, his "enemy to whom [he was] much beloved," Walt Rostow, and, eventually, John Kenneth Galbraith, his dear friend who would one day become the most prized Gerschenkron enemy of them all. Shura's first great antagonist, however, was his formative rival, his little brother.

Tolia Gerschenkron was brilliant, charismatic, witty, and joyful, and when he walked into a room everyone noticed him. Shura noticed that. Tolia became his sworn adversary; Shura said that he was driven to succeed by his brother's abilities. Then Tolia died young, with his many talents primed but unfulfilled. Such tragedies often have an iconic effect, and that was true for Tolia. In death he shone even brighter in the family memory than he did when he was alive. That may well have been truest for Shura, who always believed that Tolia's talents were far superior to his own.

There are so many ways Shura might have felt about losing his brother. One possibility is that in death, Tolia became a more formidable rival than ever; this would help explain Shura's persistent concern through life that he wasn't measuring up—an inhibiting fear that might, in turn, have had something to do with both his secretiveness about himself and the brutal public demolitions he frequently administered to people like Leopold Haimson and Everett Hagen. (By striking out so fiercely, by keeping on the attack, he was making himself both imposing and invulnerable.) Heidi says that her father had "always found rapture in contentiousness," first as a boy show-off and then through a youth punctuated by uncertainty and the loss of people and places he loved.

That turbulent early life, and perhaps also Shura's marriage to a highly intelligent, victimized woman whom he saw as both his perpetual obligation and his perpetual challenge, reinforced the idea in him that the world was a punitive place. (Like his father, he believed in the omnipresence of inimical forces.) By the time Shura got to Harvard, he was wary, a person who longed for connections in a world he felt disconnected from. Better at being a distant exemplar than a close companion, he found it easier to invest his enormous capacity for loyalty in institutions rather than in people. Abstract associations can be idealized, and they don't let you down as often as people do.

All this is part of the reason that Shura liked the Faculty Club and Eliot House so much. You could live in the present, could have congenial relationships with people while avoiding intimacy. (He and Erica dined together with Mr. and Mrs. Willard Van Orman Quine exactly once.) At Harvard he was part of no bloc, circle, or group. He moved freely, maintaining his own counsel and keeping the world at a discreet remove. He was at the center of an ideal intellectual community, sitting across the lunch table from men who were writing some of the most important books of their day, books Shura bought at Cambridge shops and carried off to his office bookshelf, where he piled them into careful stacks that hid the light switch on his wall. That these men respected him, thought he was special, meant that he was finally who he wanted to be.

"Harvard was his family," says his sister Lydia. "He felt at home there. I always had the feeling that when he left his house in the morning to go to work, the real peace came for him. A real feeling of coming home for him when he entered his Harvard office. He said the real peace and safety were there for him. He felt safe in his office. He found himself there. He was self-fulfilled."

TEN

THE GREAT GERSCHENKRON

The day is short, and the work is great, and the laborers are sluggish, and the reward is much, and the Master is urgent.

Pirke Avot ("The Sayings of the Fathers," from the *Mishna*)

THE PEOPLE MOST CURIOUS ABOUT SHURA WERE HIS GRADUate students. They were always anxious, anxious to know a little more. He began for them as a rumor. "I encountered the myth before I met the man," says Peter McClelland, who came to Harvard from Canada, where he'd gone to Queens University after growing up in a small town in Ontario.

I arrived at Harvard and discovered that there were a lot of fine people. Among the faculty could be found excellent mathematicians and excellent economists. And then there was Gerschenkron. He was spoken about with awe. You heard, "There isn't anything he doesn't know. Gerschenkron knows everything. Not only that, he speaks an infinite number of languages and reads books written in alphabets you won't even recognize." You heard that if you didn't take Economics 233 with him, you had to take an oral exam administered by Gerschenkron himself. He'd ask you to name all the books you'd read in the past year and you'd list them for him, and he'd say, "What else?" You'd think about it, and after a while you'd maybe be able to name a couple more, and he'd say, "What else?" Now you were desperate. You'd search your memory, search it and search it. Finally from the back of your mind you'd manage to come up with one more book, and he'd nod and say, "Okay. Tell me about that one." You also heard, "whatever you do, on the oral exam don't try to bluff that man or you'll be killed because he believes in honesty. A ruthless adherence to intellectual honesty." All this and I haven't met the man yet.

In Shura's day, Harvard took a three-in-hand approach to its graduate economics curriculum, with all sixty first-year students obligated to study theory, statistics, and history. That is not precisely correct. The real requirements were theory, statistics, and Gerschenkron. Various professors taught various courses in theory and statistics. Shura's lone offering was The Economic History of Europe, and every single student pursuing a graduate degree in economics spent two semesters taking it. Day one of the course caused many of them consternation. They were Americans who had enrolled at Harvard to learn the science of economics. Now they were being confronted not only by its European history, but by the business end of a quarter-inch-thick reading list.

Great university courses do not relate all the details of a subject. In their narrow interval of months they can usually offer only the choicest menu of them, and even then the real art lies in the composition. Professors, in their way, are very much like cooks. If most cooks are given a section of beef, they will prepare a tautology: beef that tastes like beef. There are only a few whose feeling for the chemistry of heat and fat and smoke and seasoning is such that they can make the meat of a thousand meals into something memorable. A great teacher will take a subject that in the hands of somebody else might be just so much information and seize his students with its larger substance and meaning. Among the reasons all great teachers can express their subjects so well is that their subjects express them. It used to be said at Harvard that students in Walter Jackson Bate's course, The Age of Johnson, "were often too interested to take notes." Bate was a delicate man whose frame appeared to be constructed of twigs and mist, and yet not many weeks into the semester, as he began the day's lecture, Bate's students would look up and see before them the ursine bulk of Samuel Johnson. Nobody ever decided that Shura looked like anybody but himself. Still, by midterm in his economic history course, they did see something fresh in him. They saw civilization.

Economics 233, The Economic History of Europe, examined the long rise of an industrial age. Particular scrutiny was given to England, Germany, France, and Russia, with additional emphasis directed toward whatever other countries Shura had become taken with at the moment. (There was a Bulgarian interlude, an Italian intermezzo, and a two- or three-year period when all roads to commercial development suddenly swerved through Stockholm.) The course had a quirky, extemporaneous feel to it. Shura presented the growth of capitalism as a broad historical narrative with a teeming dramatis personae of nobles, guild officers, plowmen, coal miners, census takers, engineers, entrepreneurs, clerks, sea captains, and financiers. On any given day he might tell the students about a newfangled horse collar that improved pulling performance, spice traders who grew rich importing powders that disguised the foul taste of spoiled food, or an order of medieval French monks who devised one of the world's first large-scale industrial plants. Or he might describe the bizarre spectacle of the countries on opposing sides in the Crimean War continuing to trade in each other's currencies even as their armies exchanged bullets. (The lesson there was that the world of stocks and bonds recognized no boundaries.) On another morning, he might give them a room-by-room, field-by-field tour of a Carolingian manor.

Along the way Shura supplied the occasional etymology—"robot" was a word first used in the Austrian provinces for slave laborers—explicated the index number problem at such length that it took on the shambling proportions of a shaggy dog story, and suggested a union catalogue's worth of "supplemental reading" to the quarter-inch-thick list—additional titles that tended to have been written in teenaged centuries. There were classes when Shura brought one of these old mercantile catechisms to lecture and read aloud from it. He'd be moving down the page, and only gradually would the students realize that although he was reading to them in English, the text was printed in

German or Dutch. It was right around then that he would look up and say, "You know, the mercantilists were just about the biggest liars there ever were before our time."

Shura's lectures were performances, and he prepared for them with the care of a Garrick polishing his part. Gerschenkron arrived at his classroom empty-handed. He never gave the same lecture twice, writing each one out fresh every summer and then studying the pages until he was familiar enough with his material to create the impression of casual improvisation. The students were getting bespoke commentary tailored just for them, but they never knew it. "He talked," says his former student Merton Peck, "as though this flow of ideas was occurring to him."

Shura lectured on Tuesday, Thursday, and Saturday mornings at 9:00 a.m. He never ate anything before he lectured—he was too keyed up—and from the moment he began speaking, the nervous energy kept him in constant motion. He paced the floor from wall to wall, sliding his hands along the edge of the desk every time he passed it, allowing the students to take in his overplump fingers—only one of the many things about him that they wondered about. Shura could be dismissive of the antic aspects of his morning: "They sit there dreaming, and the lecturer has to go into histrionics to wake them up," he grumbled once. And yet he was well aware—and well pleased—that he was in part an entertainer. All successful long runs require an occasional invigoration, and over the years Shura refined his stagecraft from time to time, making sure that, as one student says, "everybody had a favorite Gerschenkron mannerism." There were his excursions to the window to lower the shade a precise half-inch, and his peregrinations past the blackboard where he picked up a piece of chalk for a solo game of catch, underhanding it toward the ceiling as he walked. A few laps later the chalk was set down and his hand shot into his fob pocket and unwound a gold chain clasped to a costly Swiss timepiece. He did such a thorough job of consulting it that the students had plenty of time to contrast the elegant little watch cupped in his palm with his unkempt attire—his shirts so poorly ironed that sometimes chest hairs sprang through the gaps along the buttonfront like sprigs of sea grass. When the watch was returned to the fob pocket, the circuit was complete. A moment later, Shura set off again, and after he'd been several more times past the shade to make further half-inch adjustments, the students understood: he was keeping up with the sun.

In the accent that melded the sounds of Russia, France, and Germany, he told them about old Europe in vivid modern English. He invented words—the Gerschenkron term for lack of difficulty was "cinchiness"—and made suggestive remarks. One "clear factor" in the slow French economic growth during the late 1800s, he said, "was a diminished entrepreneurial vigor." Then, by way of implying that the French business community had got fat and lazy, he went on to observe that "whether it was interesting bureaucracy or interesting weekends is not clear."

Sometimes Shura would tell the students a parable. A man walking down a street late at night sees a drunk searching for something under a lamppost. The drunk is circling around and around the lamppost. Finally the man asks him, "What are you looking for?" The drunk says, "My wallet." The man makes a search himself and concludes the wallet isn't there. So he asks the drunk, "Are you sure you lost it here?" The drunk says, "No. I lost it way up that alley." The man asks, "Then why are you looking for it here?" The drunk says, "Because the light's so much better here."

The point was that knowing all the facts was crucial because human behavior is unpredictable, the result of complex and sometimes illogical variables. In this way Shura was much opposed to the latest fashion in economics—economists who scorned the library to sit in their offices thinking up models and methodologies. Models, he contended, were created to fulfill a promise. "It's as Chekhov said," he told the students. "If the rifle is hanging there on the wall in the first act, it has to go off in the last." Another year he warned, "I'm not going to do any methodology here. The methodologists are like eunuchs in a harem. They know everything about love, but they can't do anything about it." By that time economics was a field suffused in methodology. The students looked at this man telling them that methodology was emasculating, and they thought to themselves, "Here is a guy with balls."

*　　*　　*

SHURA'S PRINCIPAL NONMEALTIME BASES OF OPERATIONS AT HAR-vard were his two offices. Like other senior social science and humanities professors, he was given a private study in Widener Library, the three-million-book monolith that loomed over the rest of Harvard Yard like a massive head upon a narrow pair of shoulders. This was where he disappeared when he wanted to work without interruption. Seated deep within the stacks, amid the musty air of paper, cloth, and leather, he felt himself to be "right at the center of what Harvard was all about." There were two parking spaces at the rear entrance to the building—the only two parking spaces in the entire Yard—and so well known was Shura's devotion to Widener that, after the heart attack, Harvard gave him one of them. He could not have been more appreciative. Not only did the parking space allow him to come and go as he pleased, but it identified him as the library's special patron, something thousands of people were reminded of every day as they passed his black '57 Chevy (with fins) resting five steps from the back door. And they saw it frequently. Hour after hour, month after month, the car sat in silent rebuke: Gerschenkron is working harder than you are.

The Widener study was his scholarly sanctuary; his drawing room was his economics department office in the Littauer public policy building. You can tell a great deal about a man by walking into his office, for it is truly his room, a place unencumbered by the compromises of domestic life and appointed in exactly the way that pleases him. Shura's office was a dimly lit little tract, murky with the sweet fumes of tobacco and brandy. The furnishings were sparse: a chair or two, a pipe stand, the old globe which was sometimes complemented by a large map unfurled across a bookcase, the archaic adding machine, a chessboard, a tray with (dirty) cordial glasses, a wastepaper basket, a stray copy of *MAD* magazine. Otherwise it was all books. "Harvard faculty member" is a job description that nearly implies bibliophile, a fact that Shura seems to have taken as a personal challenge. Narrow gaps and spaces were filled in with journals. The floor-to-ceiling shelves were stacked two books deep, and every other surface was choked with them too. After the heart attack, Shura's doctor ordered him to take naps, so he cleared out some space in front of the desk and installed a ratty old sofa. In no time, it sagged with the weight of two hundred tomes. As for the desk, it was piled so high with books that they formed a rampart. When someone entered the room, the only initial evidence of Shura was a papal column of pipe smoke floating toward the ceiling.

The office obeyed the aesthetic of an English garden. It appeared to be organic, an overgrown tangle, but was, in fact, quite precisely stylized—a carefully formed wild landscape. Shura knew where every last thing was, from each book and periodical to the cunningly hidden light switch. His aim was to fashion a ruin, and when Gianni Toniolo's wife stepped inside, looked around, and whispered to her husband in horror, "*È sempre così?*" (Is it always like that?), he congratulated himself on his success.

EACH SEMESTER IN ECONOMICS 233 THERE WERE TWO FORMAL requirements for students: a written exam and a thirty- to forty-page term paper. Shura was not much for exams. Before giving them he would announce, "If the test is not fair, it will be graded fairly. And vice versa." As Shura saw it, exams were the sort of pointless exercises in maintaining poise under pressure that only an Austrian Herr Doktor Professor could love. Term papers, however, he said were "sanctified." He rhapsodized about past students whose hard work and imaginative thinking had led to the creation of original works of scholarship. To impress upon his new charges what a "wonderful opportunity" the term paper was, he required all sixty of them to schedule an individual meeting with him in his office to have their topic approved.

"Let me clear off a chair for you," Shura would say when a student presented himself in the doorway to discuss a term paper topic. Then Shura emerged from behind his desk, always moving at a leisurely gait so that the student could take a long look around. "The thing that was very impressive was his office," says a former student, the economist Albert Fishlow. "It was all designed to reflect the importance of the commitment to scholarship."

If the student proposed a paper Shura thought unpromising, he would get a distant look in his eye. "Oh," he would say. "Yes. Well, you know, I had a student once. Can't remember his name exactly. He wrote on that earlier, I believe. But to be sure, you ought to contact him directly. He's out in Waco, Texas. As I say, can't recall his name, but you can find him out in Waco, at the Waco economics department." If, however, he heard something he liked, usually it took no more than two sentences to hurl Shura into action. "Yes!" he would cry, leaping from his chair. "You might look at this!" and he was across the room in a blur, extracting a book from one of the densely planted shelves and flipping to the page he wanted. A moment later he was venturing deep into the pastures near the window to secure another volume. Then he was charging through the thickly papered meadows behind his desk, where he stretched high above his head for a third. Although these forays took him all over the office, he was a farmer who knew exactly where every straw was in his haystack, so they consumed very little time. Watching him go, the students congratulated themselves a little for their perspicacity in selecting a subject in which their teacher saw such potential.

A PLEASANT CONSEQUENCE OF SHURA'S HEART ATTACK HAD COME when his doctor recommended a daily medicinal glass of brandy. Aside from savoring the taste and feeling grateful for the way the drink relieved his anxiety about his health, Shura pounced upon the social possibilities. The office door was usually open, and when people he liked passed by, he would enthusiastically flag them down. "Come in, come in," he would say, ushering them over to a chair and and reaching into the lower desk drawer for a bottle of the finest Rémy Martin V.S.O.P.

This could get going pretty early. An hour after breakfast he might propose a quick one, explaining, "My doctor has ordered me to give up smoking and start drinking." It filled him with happiness to watch as someone like Lord Bullock of Oxford shook his head, looked in horror at his timepiece, eyed the top-shelf Rémy Martin V.S.O.P. Shura had produced, consulted his wrist again, made some kind of calculation, and submitted. When a bottle ran low, Shura would toss it into the trash basket with a small quantity of brandy still remaining. If his guest seemed to find this painful, Shura would say conspiratorially, "I always leave at least a half an inch when I throw it away. That gives the janitor a vested interest in not reporting me to the administration."

Brandy drinking offered abundant opportunities for one-upmanship. Shura was never much of a tippler himself, but he always poured his guests a liberal glass and topped it off. Sometimes he was rewarded. "It took real willpower to get out of there sober," says Jim Duesenberry.

The Rémy Martin V.S.O.P. was not the only libation stored in his desk drawer. Shura also kept a bottle of cheap Spanish brandy. When certain personages stopped by, Shura made his usual proposal of a drink. If the vistor accepted, Shura would open the desk drawer in such a way that as he took out the bottle stamped "Hecho en Jerez," his guest received a lingering glimpse of the Rémy Martin V.S.O.P. Shura was choosing not to serve him. There are still men out there bearing grudges because "he gave me the third-rate stuff and Rosovsky always got the good French cognac."

As he poured the brandy, Shura tended to take control of conversations. Quite often what Shura wanted to talk about were his own adventures in which he traveled the town as a kind of modern-day Cossack. "He bragged," says one friend, "about being a good shot and a poor driver." Shura had learned to shoot a gun at the age of nine when he received a French rifle from his father, and some of his happiest childhood days were those spent in groves of walnut trees acting out Turgenev's "Sketches From a Hunter's Album" with live ammunition. But in his office Shura did not tell these old stories. Instead, he concentrated on more recent history, recounting the morning he'd been sitting in his New Hampshire living room when he spotted a porcupine crossing the upper field. Porcupines were an abomination. They ground away at the sills of his house and the trunks of his trees, and each time his Labrador retriever, Tracy, tried to intimidate them, his charges met with predictably painful results. So Shura explained that when he'd seen "this fellow" he'd grabbed his rifle, run upstairs to the second floor, opened a window, and shot "that fellow" dead at two hundred yards.

Sometimes he took his guns to town. There were guests who arrived for appointments at the office and found Shura stretched out across the couch with a rifle in his hands. One such visitor was Shura's student Richard Sylla, now a New York University economist. "He'd aim it at the ceiling, move it around, and talk with you about shooting," says Sylla. "I once had a whole conversation with him while he was wielding the gun."

IN THE SPRING, THE STUDENTS WERE WELCOMED BACK INTO SHURA'S office to discuss their second-semester paper. When Bill Whitney came for his appointment, Shura told him how highly he'd thought of his first-semester paper. It was so good, Shura said, that they really ought to drink to it. He poured Whitney his first-ever glass of brandy. Whitney had come to Harvard from a farming community of nine hundred people in northwestern Iowa, intending to study straight economics. Whitney had arrived in a state of nerves. Now he was sitting in the office of Shura surrounded by books written in languages he couldn't identify, sipping an exotic liquor. Shura was an exceptional host, topping off Whitney's glass, asking him sympathetic questions, and, in the time-honored posture of those who wish to flatter their guests, leaning toward Whitney just a little as they chatted. Whitney had begun to feel warm and good, to feel that it was "a bigger world than I had known," when Shura hinted that he ought to consider a career in economic history. At that moment Whitney realized that this was exactly what he wanted to do with his life. He wanted to study under Gerschenkron and some day to have an office full of books of his own, and to know what was in all of them. In other words, Whitney says, "I was hooked."

In one way or another they all were. "The course was where he made decisions on who would do well and who would fall under his spell," says Paul David. "He was very shrewd." When Shura encountered someone promising, he "attracted" him, as he explained to another professor. In other words, he used his large personality to cultivate a large infatuation with his little field. Operating much like a confidence man, he was telling the students a tale, serving up a convincer, and then making the mark. As in any really sophisticated grift, most of the students never believed that anything untoward had been done to them.

Perhaps nothing had. Much as they all came to Harvard wanting to study straight economics, many students also worried that they were condemning themselves to a dismal science. Now here was Gerschenkron telling them that it didn't have to be that way. "We were drawn to him," says Henry Rosovsky. "When you think about it, economists in those days were not, by and large, fascinating human beings. They were accountants with unusual mathematical abilities. Salt of the earth, many of them, but not the most interesting people. He and his subject were so much more interesting than other economic subjects."

Beyond the field, Shura was offering them something more: an outlook, a way of life—his way of life. Sam Bowles had planned to go into politics. He came from a liberal political family. His father, Chester Bowles, had been one of President Roosevelt's most trusted economic advisers. There was always a place for a Bowles in the Democratic party. "I didn't expect to be an intellectual," Bowles says. "He convinced me that being an intellectual was a very exciting and wonderful thing to be, a life to be proud of."

It was the same for most of the others. They had never wanted to be economic historians, never once thought of it, until they encountered Gerschenkron. "He was a completely inspiring teacher," says Robert Sutcliffe. "I was so struck by the sweep of his thinking and the immense range of knowledge. Those lectures were little works of art, beautifully prepared and beautifully delivered." So Sutcliffe became an economic history graduate student, which meant that the following year he joined Shura's seminar. That turned out to be an even more stimulating intellectual experience than the lectures and also far more complicated. If the lectures lent a romantic fascination, the seminar gave life beyond, still absorbing, to be sure, but not without disillusion and woe.

EVERY TIME SHURA LECTURED HE FELT HE WAS GUILTY OF THAT most unforgivable sin for an economist, the willful denial of modern technology. "[Lectures] are Middle Ages," he complained not long after he retired from teaching. "They are altogether pre-Gutenberg. It's not an adult way. The adult way is for students to sit on the appropriate part of their anatomy" and ready themselves for a provocative group conversation. Shura contended that "what goes through the student's mind during the discussion, the need to articulate his opinion and to defend it against the other students and the instructor, are things that are likely to continue to ferment and are not easily forgotten." Shura was sure such a system was superior because he'd tested it. His graduate seminar was a weekly economic history colloquium that in its day was well known throughout the American academy as a master class for scholars.

Every Wednesday evening, eight to twelve graduate students and Shura met around a long table in a room adjoining his office to discuss a paper that everyone had been given to read the previous week. Usually the students wrote the papers, but there were also submissions by eminent economic historians Shura invited in from as far away as Europe to share their recent work. These guests were the only outsiders he permitted. This, says H. R. Habakkuk of Oxford, was because "feudal lords do not allow other lords inside their court." Whoever wrote the week's paper had a few minutes to explain himself. Then the floor was open. The best way to explain Shura's views on seminar protocol is to say that they closely resembled his notions of a good dogfight.

In the summer of 1957 Shura learned that his neighbor James Lynch had been bitten while trying to break up a scrum between the Lynches' dog and his Tracy. Immediately Shura wrote Lynch a letter. After expressing (very) perfunctory sympathy for Lynch's wounds, Shura moved on to the two dogs. He said he

> had been wondering what we can do about straightening out their mutual relations. Dogs of such size, of course, will fight until they have learned to know each other and to tolerate each other. The former tenants in your house had a big poodle, a very strong animal, and they, too, had a few fights in the beginning, and, although they never showed any particular liking for each other, they agreed to disagree and lived peaceably side by side for four or five years. I almost feel, therefore, that the proper way might be to have the two dogs out in the Square most of the time. They may have a couple more fights which will cause us heartbreak. Possibly one of them or both might have to be taken to a vet for some

treatment, as it happened to our Tracy after the poodle had dealt harshly with him. But in the end, I believe, and very soon, they will learn to accept each other and probably will jointly chase foreign intruders.

A typical seminar might find Marc Roberts presenting his paper measuring the effect of the steam engine on the eighteenth-century British coal industry. Roberts had spent weeks deep in Widener Library looking through Parliamentary documents, engineering reports, and engineering journals, counting up how many steam engines there were in England at different points in the century and then calculating how many bushels of coal various models of engine burned until "I knew more about steam engines in England at that time than anybody on the planet." All the research was used to demonstrate that the steam engine did not markedly influence the growth of the coal industry. From these statistical observations, Roberts ventured into an assessment of the relative value of the steam engine as it grew more expensive, and more efficient, over time. Then the discussion began. It was, as Paul Munyon says they all were, "an intellectual free-for-all." After only three minutes Roberts had to concede that "my argument was in pieces." The others saw that he had muddled a fundamental conceptual problem in microeconomic theory—whether capital is physical or financial—and they were prompt with their imprecations. "It was just us," says Paul David, "so we could be completely open and we didn't feel we needed to be polite. We were very hard on each other. The seminar was the place where people showed Gerschenkron what they could do. The reason it worked was because of his ability to elicit individual commitment from students to win his approval."

The strange part was that there were never any signs of this approval. Week after week Shura took his seat and puffed his pipe, a silent master looking on as his feral apprentices clawed at each other's ideas. He did not interrupt. His expressions did not change. Reactions from him were so rare that the students spent hours trying to interpret the sparse flickers and nods he gave them. Sometimes his tongue strayed into his cheek. Consensus had it that this meant disapproval. That was, in fact, the consensus for just about every twitch he made.

Only with the day's session about to end did Shura stir into motion. As the students fell silent he emptied and cleaned out his pipe, filled it with fresh tobacco, tamped it down with a silver tool, extracted a match from a little wooden box with a spring-loaded lid and a top decorated with a European pastoral scene, fumbled with the match until he got the bowl lit, took a couple of long puffs that made a strange echoing sound, stared around the room, and then finally offered a comment. Invariably it was succinct; once in a while it was also delphic. After a debate about how to quantify external costs beyond market measures, he began by saying, "You know, in my heart of hearts I would like to believe that the externalities were positive, but the brain is a more important organ than the heart." The students decided that meant that, while speculation is fine, it is only a pleasant prelude to the backbreaking job of locating unassailable proof. During another discussion someone had used the word "overview." Included in Shura's closing remark was this: "I'm not sure if you used 'overview' correctly." Then he waited a beat and said, "When a German prostitute has a client who wants to leave the lights on she says, 'Oh! You want an *Überblick*!'" There was also the day when he crowed that some documents from the Ottoman Empire had been translated into Bulgarian, "so now we can all read them!"

Did he really mean that? Nobody knew. With his students he was so elusive, always a man removed from the fray. Some evenings after the seminar, a couple of students would be invited back to the office for a postseminar sip of (Spanish) brandy—"the laying on of hands," one of them called it. Yet whether or not this was any kind of reward was never clear. Red Sox fans rather than the most promising economic historians tended to be invited.

Every few years something happened that overwhelmed Shura's aura of stately remove. Once the great British Marxist historian Eric Hobsbawm visited the seminar and gave a presentation on Latin American development. Predictably, Hobsbawm used a Marxist framework to explain Latin America. Predictably, Shura was very quickly well heated. Although he tried to mind his manners until the end of the session, there were few things he disliked more than people living comfortable lives in free societies and passing off as scholarship what he considered the dogma of repression. "See here, Hobsbawm," he said, interrupting. And then the students were treated to the sight of Gerschenkron becoming so genuinely furious that his feelings came plunging out of him like a raft passing over a waterfall. "He ripped him apart, explaining that Hobsbawm had misrepresented Marx," says Peter McClelland. It was 'You've suggested Marx said "A" but isn't it the case that . . .' and then you'd get a direct quote from memory from *Das Kapital*. The indignation was enormous. I was in the seminar for eight years, and this was the only time I heard him speak at length."

There was at least one other time. That was on the memorable evening in 1958 when Shura himself gave the paper. His subject was Bulgarian production, and in the week preceding the seminar the students prepared to take on their teacher with a feverish sense of purpose. Albert Fishlow and Paul David spent so much time scrutinizing Shura's work they hardly slept. "We wanted badly to catch him out," says David. Neither of them could read Bulgarian, but to their joy, one day they discovered that Bulgarian statistics were available in French translation. That they could read. Mining the documents carefully, Fishlow and David found what appeared to be—oh, ecstasy!—some Gerschenkron errors. When the seminar met, with much deference they pointed them out and then gleefully sat back to see what he would do. "He congratulated us," says David. "But then he told us, 'Alas, the paper's already gone to the printer.' We never laid a glove on him." Saving face that way couldn't have been completely satisfying, which is perhaps why, when Shura later learned that Fishlow and David had culled a French translation for their Bulgarian statistics, he made a great display of outrage, thundering at them that if they'd wanted to do an honest job, they should have learned Bulgarian.

SHURA'S STUDENTS WERE YOUNG MEN TRAINED ON THE FRONTIERS of contemporary theory and mathematics. By applying the most sophisticated modern methodological and data-gathering techniques to the study of the past, they would change the field of economic history. Their approach would become known as the new economic history, and they would be dubbed the cliometricians—a neologism that links Clio, the muse of history, to measurement. Truth be told, there was a lot they could teach Shura. Yet his effect upon them was such that he made what they knew seem almost beside the point. "I've never been able to explain how somebody could come into that seminar room and could be of such tremendous influence without using his own work as a guide," a former student named Richard Sutch says. "He wasn't a cliometrician, and he trained the world's best cliometricians."

"I've thought about what made his seminar work throughout my own teaching career without being certain," says former student Knickerbocker Harley. "I don't know how he did it. Somehow he created a sense of high purpose we all felt. There was a scholarly standard. It struck me that the content wasn't as important as the fundamental idea of the honesty and the worth of scholarship. It didn't matter that on technical stuff he was useless. He was an exemplar of intellectual inquiry. There was this sense that you were striving for something that had to do with quality and integrity, and when you got it you'd know it."

Many of the students sensed this: Shura had higher ambitions for them than the mere mastery of an area of economic history. He was forming them as scholars in his own image. "By a process I still don't understand, the man set an elevated critical tone that prevailed," says Peter McClelland. "Even within Harvard that seminar was special. People would say, 'Alex has nothing to do with it. If you had a tape recorder you'd find he says very little.' True enough. But the fact is that he was there. The man was a presence."

It all amounted to an education in character, the essence of which Shura expressed in a story he told his students about the death of his dog. He said that when the end was near, he had placed the weakened Tracy on the floor in the back of the car for the last drive to the veterinarian's. Throughout the trip, as Shura drove, Tracy fought to climb up onto the back seat, and throughout the trip he failed. Time after time he would come close before slipping back onto the floor. He would then lie there panting, before gathering himself and trying again. It was with unabashed admiration that Shura described that it was only at the very end of the ride with an extraordinary effort that Tracy succeeded in hoisting himself up onto the seat. Shura could, of course, have helped him, but he said that wouldn't have meant anything to the dog.

This way he had accomplished something momentous, and all on his own. It was his achievement, to take with him into death. Greatness, Shura implied, was always possible, but only possible if you made it possible. Everything was up to you.

SHURA SAW THE YEARS HIS STUDENTS SPENT IN THE SEMINAR AS their own coming of age novel. Turning graduate students into scholars was, he once confided to another professor, all a matter of "intelligent planning." They came to him young, innocent, and promising, and by the time they left him they had been fully formed as men. Along the way Shura made it his obligation to provide his students with the difficult experiences that seasoned them as people of the world. The great care with which he conceived these narratives of experience is evident in the two-paragraph letter of recommendation for a teaching position at the University of California at Berkeley he wrote for Albert Fishlow in 1960.

The letter began as a panegyric, a paragraph of praises culminating in Shura's declaration that Berkeley could not "have a better man than Fishlow for the [job.]" In the second paragraph Shura took it all back. "Let me also issue a word of serious warning," he said. This "excellent man of very great promise is also a very young man; he is not fully mature; and he still has a great many things, both very important and not so important, to learn." The twenty-five-year-old Fishlow needed to "achieve a high standard of scholarly perfection in producing a large literary work," to master more foreign languages, to read widely in foreign literature to achieve a worldy perspective, and, finally, to "shed a certain coarseness in both manner and thought. All this," Shura said, "requires time." The strong implication was that Berkeley should allow Shura to finish the forming of Fishlow before offering him a professorship. That Fishlow was the best candidate in his field for the job was beside the point.

Fishlow was not, of course, privy to the letter at the time, yet years later when he learned of it he was not surprised. "He set himself up as a model that we tried very hard to emulate," Fishlow says. "What was so powerful about his model was that he never stated the standard; he embodied it. The phenomenon was 'Look at me. This is what it takes to be a first-class scholar.' He was extraordinarily shrewd in his ability to choose students who he knew would be responsive to him. At the time I knew he felt there was more I could absorb, and what I most wanted was his feeling that I'd done my job right."

Along with Paul David, and a few months later Peter Temin, Fishlow had been one of the Gerschenkron chosen, selected by Shura as an original member of the Economic History Workshop. In late 1958 Shura learned that he had received the large grant he'd sought from the Ford Foundation to create the Workshop. Immediately he wrote a letter of thanks to the foundation's president, McGeorge Bundy, exulting that "this will revolutionize the teaching of economic history in this country, I hope." Then Shura told Fishlow and David the good news, promising that they would all receive a princely stipend and office space. The Workshop, he said, was to be a scholarly redoubt where they could write their thesis—their "large literary work"—free of interruption from anyone. That, he said, included him. He gave each student a key, wished everyone well, and had nothing more to do with them. Only once in all the years of the Workshop did he climb the three flights of stairs to actually look in on the operation. "He came," says Paul David, "he saw, he left—permanently."

For his dissertation, Fishlow had decided to study the role of railroads in the growth of the American economy. Shura approved the topic, and with that it became "your thesis." Fishlow's dissertation took him seven years to write, during which Shura never once consulted with him about it, just as he avoided speaking with any of his students about their dissertations. "The simple explanation is that he didn't give a damn," says Peter McClelland.

> But that doesn't mesh. Clearly he cared about his students, their ventures, the life of the mind in economic history. So why didn't he give direction from first to last? He felt the thesis is your work which you present to the profession to qualify for membership. It was a matter of integrity. He didn't believe in touching up somebody else's work. I remember a year I'd prepared to teach a course in American

economic history. I came in to discuss it with him. He looked shocked. "Peter," he said to me, "if it is important for you to defend what you teach to me, I have to defend what I teach to somebody else. I have no intention of defending what I teach." I see this as his dedication to freedom of inquiry, and giving you the freedom of your own pursuits.

THE EDUCATION OF ALBERT FISHLOW TOOK MANY FORMS. In 1960 Fishlow was working well on the railroads and finding himself increasingly puzzled by his mentor. Whenever he had business in Shura's office, Fishlow would see the tray of brandy glasses sitting on the typewriter table behind the desk. He knew that some students had been fed this nectar, but for Fishlow, just as there was no thesis advice, there was never any brandy either. What he did receive was an invitation with Paul David to bring their wives up to Shura's house in New Hampshire for a day. "We were conscious that this was something special, that we were to regard this as a very special thing," says David.

He was right. Shura's characteristic ability to imbue the places in his life with his personality reached its apotheosis at his little farmhouse. Shura had been very fond of his family's property outside Odessa, with its peasants, fields, and orchards, and he was soon equally devoted to southwestern New Hampshire, where the landscape of rolling hills, groves of white birches in the forests, and grassy fields reminded him of Russia. In the first few years he had rented houses, mostly in Hancock. That earned him some teasing from his friend the biologist Ernst Mayr, who said that any economist who paid out his money on leases when he could buy property was "a disgrace to the profession." Soon enough Shura had made a down payment on "Windswept," a white colonial farmhouse on a hillside in the tiny community of Francestown. All shutters, clapboard, stone walls, picket fences, red barns, and blue and green summer days, this was the very image of a classic New England small village, and Shura did nothing to clash with the scenery. He erected a sturdy pole out by the road, from which he hung a large American flag. Then he began constructing the legend of his American Arcadia.

By the time Fishlow and David got to New Hampshire, they had heard all about the clear lakes, the fresh air, the deep and cool woods, the old granite mountains which were as solid as the local people, such as the owner of the Francestown general store—extolled by Shura as a merchant who would rather die defending his cash register than give up a nickel to a holdup man. The Fishlows and Davids arrived, and a vegetable-free lunch was served. Then Shura announced from the head of the table that he was taking the boys out for some target shooting. Fishlow was astonished. Not only was he unaware that Gerschenkron was a marksman, but Fishlow had never fired a gun before in his life. David had. "I was a better shot than Al," he says. "Alex noted this. Afterward Al was worrying that his stock had gone down with Alex. This is the kind of neurotic behavior he could induce in his students, who cared so much about their standing with him. If he thought it was important, you thought, 'I should be able to do this.'"

Shura took it upon himself to referee some of the most private aspects of his graduate students' lives, including their marriages. He came down heavily in favor of wives. To Paul Munyon's wedding he sent a short letter to be read aloud that said: "Dear Wendy and Paul, I distinctly prefer married students. They are much more stable." About offspring he was far less enthusiastic. On the day Herbert Levine skipped into Shura's office crying, "Helene has given birth!" Shura frowned and said, "I really don't like children. They're disobedient and they don't respect books." In 1960 Fishlow and his wife Harriet had their first child. Six months later Harriet was pregnant again. As soon as she was showing, Fishlow heard from Shura. "He almost tried to suggest that this was a little excessive," says Fishlow. "'You have to be careful and pay attention to what you are doing,' he told me. He said I should be paying attention not to accumulate large numbers of children while I was doing my serious dissertation work."

To a degree, Fishlow could see the point. He had been an impoverished student for years, living in a shabby little apartment with no bathroom sink, conditions he found much less tolerable with the prospects of multiple infants to bathe. He decided he owed it to his family to make more money. So, with his dissertation draft nearly complete, Fishlow applied for the job at Berkeley. And, despite Shura's letter of recommendation, Berkeley made Fishlow a fine offer. "I had the two children and was desperately trying to finish my dissertation by September, when I was due to be at Berkeley," he says. "I got together a draft and showed it to Gerschenkron."

Shura looked it over and then called Fishlow into the office. "Well," he said. "If you want a degree, I'll give it to you. But I expected something better."

"His sense of disapproval," says Fishlow, "was sufficient for me to throw it away. There I was with two baby girls, going out to take a job in California, and all it took was his saying 'I don't think so' for me to put in two more years on the dissertation. It took me two years to do it over."

Fishlow handed in the revised thesis in 1963. This time Shura was well pleased. "I was truly astonished to see how greatly Fishlow has developed," he purred to Henry Rosovsky. The thesis was put up for and subsequently awarded the David Wells Prize as the outstanding economics dissertation of 1964. The next time Shura saw Fishlow, he invited him to come into the office and sit down. Taking two little glasses off the typing tray, he set them on his desk, opened the bottle of Rémy Martin V.S.O.P., and poured Fishlow a brandy. "Thank you, Professor Gerschenkron," Fishlow said. Shura gave him a subtle look. "Now it is time for you to call me Alex," he said.

Ten years later Fishlow was applying for a new job and needed a letter of recommendation. This time Shura sent off a reference describing "the most brilliant student I have ever had."

ALL THE STUDENTS WERE SUBJECT TO THESE CALCULATED DISPLAYS of dominance, but Henry Rosovsky was treated to more of them than most. Everything about Gerschenkron intrigued Rosovsky, from the brandy and the lumberjacket to more existential matters such as who exactly Shura was. Rosovsky had grown up in the Free City of Danzig (Gdańsk) speaking Russian and German. He was a Russian Jew, and he was almost sure Gerschenkron was too. "He looked like a Jewish labor leader," Rosovsky says. "And his name was obviously Jewish." Shura considered his religion to be his business, but instead of simply saying so, he preferred to provoke Rosovsky. One year at Passover, Rosovsky announced, "Professor Gerschenkron, I will not be at seminar next week because I have to attend a seder."

Shura fixed Rosovsky with a quizzical expression. "Henry," he said, "tell me. I have always wondered. What is a seder?"

Rosovsky's graduate training at Harvard was interrupted by the Korean War. On the day Rosovsky was called up to Fort Meade, he came to Shura's office to say goodbye. Shura wished Rosovsky well, and then he put a book into his hands saying that this was for Rosovsky to take with him into battle. The book was Sartorius von Waltershausen's *Deutsche Wirtschaftsgeschichte* (Economic History of Germany). Although he considered it "probably the most absurd book any American soldier ever carried," Rosovsky did keep the Waltershausen stuffed in his pack throughout his time in the service, and he found that having it with him in frozen Korea reminded him of life beyond the war.

In 1955 Rosovsky was back in the United States and engaged to his girlfriend Nitza Brown. Rosovsky had considered marriage once before, to a woman named Eliza, but he had broken things off. At the time Rosovsky had suspected that nobody was more disappointed than Shura. Gerschenkron, he knew, had a high regard for marriage. "Henry," Shura told him once, "a nagging wife is a scholar's greatest asset because it keeps him in the library." Shura did not attend Rosovsky's wedding, but a little while afterward a gift arrived at the couple's apartment. They opened the package and found a book of chess problems inscribed with a few Pushkin verses and one line of Gerschenkron: "For quiet matrimonial evenings."

Rosovsky had chosen Japan as his area of specialty "in part, because Gerschenkron knew nothing about Japan." He spent two years in Tokyo, researching a thesis on capital formation in Japan. Every few months Rosovsky sent in a chapter and never once heard anything back. Then Rosovsky mailed in a section which contained a brief discussion of index numbers. Two weeks later he opened his letter box and found a twelve-page, single-spaced reply from Shura full of delighted commentary on the Rosovsky use of index numbers.

In 1958 Rosovsky came back to the United States to take a job at Berkeley. There he finished his dissertation and sent it to Massachusetts. After some time had passed, he wrote to Shura asking if he had any information about how his thesis was being received. Did he perhaps know who might be reading it? In the return post came this: "The thesis committee is a secret and curiosity a feminine and hence despicable quality."

Later that same year, the chair in Chinese economic history was created and Shura decided to hire Rosovsky for the position. That Rosovsky was a Japan specialist who knew nothing about China did not trouble Shura. It had long been Shura's contention that Harvard ought always to hire the smartest scholars without much regard to their expertise. Rosovsky could, he pointed out, learn Chinese. Rosovsky thought the idea was ludicrous and said so. Shura did not give up. Back in Berkeley, Rosovsky's telephone rang. Nitza picked it up and reported to her husband that Gerschenkron had two other Harvard professors, Edwin O. Reischauer and John K. Fairbank, on the line for him. Reischauer and Fairbank were the country's two leading Asia specialists, and Shura had persuaded them to assist in the Rosovsky effort. Rosovsky refused to take the call and did not answer the telephone for ten days. The job was not filled until years later. "One reason I left Harvard and went to Berkeley was that I could not deal with Gerschenkron," Rosovsky says.

In 1960 the Rosovskys came through Cambridge, and Shura invited them to dinner. Now that they had been happily married for five years, he said it was time that he met Nitza. The couple dressed in their best and arrived at Shady Hill Square by taxi, and there was Shura at the door, in something worn and rumpled, kissing Nitza's hand and helping her out of her coat—his opening move in a display of charm and courtesy that lasted all evening. It was a very long evening. Erica was cooking a roast, and at 10:30 p.m. when she opened the oven yet again, her roast remained frozen solid. So they ate scrambled eggs. Outside, it had begun snowing hard and Shura announced that he would take them back to their hotel himself; he said he could drive in the snow better than any cab driver. This turned out to be true everywhere but on bridges. They were crossing the Charles River when the car became stuck. So there was Rosovsky, out in the snowdrifts in his finery, leaning into the bumper, while Shura gunned the motor and shouted out advice on pushing technique. "Henry," Shura said to him when they finally made it to the hotel, "you must call me first thing tomorrow."

The next morning, Shura answered Rosovsky's phone call in mid-thought. "You know, Henry," he said, "I always thought you should have married Eliza." Then he waited for several beats. "Until I met Nitza," he finished.

In 1965 Rosovsky left Berkeley to take a job teaching economics at Harvard. As members of the same faculty, Rosovsky assumed his relationship with Shura might change a little. In some ways he was right. Now that Rosovsky was a professor, Shura banned him from the seminar. In most other respects things were very much as Rosovsky had left them. When Rosovsky began reading Aleksandr Solzhenitsyn's *The First Circle* he told Shura, and then he made the mistake of allowing Shura to know that he was reading the novel in an English translation. As Shura's voice rose, wanting to know how Rosovsky "could understand the regional dialects of the prisoners if you don't read it in Russian?" Rosovsky achieved a different kind of epiphany. He saw that to Shura "I would always be the student, and he would always be the Master."

SHURA'S EARLY HEART ATTACK IN 1958 HAD TAUGHT HIM THAT life is short and every hour precious. Convincing young people in their twenties that the end came soon was not easy, and for much of his life Shura searched for a way to do it. Only in 1976 did the ideal means come to him. While having lunch at the Long Table at the Faculty Club, he began to feel poorly. Excusing himself, he walked through the dining room and out into the main foyer, where he collapsed. By the time the firemen from a nearby station arrived on the scene, his heart had not been beating for several minutes. The firemen began thumping on his chest, and eventually they revived him, breaking a couple of his ribs in the process.

Soon reports began drifting in from Gerschenkron's hospital room that he was spending his recovery working in bed. "He had the day so well organized," recalls his doctor, George Kurland. "In the morning he worked on economics. In the afternoon he read Shakespeare. I never had a patient who worked in bed like that but he did." After he was back to teaching, Shura began bringing his students to the Faculty Club foyer. Pointing to a spot on the floor, he would say, "That's where I died." Once he'd let that settle in, he would push his eyeglasses up onto his forehead and continue. "You know, there was nothing. No beautiful colors. No castles. No bright lights. Nothing. So, if there are things you want to say and do, don't wait. Say them and do them. You won't get the opportunity after you're dead."

Many of the students came to think that he tried to make a lesson out of everything he did. Among Shura's commandments was precision. In one of Richard Sylla's papers, Shura thought that Sylla had used a comma where a semicolon was more appropriate. Sylla was not so sure, and triumphantly produced the grammar book that had recommended use of a comma. A day or two later he received a piece of mail from Gerschenkron. Enclosed was an unequivocally pro-semicolon passage copied from Fowler's *Modern English Usage,* along with a note from Shura that described even Fowler as "much too permissive" and also urged Sylla to "throw away that incompetent book of yours." Sylla remembered that "there was a twinkle in his eye the next time I saw him, but it was very serious to him and he wasn't just thinking about my punctuation. He was striving for a Platonic ideal of excellence in everything he did and he wanted us to be the same way."

SHURA WANTED STUDENTS WHO WERE HUMBLE ABOUT HOW MUCH there was to know and yet urgent in their appetite to understand everything. The more specific wish was for his students to be as serious about scholarship as he was. Almost all of them had Albert Fishlow's experience of thinking they had finished their dissertations long before Shura thought they were done. Many of Shura's students became infected by all this intensity, sometimes to extremes. There were students who learned Greek, Latin, and Japanese as members of the seminar. There were students who taught themselves the most advanced new mathematics. There were students who wrote their entire dissertation in Shura's voice, speaking the words aloud in a Gerschenkron accent as they set them down. There were even several students who bought slide rules and began wearing them around every day in their jacket breast pockets, just as Shura did. What D. N. McCloskey took from this was that "Gerschenkron's theory of teaching was successful at making his students as crazy as he was."

He was inspiring and motivating, and yet there was a painful side. Shura was exhorting his charges to meet ideals which for many of them were unattainable, and when they realized that they could never know as much as he seemed to want them to know, the mutual disappointment could be profound. He was a person with powerful internal complexities, and there were students who foundered on his strident impulses. "He was such an awesome intellect, you had to agree if he told you you didn't measure up," says Robert Zevin. "You weren't learning new languages every two years, conducting disputes with people in different disciplines in different languages like Italian and Hungarian." Zevin eventually left economics for investment banking, a decision Shura told him was "a waste of your intelligence." Years later, when the writings Zevin had done for the seminar were published as a collection of essays, he sent Shura a copy inscribed "With love, affection, respect, and a little regret."

Paul David came to feel the same way, and also, perhaps, a bit resentful. In 1959 David began a thesis on the industrial development of the city of Chicago. He was a member of the seminar and the Workshop, and much interested in Gerschenkron. Gerschenkron, however, showed increasingly tepid concern for him. David was bothered by this phenomenon of a man who had recruited him with such warmth and was now suddenly remote. "There was a kind of come hither, back away," he says. "Drawing people in and then creating distance and suggesting you have to do something to fulfill the teacher's expectations." David was willful. He hated getting up in the morning, and he became celebrated as the one student Gerschenkron bent for; when they met for breakfast, they did so at 7:00 a.m., an hour later than usual.

In 1961 David decided to leave Harvard for Stanford "with my unfinished thesis and the knowledge that he'd responded to Stanford's inquiries about the suitability of my employment by saying he didn't think I was ready." The years passed with no dissertation completed. Occasionally he and Shura corresponded. When David received a letter from Shura that baffled him, he had the temerity to write back and say so. Shura's next communication asserted, "I thought that the meaning of my letter was as clear as a cup of chocolate and I resent the suggestion that it was not." In 1965 David sent Shura an article along with a long letter in which he confessed that he had heard that Shura was in the hospital the year before, but "I could not pen even the simplest lines on a Get Well message. The pain was augmented by the thought that this final involution of my feelings would be taken to mean that I was unconcerned with you, whereas, what I had been wanting to say was the opposite." His own and Shura's expectations for the thesis were, he said, raveling his emotions. He described how he felt at some length, conscious that this was "not the sort of letter you will like to read, from me or from any of the students whose lives, like mine, you have managed to touch. . . . But unless I venture to displease you in this candor, I shall not find it in myself to risk your possible displeasure at the contents of a completed dissertation." At another point that year, David sent in eight hundred pages of "Technical and Statistical Appendices," the quantitative foundations of his thesis on Chicago. In reply, Shura offered no comment except to say he thought it would be better to label the material "Addenda" rather than "Appendices."

In 1967, seven years into his dissertation and now an associate professor at Stanford, David asked Shura if a collection of his published essays might be accepted as a stand-in for the thesis. Shura told him that

> we should stick to Chicago. . . . When finished, it will be a very considerable book, and there is a great danger that if we accept a substitute now the book will never be completed, will be, at best, dissipated in a number of articles, and both you and the scholarly world will be so much poorer for that. It is no doubt dismaying to know that it will take another twenty months before the thesis is completed, but then when we relate the additional delay to the period that has elapsed since the day when a very young and innocent Paul David left Harvard to go out and conquer the Far West, that further delay does not look at all as forbidding as it otherwise would and should.

Two weeks later Shura tried a more conciliatory approach. "There is a Russian peasant saying: 'Never show half of the work to a saphead,'" he told David. "In short, my feeling is that you have advanced so far that you should consider the thesis one and indivisible and eventually a sort of gladness and satisfaction for all."

In 1969 there was still no thesis. Oxford now offered David an appointment, and Stanford's response was to consider David for a full professorship. Stanford solicited Shura's opinion on the matter. He thought back across the past thirteen years and this is what he wrote:

> Paul David has everything a modern economic historian should have. He is an excellent economist, has an abiding interest in economic history, and, above all, has creative ideas. He belongs to the group of three or four magnificent students which it was my good fortune to have had so far at Harvard during the two decades of my connection with the University, and I doubt very much that I can hope to produce anything remotely comparable with that group during my remaining years of active service. I think Stanford will have every reason to be proud of having Paul David on the list of its full professors, and I should like to support the department's proposal for his promotion as strongly and as emphatically as I can.

For several years it was a source of pride for David that he was a full professor at one of the world's best universities, although he held only an undergraduate degree. Shura, however, was unhappy about the situation, and when David came to Harvard one year as a visiting professor, Shura cornered him and extracted a promise that David would organize a series of his essays as a dissertation and then sit through a Ph.D. oral examination which Shura himself would help administer. "He wants to close the books on you," Henry Rosovsky told David. By now, David had begun to wonder what it was about Gerschenkron's personality that led him to have such an intense investment in a student finishing a thesis, but he agreed to the terms and received his degree shortly before he turned forty. The Chicago thesis was never completed.

"Paul may well be the best economic historian of his generation, with a number of classic works to his credit," says Knickerbocker Harley. "But he never finished. Gerschenkron was usually right. A lot does get published too soon. But Gerschenkron did have a lot of students who had difficulty completing things. Nothing was ever quite good enough. It inhibited Paul, and me too, probably."

"His interaction with his students did something for him emotionally," says David. "I had the feeling I was being manipulated. There are lots of powerful models who do that. For me, it pushed me in the opposite direction. But I so admired him that I never quite got into a state of outrage."

As David thought about it, he decided that Shura was paternal with his male students in a way that was "characteristic of the awkwardness between fathers and sons in societies with strong patriarchal traditions. I think it was the sense that relations with him were very complex and charged with the sorts of ambivalences that often complicate families." Shura treated economic history as the family business that he wanted the students to take over for him. He cultivated the students warily and uneasily, hoping that they would bring him honor, and yet always looking to outdo them himself.

Yet that wasn't all of it. Shura was also a lot like the masters from the old British and American schoolboy novels he liked so well, *Tom Brown's School Days*, *The Willoughby Captains*, and *The Lawrenceville Stories*—ferocious men with the souls of kittens. Shura liked to tell his sister Lydia how much "heart and brains" his students had. "He was so proud of them," she says. And when a professor at Yale asked him to evaluate the virtues of his students for a possible job offer, he did his best and then gave up, explaining, "Who can presume to compare the creatures of the Lord?" Beyond the stern veneer, Shura was really on their side all along. They were all his boys. In his old age he even told one of them so. When Peter McClelland finally left Harvard for Cornell, Shura wrote him a letter. "Dear Peter," he said. "The school year has started, and it makes me wistful after all those years. . . . I do miss you."

*　　*　　*

SHURA'S THEORY OF BACKWARDNESS MADE HIM FAMOUS, BUT HIS most glorious legacy is probably his students. "As I get older," says D. N. McCloskey, "more and more of my life is a scholarly imitation of his." They are all like that in some way or another, right down to the bottle of Rémy Martin V.S.O.P. cognac Henry Rosovsky keeps in his lower right desk drawer. Most of them would agree with Gianni Toniolo, who says that after he came to the United States from Italy just so he could study under Shura, "he changed my life." When he left Rome, Toniolo had his degree and a generous job offer from the Bank of Italy that he'd nearly accepted. "But I decided that being an intellectual would be more fulfilling, and, to this day, I still wonder every month when my check comes why I'm being paid to do this because I'm so very happy."

Shura produced an extraordinary succession of successful students who are now among the most prominent and influential economic historians of our time. Gerschenkron students have held appointments at Yale, Harvard, Stanford, the University of Pennsylvania, Cornell, Duke, the University of Chicago, and Oxford, among dozens of other fine universities. Shelves in libraries are crowded with large works written by students of Gerschenkron analyzing the modern economic consequences of historical evils like slavery in the United States and colonial repression in Latin America. "He trained as much of the new generation of economic historians as all the others put together," said the economist Otto Eckstein.

What no doubt would make Shura happier still is that today students of Gerschenkron's students are telling Gerschenkron stories. One of them is Charles Calomiris, who studied with Paul David at Stanford and now is a professor of finance and economics at Columbia University. "I never met Gerschenkron," he says, "but people still talk about his seminar, how exciting it was, and how exciting he was. He was a magnetic personality, and what you always come away understanding when you've heard someone like Paul David tell you about him is that it wasn't so much what he published, but who he was."

ELEVEN

A PRISONER OF HIS ERUDITION

Suppose we turn from outside estimates of a man, to wonder, with keener interest, what is the report of his own consciousness about his doings or capacity: with what hindrances he is carrying on his daily labours; what fading of hopes, or what deeper fixity of self-delusion the years are marking off within him; and with what spirit he wrestles against universal pressure, which will one day be too heavy for him and bring his heart to its final pause.

George Eliot, *Middlemarch*

THE LONGER SHE LIVED IN CAMBRIDGE, THE MORE UNHAPPY Erica became. One morning in 1955, as she leaned over Heidi's pillow to get her up for school, Erica suddenly let out a shriek and staggered out of the room. She had torn a ligament in her back, an injury that kept her in bed for the next full year. Some people had the impression that she was more content as an invalid, that it suited her state of mind in this country, where she always felt so alien and impaired. Even after she finally recovered, she remained subsumed by woe. For the rest of her life the house was littered with her heating pads. She refused to throw even the broken ones away. They were souvenirs of her sufferings, and they turned up everywhere, the way stray tumblers do in the home of a drinker.

Perhaps because Erica was so wretched herself, she was often brusque with other people. If a friend who hadn't seen her in a while rushed up, calling out greetings and clasping her hand, Erica would let out a low cry and moan, "Oh, you've hurt me," as she drew back her hand and cradled her fingers to her face. Encountering a little boy on the sidewalk who wheezed, Erica snapped at the boy's mother, "Do something about that." When she passed shaggy college couples in the late 1960s, she was prone to remarking loudly, "I can't tell them apart." Erica had very few friends, but there were people who made an effort to know her and came to find her manner amusing. "I was fond of her because she was so consistently difficult," says Jane Williams, Erica and Shura's next-door neighbor on Shady Hill Square. "It was who she was."

Erica was sometimes drawn to delinquent children. One year in Cambridge, gangs of kids from a nearby housing project took to wandering through Shady Hill Square, where they stole things and made petty mischief. Most residents gave them a wide berth, preferring to call the police and let them handle the situation. Erica befriended some of the troublemakers, played with them, invited them into her kitchen for cake, and paid them for the little jobs she thought up for them to do.

She was a person who truly did not care what other people thought of her. Even in her late sixties, she wore girlish dirndls all summer long, except for the occasional July or August New Hampshire day when she emerged from her house in a thick gray wool dress. One of her summer pastimes was planting wild strawberries and rose bushes. Another was taking her broom into the woods near the house and sweeping up the forest floor. She also maintained a policy of dragooning just about anyone who came within range to help her with chores. Guests would arrive for dinner or tea, and before they'd so much as shrugged their coats off, she had them lugging old furniture up from the basement, cutting fallen tree limbs into small pieces, wrestling with stuck storm windows, splitting firewood, moving that bureau into the next room, assisting in the flower beds, or driving her garbage off to the dump. Once a job was done, she welcomed "my helper" back in with Viennese tea cakes, although what she really considered to be her side of these transactions was permitting others to sun themselves in the company of the fascinating Gerschenkrons. Shura positioned himself as a slightly bemused observer to all of this. He sent off letters to Vienna detailing how "Erica tried to make New Hampshire into an Austrian garden. When guests would come she forced them to saw and chop."

It was an irony that Shura, raised in Russia's haute bourgeoisie with nannies and a French governess, should find himself in America hobnobbing cheerfully with shipyard workers in California and janitors at Harvard; while Erica, brought up by members of Austria's progressive intelligentsia, surrounded by Social Democrats fighting for a better life for laboring people, should have become a snob. She had little compunction about asking Francestown locals to do her menial favors. Then, when they came inside for refreshment, Erica might begin a conversation with someone else in the room in French.

Erica treated her children as her drudges. "The girls washed the floors, the girls washed the clothes, the girls prepared the food," says Lydia. "The girls did everything. Erica had a kind of inertia. She was always lying down." Erica did things to both her daughters that made her seem like a fairy tale stepmother. The Shady Hill Square house was always so packed with her pills and creams and ointments and salves that it was impossible to think of Erica's name without seeing it typed on the side of a pharmacy bottle. Yet the children's colds and flus and feminine discomforts were dismissed by their mother as "nothing." Heidi once had an allergic reaction to some aspirin at school and lapsed into anaphylactic shock. Her mother's response to a frantic telephone call from the school was to say, "Call her a taxi."

Susi grew up to become a psychologist and Heidi a teacher. When the girls were visiting their parents, Erica took frequent opportunity to find fault with psychologists and teachers. Each daughter married young. At twenty-five, Susi eloped with Anthony Wiener while her parents were away in Europe. Heidi was a college senior when she became engaged to Donald Dawidoff, who had left both college and law school after mental breakdowns. Heidi's marriage lasted seven years. Then her husband fell apart and she became a twenty-eight-year-old single mother working full-time to support two young children on a teaching salary of $4,000 a year. Erica took to making derisive remarks about "divorced women." Years later, Shura praised Heidi for raising decent children and teaching well. "You've had such a hard time, with so much struggle, and you're doing such a beautiful job." Erica, in another room, overheard. "What's so hard about it?" she called out. Nobody would insist that Erica was an evil person. Consumed with her own miseries, she was oblivious to the degree of pain she inflicted upon others. "Erica was such a child herself that as a mother she had nothing to give to her children," says Marjorie Galenson.

Shura rarely saw the way his wife mistreated his children. In part that was because Erica was careful. Around him she did not often criticize Susi and Heidi. Instead, she referred to her old friends the Bettelheims as she critiqued other people's methods of child rearing, making searching, thoughtful remarks about "the child's needs" and "what's good for the child." Inevitably, every mother she brought up in conversation was found wanting as a parent.

Erica could be hard on Shura too. They had a very different sense of aesthetics. While Erica favored clean, modernist Scandinavian lines, Shura preferred a busier decorative style. His wife jabbed at his "bad taste" for liking Victorian furnishings, pretty little music boxes, and porcelain painted with English roses. Because she never learned to keep track of bills, he handled all of their finances, with the result that he was sometimes paying too much, too little, too late, or not at all. Then he was forced to write apologetic letters to his creditors confessing that "I have been so overwhelmed that I just did not get around to attending to my bills." Household crises were also beyond Erica's capacities, and since they lived in an old house, he was always coming home from work to discover that the pipes had burst or the ceiling had fallen in. Then he'd be scrambling, calling around to find an expert who was available to make emergency repairs. He never made a fuss about any of this, and he expected his children to be the same way.

Shura always spoke of Erica as he'd long ago decided to see her, as an ideal woman. One component of the role was being a perfect mother, and so, as far as he was concerned, that was what she was. "I'd hear about how Susi had passed an exam or that Heidi had done this," says Lydia. "He always said they'd turned out so well and it was all due to Erica. She was such a wonderful mother. I don't think he thought that. He just said it. He said those things to boost Erica and make himself worthy of her. That was how he'd put it. He'd say, 'Erica, am I worthy of you?' It would upset Heidi terribly. Erica would beam and say, 'Maybe you are.' Why he did this is too deep for me."

Shura once confessed that "the only thing I would not like in this world is to outlive Erica." As for how anybody else felt about his wife, Shura did not appear to care. He was a determined enough man that, no matter what she did, he could maintain loyalty to an attractive private version of her. While writing to a friend after a heavy New Hampshire snowfall, he looked out of the window and noticed his sixty-six-year-old wife crossing a field on skis. "She looks like a very young girl," he wrote. "An optical illusion, obviously, but very pleasant." From the first, he had loved her as the beautiful, brilliant student who had regarded him with steady schoolroom contempt, and he would always proclaim that she was the same girl she'd been at sixteen. It was the most absorbing attachment anyone who knew Erica and Shura had ever seen. "I always thought that they had an eternal love affair," Simon Kuznets's daughter Judy Stein said. "They were obviously totally involved with each other, so much that it would have been hard to grow up with. All of her energy was expended upon him. He did have energy to spare for other people. He was charming, funny, and giving, but she did not have it, and with her he was completely involved. If you are that involved with each other, you are not involved with your children, and their children had a hard time."

Shura once said in a letter that he believed that "any marriage is a complicated and risky thing and I have always harbored the suspicion that most so-called happy marriages are only proof that human nature can adapt to anything. These people live in a constant state of lying to themselves but not nobly so. The few really happy marriages are a miracle which cannot be predicted before or explained afterwards." Was he thinking of his marriage as a miracle? This much is certain: he was passionate about his wife and enjoyed having such a formidable intellectual rival in the house. Whether he was bothered that she did not have a fulfilling professional career he never said. Without question he felt sorry for his thwarted wife, felt that his own source of happiness—the United States—caused her misery. That is probably why he allowed her to live as a sort of kept feminist. "Shura knew his own mother could cook, take care of the kids, keep the house in ship-shape, keep everything ironed, ready and clean," says Lydia. "One day he said to Erica, 'My mother could do it singlehanded.' Erica said, 'If your mother wants to lower herself to do that sort of thing, that's her business.' That was the one time Shura spoke that way to her."

Instead of offering Erica reproofs, he protected her. Erica even called him "Vati" (father), while he referred to her as "Pootsie" (little baby). In 1954 he sent a letter to Heidi from Rome that said, "You might try to write particularly pleasant letters to Mama. . . . If you want to bitch, put that into your letters to me. I'll be glad to read them and I'll bitch back. But do write regularly to both of us." Lydia says that "his shout to Susi and Heidi was always 'Help your mother. Help your mother.'" If Erica said something inaccurate in conversation and some-one—a son-in-law, a grandson—pointed this out, it appealed to Shura's notions of chivalry to take the person aside and caution: "Look here. You must not criticize Erica. In this house Erica is always right." The faces of whomever he was rebuking would grow scarlet with frustra-tion, but that was it.

SHURA WAS A COMPLICATED PARENT—PROUD, LOVING, WATCHFUL, and ambitious. From the first, he embraced the idea of having a loving pair of daughters gathered around him, and he was reluctant to share them with the world. He liked doing things with Susi and Heidi. With them he listened to the Red Sox on the radio, tried to buy them banana splits at diners—his success with his daughters was no better than with his students—and he carried a red taffeta dress home from abroad for Heidi to wear to dancing class. Heidi liked to read movie magazines. Every time Shura saw her with them, he would ask, "Why do you read such trash?" He did take her to what he considered serious and artistic films. In 1950 the whole family settled into seats at the Kenmore The-ater in Boston and sat through three consecutive showings of *The Philadelphia Story*. In the movie, Seth Lord (played by John Halliday) tells his daughter Tracy (played by Katharine Hepburn) that "the best mainstay a man can have as he gets along in years is a daughter . . . of his own, full of warmth for him, full of foolish, unquestioning, uncritical affection." When the Gerschenkrons finally emerged from the theater, Shura stopped on the sidewalk and sharply criticized Lord, saying that he had never hoped for daughters like that. He looked at Heidi and Susi and told them that he wanted them to challenge him, to be independent-minded, to stand up to him, to surprise him with their individuality.

A year later, Heidi was thirteen and spending a New Hampshire summer sick with polio. For weeks Shura read her short stories by Chekhov every evening. One day he came home from a trip to Peter-borough, stomped loudly up the stairs, strode into her room, threw down three movie magazines on the bed, turned around, and left. "It was special because he didn't approve," Heidi says. "He thought movie magazines were trash. I think he thought God would reward him with my recovery if he sacrificed his standards during this emergency in order to please his child." At Christmas that year, his present to her was *A Pictorial History of the Movies,* which Heidi considered "a touching sacrifice of principle for love."

Many fathers have trouble getting used to the idea of their daughters going out with men. Most eventually get over it. Shura never did. "He was so proud of having smart, pretty daughters, and he wanted them all to himself," says Heidi. "He was not happy to see us grow up and want to get married. There was hardly anybody he was happy to see us go out with. He was just so unfriendly at the door, and unfriendly in the way he called me to the phone when boys called. When Susi married while my parents were away, he flew into a rage. Before he left, he had told her to have nothing more to do with Tony. Now there wasn't anything he could do about it."

In other ways he was a nurturing parent. Heidi was very smart but not particularly confident, and from early on her father set out to encourage her. "He saw a lot in me when I didn't see a lot in myself," she says. He was working to a purpose; he had hopes for her career. "He was eager for his daughters to be like him," she says. "My sister felt pressured by him, but with me maybe he'd adjusted because I only felt encouraged. He gave me confidence academically and professionally. He motivated me and he pushed me."

Two years after Heidi got married she began the doctoral program in English literature at Columbia University. Shura was more excited about this than Heidi, who was already pregnant, eager to raise a fam-ily, and not so sure she wanted to spend years toiling in the library. "My sister and I felt he was pushing us to do the things with our lives that he had done with his life," she says. "He definitely wanted us to have careers and to have them come first. We did have careers. But neither of us wanted them to come first. It was very pointed with him. He didn't want us to be like his wife, although he made it possible for my mother to be the way she was—pampered, helpless, and immature. He didn't want that for us."

And yet after Heidi enrolled at Columbia, Shura did not talk with her about her instructors anymore. Those sorts of inquiries had, in fact, stopped years before. As soon as she entered college, Shura had begun treating his daughter the way he treated all of his promising students; her writing became *her* business. She wrote an undergraduate thesis and then began a doctoral dissertation, but Shura never read or asked about any of it.

SHURA'S OWN WRITING EXCITED HIGHLY ENTHUSIASTIC REACTIONS among professional readers. After the collection of essays *Economic Backwardness in Historical Perspective* was published in 1962, Charles Kindleberger's sprig of praises in the *Journal of Economic History* referred to "an intellectual feast of rich provender by the doyen of economic history in the United States." Equally fragrant words came from Holland Hunter in the *Russian Review*, applauding the "awesome range of concerns, combining earthly knowledge with detached ideals, amusing and devastating criticism with an almost romantic warmth and nobility of spirit." A great many more such nosegays were scattered across publications of interest general—the *New York Review of Books*— and particular—*Economica*—and collectively they created a little celebration of Shura's talents.

It was almost a debut. Shura had published essays every year, but few people were aware of them. That was because he seemed to take a perverse pride in contributing to periodicals read by nobody but experts. Such "honor," according to Goran Ohlin, did Shura place "in publishing in the most obscure scientific journals," that over the long bookless years Gerschenkron admirers began to treat prose sightings the way lepidopterists react to the spotting of an uncommon *Lycaeides*. Gerschenkron aficionados were themselves quite rare, so much so that they considered Shura to be, in a sense, their secret—something in their private collection.

Shura wrote very much the way he ate. At the table he enjoyed rich foods like fish eggs, liverwurst, sour cream, blackened sausages, hazelnut extracts, and soft, runny cheeses that smelled like the bogs. His paragraphs were just as intensely flavored; he compressed them into lush little fillets teeming with ideas and knowledge. The title essay in *Economic Backwardness in Historical Perspective* is typical, a twenty-five-page tour of Western culture in miniature. Among the spectacular bounty of thinkers Shura refers to are Seneca, Marx, Veblen, Keynes, Goethe, Saint-Simon, Arnold Toynbee, Bertrand Russell, Friedrich List, Émile Zola, John Stuart Mill, Auguste Compte, John Bright, H. T. Buckle, Matthew Arnold, Peter Struve, Thomas Malthus, and David Ricardo. There is even a cameo from Rouget de Lisle, the composer of "La Marseillaise"—as well as the nonchalant disclosure that Saint-Simon induced Rouget de Lisle to prepare an "Industrial Marseillaise." A similarly luxurious atlas of countries flashes by: the economies of Germany, Russia, England, France, Austria, Italy, Hungary, Switzerland, Denmark, Mexico, and the United States are all discussed with crisp authority. (In a footnote, the author regrets his lack of expertise in matters Japanese.)

Almost everything Shura wrote featured such exuberant displays of erudition. He was prone to offhand remarks about Polichinelle and La Palice, and could not resist garnishing his thoughts on dictatorship with Theodor Gomperz's detection of "a curious Machiavellian tone" in Aristotle's *Politics*. Within the very first two paragraphs of *An Economic Spurt That Failed*, his slim 1977 book on turn-of-the-century Austrian economic policy, there are quotations from Kipling, Ibsen, Plutarch, and Samuel Smiles, as well as a little Latin. There was almost always a little Latin, unless there was a little Greek or a little German or a little Russian or a little French or a little Italian; he had a penchant for foreign frissons. There was not, however, a corresponding bent for translating them. Any reader who was baffled by phrases like *nec unquam satis fida potentia, ubi nimia est*, or who looked quizzically at a passing reference to Otto Ludwig's *Erbforster*, was left to his own devices. Some Princeton students whose professor assigned them

Shura's books responded by preparing a trot they called "A Guide to Gerschenkron: The Latin Glossary."

There was something curious about publishing portions of books in languages most readers wouldn't know, and perhaps something assertive about it too. In a way it was showing off, just as sprinkling in all those erudite references was showing off. But in another sense it was a way for Shura to obscure himself. That could also be said about Shura's proclivity for publishing his writing in rarefied places. The effect was that he was different, he was elsewhere, he was unseen; he wasn't competing.

Broader exposures were available to him. Editors from national magazines frequently tried to assign Shura essays and articles and he waved them all away. Among the many publications he turned down were *Esquire*, the *New Republic*, and the *New York Times Magazine*. When Francis Brown, the editor of the *New York Times Book Review*, asked Shura to do some work for him, Shura astounded Brown by telling him, with some annoyance, that he had no time for an "extra-curricular activity." Book publishers were likewise brushed off, among them Alfred A. Knopf, who ran among the most prestigious imprints in the business. In 1961 Knopf invited Shura to have lunch with him in Cambridge. Writing to Knopf's secretary in reply, Shura, sounding somewhat irritable, said that "I am afraid I cannot accept. It so happens that this is the beginning of the term in the University, which is always a busy time of year. Nevertheless, if Mr. Knopf has something on his mind which he would like to discuss with me, I may be able to make an appointment for him to see me in my office."

An economist once walked into that office, had a look at the stacks of reading material covering every available cranny of wall, desk, and floor, and observed, "Ah, I get it—high capital to output ratio." That must have smarted, because there was no talking around it, Shura was a long time between books. After *Bread and Democracy in Germany* was published in 1943, nineteen years passed before his next work, *Economic Backwardness in Historical Perspective*, finally appeared. In later years he would publish two collections of his lectures and another volume of essays. What never came was something longer.

Therein lay the rub that vexed Shura's professional life. The Big

Book—"Za Beeg Buke," as it came out in the Gerschenkron elocution—was Shura's El Dorado, his holy grail, the pot of coins at the end of the great scholarly rainbow. He goaded his students to complete "a large literary work," making them feel that they were nothing until they did. Meanwhile, he never published one himself.

SHURA ALWAYS APPEARED DESTINED TO TAKE ON A LARGE AND important subject and write about it with such originality and freshness of purpose that the subject became, in a sense, his. Such a work was so much the logical thing to expect from Shura, who knew and loved books better than just about anyone, that, as he grew older, people speculated about when Gerschenkron would at last unveil his masterpiece. There were rumors that after years of careful construction behind drawn shades and locked doors it was nearly done. Unconfirmed reports said Shura had created a polished intellectual gemstone, a work of scholarly perfection. After a while, when nothing seemed to be forthcoming, people wondered what had gone wrong. "I don't know what happened to him," says Albert Hirschman. The backs of a few hands began to conceal whispers that Gerschenkron was "a dilettante." He was, everyone agreed, a brilliant man and a spellbinding talker, "But, you know, he's never produced that big book."

Over the years there were always large-scale projects Shura was working on. Among them was the history of European industrialization he'd made motions toward writing in the early 1950s. Then came a flirtation with an economic history of Italy, followed by his more serious dalliance with an economic history of Russia. The prospects of such a book written by Gerschenkron, the great Russian-born economic historian, led publishers to write him frequently over the years, each of them eager to know how the book was going.

It was going sideways. In 1950 he confessed to an editor that the project had "deflected somewhat from the path of straightforwardness." Nineteen years later, when Shura was sixty-five, he wrote to his friend the Cambridge University economic historian Munia Postan of his future plans: "I shall finish—God knows when—the economic history of Russia. I must then write a book on economic history and belles

lettres. As Tolstoy used to say, there is work for twenty years, but . . ."
Six years after that he was informing his old student, the future librarian of Congress James Billington, that he was poised to embark upon a new project "the idea of which has been on my mind for a fair number of years. The name of the project is 'Time Horizon in Economic History.' . . . Time horizon refers to the willingness and ability of people who make economic decisions to look into the future." Only a year later, however, when Shura spoke with the *New York Times*, the horizon was dim. "Whether I'll be able to swing it is an open question," he said. He did not swing it, just as he did not swing any of them.

SHURA'S THEORY OF THE ADVANTAGES OF BACKWARDNESS WAS such an original insight into the origins of economic growth that a lengthy study by Gerschenkron on that topic alone would have been a seminal contribution to the field. Shura's "approach" has implications that carry well beyond the channels of economic history. Something called "The Advantages of Backwardness" could have integrated philosophy, psychology, history, literature, and even linguistics into a consideration of how generations of citizens had contended with adverse circumstances. Here was a way for him to reconcile his many interests and lend them focus, a vehicle for him to present his vision of human nature struggling against the nature of the world. Here he could select a fictional character like Dostoyevsky's Gambler, who scorns the ruthlessly systematic German way of doing business ("I shall not worship the German method of accumulating riches," cries the Gambler. "I prefer to squander riotously à la russe or to get rich through the roulette"), and pair the literary reference with more traditional economic sources to support his belief that a native loathing for discipline made nineteenth-century Russians reluctant to embrace the codes of conformity that are necessary for industrial progress. Through the varied experiences of farmers, bankers, insurance men, shop owners, tax collectors, lords, serfs, thieves, touts, and kings, Shura had the means of revealing the complicated story of relative commercial progress: the regional customs, the national attitudes, the problems of geography, climate, resources, and a thousand other variables that explain why the

Russian industrial experience differs from the German, the Italian, the British, the Austrian, the Dutch, and the French. What he really would have been describing is the divergent progress of men. For Shura, whose very autobiography was called "The Uses of Adversity," backwardness was a subject ideally suited to express his most abiding intellectual interests and scholarly concerns.

He never mentioned even the possibility of such a book. Still, the broad cultural exploration of his greatest idea must have occurred to him. How else to explain his preoccupation with time horizons? In his letter to James Billington, he says that "the problem of time horizon transcends the economic aspects thereof and extends to very broad problems which may be called philosophical. . . . Time horizon covers man's attitude to the length of his life span and accordingly to death and the succeeding generations." Time horizon was economics as a window into the human sensibility—a measure of the ability of different men to look beyond their present and envision something better. Shura believed that backward people have low time horizons and small expectations for the future. Their life is in the moment. He thought that progressive men, by contrast, have their eyes on the distance. As perceptive as this observation may be, it serves as only a single filament within a larger body of inquiry—one means among many of pondering the questions Shura asked throughout his professional life: Why have some men lived better than others? How did those who lived less well feel about their circumstances? What did they do to change them?

Shura had resources, energy, skill, ambition, and pride. His expectations for himself were the same ones others had for him. So why didn't he do it? Why does a man of great talent fail to accomplish the one thing in life he seems to aspire to above all others? Among his many problems was that he knew too much.

SHURA WORKED LIKE A DOOMED MAN, AND THAT IS HOW HE FELT. Not only had political repression in Austria cost him his professional youth, but a doctor had told him in 1958 he had only two years to live. It's no surprise that the subject of time horizons interested him because his own limited future was a source of distressed preoccupation. When friends recommended books to him, he pressed them to be sure they were really good, because "I have only so much time left and I don't want to waste it." Most people catch their breath and loosen their imaginations while taking short train rides, waiting in lines at the bank, standing on street corners, or convalescing in bed. Not Shura; he was always reading and taking notes. Traveling companions noticed that even when Shura walked into public rest rooms he always had his face in a book, as he still did when he emerged, two minutes and one page later.

Nothing interfered with Shura's work. His colorful hobbies added to his reputation and brought him pleasure, but none of them—not even chess—took up much of his time. Universities, foundations, and organizations were always sending him invitations to speak and attend, which he turned aside like a man of means putting off favor seekers. "Pedagogical pleasure trips are not for me," he told a former student, the Yale economic historian Bill Parker.

It was not only because of his heightened sense of mortality that these invitations did not interest Shura. Convivial professional gatherings and mainstream publishing did not fit within the Gerschenkron rubric of serious scholarship. Heidi describes her father as someone who "limited himself in what he could do because he held himself compulsively to the most rigorous scholarly standards." He was an intellectual Trappist, a man who took his responsibilities to the scholarly life so seriously that he implied that taking a break—or placing his prose in a widely read medium—would compromise his intellectual integrity.

Shura extended this self-imposed charge to be the model and keeper of the standards of the scholarly community to dramatic extremes. Not only did he scuttle most candidates for Harvard economics department positions, he stalked talent like a particularly motivated bloodhound. (Simon Kuznets and Abe Bergson were two of the scholars he brought to Harvard; his greatest recruiting disappointment was that Paul Samuelson always remained at M.I.T.) Shura was the only member of the economics department who reacted to Hendrik Houthakker's announcement that he was leaving Harvard and scholarship to go to work for the Council of Economic Advisers by telling Houthakker that he had disgraced himself. "It's like taking your pants down in Harvard Square," Shura said to him.

Yet, much to his distress, Shura was not above secular temptation himself. When he gave in to his desires, forsook economic history for a while, and wrote about Shakespeare or Nabokov, he was overcome with shame. Both he and Heidi were fans of Flaubert's *Bouvard and Pécuchet*, to which the author attached a satirical *Dictionary of Received Ideas*. After Heidi became a teacher, she and her father decided to compile a dictionary of received ideas held mutually by their students. "I hope you do not disapprove of this little bit of irresponsible fun," Shura wrote guiltily to his friend, the historian Franco Venturi. "I find it enjoyable to write something jointly with a daughter of mine." After one of his economic history students read the *Hamlet* essay and sent him an admiring letter, Shura wrote back fast. "You will not get any literary escapades out of me for a long time," he told the student. "From now on I shall keep my nose to the grindstone. Thus there is no cause for alarm."

The same sense of obligation to the profession also led him to spend a great deal of time producing lengthy reviews of terrible books. In a letter to Sylvia Thrupp at the University of Michigan, he described writing his critique of Elizabeth Beyerly's *The Europecentric Historiography of Russia*, telling Thrupp of the "weeks and weeks" it took him to "study the book and to write the review. The book is an unbelievable concoction, arrogant and ignorant and incompetently published to boot. But a long critical review had to be written so that the author knows and also other people know that you cannot get away with superficialities, misinformation, and horrible inaccuracies of this sort." This line of thinking baffled Paul Samuelson, who felt Shura was wasting his time. Samuelson remembers the day Shura proudly told him that he had "just annihilated at length an incompetent book by a Soviet historian." Samuelson asked him, "Why, Alex, did you spend the time to do that job so thoroughly?" To such questions Shura always replied that writing books is a serious business and people who produce something not serious "need to be punished." He saw himself as a scholarly Ivanhoe, striking out to defend the ideals of his community. To many it seemed an empty victory, Ivanhoe killing off paper knights while his own book languished unwritten.

Any man who positions himself as the custodian of lofty standards is going to have some concern about meeting them himself. Shura thrived on winning debates, but he hated to be criticized, and some people who knew him think that he never wrote a big book because he feared he couldn't do it well enough. Many writers experience a crippling addiction to admiration, a condition that is close cousin to a paralyzing fear of rejection. Some of Shura's peers speculated that for Gerschenkron it was more comfortable to do what he knew he could do uncommonly well than to strike out and try something difficult, time-consuming, and uncertain. If he had written a book that somehow failed to meet his expectations, he wouldn't have been a model anymore.

It's also true that he was comfortable writing short pieces. Like his friend Isaiah Berlin, who never wrote a big book either, Shura was an essayist by instinct. Writing at concise length guaranteed that he would finish what he began, an important consideration for someone who thought every day might be his last. The essay also fit his nature, which was, as he told his sister, "to crystalize something to the essence of it." He enjoyed conceptualizing an intellectual problem and then teasing out the causal forces and their consequences.

The Gerschenkron essays, what Shura referred to as his "contributions to the field," make an impressive collection. Among them is the hundred-page chapter on "Agrarian Policies and Industrialization in Russia 1861–1917," which he wrote in 1965 for the *Cambridge Economic History of Europe*. This is a meditation on Russia's economic history from the emancipation of the serfs to the Stolypin reforms, which explains in detail why cultural and political backwardness retarded economic growth. Adam Ulam called it "a masterpiece of scholarship. He knew more about it than anybody else. Fastidious detail." Walt Rostow, Shura's old whipping boy, read the chapter and wrote Shura to say that he had produced a "remarkable" piece of work. "I don't know when I've enjoyed an essay more." Thirty-five years after Shura published the essay, the Russian historian Daniel Field says that "[Gerschenkron's] work on Russia's pre-revolutionary agrarian policies is still unmatched."

"Agrarian Policies" became the centerpiece of *Continuity in History and Other Essays*, Shura's second collection of essays. *Continuity* emerged as a worthy companion volume to *Backwardness*. They are both exemplars of serious intellectual inquiry on a variety of subjects that embrace a uniform intellectual outlook. Even so, for anyone who knew Shura, there is something vaguely disappointing about these books. In conversation he could be dynamic, forceful, witty, and creative. Between covers he is so self-consciously restrained that his personality is reduced. He concentrates on a problem of history or on one of historical method and burns it down to the essence of what he wants to say, using facts that are beyond reproach, arguments that are laid out with scientific care, and prose that is always clear and sometimes lively. "I've always felt the books are good, but they don't quite capture the richness of his mind," says Dwight Perkins.

Perhaps it was his vast fund of knowledge that functioned as the impediment. For all of his extreme work habits, Shura was undisciplined. So much in the world engaged his curiosity that he was always wandering off the trail to make private studies of symbolist poetry or Venetian epigrams. He was a man who could say in a letter that "there is, incidentally, considerable similarity between some Italian and Russian proverbs, particularly with reference to poverty and wealth." Knowing such things made him unusual, but it also made him a man with limited time for big projects. Long books are written by patient people. Shura was, at heart, the owner of a restless mind—an intellectual skylark. He didn't want to focus, he wanted to explore, so much that he had to force himself down to produce even an essay. The scholar of the Renaissance Walter Kaiser thinks that because Shura's mind "was so wide-ranging and acquisitive," he made a conscious choice to avoid committing himself to "some huge book." With all those intriguing things out there to know about, Kaiser speculates that spending years on one idea might have demoralized Shura.

It wasn't only his curiosity that affected his writing. Since nobody knows everything about anything, there is a way in which any attempt to write definitively on a subject is inherently brazen. This fact doesn't constrain most writers, but Shura could never quite get over his inability to be an authentic master of his material. He proclaimed "the basic article in the scholar's code" to be—as he paraphrased it from Wittgenstein—"What I do not know, I must remain silent about," and he routinely began guest lectures by confessing his "considerable uncertainty and uneasiness" about commenting at all upon his subject. This was true even when he was talking about something like *Doctor Zhivago* or European industrial development, things about which he was an acknowledged expert. In 1956, when the Senate Committee on Foreign Relations asked him to write them a memo on Soviet industrialization, he said he would do it as long as the senators promised to keep his remarks out of the public record, because they were "so conjectural and uncertain." The committee chairman, Hubert Humphrey, received Shura's report and was so pleased with it that he wrote Shura a letter urging him to reconsider his terms. Shura refused, explaining that, although he had spent ten years studying the subject, he was "reluctant" because he did not have the "requisite competence." Then he said that the only reason that he had sent in anything at all was that he had considered it his "public duty" to do so.

He was, in the words of Peter McClelland, "a prisoner of his erudition." In the spring of 1969, at the end of his year in residence at the Institute for Advanced Study in Princeton, Shura wrote a letter to the director Carl Kaysen, describing the way he'd spent his time. "I did not," he said to Kaysen,

> read the 150 "must" books and articles that are still on my list, and which would have transformed me into a well-educated man thoroughly informed of the recent accretions to the literature in economics and economic history. Nor did I advance my work on the economic history of Russia (which, when eventually completed, will make further work on the subject unnecessary) beyond some work on the chapter on foreign trade. But I did do some reading, the most important among which was working through a book on econometrics and perusal of the seven volumes of letters by Turgenev. My ambition to have read through all of the diaries of the Goncourts was frustrated, as I did not read more than the first volume. The least important thing I have read during the period was the volume by Holroyd on Lytton Strachey, which you so kindly and so unnecessarily lent me.

With Shura, nothing got in the way of what always came first for him—his reading. If Shura had ever really come out and admitted it, he would have said that what made him special was that he'd read more books and got more out of them than other people. Much as he may have intended to be an Archilochean hedgehog, to master one big thing, he was by instinct a fox with an insatiable desire to know many things. Within the stacks of Widener Library he behaved the way the novelist Thomas Wolfe said he had done during his own years in Cambridge, "like some damned soul, never at rest—ever leaping ahead from the pages I read to thoughts of those I want to read." Shura finished entire volumes while standing in Cambridge bookshops, read hundreds of pages while seated in the Widener men's room, and sometimes failed to step off the curb because he was about to finish a chapter. "His relation to the book was one of the more extraordinary things I have ever seen," says Walter Kaiser. "He couldn't go anywhere without four or five books. I had a friend who was having lunch with him in Harvard Square. The only thing they were going to do was go out the Widener door, cross the street, go to the restaurant, have lunch, and go back across the street to Widener. When my friend arrived to pick Alex up, Alex got up, stuffed a book or two in each pocket, took two more in his hands and said, 'Okay, let's go.'"

Shura told Oscar Handlin that it was his ambition someday to read all three million books in Widener Library. The fact that he'd made some honest calculations with a pencil and knew he could get through only 100 to 110 books a year tormented him. He kept lists of the writers whose titles he finished. "Hegel, Saint-Exupéry, Hobbes, Swift, Catullus, Goldsmith, Anatole France, Cowper, Calvino, Turgenev, George Eliot, Gide, Mallarmé, Blake, Ibsen, John Clare" occupied part of a typical stretch of notation. When his choices were slightly less ambitious, he berated himself for sacrificing his time to mediocrity, and then he fell into ever-deeper ennui as he thought back on all the dreadful things he'd read in his life. In an essay he wrote for the *American Scholar* that he called "On Reading Books: A Barbarian's Cogitations," he flayed himself for his literary debaucheries: "Why did I not follow a careful program? Why did I give free reign to my curiosity? Why did I

allow myself to engage in those wild sprees of desultory and promiscu-
ous reading? Why did I not limit myself to strictly *good* books?"

All the reading sated Shura's need to know. But much of what he
read was great fiction, books that were filled with ideas rather than
scholarly facts. "I was always struck that he was always reading novels,"
says Paul David. "He read Calvino's *Baron in the Trees,* and it really captured his imagination and he wanted to tell me all about it." He was the
same way with other new literary discoveries. When he read the works
of Nadezhda Mandelstam, he was ecstatic, proclaiming that he had "the
greatest possible admiration for the author, for her magnificent use of
the language, for her incisive mind, and above all for her courage." Of
War and Peace he said that "on every perusal I never fail to discover
something new in this inexhaustible store of observations, insights,
ideas, and images that the previous readings have failed to reveal."
Another time, speaking of the same book, which he may well have read
more than twenty times, he said, "You still find new things every time
and experience the enjoyment of gliding along that enchanted stream."

By reading a volume of Tolstoy, Shura was giving way to something
more powerful than the expectation of being educated or entertained.
He could open himself up in a personal way to the men and women he
encountered in books. Characters like Pierre, Pip, Hans, and Fédéric in
the novels Shura loved by writers like Tolstoy, Dickens, Mann, and
Flaubert were very real to him, and his feeling for them deepened as he
returned to them again and again across his life. "My father said he had
known the Brothers Cheeryble from *Nicholas Nickleby,* that he himself
had truly seen them," says Heidi. As Shura observed these old literary
acquaintances grappling with their inner selves—with love and hardship and emotional complication—he vicariously contended with his.
When Levin and Kitty have their child, and for Levin there is "nothing
cheerful and joyous in the feeling; on the contrary, it was a new torture
of apprehension. It was the consciousness of a new sphere of liability to
pain," Shura knew exactly what Levin meant, and he felt better about
his own worried nature, the way a man is soothed by the realization that
there is somebody else who has felt what he has felt. Shura was a person
who lived his emotional life across the pages of great books; fictional

characters allowed him to examine his real self in the safety of solitude. Literature let him engage the inconsistencies and complexities of his feelings—things he couldn't share with real people. Sacrificing something that essential for the sake of his writing he could not do.

SHURA DID COMPLETE ONE FAIRLY LARGE WORK. THE TYPESCRIPT OF "The Uses of Adversity," his childhood memoir, is over three hundred pages long. He wrote it in the early 1960s and showed it rather furtively and unofficially to someone from the Harvard University Press. When that man expressed reservations, Shura did not pursue the issue. What he wrote is spirited but essentially flawed: a piece of personal writing that is not very personal. It would have taken real effort for a secretive man like Shura to set down the details and reflections of his youth in such a way that they animated the experiences of an ordinary person into literature. Instead of expending that effort, he placed the manuscript in his filing cabinet and left it there.

TWELVE

THE MOST
UNBELIEVABLE THING

And then suddenly all that was gone.

Boris Pasternak, *Doctor Zhivago*

Iₙ 1965, when Shura turned sixty-one, a group of his
former seminar members arranged to celebrate his career with a
festschrift—a book of essays written in honor of a great scholar by
his students and peers. The festschrift is a tribute that rewards only the
most exceptional intellectual lives, an obeisance in paper to a professor
who has inspired unusual admiration and affection. Yet accompanying
all the glory of inspiring a group of accomplished people to create a
book in your name comes an unspoken truth: for the recipients of
festschrifts, the evening is near.

Long before Shura considered himself to be an old man, people
thought of him as an old man, and he was an old man. When Shura
received Henry Rosovsky's letter telling him that a group of his finest
students would like to present him with *Industrialization in Two Systems:
Essays in Honor of Alexander Gerschenkron* during a private dinner at the
Harvard Club of New York toward the end of December, his response
was not to respond at all. Rosovsky was far away at the time, a visiting
scholar in Israel, and as he sat in his Jerusalem apartment with the days
passing and no delighted letter back from Gerschenkron, Rosovsky
grew anxious. In late November he wrote again to Shura, begging him
to say whether he and "his lady" would be there for the dinner, because

"we simply cannot operate without a guest of honor." This time he received a reply, albeit not a terribly gracious one. "Barring unforeseen contingencies," wrote Shura, "we should be happy to attend the dinner."

When the grand day arrived, eight contributors appeared in New York from all over the country dressed in their best clothes—Rosovsky had a suit of blue worsted wool custom-tailored for the occasion in Jerusalem—to join Shura and Erica for an elegant, full-course meal to be followed by toasts and remarks. The evening was, says Peter Temin, "a downer." Although the weather was dry that day, Erica, in sullen spirits and suffering from a game ankle, appeared in galoshes. Shura conveyed a similar lack of ceremony. During the supper he made only the most grudging conversation. Afterward he stood and, says Paul David, "chewed us out" with a churlish speech of which the dismayed Rosovsky remembers that "he said 'I wish that when you are old you will endure this experience.' We were taken aback. We had gone to great expense and thought we'd done a wonderful thing, but he did not want to go gently." It took Shura months before he began reading the essays, an oversight he excused to Goran Ohlin by saying, "I felt somewhat embarrassed by the volume." Shura often used the word "embarrassed" as a trope for uncomfortable emotions that he didn't want to explain. It wasn't that he was flustered, and he wasn't really angry with the students either. His quarrel was with his years.

Shura thought of himself as a middle-aged man with so much still to accomplish, but, of course, his watch was slow and part of him must have known it. Not only was he sixty-one, he was an old sixty-one, an aging engine with different parts breaking down or rusting away all the time, and so he was left in a perpetual state of sputtering, listing, and stalling as he tried to accelerate through the days with his usual gusto. His digestion was bad and his thyroid gland worse. His prostate was enlarged, he had jaundice, faltering eyesight, that cranky gallbladder, and—most serious—the patchwork heart that broke down time after time. The allowances he was supposed to make for the various afflictions oppressed him: he shouldn't exert himself, was absolutely forbidden to eat this and really shouldn't lift that. There were too many glasses of prune juice, too many naps on the blue daybed, and too much fumbling with pill boxes. His rifle now required a Kentucky windage to

help him sight the target. He was prescribed anticoagulants for his heart, several tablets at a time, and he could never remember whether he'd taken them or not. His doctor, George Kurland, would shake his head and say, "You are my smartest patient, and you are the only one who can't count."

Shura was fortunate to have this physician, who understood people as well as he did science. Dr. Kurland would see Shura coming into his office, tuck away his stethoscope, and begin a conversation about Shakespeare. Along the way he'd work in a few orders concerning balking arteries. "Shura never let his illness hold him back," Kurland remembered. "He had the most terrible-looking electrocardiagram. It looked like he shouldn't be walking, but he kept a regular schedule." Whenever Shura checked into the hospital for a procedure, the doctor raised no objections as Shura made his bed into a recumbent study where he sent up columns of pipe smoke as he read and wrote all day. "Dr. Kurland understood that a heart condition is as much a psychological condition as a medical one, and you have to look out for a man's spirits," says Heidi. "He succeeded in drawing a fine line between encouraging my father to be active and adventurous, and getting him to accept some limitations. He understood that imposing too many limitations on this patient would depress him, and the depression would be more dangerous than a little too much running around being vigorous."

What Kurland couldn't ease were the deeper emotional aches. It was increasingly difficult for Shura to retain his chosen image of himself. For so long he had been a self-sufficient, self-contained person, and now that autonomy had been undermined by illnesses that imposed the outside world of doctors and medication upon him. Making things worse was his sense that the outside world had become as diseased as he was.

IN THE EARLY 1960S, WHEN THE KENNEDY ADMINISTRATION FIRST began sending equipment and advisers to South Vietnam, most people who noticed at all took it on faith that if the United States was involved, the cause must be necessary. Shura was this way to the extreme, an unwaveringly patriotic member of the Second World War generation of optimistic middle-class citizens who considered the country to be the embodiment of all things noble. His basic view of foreign relations, informed by his experiences in Russia, in Austria, and in the United States during the 1950s, was this: freedom is good, tyranny must be resisted. Shura saw the American government's desire to create a functioning democracy in Southeast Asia as an obligation, the right thing to do in a distant place threatened by a spreading Communist movement. Like most people at the time—including, it would turn out later, many of the hawkish cold warriors in Washington—he was increasingly apprehensive about the prospects of a guerrilla war in a distant place. He was, of course, right to worry. As the years passed, with monks lighting matches to their gasoline-soaked robes in the streets of Saigon, the troop escalations and the defoliation campaigns, Ben Tre destroyed "to save" Ben Tre, the government dissembling, the five-column exposés, and the welter of casualties, it gradually became as clear to Shura as it was to the conflict's most vigorous opponents that "this horrible war," as he began referring to it, was a doomed enterprise. In seeking to do something virtuous, America had corrupted a country.

Since Shura could not bring himself to hold the United States culpable for anything wicked, he responded to the war gone wrong in the same way that he treated Erica when she seemed to be at fault for something: he was indignant at those who would accuse her. For Shura, it was always a question of "Are you for your country or are you against it?" It was as though he worried that the things he most cared about were too fragile to withstand the scrutiny of criticism, and he hoped to firm them up with his devotion. Placing blame for the disaster in Southeast Asia, he looked beyond Washington and found the perpetual villain. "The Soviets wanted to make hay in the Mediterranean," he said, "so they lured us into Vietnam and we fell right into the trap."

On summer mornings in Francestown in the late 1960s, when Shura walked down his dirt driveway to the edge of the road and raised his American flag on its slim wooden pole, he was a lot like men and women in small towns all across the heartland, hanging out their flags as an expression of faith, not just in the military, but in the country. Yet as Vietnam lasted the decade, droning on like a dog that wouldn't stop barking, the faraway war became an oppressive daily presence. It was difficult to watch the evening news without feeling somehow complicit in the events at My Lai, and since the images were so disquieting, the idea that the United States was capable of an enormous evil slowly took hold. Once that happened people began noticing American treachery in many places across the globe and then also in their own towns. As the war brought the squalid American underculture of poverty and discrimination into sudden focus, large numbers of citizens began to express their outrage with a passion that made Shura miserable, because he found the dissent to be as intolerant as the intolerance it opposed. He felt that a foolish war had made a great country half mad, and not only was that country now in danger but, by extension, so again was he.

IN LATE 1964 SHURA RECEIVED A LETTER FROM HENRY ROSOVSKY, who wrote that he was resigning his professorship at the University of California because the "Free Speech Movement" had made chaos of the Berkeley campus. Crowds of students staged daily demonstrations, screaming through megaphones about the "respectable bureaucracy" that wanted to obstruct their efforts to create a better society. After watching five thousand young people rally at the student union, led by speakers who addressed them from the roof of a captured police car, Rosovsky told Shura that "I have managed to do no work in the past two months. . . . I cannot take this any longer." Rosovsky had lived through Nazi tyranny as a child in Danzig, where he had been barred from public schools and harassed by members of the Hitler Youth. Seeing these American kids who had it so good playing the role of subjugated Danzigers incensed him. He came east and went to work at Harvard, telling Shura how relieved he was to be away from all that.

Shura admired the Harvard students who left town to volunteer in the national war on poverty, as he did those who went south in the 1960s to join the sit-ins and freedom rides of the civil rights movement. In the late 1960s, at morning prayers in Harvard's Appleton Chapel, he delivered his talk on the similarity between Martin Luther King, Jr.'s methods of nonviolent protest and those of the Austrian workers' movements. "The way shown by Martin Luther King," he said that day, "resembles astonishingly that traveled by Austrian labor, and I believe we must pray that in the end it alone will be followed and that it will lead to a successful eradication of age-long injustices and enable us to live in accordance with the precepts of the American creed and the teachings of our Lord."

For the most part, however, in those years the actions of people Shura respected did not claim his attention. He fastened instead upon the unruly trappings of an unruly time, the gradual decline in civility and the occasional moments of raw confrontation. What he saw drew from him a daily obloquy.

In 1966, when the senior Vietnam policy maker, Secretary of Defense Robert S. McNamara, visited Harvard, a mob of angry students, shouting antiwar demands, surrounded his sedan, rocking the car, leaping onto its hood, and refusing to let him speak. Two years later, a recruiter for the Dow Chemical Company, which manufactured napalm on one of its defense contracts, was held hostage in a chemistry department classroom. But the target of the most vigorous campus displeasure was the Reserve Officers Training Corps (ROTC), a military program that financed students' education in exchange for a commitment to future service. Radical students wanted the program eliminated because they thought Harvard should not be supporting the so-called military-industrial complex. Late in 1968, students broke up a faculty meeting about ROTC in the Paine Hall music building. On a scale of insurrections, this didn't seem like much, but genteel Harvard was unused to subversion of any kind, and Paine Hall became a harbinger of bigger things to come.

In 1968, the year both Martin Luther King and Bobby Kennedy were murdered, the success of the Vietcong's Tet offensive led President Johnson to sharply reduce draft deferments for students. Opposition to the war and fear of being forced to serve in it galvanized a more general desire among Harvard radicals to reform "a corrupt and repressive society." Many of the members of Students for a Democratic Society (SDS), the leading student radical group, came to view themselves as the allies of underpaid Cambridge workers, minorities, women, and the poor. Some went further. By 1968 Harvard undergraduates were referring to themselves as victims of oppression and campaigning against such "discriminatory" practices as dress codes, grading, exams, and courses they didn't like. A yearbook entry from the time describes a young woman who "is interested in anthropology and believes in revolution." Another pronounces: "You're still a virgin until you've been laid stoned." The walls of Harvard Yard were plastered with Marxist-Leninist propoganda posters, and the lawns became a dust bowl, all the grass trampled away by the many rallies and by walkers who followed an edict holding that "the shortest distance between two points is the revolutionary distance."

Much of the student animosity was directed toward "authority," and at a university, authority is the teachers. "I had to have a police escort to get to class," recalls the government professor Arthur Maas, who taught a course on the presidency and Congress. Radcliffe president Mary Bunting was spat on and derided as "an opting-out bitch." The playwright and English professor William Alfred remembered a crowd of antiwar students picketing a classroom building and chanting "Hitler!"

at the professors who walked past them. "The students," says Alfred, "were angry at the faculty the way you would be at the head of your family for not stanching a bad thing."

The man at the head of the faculty became more unpopular with radical students than just about anyone. In 1953 Nathan Pusey had been confronted with Senator Joseph McCarthy's declaration that Harvard was "a smelly mess" of Communists and that all faculty members who wouldn't swear they weren't Red should be fired. Pusey's response had been to refuse, asserting that "it would be a sorry thing if in resisting totalitarianism we were to follow the counsels of the frightened and adopt its methods." The Harvard president was a devout, restrained man, an Aristotle expert whose preoccupations were ethics both theoretical and practical. Fifteen years after McCarthy, Pusey had even less patience with Harvard students on the barricades than he'd had with a senator on the rampage. "Walter Mittys of the left," is how Pusey described them, adding, "They play at being revolutionaries."

Shura respected Pusey and was not bothered that the president seemed to some people to be constitutionally incapable of emotion. "Pusey stood up to McCarthy" is what he always said when people made fun of the president's stiff collar. He also sympathized with Pusey's view of the students. The memory of the throngs of young Americans who'd joined Shura in California, volunteering to go to Europe and fight Hitler, was fresh in his mind, and he found it baffling that whereas then someone who'd stayed out of the army was a coward, now a student draft avoider was a person of conscience. Listening to the SDS radicals talking about their hopes of liberating the exploited American working class took Shura back to his Social Democratic party days in the Vienna workers' rights movement, fighting segregation, starvation wages, and the housing shortages. Those were truly desperate times. People he knew had been cut down in rows for their trouble. The idea of Harvard students claiming solidarity with such martyrs told him that Harvard students knew no history. He wondered about their bravery too. After all, tearing apart Harvard Yard was nearly as risk-free as digging up your parents' lawn.

That the students might be serving useful social functions by hastening the end of a bad war and asking pointed questions about the lack of inclusion of minorities and women in a so-called democracy was a possibility Shura never entertained once they began breaking things. He saw them as faux-revolutionaries, "the sons and daughters of the petty bourgeoisie" who had been given some of the most generous opportunities the world had to offer. When he heard them refer to themselves as "oppressed people" and proclaim, "You've got to stand with the working people or against them," he wanted to shout, because he felt the students were "trying to impersonate what they emphatically were not—the penurious, exploited, and oppressed laboring men of the 1840's." He complained that the Harvard radicals "did not even have the horse sense not to cry out against elitism, being a privileged group . . . who pretended to belong to the working class but never had the guts or the gumption to take a job in a factory or on a construction site and had to confine themselves to simulating holes in their pants."

Large numbers of the leading SDS activists were Social Studies concentrators. "The Vietnam war hit Harvard hard and Social Studies hard in particular," says Stanley Hoffman, a government professor on the original Social Studies committee. "Many of the brightest students were left liberals rebelling against their liberal parents. They felt their parents had gone soft, sold out their own youth and become middle class. These kids went much further left, flirted with every variety of Marxism on the market. Social Studies was the revolutionary hotbed of the university." Shura was aghast to hear these future scholars, the hand-picked beneficiaries of the program he himself had created, telling him about the wonders of Marx, Castro, Trotsky, Lenin, Stalin, and Mao, and he was equally astonished to learn that America was repressing the students. One boy Shura had lunch with told him that "here everything is impossible because the United States is not a free country."

"So where are things better?" Shura asked him. "Where is the truly free society?"

"Peking," said the student.

Shura reported that he'd been too speechless to say what he thought. "You speak of China," he said he'd wanted to reply, "but Hitler too abolished unemployment and much hunger in Germany and Austria while destroying freedom and denaturalizing and distorting the concept of freedom."

He did not often hold back. Upset as the students made Shura, he was a teacher, and his impulse was to educate. In those years he spent many nights each week—always at the students' invitation—talking and arguing with students in their homes and meeting places. When they told him that grades were "antiegalitarian," he chided them for being naive, pointing out how many centuries it had taken for grades to replace aristocratic birth as the criterion for measuring youthful promise. When the students enthused about the virtues of Marxism, he disputed their assertions with passages of *Das Kapital* quoted from memory. Then he drew from personal experience, describing for the students the initial sense of destiny Russians had felt in Trotsky and their feelings of betrayal as the Soviet Union took shape. The student revelation that you couldn't trust anybody over thirty was a dull saw to Shura, who said that young people have always had a passion for regarding their elders as senile. He repeated for the students the passage in *Faust* (Part Two) where Goethe has the student Baccalaureus explain to Mephisto, "When one is over thirty, he is already as good as dead. The best thing would be to slaughter you [the teachers] at an early point." Mephisto, only disguised as a professor, then responds: "The devil has nothing to add to this."

Although Shura made no effort to hide from the students the contempt he had for their activities, many of them looked forward to talking with him anyway. A former radical student leader named Herbert Gintis recalls, "I felt betrayed by my professors for not defending themselves. The way they behaved was defensively, except for Gerschenkron. He thought we were spoiled brats who benefited from the freedom-fighting of people all over the world, and at the time I thought he was right. I admired him and he hated me."

One evening Shura let himself through the rear entrance of a packed Winthrop House Junior Common Room. At the front of the room, looking like an elderly pugilist with his lined face and bulbous nose, stood the radical political philosopher Herbert Marcuse. Seated before him was the entire student enrollment of the Social Studies program.

Marcuse was a leading intellectual mentor to the New Left, a first-rate controversialist capable of pronouncements like "the world of concentration camps was not an exceptionally monstrous society." Anyone who disagreed with him, which sooner or later was just about everyone, he referred to as "an *Untermensch*"—a brute. He had fled Berlin in 1933, come to the United States the following year, and since then had occupied himself with critiques of democracy and capitalism that were, according to the sociologist Barrington Moore, "so far left he was contemptuous of the Communists—a sort of one-man movement."

In his thick German accent Marcuse was holding forth on "Educational Dictatorships." The students were rapt as Marcuse argued that dictatorship was justifiable if it functioned in support of "a progressive cause." Similarly, he said, intolerance was acceptable if the progressive people were intolerant.

It was there that Shura interrupted. "Look here, Marcuse," he said. The whole room turned. In a crisp voice, Shura proceeded to explain that he was "appalled" by what he was hearing because he did not understand how a man who was savoring the benefits of life in a free society could be hatching ideas that were so contrary to the spirit of freedom. "Your very title, 'Educational Dictatorship,' is an oxymoron," he told Marcuse. A heated debate ensued: Shura feinting—"Have you thought of this?"—and then jabbing—"You must have considered that"; Marcuse striking back—"Yes, yes"—sure that he was "handling him," as Marcuse told his wife afterward. "Alex took on Marcuse in a very intellectual way," says Richard Hunt, then the director of Social Studies. "The students were fascinated." So was Barrington Moore, who was present. "It was quite a time for me," he says. "Two of my best friends at each other's throats. The world was at each other's throats."

People like Moore tried to appease Shura about the students, telling him, "Shura, you just watch. In a few years they'll all be working on Wall Street." But he could never believe that, because so much of what was happening in Cambridge reminded him of his own college years when fascist fanaticism and organized bigotry took hold on the campus at the University of Vienna and infected the country. Walking through Harvard Square one day with Peter McClelland, they came upon a thick swastika chalked on the sidewalk. "He stopped dead in his tracks

as though he'd been hit with a baseball bat, and he said 'Oh my God,'"
says McClelland.

That such things were going on in Cambridge seemed to Shura even
more frightening than what he'd experienced in Vienna and in Odessa,
because Harvard students were the people who most should have
known better. *Corruptio optimi pessima*, he thought to himself over and
over as he walked through Cambridge. (Nothing is so evil as the cor-
ruption of the best.) His afternoons began to be disturbed by Vienna
flashbacks.

SHURA HATED MANY THINGS ABOUT THE LATE 1960S, BUT MUCH
more troubling to him than excesses of drugs, sex, foul language, or
anything else the students were experimenting with was the way many
of his Harvard colleagues were swept up in a culture of youthful per-
missiveness. Shura was sure that the university was going over to the
barbarians. At the Faculty Club, he felt that the sparkling intellectual
discussions he had always looked forward to had deteriorated into ideological contests where opinions masqueraded as ideas and feelings were
passed off as thoughts. "It is truly astonishing and at times quite shock-
ing to me how much of conversations among professors nowadays deals
with subjects that require neither previous study nor any real knowledge," he said. He was left with the sense that the "difference between
what is and what is not a scholarly statement has been considerably
eroded. The elusive and ambiguous thing called judgment has tended
to replace scientific inference." At the Long Table, he winced when
people who'd spent their lives on leafy American campuses played academic parlor games, constructing scenarios in which it was preferable
to be a prisoner in a Soviet labor camp than to be free.

When a group of professors urged Shura to join them in speaking
out against the war, he wrote to his colleague André Daniere, explaining that

> it is quite improper for a man expressing his political opin-
> ions to be identified as a member of a university faculty, that

is to say, a scholar. When this is done, a very misleading impression is created that what such a man says is not simply an expression of his political opinion, but somehow the result of his scholarly knowledge and interpretation. I find this highly reprehensible. The fact of the matter is that my barber in Peterborough, New Hampshire, who used to fight in Korea, probably has a much deeper understanding of the military and political problems in Vietnam than I can ever hope to attain.

In 1969 Shura's friend Alex Inkeles's social relations lecture course was continually disrupted by radicals who wrote "Fuck Authority" on the blackboard, derided the professor as "totally dead" and as "a desexualized being," and then, in a final burst of hostility, thrust a banana toward Inkeles's mouth and watched gleefully as he bit into it. Later that day Shura telephoned Inkeles and reached his wife Bernadette.

"I heard Alex ate a banana," Shura said.

"Yes," she said, and began to tell him about it.

"If someone had offered me a banana," Shura interrupted, "I'd have shoved it down his throat." Later he reflected to himself on the Aretino heroine who said, "I did not realize he was raping me; I thought he was just measuring."

In those years Shura would come home at the end of the day seething about Daniere or Inkeles or the physicist George Wald, whom he considered a shameless ingratiator. "Do you know that he asks the students to call him George!" he would burst out. "Then he says to them, 'I'm a Nobel physicist and I'm telling you you're right!'" Shura blamed professors like Wald for a lot, for tolerating the students when they were disrespectful, for taking pleasure in their rebellious behavior, and for encouraging them to do destructive things. He thought adults who wanted everybody to know they were cool, young, sexually liberated, antiwar, and as hip to marijuana as the students were ridiculous, and the idea that "mixed-up children" had something to teach Harvard professors about morality and politics made him cringe. He began to lob insults at them. "I was pretty far to the left, and he made fun of me as a revolutionary," Albert Hirschman says. Hirschman wasn't the only one. "I have seen," Shura said, "a fair number of faculty members who, when somebody spit in his face, looked up at the sky and wondered whether it was raining." Such professors became the "middle-aged popularity kids," who were willing to forfeit the high standards of the university to curry favor with young rowdies and mischief makers. Hirschman says that after a while, Shura "was considered by some of us to be the enemy."

That among the people Shura was condemning were treasured friends made no difference to him. Shura was often attracted to people who were more liberal than he was, and because he could never agree to disagree, in the last years of his life he would sever ties with many of the people he cared most about. These ruptured relationships came at great emotional cost, yet Shura never allowed himself to mourn them because he thought of each division not as a matter of choice but rather as an act of conscience. Confident that those who did not think as he did were revealing a serious moral flaw, he isolated himself, maintaining his sense of his own integrity as his community disintegrated around him.

The estrangements were often as sudden as they were drastic. When Barrington Moore said in a conversation that the most serious threats to Harvard came not from the student movements but from "the military-industrial complex," Shura was all but finished with him. During lunch one day at Eliot House, Monroe Engel listened as Shura responded to a young professor's enthusiastic remarks about the political concerns of the students. "Alex began tearing him to pieces," says Engel. "It was awful. He had about 5 percent of Alex's verbal powers. I was sitting there and I said something I shouldn't have. It was presumptuous. I said, 'Alex, this is unworthy of you.' The temperature went down seventy-five degrees. He said, 'I will decide what is unworthy of me.' I never again had a sustained conversation with him after that."

Easily the most painful break was with John Kenneth Galbraith. Shura truly loved Galbraith, and when he experienced such strong feelings for someone, he needed that person to see and think about the world in the ways he did. If that didn't happen, he was capable of conflating a difference of opinion or style with disloyalty—you weren't with him. Shura took personally to the point of outrage things Galbraith did that he thought Galbraith should not do, things that usually had nothing whatsoever to do with Shura.

One of Galbraith's gifts was a shrewd ability to size up a moment and offer commentary that was timely, serious, digestible, and provocative. At heart he was a pamphleteer in the best sense of the term, a worldly man about whom it was once said that "his natural literary form is the letter to the editor." He didn't want to be a scholar, to hunker down in a university study spending years mastering a single arcane topic. He wanted to think big and broad, to write for the leading opinion pages and the best magazines, to be quoted in newspapers, to be part of a national conversation, or, better yet, to begin one.

In 1958 he did just that. That year Galbraith published *The Affluent Society*, a fluid activist critique of the American economy in which he argued that by relying upon the capital market system and Keynesian production theories, America had become a country unfairly divided between great wealth and chronic poverty. The book appeared in a day when Americans were just becoming receptive to the idea that a prosperous country where many are poor is a morally impoverished country, and enough people bought it that Galbraith won a dinner from the publisher, who had bet him that the book would not make the author the rare best-selling economist.

Shura thought that Galbraith had the ability to be a great scholar and so should be one. For *The Affluent Society* he had only disdain. "He felt," says Heidi, "that Galbraith was wasting his mind on popular economics. He thought that people who were trained to be scholars shouldn't be writing popular books. He felt that Galbraith liked the adulation and that he was vain." Over the years Shura missed few opportunities to dig at Galbraith for his self-importance. Once he wrote to his friend, asking him to make a donation to Harvard's new Mather House library. Would Galbraith be willing, Shura wondered, to give "those of your books which in your opinion a house library should have, which naturally means all the books you have published." Then, he added, "A grain of egotism is the proper yeast for the dough of philanthropy."

People often abominate the flaws of others that they see in themselves. Shura was no less egotistical than Galbraith; he was simply less overt in the way he expressed it. If Galbraith liked to be the most famous Harvard professor, Shura was just as proud of being the most scholarly Harvard professor. It was a kind of vanity that made him eschew assignments from the very magazines Galbraith wrote for, just as it was vanity that made him litter his writings with recondite quotations in obscure languages and then never, ever provide an English translation for them. He didn't really expect his readers to know Swedish, Italian, and Bulgarian. He expected them to notice that he did and they didn't. It injured that vanity to see Galbraith forsaking the scholarly life, scorning the soft lamps of the library for the bright lights of the world.

It was the same way after Galbraith left Harvard to become ambassador to India. Although Shura had loyally intervened when President Pusey didn't want to give Galbraith his job back upon his return from New Delhi, Shura always took it personally when an economics department colleague went to work for the government. Shura was far less pleased when several years later, Galbraith went to see Pusey himself on less-than-diplomatic business. The economics professor Otto Eckstein had founded a consulting company called Data Resources Incorporated, and DRI became a phenomenal success. Eckstein continued to carry perhaps the heaviest course load in the economics department, but his successful moonlighting bothered Galbraith so much that he complained to Pusey. Shura found out what Galbraith had done and was furious. "When his break came with Ken Galbraith it was because Ken Galbraith committed the unforgivable sin of tattling on a co-worker," says Paul Samuelson. "Alex said to me that 'tattletaling was the unpardonable sin both at the shipyard and when I was a worker in the Social Democratic party in Vienna.'" Samuelson says that when "I pointed out the irony to Ken of his being the one to complain, he replied, 'Otto does it for money. I do it for the public good.'"

But Samuelson was not quite right. That was not the breaking point. It was one stress among many that slowly and gradually weakened the friendship like an overburdened beam until it split, done in at last by the same burden that divided so many Americans—the war. In 1961

Galbraith was sent by President Kennedy on a covert mission to Vietnam. The president had received forceful reports from the likes of General Maxwell Taylor and Walt Rostow—who had left M.I.T. to join the presidential cabinet—urging Kennedy to increase the American presence in Southeast Asia. "The president sent me knowing I did not have an open mind," says Galbraith. "I was aware of the irrelevance of Communism in a jungle village community, which is all Indochina was." That is exactly what he told Kennedy, but it was advice not taken. For a while Galbraith kept his opinions to himself. Eventually he did not wish to, and he says that it was after "I went public on Vietnam" that his friendship with Shura was lost.

Most men become more conservative as they get older. Galbraith went the other way. He followed up his pronouncements against the war by publicly declaring, in 1967, that his friend and former employer, President Lyndon Johnson, had to be defeated. Johnson considered that a betrayal and Shura was inclined to agree. Worse, by Shura's reckoning, Galbraith then went ahead and became one of the architects of Minnesota senator Eugene McCarthy's anitwar challenge to Johnson's renomination in 1968. McCarthy announced his candidacy inside Galbraith's pink Cambridge mansion. The senator's surprising success in the New Hampshire primary—he lost by only 230 votes—pushed the president to withdraw from the race two and a half weeks later. Galbraith then hit the campaign trail for McCarthy, returning to Cambridge each week to teach his class. In August, Galbraith seconded McCarthy's nomination on the floor of the Democratic convention in Chicago. McCarthy was against the war, but what did he stand for? Shura thought that McCarthy himself had no idea, and he concluded that McCarthy was a spoiler, content to run a casual race that, in the end, would only ruin the Democrats' chances in November. By late 1968 Galbraith was Cambridge's most visible antiwar activist, and the sight of his tall, lanky frame making its way through Harvard Yard became recognizable as a spire of faculty sympathy with the students. He spoke out vehemently against President Pusey, President Johnson, and Secretary of State Rusk, and he encouraged the students to do the same—encouraged them to shake up the life of the university.

Galbraith tried to retain cordial relations with Shura through this time, but it wasn't easy. When Shura was at Princeton for the academic year 1968–1969, Galbraith sent him a book and a Christmas card. In response, Shura mailed his sixty-year-old friend a cheerful poison-pen letter. "I am an old admirer of your deeply latent talents," he wrote.

> It is the more patent ones I object to, such as the one that made you speak with abominable satisfaction of the persecution of the Secretary of State by a bunch of neurotic and hysterical youngsters whose favors middle-aged popularity kids stoop to court. I am now eating the sweet bread of exile, but when I return to Cambridge, I shall challenge you to a public fist fight in front of University Hall. It will be a case of longer reach against greater mental and physical agility. And may the highest qualities win. For the rest, and despite everything, I remain as fond of you as I was when we used to be closer friends.

Galbraith was pained by Shura's hostility and also felt somewhat resentful. "I never accused Alex of error," he says.

> It was he accusing me, deliberately, and with some violence of manner for my position in support of those opposing the war. Alex was very much a person of his background and nothing was so important as the suffering, disturbance, disorder, and danger he'd experienced in Eastern Europe and from Communism. When the Vietnam War came, Alex thought that, given my background, I simply didn't understand the dictatorial threat that came from Communism. Alex saw it in stern revolutionary terms as the extension of Russian power and Communist power, as did many, perhaps most, concerned with the problem of the Cold War. I saw it as a local tribal conflict where the established view of Communism and capitalism was wholly irrelevant. It's fair to say that history has justified that view. Vietnam was not a casual thing with me. I was emotionally involved. So was he. He

regarded my views on Vietnam as wrong and beyond the pale, not subject to discussion. There was absolutely no chance of talking about it with him. Similarly, my tolerance of the student revolt. Alex Gerschenkron could not separate difference of belief from friendship. If you were different in belief, you could not be on good terms. He lowered the curtain.

EARLY ON THE SUNNY SPRING AFTERNOON OF APRIL 9, 1969, A procession of three hundred students and a few professional activists carrying banners, signs that read "Fight Capitalists—Running Dogs," bullhorns, metal chains, crowbars, sleeping bags, knapsacks full of homework, a guitar, and a tambourine crossed Harvard Yard and walked up the steps to University Hall. They announced that they were taking over the administration building "in the spirit of Martin Luther King." As quickly as nonviolence was advertised, it was renounced. Moving from office to office, the students expelled all the deans, ordering the men out from behind their desks and hustling them along corridors toward the exits. A couple of administrators were shoved down flights of stairs, and others were showered with profanity. One unfortunate assistant dean found himself slung over somebody's shoulder like a duffel and carried outside. Some students burst into the office of Franklin Ford, dean of the Faculty of Arts and Sciences, and told him to leave. Ford had fought Germans during the Second World War, which he thought about as he took his time deciding what to do. He left, but not in any hurry.

Michael Kazin, an SDS leader who is now a professor of history at Georgetown, says that the students felt "a certain glee at authority figures' being toppled. I wish we'd kept it completely passive and just sat down in there but, like any history, it has to be understood in the context of the times. So many people were angry about the war. We felt Harvard was connected to the American power structure and that there were lots of ways that Harvard was connected to the war. This was an issue that was tearing American society apart, and we thought why shouldn't it tear Harvard apart? And it did."

With its grand second-floor meeting room filled with portraits and busts of men like William James, Henry Wadsworth Longfellow, Louis Agassiz, and other great professors past, University Hall was the ancestral home of the Harvard faculty. It was also the custodian of Harvard's family secrets, for the file cabinets inside University Hall held all the intimate details of the administration's dealings with troubled teachers. There were letters and confidential memoranda telling stories of debts, alcoholism, and mental breakdowns. When all the deans and secretaries had been evicted, the students padlocked the doors, renamed the building "Che Guevara Hall," and announced that it would be held until a series of "nonnegotiable demands," including the immediate abolition of ROTC, were met by the Harvard governing board.

While word of the occupation spread across the campus, inside University Hall the students held strategy sessions and broke into the locked file cabinets, where they searched for evidence that Harvard was in league with the CIA or for anything else that might prove humiliating to the administration. (Some of these documents would soon turn up in *The Old Mole*, one of the radical gazettes that circulated around Cambridge.) They also scrawled "Fuck Authority" on the walls in crayon, drafted "anti-imperialist" political screeds, and used official stationery to type fake admissions acceptance letters and send them to all the names on a list of high school applicants somebody discovered.

Harvard Yard quickly became crowded with students and professors, for everyone was turning out to watch. The mood was disbelieving. Some students burned SDS members in effigy. With the occupants refusing all entreaties to leave the building, President Pusey became increasingly concerned about the prospect of students' making public the private records of Harvard's teachers. Since Harvard did not yet have a real police force of its own, sixteen hours into the occupation Pusey placed a call downtown and soon there were four hundred Cambridge patrolmen and state troopers massed in the Yard carrying truncheons and shields and wearing robin's-egg blue helmets on their heads. After a final warning which some of the occupying students later said they hadn't heard, at 5:00 a.m. the police smashed in the door to University Hall.

The Cambridge police department had never felt much affection for

Harvard students to begin with, and now, when they confronted a mob of them taunting *Sieg Heil* and throwing bottles and doorknobs, the officers were less than gentle in response. Wading in with their nightsticks high, they swung hard and seldom missed. Some occupants climbed out of windows, leaped to the ground, and ran away. Barrington Moore spotted one of his former students, an SDS leader, slipping off into the crowd. Moore went up to him. "How can you do this?" he asked. "I'm protecting my leadership," the boy replied. "I told him he was exposing other students to what he didn't want to take," says Moore. There were close to 50 injuries and nearly 200 arrests. Several policemen were hurt, two of them suffering bite wounds. In the end, the spectacle of armored cops treating unarmed students like violent desperados left many people who'd felt nothing but contempt for the SDS action now even more disgusted with the administration. "Pusey engendered sympathy for brigands," says the scientist Stephen Jay Gould. Shura was still in Princeton and saw nothing. When he learned what had happened, he told a colleague that "incredulity preceded horror." Then he got into his car and drove home to Cambridge.

The next day an emergency faculty meeting was called to talk over the Bust, as it became known. Harvard faculty meetings were such notoriously dull events that the Faculty Room in University Hall could always seat the small percentage of the professors who showed up for them. But on April 11, 1969, with well over five hundred people expected to turn out to hear what their peers thought should be done about students who had behaved so impudently and who then had been so brutally dealt with, the professors were directed to the large auditorium inside Harvard's theater, the Loeb Drama Center. Nobody anticipated the meeting with anything resembling pleasure. Yet with tear gas still drifting in the air, with thousands of students now declaring that they were on strike against the university and refusing to attend their classes—"Strike because you hate cops. . . . Strike to seize control of your life. . . . Strike because they are trying to squeeze the life out of you," urged an SDS poster—with students screaming that Pusey should be put to death, and with more violence perhaps in the offing, even the most politically detached faculty members made their way to the theater with an uneasy sense of expectation.

While President Pusey was led into the Loeb through a rear loading dock, Shura was strolling to the meeting with Jerry Bruner. As the two men moved past rows of student protesters silently lining the walkway outside the front doors of the theater, he was telling Bruner that one of the great sources of evil in the modern world came from the belief that you could attain a Utopian goal. Shura speculated that the students' nonnegotiable demands were based upon Utopian conviction, a draconian idealism that became the source of confrontation and cruelty. "You know," he said, "nobody could describe me as antistudent, but I am anti-Utopian."

One of the many ironies of this afternoon when a patrician Yankee institution searched for its soul was that the most emotionally charged contributions came from European refugees. The stated agenda for the meeting called for votes on two proposed responses to the building seizure, one written by the Russian-born economist Wassily Leontief and the other by the Russian-born scientist George Kistiakowsky. Before the motions were introduced, however, Dean Franklin Ford stood up on the stage, where he had been sitting with the other members of the administration, and gave a speech in which he compared the students to "storm troopers" and said that, although there were people telling him that the past few days had been "very interesting, even exciting," he found them "sickening." (Five days after the meeting, the dean did fall seriously ill, suffering a stroke that landed him in Massachusetts General Hospital.)

When Ford was finished speaking, President Pusey stood to defend what he called "a regrettable thing," on the grounds that Harvard could not allow "force or violence" to disrupt the life of the university. Pusey's manner of speaking was placid as ever, but his words stirred a range of strong emotions around the room. The scientists, for instance, were mostly to the left politically, and they looked at the president with loathing. Much more in sympathy with Pusey, and generally more conservative on the subject of the students, were the social scientists. There were exceptions. Galbraith was one. Another was Leontief, who'd been arrested during his own student days in Saint Petersburg for hanging posters criticizing the tsarist regime. After conceding that the students needed to be punished, Leontief closed by attacking President Pusey, saying that the confidence of many members of the faculty in their administration had been "undermined, if not entirely destroyed."

Kistiakowsky followed Leontief. As a young man, Kistiakowsky had been a cadet in a gentlemen's regiment in the White Russian army. While his sensibilities remained much less liberal than Leontief's, like the economist, Kistiakowsky equivocated, saying he was "troubled" both by the student "extremists" and by an administration that had furthered "the intellectual fragmentation" of Harvard by sending in the police.

The next speaker was Shura, and the charged private disagreement between two old friends was now to play out in a very public way. Shura had always been a man who actively resisted showing his feelings to the world, but now, feeling that his community was threatened, he struck out against the danger.

Because he was spending the semester away at Princeton, and because he never said anything at faculty meetings, many people were surprised to see Shura getting to his feet. "The great unexpected guest was Alex," says Sam Beer. Shura carried no written draft of his remarks. His hands were clasped as he began.

"Mr. President," he said, "I am afraid that you are now condemned to hear a third exotic interpretation of the Harvard accent, but this cannot be helped." There was laughter, but Shura ignored it. "For the rest," he said,

> I don't mean to be humorous, because I don't feel humorous at all. I feel this is a critical hour as far as this university is concerned, a critical hour in its history, and this no doubt is the most critical meeting of this faculty which I have attended in the last twenty years since I have joined this faculty. I have been now away from Harvard for this year, but I have been watching, watching developments here rather closely, even though from far away, and I have accumulated, I have accumulated thoughts and feelings which I am afraid now I have to disgorge, I have to unload on you. And I am afraid also this will take some time.
>
> I have come to speak, and I have come to speak out candidly, and I am not going to mince any words. I feel that

what has happened, with the invasion of privacy, the occupation of a building, the manhandling, however gentle, of the deans, the theft of papers and documents, the rifling of files—I think this is legally criminal and morally outrageous, and I think the action to punish it was perfectly correct. Force and crime must be met by force, and I think that was done, and I think it was well done.

For a second there was clear silence in the room. Then came a crack of applause loud enough that Shura was forced once more to pause until the clapping subsided. He waited impatiently, and after that he spoke in a way that suggested he did not wish to be interrupted again.

Let me say that we all in this room should understand that this business must be stopped. This business must not be allowed to go on, because if it is allowed to go on, then anyone in this room will face the same experience as the officers of University Hall faced. Anyone can be then dragged out, carried like a sack of potatoes out of your lecture room and dropped over the stairs of Emerson Hall or Sever [Hall], or whatever it be, unless, unless indeed he submits meekly, submits meekly to demands, to preposterous demands and is willing to allow himself to be raped, symbolically, as happened two weeks ago when a member of this faculty had a banana put into his mouth. I think this is outrageous, and particularly outrageous if you think what the issues are, how preposterous, how irrelevant the issues are about which we are talking here.

Sitting in the audience was John Kenneth Galbraith, who had left his son's wedding rehearsal dinner in California and flown back to Cambridge for the meeting. At this moment, Galbraith experienced the certain sensation that of all the hundreds of faces in the room, Shura had picked his out and was glaring at him. "That's just Ken's ego," says the former dean of students John Fox, but Shura could well have been looking at his old friend, for now he continued:

I hear all this talk about the imperialist war machine, but any man in reasonable possession of his reasonable powers must understand that this is all bunk, this is mendacious, low, political talk. The ROTC! The American war machine! The American war machine, whatever else happens, is now protecting the freedom of Western Europe. The American war machine is protecting the freedom of India. The former ambassador to India, who happens also to be a member of this faculty, while during his term of tenure, his finest hour, his proudest moment, was when he was able to get American bombers to fly over New Delhi in order to ward off the Chinese invasion of the country. And here we are talking about ROTC. Those pilots he was so proud of may well have been trained originally in one of those ROTC camps.

The meeting was broadcast on the radio, and drivers began pulling their cars out of traffic to listen by the side of the road. Groups of students listened in their rooms. People throughout Cambridge and Boston paused at what they were doing, leaning on their brooms or pencils and staring at the radio. And the professors seated in the theater, even those who could not agree with a word Shura was saying, took everything in so carefully that thirty years later they could still recall it.

I think [Shura continued] we all must understand that in historical experience, this faculty in critical times is not the proper guardian of academic freedom. That is true for a number of reasons, and history has proved that. Remember, and many of you are old enough to remember, that sixteen, seventeen years ago, when the academic freedom was threatened brutally and viciously, not from within, indeed, but from without, it was not the faculty that stood up against the threat. I do remember the mood of the faculty at that time. The faculty was subdued. The faculty was scared. And if, at that time, if at that time a conservative member of this faculty had gotten up and said, "Look at those people, they are lying before congressional committees and we are all here dedicated to truth, let us fire them," the faculty would have fired them. And if those people were not fired, that was the merit, that was the desert of the administration of Provost Buck first and then of President Pusey and then of the much-maligned governing boards of this university. I remember well. I remember well how President Pusey, a much younger President Pusey, way back in 1952 or 1953, had his first meeting in Eliot House with the students, and a student asked him: "Oh, why should we really bother about Senator McCarthy, just a junior senator from Wisconsin and here is Harvard?" President Pusey pounded the table and said: "This is evil, and when I see evil I fight it." And that is what he did. He did it then as he did it now also this week.

Gazing out at his colleagues, Shura now began to talk in a general way about character and, quite bluntly, to question theirs. Their response was odd—they applauded him. That, says a younger professor who was there, was because each member of the audience knew himself to be quite incapable of deceit and was sure, therefore, that Shura was exposing the next fellow. (The perfidious are connoisseurs of courage.)

Let us take once, once a candid look at ourselves, at this faculty, and see why the faculty is really not apt to protect academic freedom and must leave it at critical times to the administration. Look at all the decisions that have been made so far. Look at the hesitance, look at the uncertainty, look at the vacillation. Why? There are many reasons for that. Some of them at least are respectable; others are not. There are a number of people, no doubt, so preoccupied with their research work, with their scholarly work, that they will have nothing to do with administrative affairs and with the management of the university, however important. But there are also other people at this university and other tendencies and motivations, and let us not close our eyes to them. There are the middle-aged popularity kids who have

done considerable damage to this university. In addition to
the popularity seekers, there are also the fearers of unpopu-
larity, and well they may fear in the atmosphere of terror and
tension that is being created—fear of boycotts, fear of the
reduction of election in their courses. There are other
people, people between forty-five and forty-six—

The chuckle of laughter that came in response to this slip sounded
dissonant in the face of a man upbraiding his entire community. Shura
quickly corrected himself:

—between forty-five and fifty-five, as likely as not they have
children of college age. They have lousy parent-child relationships and they don't want to louse them up some more.

To be sure it was a performance, but only in the sense that this was a
great lecturer giving his greatest lecture. And it worked so well because
his emotions overwhelmed any formal rhetorical technique; emotion
became his technique. There was a musical quality to his speaking. The
plangent Russian cadences, the shifting tempos, the repetitions of
phrase, the way he applied limpid emphasis to some words and found
rushes of feeling slurring others nearly to the point of unintelligibil-
ity—all gave his voice the quality of a horn making its way into the core
of a theme. More even than the words themselves, it was the sound of
his voice that conveyed his feelings. He spoke in a tone that was resonant
and sonorous and yet so without varnish that the timbre alone betrayed
feelings he had locked away for decades. It was all there: the losses, the
disappointments, the dangers, the fading hopes, the anger at what the
world was not, the broad capacity for love, and the tired expectation of
heartbreak now, even here, even in America, even at Harvard.

For the first time since he'd come to America, he was heard to admit
that the country was flawed:

I think what we have to consider, what we have to consider
here is that the whole set of problems that we face here in
this university and in this country with regard to the univer-

sities is altogether incongruous. You see, I am not Pollyanna. I know quite well that there are many things in the United States, many things in America that are horribly wrong, but I know also that there are many things that are wonderfully right with the United States. And among those things are the great universities of this country, and among them, Harvard, like what there is nothing comparable, there is no counterpart anywhere in the world. And to try to destroy, to disrupt, to destroy, to attack this university, this is criminal. This is done precisely because as the Roman lawyers used to say of the Conditio Occasionis, a criminal steals a watch just because it is lying there. Just because they are in the vicinity of the university, just because they are in the proximity of the university, they attack the university. They attack something that is really the finest flower of American culture.

And then, in his peroration, the part people remember best, he gave them his culture:

What I must tell all of you is that what you must do is to read the literature of the subject and I am sure that most of you have failed to read the literature. [Much laughter.] I am not going to give you a long reading list. But I am going to tell you about one single item on that list which you must read even though I am going to summarize it for you now in conclusion. This is a fairy tale by Hans Christian Andersen, a fairy tale which the Danes, in the dark days of the Nazi occupation, used so subtly and so effectively. That fairy tale is called "The Most Unbelievable Thing." It deals with a kingdom, and in the kingdom there was, of course, a king, and he had a princess, and he was interested in the progress of arts. And at a certain point he announced that he would give the princess in marriage to the man who had accomplished the most unbelievable thing.

And there was a tremendous competition in the land, and

finally the great day came when all those prepared works had been submitted—many marvelous things. But towering, towering high above them was a most wonderful thing. It was a clock, a clock produced by a handsome young man. And that was a most wonderful mechanism, showing the calendar back and forth into the past and into the future, showing the time, and around it were all the great spiritual and intellectual figures in the history of mankind. And whenever the clock struck, those figures exercised most beautiful movements. And everybody, the judges and the people, said, "Yes, to accomplish a thing like that is the most unbelievable thing." And the princess looked at the clock, and she looked at the handsome young man, and she liked them both very much. And the judges were just about to pronounce their judgment when a new competitor came, a low-brow fellow. He also carried something in his hand, and that was a sledgehammer. And he walked up to that clock, and he swung out, and with three blows he smashed up the clock. [Shura made violent chopping motions.] And everybody said, "This really—why, this is the most unbelievable thing to happen," and the judges also had to adjudge that.

And this is relevant to the present situation of Harvard. And unless you do something about it, it will remain relevant. Except that Andersen also has a happy end to his story which may, I am afraid, not be relevant for us. Because what happened in the story was that the king, of course, had to remain true to his word. There was the wedding day and the church bells and the low-brow fellow stood at the altar, and the princess was marching down the aisle. And then, and then at that moment, the spirits, the spirits of all those intellectual and great spiritual figures in the history of mankind, they suddenly arose. All those allegedly smashed-up figures, their spirits arose. They fell upon the low-brow guy. They smothered him, and in the end the princess got the young man. And I can only hope that the spirits of this faculty, the spirits of this faculty will rise, will rise and smash up, and smash up all this criminal nonsense that is going around in the country.

Don't forget, it is now one hundred years since President Eliot started converting what after all was an ancient but rather obscure college into a great university, the greatest university in the land. This, like the clock in the story, like all great works of art, this is frail, a frail and fragile creation, however beautiful, and unless you do something about it, and unless you let the administration do something about it if you are unable to do something about it, then this wonderful work of art will be destroyed and the guilt will be yours.

HE HAD TAKEN TWENTY MINUTES. THE MEETING THAT DAY WOULD last another three hours. The speakers ranged from the quiet Russian-born archaeologist George Hanfmann, who told of his horror at inhaling "the smell of violence, which I have smelled before, in 1918 to 1921 when young men in jackets ran around filling the basements of Lubyanka with gore," to the radical philosopher of science Hilary Putnam, who said, "I think one might make the case that *we* have the right to be civilly disobedient, having . . . tried to get the Corporation to do what we want done about ROTC and having been no more lucky than the students." But afterward what people talked about was Shura. He had taken the measure of a crisis and responded in a way that was equal to the moment, so that the moment became his. Nobody remembers Harvard faculty meetings except for this one, and mostly what they remember about it is what a man named Alexander Gerschenkron had to say.

They also remember how he said it. People found meaning in Shura's voice that existed apart from what he said. That perhaps explains why not everyone recalled the speech in the same way. There was a professor who thought Shura's delivery was "quite quiet, his voice trembled." Another felt Shura was so angry he was "hyperventilating." A third became convinced he was listening to the reasoned tones of "a child of the Enlightenment." Others were sure he talked of things—remarkable things!—that never passed his lips. According to one man, the climax of the day came with "the parallel he made between the Bolsheviks taking over in Russia and the Harvard students taking over the building, and the only thing to do was beat them! beat them! beat them!"

The impact of the speech carried well beyond Loeb. The text was reprinted in various newspapers and magazines—an essay in the *New York Times Book Review* quoted from it at length—with the result that Shura found his movements interrupted by a swarm of handshakes, telephone calls, telegrams, and even autograph requests. For weeks the postman overburdened his letter box with hosannas from friends, enemies, and colleagues. The biologist Edward O. Wilson wrote to tell him how "courageous" he was; an excited Harvard alumnus compared the speech to "Churchill's radio talks during the Battle of Britain"; and from "the outside," as he situated himself, White House budget director James Schlesinger exclaimed, "Amen, bravo, bully for you." The students who wrote tended to describe "how gratifying" it was to see at least one faculty member taking a firm stand.

The speech seems to have meant the most to the older people who heard it. It was oratory, not formal prose, and yet it had all of the passion and personality that Shura kept out of his books and articles, so that like a short story or a novel it captured feelings that many people were experiencing but could not quite articulate themselves. Quite a few of those in the audience heard it not as a jeremiad, but as a celebration of traditional American democratic values, in particular the concept of progress—the optimistic liberal view that the story of America is the story of improvement within a just, responsive system. To subvert the system, to operate by force or fiat, accomplishes change but not progress. William Alfred thought of the speech in this way. "There is an important part of human nature that manifests very early when children take great joy in building things and then kicking them down," Alfred said. "It's part of our animal reality. Shura certainly dramatized this in that speech. His speech was a stand for sanity, probity and higher integrity. He was the way we all were and what we felt inchoately he expressed for us. A terror for people like me who live a life of books is that books don't matter. That's why we were so worried—that reason would go by the board. The speech released the ongoing sense of the beauty of the moral."

There were also plenty of people who felt, as Stephen Jay Gould did, that Shura's view was too romantic, that America and Harvard weren't as fragile or as pristine as Shura claimed they were. "It was such an idealization of what Harvard was," Gould says, "and I was moved by it, but there never was a clock like that." Monroe Engel found the speech "painful to watch because I admired him so much." Engel believed that Shura simply did not understand the United States. "He was equating it with Germany," he says, "but this wasn't Germany." Out at Berkeley, the cultural historian Carl Schorske was thinking the same thing. "I saw this in a number of émigré professors," he says. "They massed together in anxiety as they saw the 1960s unfolding and kind of misjudged it."

When Shura himself reflected upon his speech in the weeks following it, he took to using a pessimistic couplet he'd worked up: "I feel I have done my bit, but it didn't do a bit of good." In a sense he was right. The students who took over University Hall received the mildest of punishments, and the unrest at Harvard did not subside. In a scathing letter to Galbraith written in late April, Shura predicted that the revolution the radicals were really inciting was a national conservative backlash—a "*Reegan*" revolution. "If on April 11 the Faculty had rallied behind the administration and condign punishment had been swiftly meted out to the perpetrators of the outrages, then, after one or two more disorderly episodes, the air would have been cleared at Harvard and a trail of sanity blazed for other universities. As it is the student unrest will continue and with it the swelling wave of reaction in the country. Berkeley aided by Watts put Reagan into Sacramento. Further student unrest plus Negro riots may well put him into the White House."

Heidi remembers Shura talking that way as well. "As I think back upon my father in those days, he proved to be prophetic," she says.

> I think it is precisely because of his background that he had perspective and understanding of America that natives didn't have. He saw signs and read consequences into them

that liberal natives didn't take seriously. Those people who say he was confusing the student movement with violence in Nazi Austria are wrong. He was afraid that the radical left excesses would be the impetus for a different kind of excess, the radical right. My father knew all about Ronald Reagan, and he thought Reagan was dangerous, that he was indifferent to all but the rich whose taxes he would cut at any cost. My father used to talk about the homeless people who would be all over the streets in the wake of those tax cuts, and he'd get furious and go on and on about how dangerous Reagan was, that the progressive Democratic party was going to be destroyed by him, and what was left of the New Deal dismantled.

When John Kenneth Galbraith took to the op-ed page of the *New York Times* that spring, he was not nearly as alarmed. "Let us not be too depressed," he wrote. "Universities are going to survive." That was the essential difference between Galbraith's view of America and Shura's. Shura lived for books and by the book, and he thought others should too. Perhaps because, as Shura's friend H. R. Habakkuk of Oxford says, "the world for him was a very uncertain place," when people couldn't be as morally consistent as Shura wanted them to be, he became apocalyptic. Galbraith was principled too, but those principles were accompanied by his political nature and his skepticism. Galbraith took a calmer view and didn't worry so much. Thirty years after he denounced Lyndon Johnson, Galbraith would call a news conference and admit that he'd been wrong about the president. Galbraith had faith in the turmoil of process. He knew there would be another tomorrow and another paper on the newsstand. Shura could never be so sure.

"If I had gone through what Alex Gerschenkron had gone through I probably would have had stronger, more vital reactions on issues than I did," Galbraith says. Shura could not say anything so conciliatory, could never forgive Galbraith for anything, just as he could never forgive the 1960s. "Come on, Alex, let's bury the hatchet," Galbraith said to him one day after the Vietnam war was over. "I am not prepared to do that," Shura replied. Another time they passed each other on the sidewalk. "Good morning," said Galbraith. Shura let out a low growl and kept right on going. They never saw each other again.

AT THE END OF 1969, SHURA TURNED SIXTY-FIVE, HARVARD'S mandatory retirement age, but, by special invitation of the president, he was given another five years at the university. That honor gratified him. Little else in those years did. Many old men look back across their lives and conclude that they were young in a better time. Shura had always felt quite the opposite, but now he was reconsidering.

As America, the Harvard faculty, and, he began to feel, everything else too disappointed Shura, the one thing that never let him down was Christianity. Many times in the years after 1969 he got up early and walked along the damp, reseeded lawns of Harvard Yard on his way to Appleton Chapel for the morning order of worship. He had come increasingly to depend upon his belief for solace, for uplift, for balance, and for the encouragement to keep on. In remarks he wrote and gave at morning prayers, he described how his spiritual faith grounded him during his difficult times. "We waver uncertainly," he said, "between exultation and gloom, between certitude and doubt. But the clearer we recognize that our world is a world of relativism where everything can—nay, must be—doubted, questioned, criticized, and refuted, the more urgent is our need for something within ourselves that we can accept once and for all, that we shall never question, never criticize, never doubt; the more urgent, I say, is our need for simple absolute truth, which is the rock upon which our world must stand. This to me is the primary meaning of religion."

From 1969 to 1971 Shura spent several nights of almost every week talking with students about the problems of society. He always came at their invitation, and, as they listened, he explained why he felt that they were all mixed up about politics and society and economics. Afterward he concluded that it had all been "a prodigious waste of time." As he looked around him, he saw antiwar demonstrators shattering every window in Harvard Square; policemen waving guns at students in Adams House; a bomb going off at Harvard's Center for International Studies; a fire set at the ROTC building; and students in Quincy House proclaiming that they would no longer eat their meals unless cookies were served at lunch. "A lot of that shit was juvenile," says Herbert Gintis, "and he let it make him bitter."

When unhappy news reports arrived from Cambodia, from Kent State and Jackson State, and from the Watergate Hotel, they damped down much of what remained of Shura's optimism. Even when things were going well in his own life, Shura had always taken the country's tribulations hard, and now personal setbacks slapped at him like sheets of cold rain. In 1970, pleading "our budgets," the Ford Foundation cut off its funding for the Economic History Workshop, putting it out of business. The next year Shura and Erica's landlord said he was selling the house in Shady Hill Square and they ended up in a modest Harvard Faculty town house. A year after that, Harvard University Press rejected Shura's third collection of essays, criticizing it as "hors d'oeuvres disguised as an entree." He was told that he owed his readers "a more sustained and focused view of an historical problem." In other words, the editors thought he should have written a big book. The essays were published in several European countries, but never in the United States.

At the same time the economics department was in an uproar. With the support of patrons like Galbraith and Leontief, politically minded young radical economists wanted to make their work into a formal critique of the American consumer society by dividing the department into Marxist and capitalist sections. And then, in 1973, the students were attacking his course. There were no other requirements left in the department, they complained. Why was The Economic History of Europe an exception? One student stood up in a meeting and said, "Economic history is my favorite subject. I just don't think I can make a living at it." Abe Bergson was put in charge of a committee to decide what to do. He sided with the students, whereupon Shura lost his fiefdom and Bergson lost his friend of thirty years. "The warmth was gone," Bergson says. "I was bereft."

Shura had grown up in a culture that revered men who had spent a lifetime accumulating knowledge. To him the professorial ideal was, as he said in a letter to his former teacher, Hans Kelsen, "an old, tall, broad-shouldered man with a big grey beard, clad in a solemn black cloak." Now youth was everything and he felt discarded and betrayed.

Increasingly Shura was on bad terms with people, spoiling for arguments, dispensing bile at the mildest provocation. Elena Levin saw him
explode at a clerk in the library. Another day, when he was fined for
keeping books out too long, he fired off several vituperative letters,
including one to the director of the university library in which he went
on at great length. The library was "arrogant and unreasonable." It was
"reckless." It was "offensive." It was nasty phrases in German (they
were not translated). It was nasty phrases in French (also not translated). "This is very German and very French," Shura continued, "but
it is downright un-Harvard and downright un-Widener. I regard the
whole thing as part of the general assault on the Faculty and the Faculty
privileges—an emanation of the atrocious *un-Geist* that was so much in
evidence in the last few years."

He had always been contentious and proud, but in the past these
qualities had been tempered with charm. Now, because he was feeling
underappreciated, passed over, and passed by, the tone had lost its balance. A professor from Toronto showed him something he'd written,
and Shura replied harshly, "I always have had nothing but contempt for
gossip when it is masquerading as scholarship. Kindly spare me further
offerings of your products." Then came this gratuitous barb: "Has your
German improved since the day when you appeared in my office unable
to read a letter written in very clear German?" There were many occasions upon which he was completely recalcitrant. He screamed at other
people's secretaries, and he shouted at Russian Research Center director Richard Pipes so often that Pipes finally wrote to tell him that "if
you wish to retain relations with me, please do not again raise your
voice at me or order me what I must or must not do." After Zeph Stewart offended him in a faculty meeting, they never spoke again. When
Simon and Edith Kuznets wanted to visit, Erica told them to stay
home. "Your Simon is so sarcastic," she told Edith.

Peter McClelland watched all this with alarm. McClelland blamed
what was happening to Shura on Harvard:

> There are a lot of tragedies at Harvard. It's an unnatural
> community, and it destroys a lot of people. Harvard is an
> unbelievably demanding place full of narrow specialists, and

the pressure on most people there to prove that they belong is enormous. The very intellectual intensity of Harvard can squeeze out the humanity of the place. There is a notable absence of warmth because there isn't time for warmth. In the early 1960's, Shura could reside in this community and achieve its collegiality—he was "Good Old Alex." Then, a decade later, in the wake of the Bust, that community turned out not to be bound terribly tightly, and the collapse was astonishing. The disintegration of acquaintances meant the community fragmented. Alex was caught up in it. He brought a special European lens to the situation and he misread it and his misunderstanding could not be forgiven. Alex was faced with an unreasonable, uncharitable collection of human beings. He became isolated and he became angry. That Alex, the irascible, isolated Alex, would have been a disappointment to the Alex I first knew in the early 1960's, a man of extraordinary graciousness and perceptiveness. Back then, he didn't have corners you collided with.

AS HIS CAMBRIDGE CIRCLE NARROWED, SHURA TOOK AN INCREASING interest in his daughters. He looked forward to their visits more than ever. After her divorce, Heidi taught high school English in New Haven, and she came to see him often. As intense and full of strong convictions as her father, she shared his love for French, Russian, and English nineteenth-century novels, for Victorian armature—they bought each other music boxes—and for Democratic politics. Their conversations about Anthony Trollope and Franklin Roosevelt could last entire afternoons. Susi lived farther away, in Croton-on-Hudson in New York's Westchester County, and her trips to Cambridge and New Hampshire were less frequent. When she came it was always an occasion. Susi was a warm and joyful person, blonde, plump, physically affectionate, and always dreaming up little events for her father. There might be a poem or skit about him to be performed by the grandchildren, or a concert of Austrian folk songs that she'd taught everyone during the five-hour drive to his house, or a sudden pie in a grandson's face. Afterward, while

Erica busied Susi's husband Tony with assorted tasks, Susi would plunk down on the couch across from Shura in his white chair, and while the grandchildren played on the carpet, she'd make him laugh. Whenever either daughter left to go back home, Shura always looked so forlorn that they felt that, by leaving him, they were breaking a little more of his heart.

In 1974 Shura traveled to England to receive an honorary degree from Oxford. During the presentation ceremony, he was described as a man of many parts who knew four languages. Standing there, receiving the highest of honors from the most famous university in the world, Shura became visibly agitated. The problem was that he knew ten languages. Possibly even twenty languages! Here it was, the great tribute to his scholarly life, and he had been underestimated. Later, with all the casual unconcern he could muster, he let the vice-regent of Oxford know the truth of the matter.

Swarthmore College also wanted to give him an honorary degree in 1974, and asked him to be the Commencement speaker. He prepared remarks, but then he was told by his doctor that he was too weak to tolerate the demands of the trip. A year later he was given a second chance by Swarthmore's president Theodore Friend, and once again had to send regrets. His health also brought him humiliation. The enlarged prostate forced him to begin wearing a catheter and a drainage bag on his leg at all times, which he thought was "dirty" and embarrassing for his wife to see. He who had always scorned the winter by striding around coatless in deepest January now found the wind was sometimes too strong for him to venture outside. These matters he tried to keep secret. "He did not want anyone to know how sick he was," says Heidi. "He did not want to be the invalid."

In June 1975 he retired from teaching, claiming to be glad about not having to lecture anymore. His head was full of plans to write the time horizon book; he was going to show that Harvard Press. "I think retirement is a joyous expectation," he told the *New York Times*. To his friend Herbert Block he elaborated: "I feel no regrets at all, and am looking forward to a great deal of pleasant work. . . . I always wanted a free year in Cambridge because of Widener Library and never could have it. And now, deo volente, I can have it."

The Lord was not willing. In 1976 he suffered the heart attack that sent him into cardiac arrest at peak lunch hour in the middle of the Faculty Club. This stay in the hospital was even more painful than it might have been, because it told him how isolated from his community he had become. "I don't think he felt he had a great many friends here," says Donald Fleming, who came to visit. "I didn't have the impression many people went to see him."

Soon after he recovered, he was struck again. Susi was on her way to the dry cleaners one day in the spring of 1977 when she experienced mild chest pains. She came home and got into bed. While Tony was calling an ambulance, she suffered a fatal heart attack. When word that she was dead reached Cambridge, Nancy Dorfman and her daughter Ann arranged to drive Shura and Erica to Croton-on-Hudson. "They sat in the back seat," says Nancy,

> and it was as though we were off on an outing except that every so often Erica would burst into tears and Alex would say tenderly but pretty insistently, "Don't do that. You're not allowed to cry." At lunch we went to this roadside place to eat, and I had this weird feeling that it was like a picnic. It was as though we weren't supposed to admit it was an unpleasant occasion. Erica would cry, and he'd tell her not to, and he kept up a cheerful conversation the whole way down. Then we got there and Alex walked into Susi's house and suddenly let out a primal scream. He couldn't hold it all in anymore.

Erica distributed gifts of books to the grandchildren, and then she and Shura went off to the funeral home, where he forced himself to view the body and say goodbye. Sinking to his knees beside his dead child, he recited the Russian Orthodox liturgy he'd known since boyhood. "She looked very dead," he reported later with a little of the old bravado. Back at the house, he took Susi's fourteen-year-old son Jonathan aside and told him to be optimistic: he would overcome this; Jonathan had his whole life ahead of him. Then Shura went home and gave up.

*   *   *

PEOPLE WHO VISITED SHURA DURING THE LAST YEAR OF HIS LIFE remember a pall over his household. The time horizons were put away forever. He had no interest in thinking about how people measured their future when his daughter was dead of a weak heart given to her, he was sure, by her weak-hearted father. His guilt was intense, as was his misery. Outliving a child is something no parent ever expects, and when it happened to Shura and Erica, it was one tragedy too many for both of them.

In October 1978 Shura went into the hospital for prostate surgery. His body was so frail that he was warned that there was a good chance he wouldn't live through the procedure. Nancy Dorfman took Erica to see him the day before the operation. "I walked in," she says, "and he said, 'Oh, Nancy!' and he put on such a show. He was so alive. It was such a great thing to see me. He was so excited, so upbeat, so animated, telling stories. Then he turned to Erica and he said, 'Now Erica, tomorrow you'll come in here and they're going to tell you what happened, and no matter what they tell you, you are not to cry.' He was so serious. It seemed so deep in the heart of him. Nobody was to get upset about him." The surgery went well, but two days later a blood vessel ruptured in his groin. When the doctor told Erica that they had lost him, she did as Shura had asked. Dry-eyed she requested a last look at him, and then, when she saw his face, she wept.

Not long after Shura died, Erica visited Austria. At age seventy-four, she was thinking that perhaps she'd like to move back. As she traveled about Vienna, everything she saw offended her. She said she found "those" Austrians tactless, xenophobic, and undemocratic. And so she returned to Cambridge.

Shura found a way to watch over her even after he was gone. Years before he died, he went to an insurance company and purchased a special annuity designed just for Erica. The terms were that upon his death she would be guaranteed a comfortable fixed annual income for as long as she lived. Once she died, if anything was left, it all reverted to the insurance company. The insurance people were gambling upon how long Erica would live, and they turned out to know their business. It is possible to die of grief and that is what happened to Erica. She lived a helpless eighteen months after Shura died, during which she hired a handyman who swindled her out of thousands of dollars. Erica told Marjorie Galenson that she'd never been so lonely and had never imagined she could feel so lonely. Erica hardly ever went to New Hampshire after Shura died. One of the few times she did go was with Heidi. One evening Heidi took her mother to see a play, a comedy. Erica cried all the way home. "She was inconsolable," says Heidi. "She had grieved all her life for her dead mother and the loss of her country and now he was gone. I knew she'd never welcome anything in life after my father's death."

Until her death Erica was never stoic in the way Shura expected of others. It was during the last few weeks, as she lay dying of heart failure in Cambridge city hospital, that she became as noble as he always insisted she was. For weeks her lungs slowly filled with fluid and she did not once complain about the excruciating pain and the scary losses of breath. In her final hours she fell into a delirium, muttering incomprehensibly in German. At one point she switched to English and reviled the Austrians for the dreadful things she'd seen them do to the Jews in 1938.

PEOPLE WHO KNEW SHURA OFTEN TALK ABOUT HIM BY COMPARING him to characters in books they love. When he said to the *New York Times* upon his retirement that he missed the shipyards because the life there didn't "follow you home at night into your leisure and your dreams," it told people how difficult Shura must have found it to be always so morally invested in everything. In that way he was like Henry James's duped and disappointed Isabel Archer, of whom the countess Gemini says, "You seem to have so many scruples, so many reasons, so many ties. . . . My poor Isabel, you are not simple enough." To others Shura was Cyrano de Bergerac, a romantic idealist with unusual power and artistry of language using his love for words, his sharp wit, and his sharp sword to overcome his disadvantages. Or perhaps he was

Chekhov's Ivanov, a man built of so many wheels and screws that he was as inscrutable to other people as he was to himself. Nobody was ever surprised that Shura enjoyed *The Pickwick Papers* so much because, like Pickwick himself, Shura was such an appealing and thoroughly principled gentleman. Mostly, however, Shura seemed like a man out of a Russian novel. Visible in him were the sorrows of Zhivago, the valor and decorum of Prince André, and the flights of joy pulled down by the brooding conscience of Levin.

Really, of course, he was none of them and all of them. And just as Shura read all those books for pleasure and also for personal edification, he himself served that same kind of function for the real people who knew him; they experienced him the way he experienced books. To his friends, he was a living, breathing literary figure, an extraordinary, ordinary man of many parts. You could enjoy or object to Gerschenkron, but you couldn't exactly say it was this way or that way with him. Yet if other people didn't think they exactly knew him, it didn't stop them from regarding him as a prism that strangely helped them see into themselves.

Since he didn't talk about so much of himself, how well Shura knew himself is a mystery. It was perhaps more important for him to know the characters in books. He liked to make dismissive comments on the subject. "Know thy self is the worst advice given to us by the old Greeks," he once wrote to Ruth Scheurer. "By looking at yourself one doesn't get far. . . . Don't torture yourself." It was ironic, and true to form, that Shura's most notable public display of personal introspection perhaps came unbeknown to him, in the preface he wrote to accompany his translation of Eli Heckscher's *Economic History of Sweden*. In life, Heckscher was a somewhat colorless workaholic, a kind and intelligent enough man, but a slogger who wrote all day every day and spent his spare time reading detective stories. When Shura wrote about him, however, Heckscher was transformed into a dashing figure of truly incandescent parts. Shura was only fifty-two when he wrote the Heckscher preface, but given the proximity he always felt to death, it's possible he was resorting to an unconscious subterfuge: he was using Heckscher as a means of elegizing himself.

In a sense [Shura wrote], Heckscher himself was a great figure of the nineteenth century. His immense erudition, his
classical background, his modesty, his fierce independence,
his willingness at all times, in the words of his beloved
Horace, to step on the treacherous ashes covering the smol-
dering fire of conflict and controversy, and, above all his
severity to himself, his supreme sense of duty—these qualities of a very great scholar are less readily produced by our
age of anxiety and instability. To the very end he remained
faithful to his mission and continued to labor in the knowledge that the night cometh when no man can work.

EPILOGUE

Grandpa Vati

His chief pleasure and delight was in the children,
with whom he was a child himself, and master of the
revels.

Charles Dickens, *Nicholas Nickleby*

LIKE MOST HUMAN BEINGS, MY GRANDFATHER WAS A PERSON
of contradictions. He understood two dozen languages, but
expressed scant desire to understand himself. He spent his life
thinking about problems of backwardness, even as there was always
something held back about him. He was a dazzling presence and a distant presence—passionately engaged in the world and stiffly withdrawn
from it. Sentimental and unsympathetic, fragile and bullying, modest
and strutting, romantic and worried, gregarious and ill-tempered;
nothing about him was straightforward. What most distinguished my
grandfather from other men was that his qualities and inconsistencies
were so pronounced. Many people are complex. Few are so vivid in
their complexities.

My grandfather lived through horrible times, and once those times
were over, he never really talked about them with anyone, including, so
far as I know, his wife. In this way, he rarely admitted the obvious—that
they made him unhappy. Such is the nature of human beings that
because he could not say he was unhappy, his unhappiness remained
with him.

Probably nothing pained my grandfather more than losing Russia. It
was typically Russian to shrug off hardships and disappointments, and

that is what he tried to do; he became an expert on the Soviet economy who locked away his Russian boyhood. But the country of his past was always a part of his present. His younger daughter was called by her nickname, Heidi, but she noticed that when her father was feeling most buoyant, he referred to her by her Russian patronymic, Marya Alexandrovna. All his life my grandfather rode only one-speed bicycles, explaining that this was the Russian style. (He was sometimes heard to proclaim, "Russians don't need gears.") Up in New Hampshire, where the geography and the summer temperatures reminded him of the Russian countryside, he once pointed to some exposed beams in a friend's house and said that Russian peasants built their houses that way, but they did a much better job of it. When people my grandfather knew made visits to the Soviet Union, he begged them to bring him back sunflower seeds and striped Russian sailor's T-shirts.

My grandfather once set down some of his feelings about life after Russia in a letter he wrote to a man he venerated, Aleksandr Solzhenitsyn. My grandfather never met the great Russian writer, but he read his books carefully enough to feel he had. That sense of familiarity was such that just after Solzhenitsyn was exiled from the Soviet Union in 1974, my grandfather took it upon himself to welcome the novelist to the West. In his letter he offered the words he said he himself had lived by: "Don't be sad about the Russia you lost, because wherever you are there is Russia."

The most important way my grandfather found consolation for his lost country was through the works of the great Russian writers he'd read in Odessa with his friends. "Rereading favorite books from childhood," he once wrote, "serves to recall to us ourselves as we were a long time ago." Tolstoy, Chekhov, Turgenev, and Pushkin accompanied him through life. Every time he slipped into *Anna Karenina* or *Eugene Onegin*, he felt himself overcome with a simultaneous twinkling pleasure and a bleak sadness. Seated in his large upholstered reading chair with Tolstoy in his hand, he was not only recapturing the feeling of his Russia, he was cheered and soothed in ways that no human was ever permitted to do for him. His was in many ways a private life, and he took his comforts privately, in Cyrillic. His confidantes were Russian literary characters. In this way, as infrequently as my grandfather talked about

Russia, I think that Russia formed his inner life and he always remained a Russian in that inner life. When I proposed this to Isaiah Berlin, he thought for a moment. Then Berlin nodded and said, "Fundamentally he was Russian, culturally he was a Russian, but his home was not Russia. It was Russian literature."

MY GRANDFATHER DIDN'T COMMAND ARMIES OR LEAD GOVERNMENTS or win pennants, but he was big, big in his qualities. I think of him as a real-life character, someone who was not like everybody else precisely because in him you could see so much of other people. There was a purity about him. He thought about what it meant to be a man of strong personal attributes and he had them in full measure. When he was brave, you could say, "That is courage." When he was harsh, you could say, "That is unkindness." When he stood by his principles, he embodied probity. And then when he strained those rules, you were intrigued, wondering what would impel somebody who was so emphatically honorable to go and do *that?* In the end, he was a person who made other people curious about him, and he usually lived up to the invitation.

Certainly for me he always did. When I came to visit, we played a lot of chess. He liked to position himself as both my teacher and my critic, responding to my moves with elaborate grunts and vivid mumblings. After a move that he particularly approved of, he would puff on his pipe and say, "Possible, Nicky Boy . . . *possible*." He always won these matches, except one day before supper. The two of us were in the middle of a game, and somehow my grandfather's queen was taken. He looked genuinely shocked. A moment later he suddenly reached out and cleared all the pieces off the board. "*Num-num*," he said, meaning it was time to eat.

That was an astonishing thing to see, and such an aberration in an otherwise doting relationship that I could make no sense of it until many years later when I began to hear about what kind of a croquet player he was. Many things in life were complicated for Alexander Gerschenkron, but being a grandfather wasn't one of them.

He became a grandfather twice in 1962, the year my cousin Jonathan and I were born three months apart, but as a man who was outspoken in his dislike for babies, he didn't really get interested in me until the later 1960s, when things in his own life were increasingly difficult. I imagine him to have been a lot like Alexander Herzen's father, whose balled fists and jangled nerves relaxed in the presence of his young son as "he found rest from the incessant agitation, conflict, and vexation in which he had kept himself."

After my parents divorced, my grandfather worried a lot about how I would "turn out without a male image," as he once put it to his former student, the Harvard economist John Meyer. He encouraged other former students to visit me whenever they were in New Haven—I remember being curious about the sudden appearances of these emissaries from the Gerschenkron north—and Meyer says that my grandfather devoted a lot of time to thinking about how to get close to me himself: "He made a real effort for you." All I knew about that was that my visits to my grandfather were some of the best days of my youth.

I was like most people in the sense that I found my Grandpa Vati (*fah*-tee), as all of his grandchildren called him, to be a person of irresistible charms, the most interesting man I had ever met. It was with my grandfather that I saw lightning split a tree. The russet-coated animal we glimpsed tracking across a snowy field was my first fox. But any boy would remember those events. My grandfather's special ability was to make regular daily activity part of the dramatic narrative of his life. Things were not just done, he was doing them, and that active spirit made him very much the hero of his own life story and my hero too.

He took me to his barber shop, to his newsstand, his pastry shop, his diner, and his bookstore, and I could tell—as anyone could have—that he aspired to loyalty and believed in it. He made it clear that every thing and every moment was important and in that way he showed me how all of life could be filled with meaning. But probably there was even more than that going on. Something my grandfather and I shared was that we had both been forced to leave our childhood homes after sudden, disturbing events. I think that all of those loyal attachments he made in Cambridge can be described as his effort to create a community, and I believe that by showing me how much value he placed on that community, he was urging me to create one for myself. You find your place in the world by finding your places.

Another concern of his was making sure that I developed good taste. I remember a conversation about Tolstoy when my grandfather told me that some day I would read *War and Peace* and that afterward I would want to read *Resurrection* because *War and Peace* was so good, but that I should avoid *Resurrection,* because it was a "second-rate book by a first-rate writer." When I showed up at his house with a copy of Machiavelli's *Discourses* (carefully chosen and purchased in the hopes of impressing him), and then casually produced it in his living room, my grandfather advised me to put *that* away and sent me off to buy myself a copy of *The Prince.* Anybody who is called Nicholas Nickleby by his grandfather—as I was—and is presented with a copy of *David Copperfield* at the age of eight by his grandfather—as I was also—learns quickly what will please. Some months after my grandfather gave me the *Copperfield,* I reported truthfully to him that I'd read every word, and I could see the excitement in his eyes. "Is that so, Nicky Boy?" he said, and that made all the uncomprehending hours worth it. Then he began to ask me questions about the novel and I didn't know the answer to any of them. Yet beyond a little sigh from him, there was no sign that perhaps both people in the room wished I would grow up faster than I could.

He never made me feel bad for my inadequacies. At age fourteen I wrote a history class term paper which I called "The British Wool Industry: An Economic and Social Review"—a title I hoped he would like. My grandfather took this little effort very seriously, praised it to the skies, and then presented me with his copy of Paul Samuelson's *Economics* textbook. I found out later that after I returned home, he went around Cambridge telling people that "my young grandson is reading Samuelson and already has mastered the post hoc, ergo propter hoc fallacy."

By then it was abundantly clear that I was no mathematician, so I'm sure he knew I wasn't going to be an economist. I don't think he cared. What made him so special as a teacher of economic history had never been his mastery of economics. He was a humanist in the halls of science. For other people—and for me—he represented the importance of creativity, curiosity, and enthusiasm. The world for him began as a flat place and developed its contours through the power of what a person's imagination could do with all that space.

Many of my grandfather's fascinations became mine, from Tolstoy right down to Pieter Bruegel, a painter beloved by all his grandchildren. On the walls of his house were reproductions of the paintings he'd gone to see in Vienna museums as a young man, and when I admired them, he showed me books full of Bruegel's picaresque renditions of peasants, skaters, haymakers, beekeepers, rabbit hunters, lechers, cuckolds, and naughty children. Bruegel and my grandfather seemed to be of a piece. With his bright eyes and textured face, my grandfather looked to me like one of Bruegel's cunning village elders. Eventually all of us grandchildren had copies of *The Harvesters* or *Hunters in the Snow* on the walls of our homes.

Whether he was forming interests in me or cultivating what already existed I'm not sure. What gets passed on is such an elusive matter. Would I have liked Bruegel and Tolstoy without him? Do I enjoy eating sunflower seeds, wearing striped T-shirts, and playing Ping-Pong because my grandfather did? Now that I know so much more about him, one of the things I see is the value he placed on optimism. Even in his very last years, when life was slowly wearing him down, I notice now that he was busy urging all of us grandchildren to be hopeful about the world. After Susi died, he implied that the best way for us to honor her life was to overcome our loss of it.

I also notice ways that he made life hard for himself. In the years since his death, whenever I have been in New Hampshire, I have gone by the Francestown village cemetery, where he is buried, to spend some time at his grave. Not long after I began making these visits, I fell into the habit of talking to my grandfather's tombstone, filling him in on what I'd been doing with myself, telling him how things were going. Since I was standing in a corner of a remote country graveyard and speaking quietly, I was always about as alone as possible, but even in these solitary moments with my grandfather, there is one thing I never discussed with him—my father.

My father responded to the pain and frustration of severe mental illness by subjecting just about everyone who came near to bizarre and often vicious outbursts. I absorbed my share. Having such a sick father

seemed so frightening and so shameful to me that it wasn't until he died, at age sixty-five, that I could see the character in a person who retains his will and regains his hopes breakdown after breakdown.

In the days after my father's death, I spent as much time thinking about my dead grandfather as my dead father, two unusual men who had encountered so much adversity and who had suffered so much. I began to grasp that in my inability to talk about my father for all those years, I was very much like my grandfather, who kept to himself all the things that brought him pain. By then I'd spent enough time looking into my grandfather's life to know that barricading himself from his past had cost him plenty, and I could now see how the same might be happening to me.

IN THE END, MY GRANDFATHER GAVE ME SO MANY THINGS, AND sometimes I wonder what I gave him. I know that he found the company of a young innocent with most of his years ahead of him very soothing as his own allotment neared their conclusion. It was characteristic of my grandfather's rich and often difficult life that his ambitions to serve for other people as a teacher and a model sometimes inhibited his natural affections. That wasn't true with me. I could always feel his warmth and his concern. His friend and former student Barbara Solow told me that "when you came along, a plug was pulled, and all this love came out of your grandfather." It must have been pleasant indeed, as he would have said, for him to have had such an adoring convert, a young grandson, not yet nine, who came to his house and brought conversations between my grandfather and his friends to an abrupt halt by piping up with "Grandpa says people don't talk about religion." After the myriad conflicting feelings he experienced in his relationships with just about everyone he knew, it was probably nice for him to feel such simple, unconditional affection for someone.

One year when my mother, Sally, and I got up to New Hampshire for our annual summer visit, there was something new by the side of the road. My grandfather had asked the state to install yellow warning signs, one in each direction. They read "Slow—Children At Play," and had on them the silhouette of a child. Nobody ever drove fast on that road; almost nobody ever drove on it at all. But those signs made him so excited. He couldn't wait for me to see them, and after I had, he always pointed them out at the beginning and the end of our drives in the old blue Plymouth. It gave me such pleasure that, no matter what wonders we'd just discovered, the last thing this extraordinary man wanted to show me was me.

Source Notes and Acknowledgments

This book is a biographical memoir, a work of reconstruction. My own fond memories of my grandfather made me want to know what his life was like and, indeed, what he was like. It took a long time to do this, and over the many years I was helped by many books and many people, both in New York, where I live, and in the places my grandfather lived that I visited in the course of the project—Odessa, Vienna, Stockerau, Ramseiden, Oxford, Berkeley, Washington, Cambridge, and Francestown.

If my grandfather can be said to have lived for anything, he lived for books, and as I tried to get to know him retrospectively, I read the books he most cared about. I also read books about his work and his times. The books on which I have relied for background, facts, quotations, or inspiration include:

Max Adler, *A Socialist Remembers*
Hans Christian Andersen, *The Fairy Tales of Hans Christian Andersen*
Neal Ascherson, *Black Sea*
Isaac Babel, *Collected Stories*
Ilse Barea, *Vienna*
Elisabeth Barker, *Austria 1918–1972*
Ernest Barker, *Father of the Man*
Walter Jackson Bate, *John Keats* and *Samuel Johnson*
Leopold Bellak, *Confrontation in Vienna*
Steven Beller, *Vienna and the Jews 1867–1938*
Maxine Berg, *A Woman in History: Eileen Power 1889–1940*
George E. Berkley, *Vienna and Its Jews: The Tragedy of Success*
Isaiah Berlin, *Karl Marx, Personal Impressions, Russian Thinkers*, and
     Conversations with Isaiah Berlin (with Ramin Jahanbegloo)
Paul Berman, *A Tale of Two Utopias*
Thomas Bernhard, *Gathering Evidence*
Piero Bianconi, *Breugel*
Alexander Blok, *Selected Poems*
Mark E. Blum, *The Austro-Marxists 1890–1918*
James Boswell, *The Life of Samuel Johnson, LLD*
Brian Boyd, *Vladimir Nabokov: The Russian Years* and *Vladimir Nabokov:
     The American Years*

Christian Brandstatter and Werner Schweiger, *Das Wiener Kaffeehaus*

Vera Brittain, *Testament of Youth*

Gordon Brook-Shepherd, *The Austrians: A Thousand Year Odyssey*

James MacGregor Burns, *Roosevelt: The Lion and The Fox* and *Roosevelt: The Soldier of Freedom*

Wilhelm Busch, *Max and Moritz* and *A Wilhelm Busch Album*

Joseph Buttinger, *In the Twilight of Socialism: A History of the Revolutionary Socialists of Austria*

Italo Calvino, *The Baron in the Trees*

Elias Canetti, *The Play of the Eyes*

E. H. Carr, *The Romantic Exiles*

F. L. Carsten, *The First Austrian Republic 1918–1938*

Richard Charques, *The Twilight of Imperial Russia*

Anton Chekhov, *Five Plays* and *Selected Stories*

George Clare, *Last Waltz in Vienna*

Lewis A. Coser, *Refugee Scholars in America*

Edward Crankshaw, *Vienna: The Image of a Culture in Decline*

Rex Crawford, editor, *The Cultural Migration: The European Scholar in America*

Robert C. Delevoy, *Breugel*

Charles Dickens, *David Copperfield, Great Expectations, Nicholas Nickleby,* and *The Pickwick Papers*

David Donald, *Look Homeward: A Life of Thomas Wolfe*

Fydor Dostoyevsky, *The Gambler and Other Stories*

Lawrence Eichel and others, *The Harvard Strike*

George Eliot, *Middlemarch*

Helen Epstein, *Where She Came From*

Harold Evans, *The American Century*

Laura Fermi, *Illustrious Immigrants: The Intellectual Migration from Europe 1930–1941*

Frank Field, *The Last Days of Mankind: Karl Kraus and His Vienna*

Michael Florinsky, *The End of the Russian Empire*

Ian Frazier, *Family*

Willi Frischauer, *Twilight in Vienna*

Paul Fussell, *The Great War and Modern Memory*

John Kenneth Galbraith, *The Affluent Society, The Galbraith Reader, A Life in Our Times, The New Industrial State,* and *Who Needs the Democrats?*

Sheldon Gardner and Gwendolyn Stevens, *Red Vienna and the Golden Age of Psychology*

Peter Gay, *Freud: A Life for Our Time*

G.E.R. Gedye, *The Fallen Bastions*

Todd Gitlin, *The Sixties*

Johann Wolfgang von Goethe, *Faust* and *Faust Part II*

Nikolai Gogol, *The Collected Tales*

Ivan Goncharov, *Oblomov*

Maxim Gorky, *My Childhood*

J. D. Gregory, *Dollfuss and His Times*

Helmut Gruber, *Red Vienna: Experiment in Working-Class Culture*

Frederic Grunfeld, *Prophets Without Honour*

Charles Gulick, *Austria from Habsburg to Hitler*

David Halberstam, *The Best and the Brightest*

Brigitte Hamann, *Hitler's Vienna*

F. A. Hayek, *Hayek on Hayek*

Eli Heckscher, *History of Economic Sweden*

Robert Heilbroner, *The Worldly Philosophers*

Patricia Herlihy, *Odessa: A History, 1794–1914*

Alexander Herzen, *My Past and My Thoughts*

Albert Hirschman, *The Passions and the Interests* and *A Propensity to Self-Subversion*

Paul Hofmann, *The Spell of the Vienna Woods* and *The Viennese: Splendor, Twilight and Exile*

Samuel Hymes, *The Soldiers' Tale*

Michael Ignatieff, *Isaiah Berlin* and *A Russian Album*

Henry James, *The Portrait of a Lady*

Allan Janik and Stephen Toulmin, *Wittgenstein's Vienna*

William Johnston, *The Austrian Mind*

Ernest Jones, *The Life and Work of Sigmund Freud*

E. J. Kahn, Jr., *Harvard Through Change and Through Storm*

John Keegan, *The First World War*

John L. H. Keep, *The Russian Revolution*

Steven Kelman, *Push Comes to Shove*

John Maynard Keynes, *Essays in Biography*

Thomas Kuhn, *The Structure of Scientific Revolutions*

Carl A. Landauer, *European Socialism: A History of Ideas and Movements*

David Landes, *Bankers & Pashas* and *The Wealth and Poverty of Nations*

John Lawrence, *A History of Russia*

Gustave Le Bon, *The Crowd*

Mikhail Lermontov, *A Hero for Our Time*

Library of America, editors, *Reporting World War II* and *Reporting Vietnam*

Niccolò Machiavelli, *The Prince*

Norman Maclean, *A River Runs Through It*

Nadezhda Mandelstam, *Hope Against Hope*, and *Hope Abandoned*

Herbert Marcuse, *Soviet Marxism*

Karl Marx, *Das Kapital*

David Maurer, *The Big Con*

William Maxwell, *Ancestors*

Ved Mehta, *The Fly and the Fly-Bottle*

James Miller, *Democracy Is in the Streets*

Alberto Moravia, *The Time of Indifference*
Frederic Morton, *A Nervous Splendor*
Robert Musil, *The Man Without Qualities*
Vladimir Nabokov, *Ada, or Ardor, The Defense, Eugene Onegin*
   (translation), *The Gift*, and *Speak, Memory*
Johann Nestroy, *Works*
George Packer, *Blood of the Liberals*
Boris Pasternak, *Doctor Zhivago* and *I Remember*
Bruce F. Pauley, *From Prejudice to Persecution: A History of Austrian
   Anti-Semitism*
Robert Pick, *The Last Days of Imperial Vienna*
Karl Popper, *Unended Quest*
Thomas Powers, *Vietnam: The War Comes Home*
V. S. Pritchett, *Chekhov*
P. G. J. Pulzer, *The Rise of Political Anti-Semitism in Austria*
Alexander Pushkin, *Eugene Onegin* and *Boris Godunov*
Anson Rabinbach, *The Crisis of Austrian Socialism: From Red Vienna to Civil
   War 1927–1934*
Arthur Ransome, *Old Peter's Russian Tales*
Talbot Baines Reed, *The Willoughby Captains*
F. D. Reeve, *Aleksander Blok: Between Image and Idea*
Richard Rickett, *Austrian History*
Herbert Rosenkranz, *The Anschluss and the Tragedy of Austrian Jewry
   1938–1945*
Henry Rosovsky, editor, *Industrialization in Two Systems: Essays in Honor of
   Alexander Gerschenkron* (Gerschenkron festschrift)
W. W. Rostow, *The Stages of Economic Growth: A Non-conformist Manifesto*
Joseph Roth, *The Radetzky March*
Paul A. Samuelson, *Economics* and *Foundations of Economic Analysis*
Arthur Schnitzler, *My Youth in Vienna* and *The Road into the Open*
Carl Schorske, *Fin-De-Siècle Vienna*
Joseph Schumpeter, *Economics Doctrine and Method* and *History of Economic
   Analysis*
Kurt von Schuschnigg, *My Austria*
Victor Serge, *Memoirs of a Revolutionary*
William Shakespeare, *Hamlet, Prince of Denmark*
Aleksandr Solzhenitsyn, *One Day in the Life of Ivan Denisovitch* and
   The Gulag Archipelago
Wolfgang Speiser, *Socialist Students of Vienna*
Friedrich Stadler and Peter Weibel, *The Cultural Exodus from Austria*
Karl R. Stadler, *Austria*
Adolf Sturmthal, *Democracy Under Fire: Memoirs of a European Socialist*
Richard Sylla and Gianni Toniolo, editors, *Patterns of European
   Industrialization: The Nineteenth Century*

Leo Tolstoy, *Anna Karenina, The Death of Ivan Ilych and Other Stories,
The Kreutzer Sonata and Other Stories*, and *War and Peace*
Calvin Tomkins, *Duchamp*
Calvin Trillin, *Messages From My Father*
Lionel Trilling, *The Liberal Imagination*
Leon Trotsky, *My Life: An Attempt at Autobiography*
Ivan Turgenev, *Fathers and Sons, Sketches from a Hunter's Album*, and
First Love
Mark Twain, *A Tramp Abroad, The Innocents Abroad*, and *The Adventures
of Tom Sawyer*
Adam B. Ulam, *The Bolsheviks*
Thorstein Veblen, *Imperial Germany and the Industrial Revolution* and
The Theory of the Leisure Class
Richard von Warton, unpublished reminiscences
Bernard Wasserstein, *The Secret Lives of Trebitsch Lincoln*
Max Weber, *The Protestant Ethic and the Spirit of Capitalism*
Joseph Wechsberg, *Vienna, My Vienna*
Ted Williams with John Underwood, *My Turn At Bat: The Story of My Life*
and *The Science of Hitting*
C. Vann Woodward, *The Strange Career of Jim Crow*
Virginia Woolf, *Mrs. Dalloway*
Avrahm Yarmolinsky, *The Poems, Prose and Plays of Alexander Pushkin*
Daniel Yergin, *Shattered Peace: The Origins of the Cold War and the National
Security State*
Harry Zohn, *Karl Kraus*
Stefan Zweig, *The Burning Secret and Other Stories* and *The World of
Yesterday*

Particularly helpful articles were:

Svetlana Alliluyeva, "To Doris Leonidovich Pasternak," *Atlantic Monthly*
American Academy of Arts and Sciences, "The Hundred Most Influential
Books Since the War," *Bulletin of the Academy*
Marilyn Berger, "Isaiah Berlin, Philosopher and Pluralist, Is Dead at 88,"
New York Times
Kenneth E. Carpenter and Afred D. Chandler, "Fritz Redlich: Scholar and
Friend," *Journal of Economic History*
John Cassidy, "Height of Eloquence," *New Yorker*
J. M. Coetzee, "The Genius of Robert Walser," *New York Review of Books*
Daily Telegraph, "Sir Isaiah Berlin, OM"
David C. Engerman, "Russia as a Developing Country: Economic Soviet-
ology and the Question of Development," draft workshop paper
John H. Fenton, "A Russian Defector, Student at Harvard, to Return to
Soviet," *New York Times*
John Haag, "Blood on the Ringstrasse: Vienna's Students 1918–1933,"
Wiener Library Bulletin

Gottfried Haberler, "Alexander Gerschenkron," *American Philosophical Society Yearbook (1980)*

Patricia Herlihy, "Commerce and Architecture in Odessa in Late Imperial Russia," draft paper

Albert O. Hirschman, "Fifty Years After the Marshall Plan: Two Posthumous Memoirs and Some Personal Reflections," paper presented at Woodrow Wilson School of Public Affairs, Princeton University

Gerald Holton, "Ernst Mach and the Fortunes of Positivism in America," *Isis*; "From the Vienna Circle to Harvard Square: The Americanization of a European World Conception," in *Scientific Philosophy: Origins and Developments*; and "On the Vienna Circle in Exile: An Eyewitness Report," *Foundational Debate*

Michael Ignatieff, "First Loves," *New Yorker*

Aileen Kelly, "Chekhov the Subversive," *New York Review of Books*

Christopher Lehmann-Haupt, "W. V. Quine, Philosopher Who Analyzed Language and Reality, Dies At 92," *New York Times*

J. Anthony Lukas, "A Fairly Old Grad ('55) Looks at Harvard (in '69)," *New York Times Magazine*

Alfred Magaziner, "Michael Schacherl: Kampf dem Alkohol," *Rentner und Pensionist*

Donald McCloskey, "Alexander Gerschenkron," *American Scholar*

John Meyer, "Notes on Cliometrics' Fortieth," *AEA Papers and Proceedings*

Jeffrey Meyers, "The Bulldog and the Butterfly: The Friendship of Edmund Wilson and Vladimir Nabokov," *American Scholar*

Albert Mueller, "Uses of Adversity," draft paper

Vladimir Nabokov, "Reply to My Critics," *Encounter*

Cynthia Ozick, "A Buried Life," *New Yorker*

M. F. Perutz, "A Passion for Science," *New York Review of Books*

Henry Rosovsky, "Alexander Gerschenkron: A Fond and Personal Recollection," *Journal of Economic History*; and "The Most Famous Professor at Harvard," in *Unconventional Wisdom* (John Kenneth Galbraith festschrift)

Alan Ryan, "Memories of a Captivating Conversationalist," *New York Times*

Paul A. Samuelson, "Alvin Hansen as a Creative Economic Theorist," *Quarterly Journal of Economics*; and "Gottfried Haberler 1900–1995, *Economic Journal*

F. M. Scherer, "The Emigration of German-Speaking Economists After 1933," *Journal of Economic Literature*

Arthur Schlesinger, Jr, "On JFK: An Interview with Isaiah Berlin," *New York Review of Books*

Lydia Seward, "The Flight from Russia," unpublished memoir

Israel Shenker, "Harvard's 'Scholarly Model' Ends His Career," *New York Times*

Patrick Smith, "Letter from Tokyo," *New Yorker*

Gleb Struve, "Notes on Nabokov as a Russian Writer," *Wisconsin Studies in Contemporary Literature*

Louis Uchitelle, "A Challenge to Scientific Economics," *New York Times*

Raymond Vernon and others, "Edward Sagendorph Mason," *Proceedings of the American Philosophical Society*

Michael M. Weinstein, "Students Seek Some Reality Amid the Math of
Economics," *New York Times*

Leon Wieseltier, " 'When a Sage Dies, All Are His Kin,' " *New Republic*

Andrew L. Yarrow, "Nathan Pusey, Harvard President Through Growth
and Turmoil Alike, Dies at 94," *New York Times*

Igor Yeykelis, "Odessa 1914–1922," unpublished Ph.D. thesis

The following institutions supplied me with important
materials or assistance:

The Board of Governors of the Federal Reserve System; the Bobst Memorial
Library at New York University; the Federal Bureau of Investigation; the Harvard University Alumni Office; the Harvard University Archives at Pusey
Library, where the Alexander Gerschenkron papers are stored, and where I
thank Harley Holden and Talar Kizirian; the Davis Center for Russian Studies
at Harvard University; the Harvard University Department of Economics
library, Littauer Center; Widener Library at Harvard University; the Harvard
News Office, where I thank Marvin Hightower; the Leo Baeck Institute, where
I thank Ursula Muenzel; the New School Fogelman Library; the Odessa Philharmonic Orchestra, Hobart Earle conductor; the Princeton University Information Office; the Center for Advanced Study, Princeton University; the Pushkin
Museum, Odessa; the Richmond (California) Historical Museum, where I thank
Kathleen Rupley; the Richmond (California) Public Library, where I thank Maria
Brooks; the Kunsthistorisches Museum (Museum of Fine Arts), Vienna, where
the Bruegel collection is in Gallery 10 of the East Wing; the University of Vienna.

For news coverage of Odessa just after the turn of the century, I consulted
Odesskij Listoc. For news reports of the 1960s at Harvard I relied upon the coverage in the *Boston Globe*, the *Harvard Crimson*, and the *New York Times*. John
Fox supplied me with a tape of my grandfather's speech at the Special Meeting
of the Harvard Faculty of Arts and Sciences on April 11, 1969, and also with a
transcript of the entire meeting. I consulted Harvard University yearbooks
from the years my grandfather was at the university. John Habakkuk sent me
his address conferring an Oxford honorary degree on my grandfather in 1974.
Newspaper reports concerning my grandfather's article "Economic Relations
with the USSR" appeared in February 1945 in the *New York Times* ("Outlines
Program for Russian Trade"), the *New York Herald Tribune* ("Three Forms of
Soviet Payment for U.S. Exports Found Possible"), and the *Daily Worker*
("Bankers with Schizophrenia").

These are the major writings of Alexander Gerschenkron
(many of his finest essays appear in the 1962 and 1968 collections):

1943: *Bread and Democracy in Germany* (University of California Press)

1945: "Economic Relations with the USSR" (Committee on International Economic
Policy, Carnegie Endowment for International Peace)

1947: "The Rate of Industrial Growth in Russia Since 1885," *Journal of Economic History*

1951: *A Dollar Index of Soviet Machinery Output* (Rand Corporation)

1952: *A Dollar Index of Soviet Petroleum Output* (Rand Corporation)

1953: *A Dollar Index of Soviet Iron and Steel Output* (Rand Corporation)

1954: *A Dollar Index of Soviet Electric Power Output* (Rand Corporation)

1953–1954: The Landes/Sawyer feud was conducted across four issues of *Explorations in Entrepreneurial History*

1954: "Eli F. Heckscher," foreword to *An Economic History of Sweden*

1955: "Soviet Heavy Industry: A Dollar Index of Output 1927/28–1937," *Review of Economics and Statistics*

1962: *Economic Backwardness in Historical Perspective* (Harvard University Press)

1968: *Continuity in History and Other Essays* (Harvard University Press)

1970: *Europe in the Russian Mirror* (Cambridge University Press)

1970: "Soviet Russia: Literature and Life," *World Politics*

1970: "Reflections on European Socialism," Carl Landauer festschrift

1971: "Ideology as a System Determinant," in *Comparison of Economic Systems*

1971: "The Concept of Continuity in German Anthropology," *Comparative Studies in Society and History*

1971: "Soviet Marxism and Absolutism," *Slavic Review*

1973: *Mercator Gloriosus and Other Essays* (De Nederlandsche Boekhandel, Antwerp)

1974: "The Legacies of Evil," *Daedalus*

1975: "Time Horizon in Russian Literature," *Slavic Review*

1976: "Getting Off the Bullock Cart: Thoughts on Educational Reform," *American Scholar*

1977: *An Economic Spurt That Failed* (Princeton University Press)

1978: "Samuelson in Soviet Russia: A Report," *Journal of Economic Literature*

1978: "On Reading Books: A Barbarian's Cogitations," *American Scholar*

Undated: "The Uses of Adversity," unpublished memoir

Many people were kind enough to share with me their memories of my grandfather, or to talk over aspects of his life. Some of them also allowed me to see their correspondence with my grandfather. They include:

William Alfred, Robert Allen, Alfred Appel, Walter Arndt, Kenneth Arrow, Alan Auerbach, Leonid Averboukh, Werner Baer, Bernard Bailyn, Nancy Barrett, Walter Jackson Bate, Samuel Beer, Abram Bergson, Isaiah Berlin, Joseph Berliner, Harold Berman, Connie Bicknell, Leighton Bicknell, James Billington, Caroline Bloomfield, Samuel Bowles, Henry Broude, Debbie Brown, Jerome Bruner, Edward Brunner, Charles Calomiaris, Robert Campbell, Ann Carter, Richard Caves, Robert Chapman, Thomas Conners, Uri Dadush, Paul David, Bruce Davie, Gregson Davis, Lance Davis, Heidi Dawidoff, Robert Dawidoff, Sally Dawidoff, Alan Dershowitz, Alexander Dolinin, Evsey Domar, Nancy Dorfman, Peter Dorfman, Robert Dorfman, James Duesenberry, Margaret Duesenberry, John Dunlop, Richard Eckaus, Rick Edwards, Monroe Engel, David Engerman, Stanley Engerman, Joseph Fabry, Charles Feinstein,

Martin Feldstein, Valerie Fellner, Stefano Fenoaltea, Daniel Field, John Finley III, John Finley IV, Albert Fishlow, Donald Fleming, Franklin Ford, Marjory Foster, John Fox, Benjamin Friedman, Milton Friedman, Mildred Furiya, John Kenneth Galbraith, Alice Galenson, David Galenson, Eleanor Galenson, Marjorie Galenson, Walter Galenson, Mary Garland, Gloria Gerrig, Herbert Gintis, Abbott Gleason, Ben Zion Gold, Jim Golden, Marshall Goldman, Peter Gomes, Stephen Jay Gould, Paul Gourary, Stephen Graubard, Alla Grebennikova, Jerry Green, Zvi Griliches, Gregory Grossman, Penny Graham Gustofson, John Habakkuk, Sarah Habakkuk, Leopold Haimson, Oscar Handlin, Charles Harley, Knickerbocker Harley, Richard Harmstone, Alan Heimert, Patricia Herlihy, Randall Hinshaw, Albert Hirschman, Sarah Hirschman, Stanley Hoffman, William Holt, Gerald Holton, Franklyn Holzman, Mathilde Holzman, Hendrik Houthakker, Richard Hunt, Alex Inkeles, Bernadette Inkeles, Marie Jahoda, Marilyn Johnson, Dale Jorgenson, Walter Kaiser, Edith Karel, Walter Kasparek, Carl Kaysen, Michael Kazin, Edward Keenan, George Kennan, Anne Reitmayer Kennedy, Robert Kiely, Charles Kindleberger, J. Burke Knapp, Gusti Kollman, Larry Kotlikoff, George Kurland, Edith Kuznets, Bob Lamont, David Landes, Marge Leibenstein, Elena Levin, Estelle Leontief, Wassily Leontief, Herbert Levine, Joseph Losos, Horace Lunt, Anne Lynch, Arthur Maas, Arthur MacEwan, Pricilla MacMillan, Stephen Marglin, Toni Mark, Edward Mason, Jr., Peter McClelland, Deirdre McCloskey, Sandra Heald McCluney, Heinz Meier, Tanya Meier, Marian Hanson Merrifield, John Meyer, Gerti Miksch, Franco Modigliani, Serena Modigliani, Barrington Moore, Albert Muller, Karl Muller, Paul Munyon, Peggy Musgrave, Richard Musgrave, Lois Natchez, Diane Luongo Nigro, Nancy Nimitz, Douglass North, Guy Orcutt, William Parker, Merton Peck, Martin Peretz, Dwight Perkins, Richard Pipes, Charles Price, Nathan Pusey, William Van Orman Quine, Anson Rabinbach, Estelle Raiffa, Howard Raiffa, Erica Reitmayer, Lloyd Reynolds, David Riesman, Marc Roberts, Roger Rosenblatt, Peter Rosner, Henry Rosovsky, Nitza Rosovsky, Walt Rostow, Winnie Rothenberg, Nancy Sabra, Paul Samuelson, Joyce Sandberg, Lars Sandberg, Thomas Schelling, Ruth Scheurer, Arthur Schlesinger, Jr., Martin Schneider, Susi Schneider, Carl Schorske, Ben Schwartz, Bernard Sears, Elmar Seibel, Lydia Seward, Marshall Shulman, Robert Solomon, Barbara Solow, Robert Solow, Arnold Soloway, Monique Spalding, Friedrich Stadler, Michael Stanislawski, Judy Stein, Lilly Stepanek, Carol Sternhill, Walter Stettner, Alexander Stevenson, Zeph Stewart, Wolfgang Stolper, Eric Streissler, Barry Supple, Richard Sutch, Bob Sutcliffe, Richard Swedberg, Richard Sylla, Peter Temin, Lester Thurow, Calvin Tomkins, Gianni Toniolo, Adam Ulam, Eliza Van Hollen, Raymond Vernon, Evon Vogt, Nan Vogt, Michael Walzer, Carl Watkins, Andre Weil, Richard Weisskoff, Martin Weitzman, Stanislaw Wellisz, Morton White, Charles Whitlock, William Whitney, Anthony Wiener, Jonathan Wiener, Lisbeth Wiener, Jane Williams, Wendy Wolcott, Robert Paul Wolff, Charles Wollenberg, John Womack, Robert Zevin.

* * *

From Gregory Grossman I received a tape of an interview about my grandfather that he conducted with Charles Gulick. From Richard Swedberg I received a tape of an interview about my grandfather that he conducted with Goran Ohlin.

I received helpful correspondence from a large number of people. They are:

Abram Bergson, Isaiah Berlin, Reinhold Beuer-Tajovsky, Connie Bicknell, Eve Bigelow-Baxley, Derek Bok, Alan Bullock, Meredith Burke, Robert Campbell, Charles Clotfelter, J. M. Coetzee, Robert Coles, Erik Dahmen, Gloria Dalton, Paul David, Bruce Davie, Rupert Davis, Heidi Dawidoff, Nancy Dorfman, Peter Dorner, Ruth Earle, Rick Edwards, Monroe Engel, David Engerman, Joseph Epstein, Martin Feldstein, Sheppard Ferguson, Daniel Field, John Fox, Milton Friedman, John Kenneth Galbraith, Peter Gay, Abbott Gleason, Jim Golden, Marshall Goldman, Peter Gomes, David Good, Alexander Gordeuk, Paul Gourary, Ditta Gourary-Roque, Oleg Grabar, Stephen Graubard, Nachum Gross, Gregory Grossman, Joan Grossman, Joan Hanchett, Oscar Handlin, Charles Harley, Richard Harmstone, Patricia Herlihy, Albert Hirschman, E. J. Hobsbawm, Harriet Hoffman, Stanley Hoffman, George Holmes, Gerald Holton, H. Stuart Hughes, Walter Kaiser, Morton Keller, Robert Kilpatrick, Charles Kindleberger, Jean Martin, Ernst Mayr, Peter McClelland, John McFarland, John Meyer, Gerti Miksch, Foster Palmer, William Parker, John Pencavel, Peter Raven-Hansen, Robert Rennie, David Riesman, Henry Rosovsky, Martin Rundstuck, Nancy Sabra, Paul Samuelson, Thomas Sargent, Ruth Scheurer, Susi Schneider, Lydia Seward, David Shannon, Monique Spalding, Alexander Stevenson, Zeph Stewart, Paul Streeten, Erich Streissler, Barry Supple, Richard Swedberg, Richard Sylla, Roman Szporluk, Peter Temin, Morton White, William Whitney, Jonathan Wiener, Jane Williams, Thomas Wilson, Mary Yoe.

For their help on this book I am indebted to Sarah Boxer, Paul Feinberg, Ayako Harvie, Walter Havighurst, Chris Hiebert, Anthea Lingeman, James Mulholland, Susan Norton, Helen Updike, and Jennifer Weh. When my computer crashed, my friends Ben Miller and Joel Roodman rescued my grandfather from the wreckage. For assistance with the final checking of facts I owe many thanks to my friend Natasha Stovall. (Any errors are, of course, my responsibility alone.)

I have received generous support for this project from the MacDowell Colony, the John Simon Guggenheim Foundation, and the American Academy in Berlin.

Those fine sirs Jeff Frank and David Remnick have been wonderful to me at the *New Yorker*, as has Lauren Porcaro. Likewise Ann Fadiman of the *American*

Scholar. I had a ball with Jim Gibbons, Cheryl Hurley, Goeffrey O'Brien, and Max Rudin, the heart of the order at the Library of America.

To care about books is to be glad there are booksellers around like Richard and Lisa "Night Mayor" Howorth of Square Books in Oxford, Mississippi, and Jill Dunbar and Jenny Feder (booksellers emeritus) of Three Lives and Company, New York.

I write by myself, but I'm never alone because of friends like Roger Angell, Kevin Baker, Maria Bennett, Patrick Bennett, Ted Conover, Tommy Davidoff, Nancy Dorfman, Patty Frank, Sue Halpern, Larry Harris, Jonathan Losos, Gerry Marzorati, Tom Powers, Tom Reiss, Henry Rosovsky, Susi Schneider, Steven Sherrill, Chuck Siebert, the Springsteen family, Melanie Thernstrom, Colson Whitehead, Jamie Wright, and Kevin Young. All of them contributed something specific to this book.

Every day I feel grateful that I have an agent so loyal and so wise about the world as Kathy Robbins, and an editor as intelligent and devoted to ideas as Dan Frank.

This is a book about family and mine treats me and my work with generosity and kindness. I'm thinking of all of you, Grandma Rebecca, but I'm especially indebted to the Gerschenkrons—my fabulous sister Sally Dawidoff, my cousinful ones Jonathan and Lisbeth Wiener, my beloved great-aunt Lydia Seward, and especially my mother, Heidi Gerschenkron Dawidoff, a truly decent person who was big enough to let me see her father just the way he was for me.

I wish my grandfather had met my wife, Rebecca Carman Dawidoff. I know that he too would have loved her very much.

About the Author

NICHOLAS DAWIDOFF graduated from Harvard University. He is the author of *The Catcher Was a Spy: The Mysterious Life of Moe Berg* and *In the Country of Country: A Journey to the Roots of American Music*, the editor of the Library of America's *Baseball: A Literary Anthology*, and a contributor to the *New Yorker*, *The American Scholar*, and the *New York Times Magazine*. He has been a Henry Luce Scholar, a Guggenheim fellow, and a Berlin Prize Fellow of the American Academy. He and his wife live in New York.

*The
Gerschenkron
Family
Genealogy*